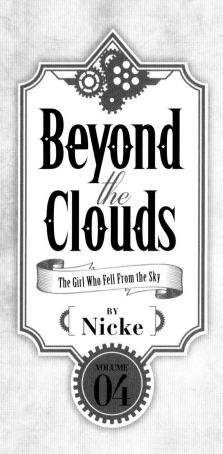

Beyond the Clouds

the

The Girl Who Fell From the Sky

BY

{ Nicke }

VOLUME

04

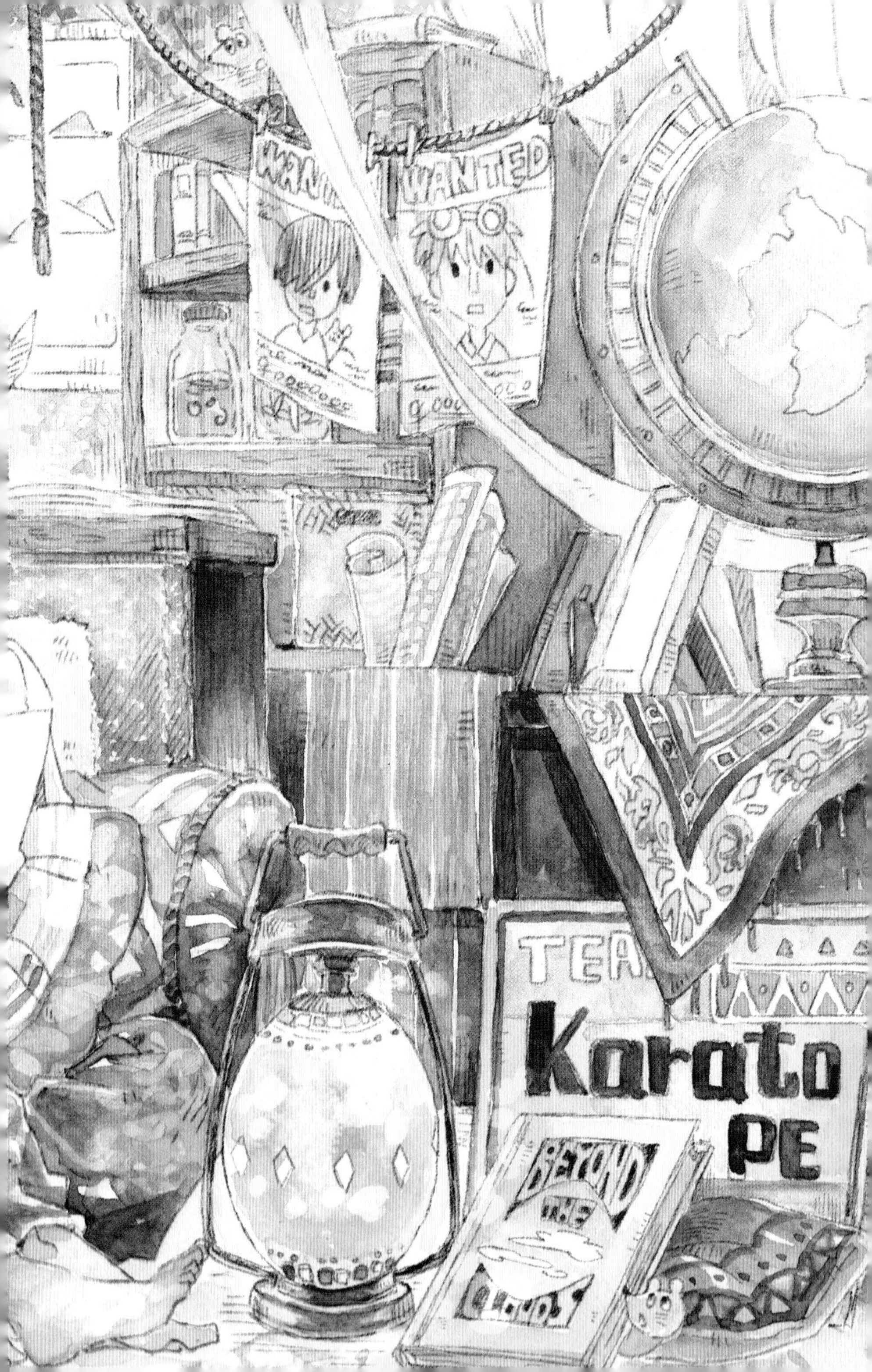
WANTED
TEA
Karato
PE

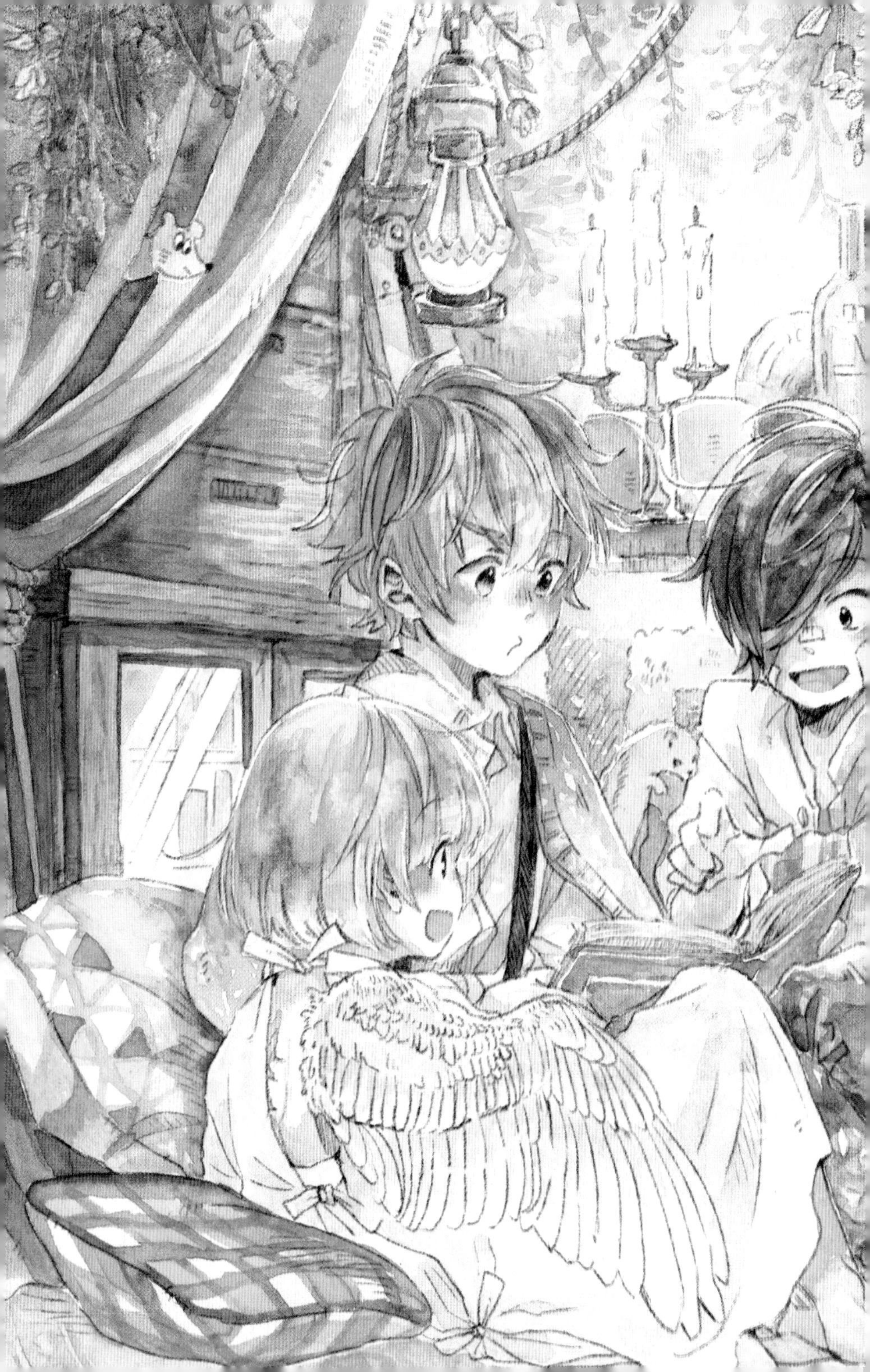

Table of Contents

Chapter 16: The Charlatan's Repentance

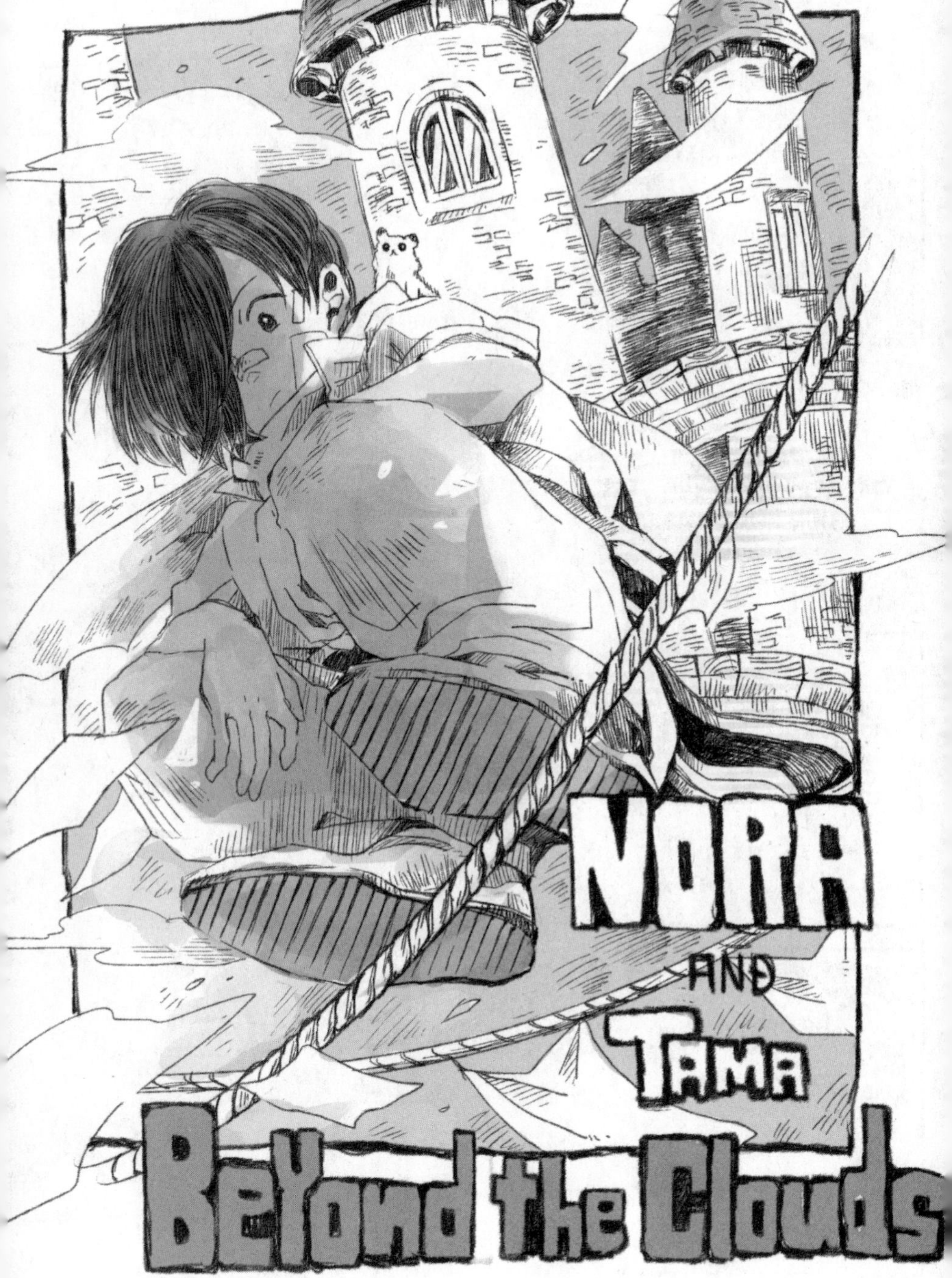
NORA
AND
TAMA
Beyond the Clouds

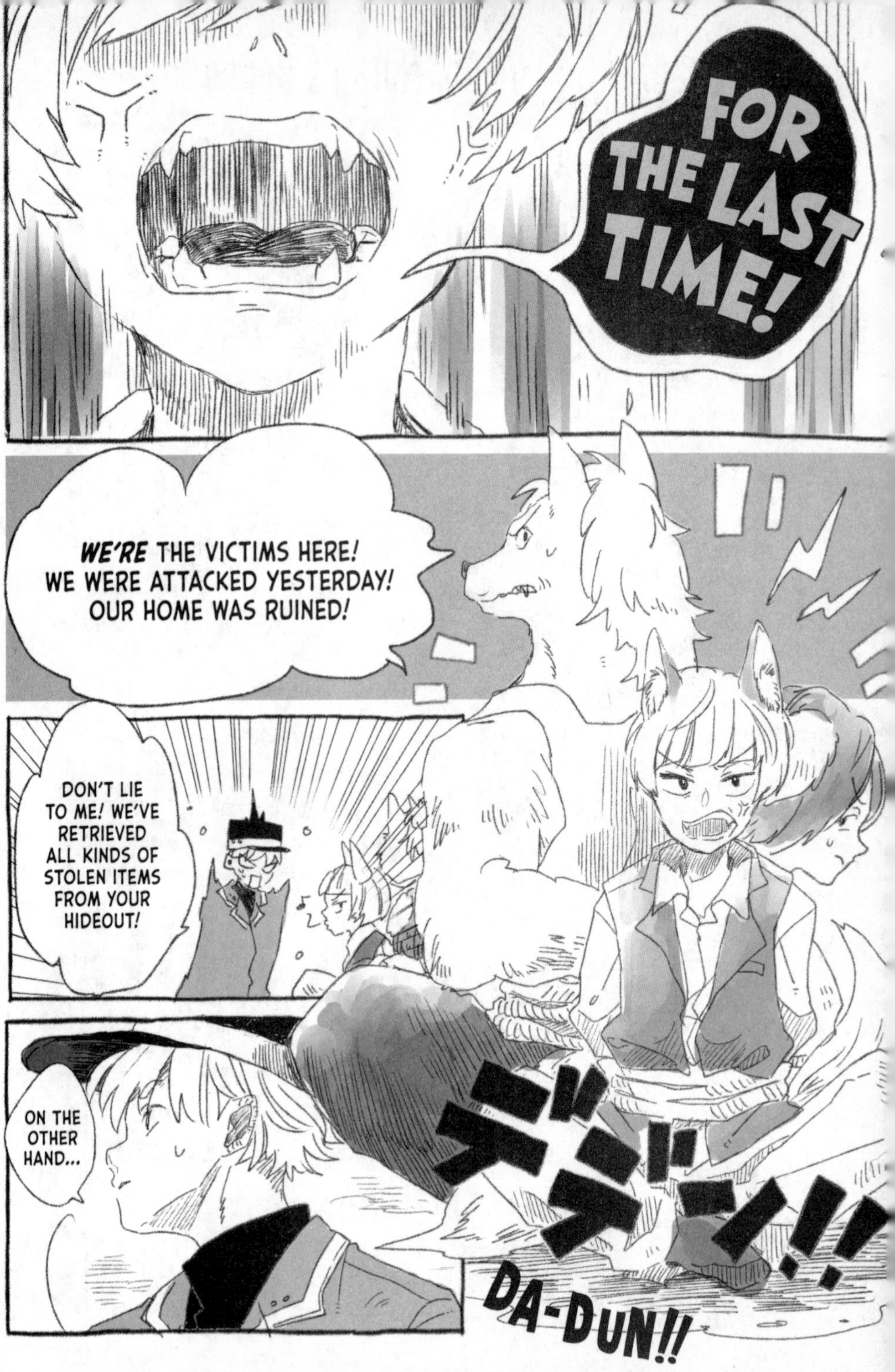
FOR THE LAST TIME!
WE'RE THE VICTIMS HERE! WE WERE ATTACKED YESTERDAY! OUR HOME WAS RUINED!
DA-DUN!!
DON'T LIE TO ME! WE'VE RETRIEVED ALL KINDS OF STOLEN ITEMS FROM YOUR HIDEOUT!
ON THE OTHER HAND...

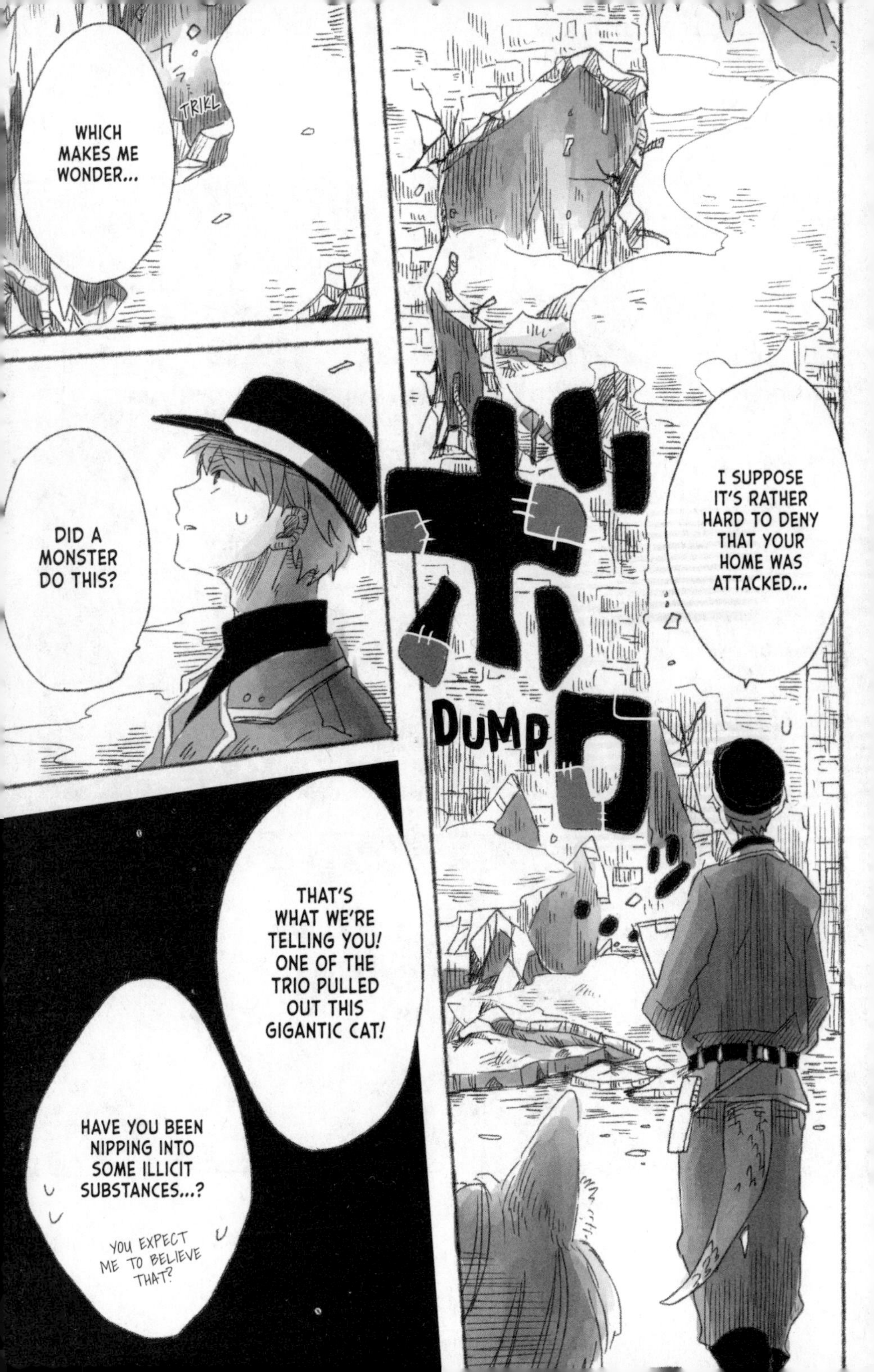
I SUPPOSE IT'S RATHER HARD TO DENY THAT YOUR HOME WAS ATTACKED...
DUMP
WHICH MAKES ME WONDER...
TRIKL
DID A MONSTER DO THIS?
THAT'S WHAT WE'RE TELLING YOU! ONE OF THE TRIO PULLED OUT THIS GIGANTIC CAT!
HAVE YOU BEEN NIPPING INTO SOME ILLICIT SUBSTANCES...?
YOU EXPECT ME TO BELIEVE THAT?

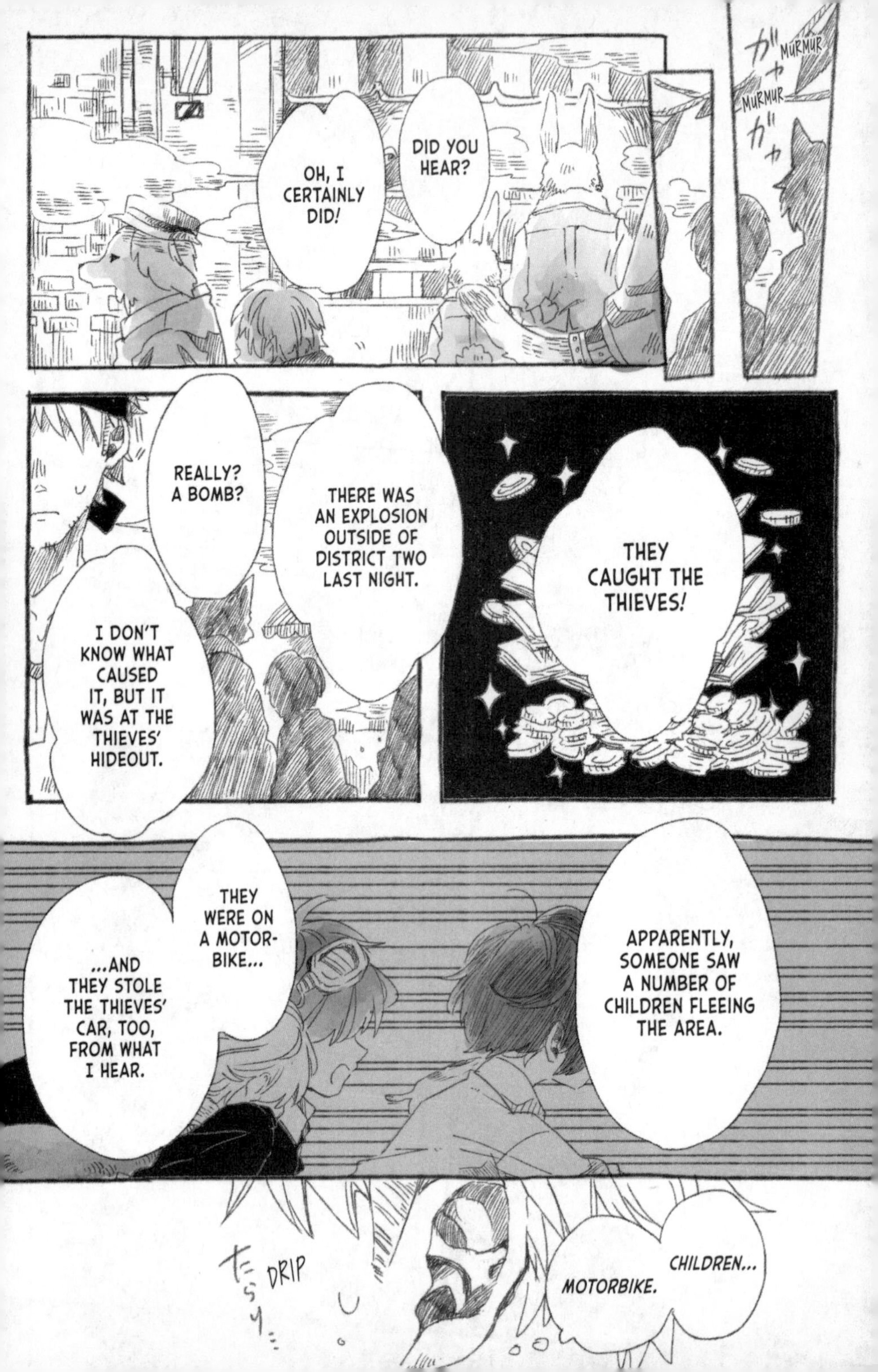
MURMUR
MURMUR
DID YOU HEAR?
OH, I CERTAINLY DID!
THEY CAUGHT THE THIEVES!
THERE WAS AN EXPLOSION OUTSIDE OF DISTRICT TWO LAST NIGHT.
REALLY? A BOMB?
I DON'T KNOW WHAT CAUSED IT, BUT IT WAS AT THE THIEVES' HIDEOUT.
APPARENTLY, SOMEONE SAW A NUMBER OF CHILDREN FLEEING THE AREA.
THEY WERE ON A MOTORBIKE...
...AND THEY STOLE THE THIEVES' CAR, TOO, FROM WHAT I HEAR.
CHILDREN...
MOTORBIKE.
DRIP

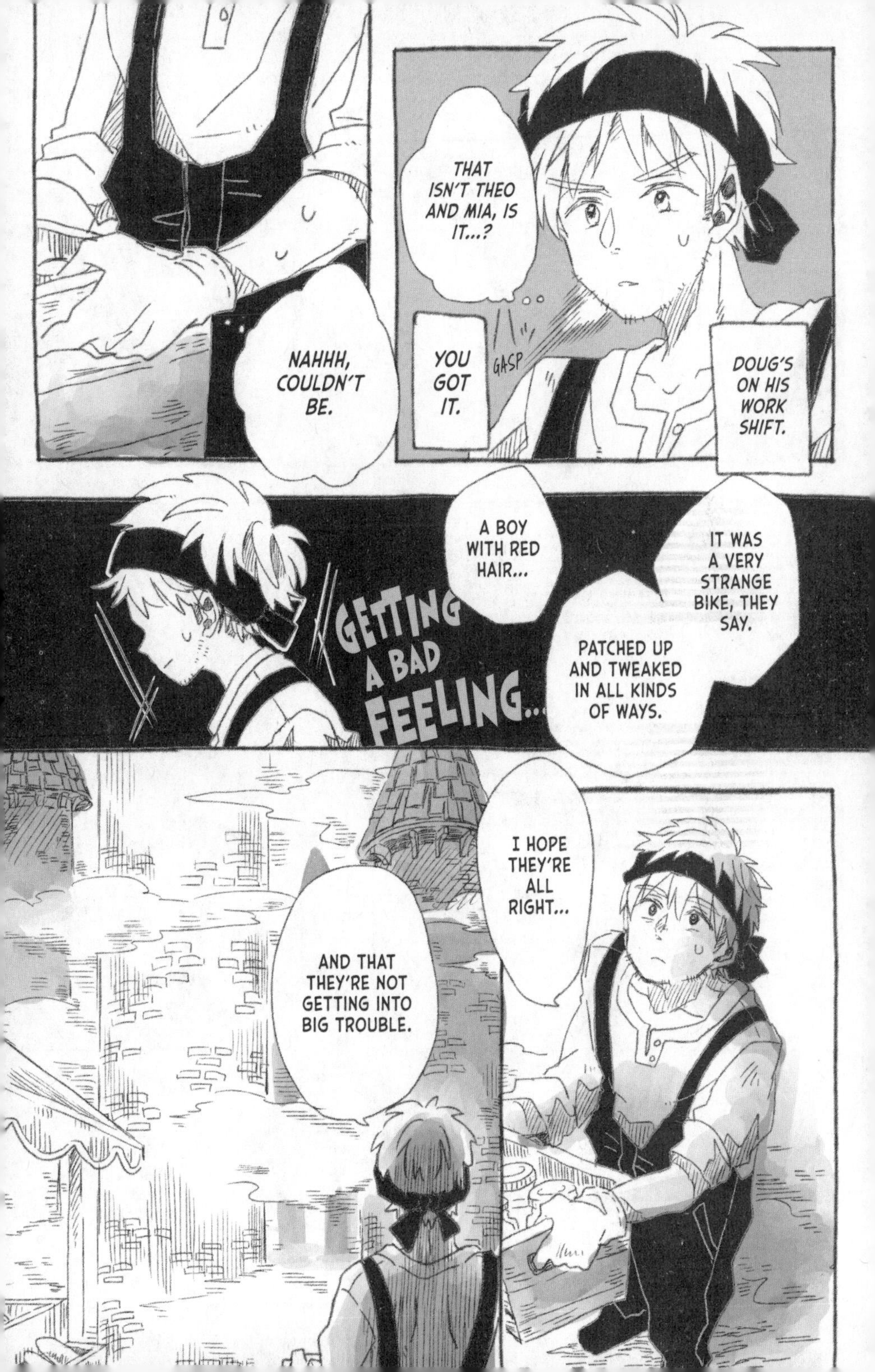
DOUG'S ON HIS WORK SHIFT.
THAT ISN'T THEO AND MIA, IS IT...?
GASP
YOU GOT IT.
NAHHH, COULDN'T BE.
IT WAS A VERY STRANGE BIKE, THEY SAY.
PATCHED UP AND TWEAKED IN ALL KINDS OF WAYS.
A BOY WITH RED HAIR...
GETTING A BAD FEELING...
I HOPE THEY'RE ALL RIGHT...
AND THAT THEY'RE NOT GETTING INTO BIG TROUBLE.

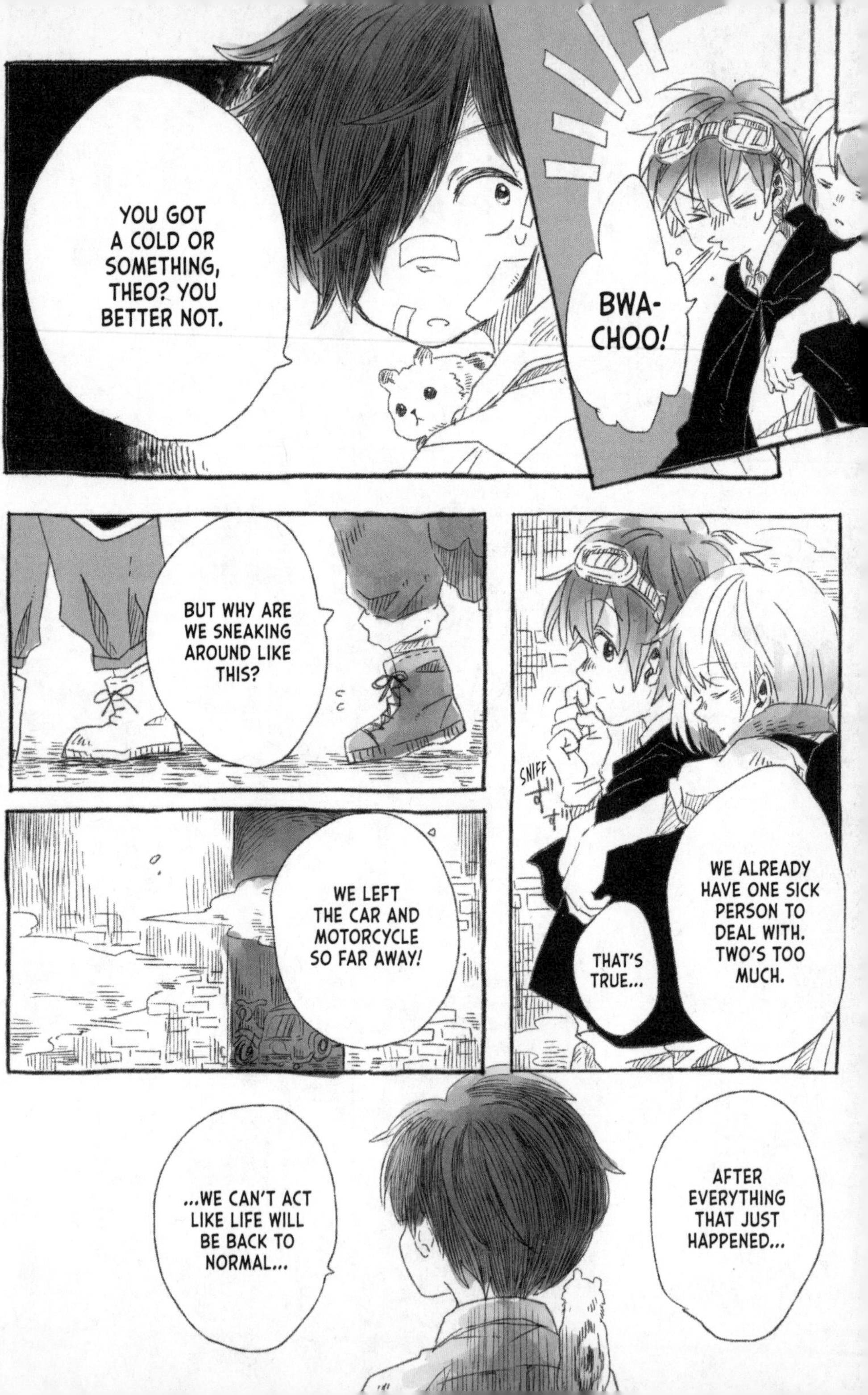
BWA-CHOO!
YOU GOT A COLD OR SOMETHING, THEO? YOU BETTER NOT.
WE ALREADY HAVE ONE SICK PERSON TO DEAL WITH. TWO'S TOO MUCH.
THAT'S TRUE...
SNIFF
BUT WHY ARE WE SNEAKING AROUND LIKE THIS?
WE LEFT THE CAR AND MOTORCYCLE SO FAR AWAY!
AFTER EVERYTHING THAT JUST HAPPENED...
...WE CAN'T ACT LIKE LIFE WILL BE BACK TO NORMAL...

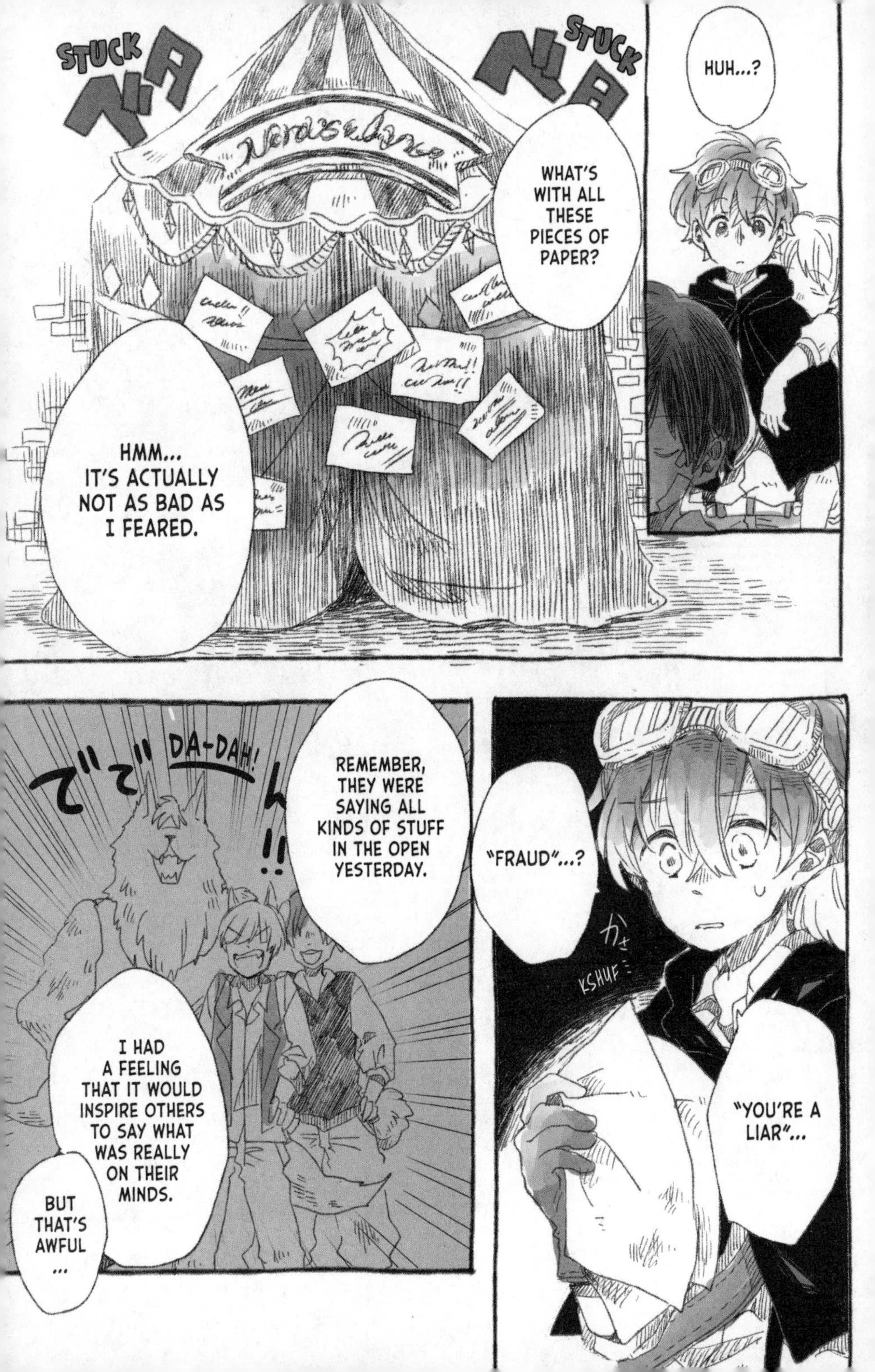
HUH...?
STUCK
WHAT'S WITH ALL THESE PIECES OF PAPER?
STUCK
HMM... IT'S ACTUALLY NOT AS BAD AS I FEARED.
"FRAUD"...?
KSHUF
"YOU'RE A LIAR"...
REMEMBER, THEY WERE SAYING ALL KINDS OF STUFF IN THE OPEN YESTERDAY.
DA-DAH!
!!
I HAD A FEELING THAT IT WOULD INSPIRE OTHERS TO SAY WHAT WAS REALLY ON THEIR MINDS.
BUT THAT'S AWFUL ...

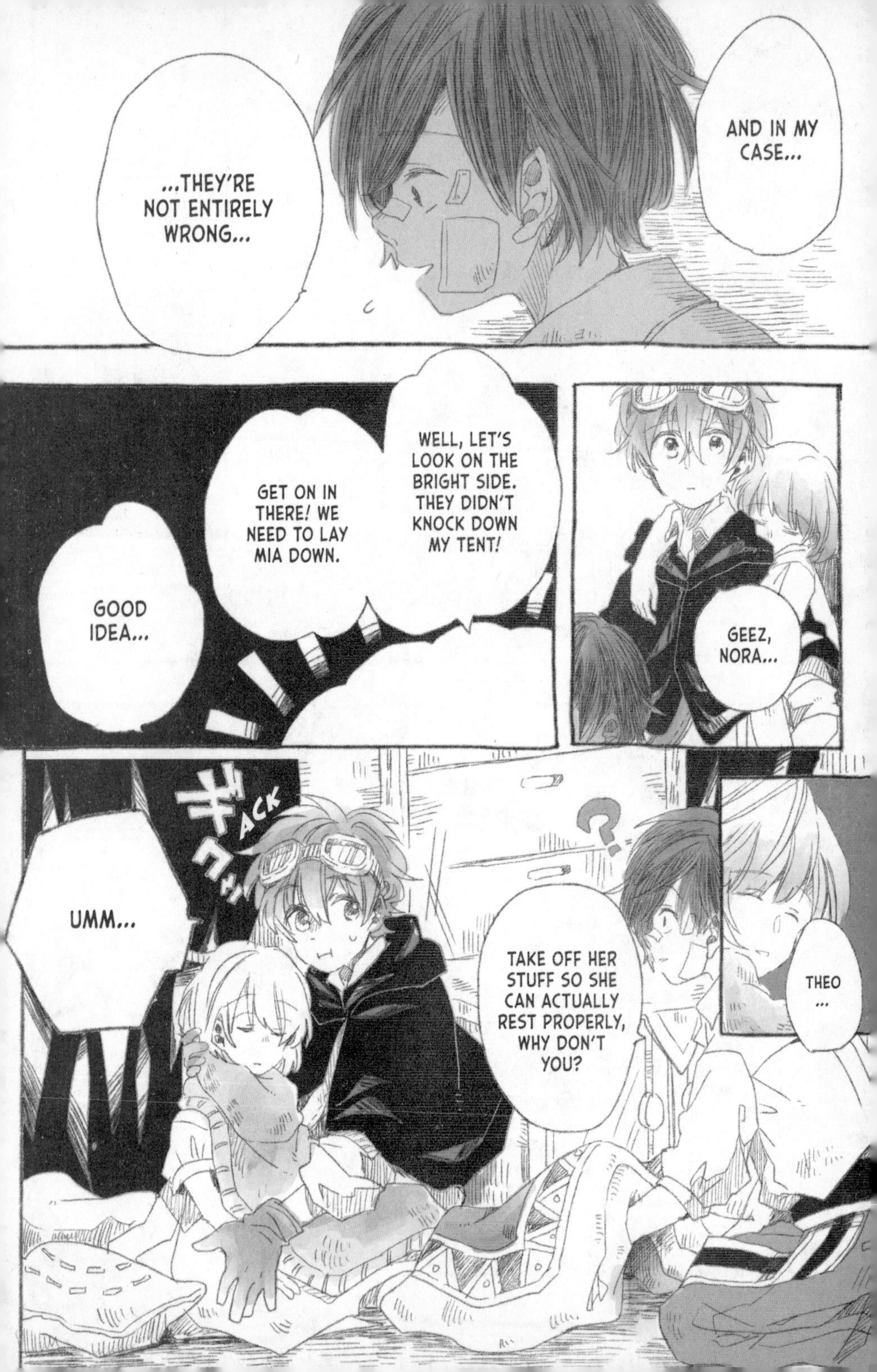
AND IN MY CASE...
...THEY'RE NOT ENTIRELY WRONG...
GEEZ, NORA...
WELL, LET'S LOOK ON THE BRIGHT SIDE. THEY DIDN'T KNOCK DOWN MY TENT!
GET ON IN THERE! WE NEED TO LAY MIA DOWN.
GOOD IDEA...
THEO ...
TAKE OFF HER STUFF SO SHE CAN ACTUALLY REST PROPERLY, WHY DON'T YOU?
ACK
UMM...

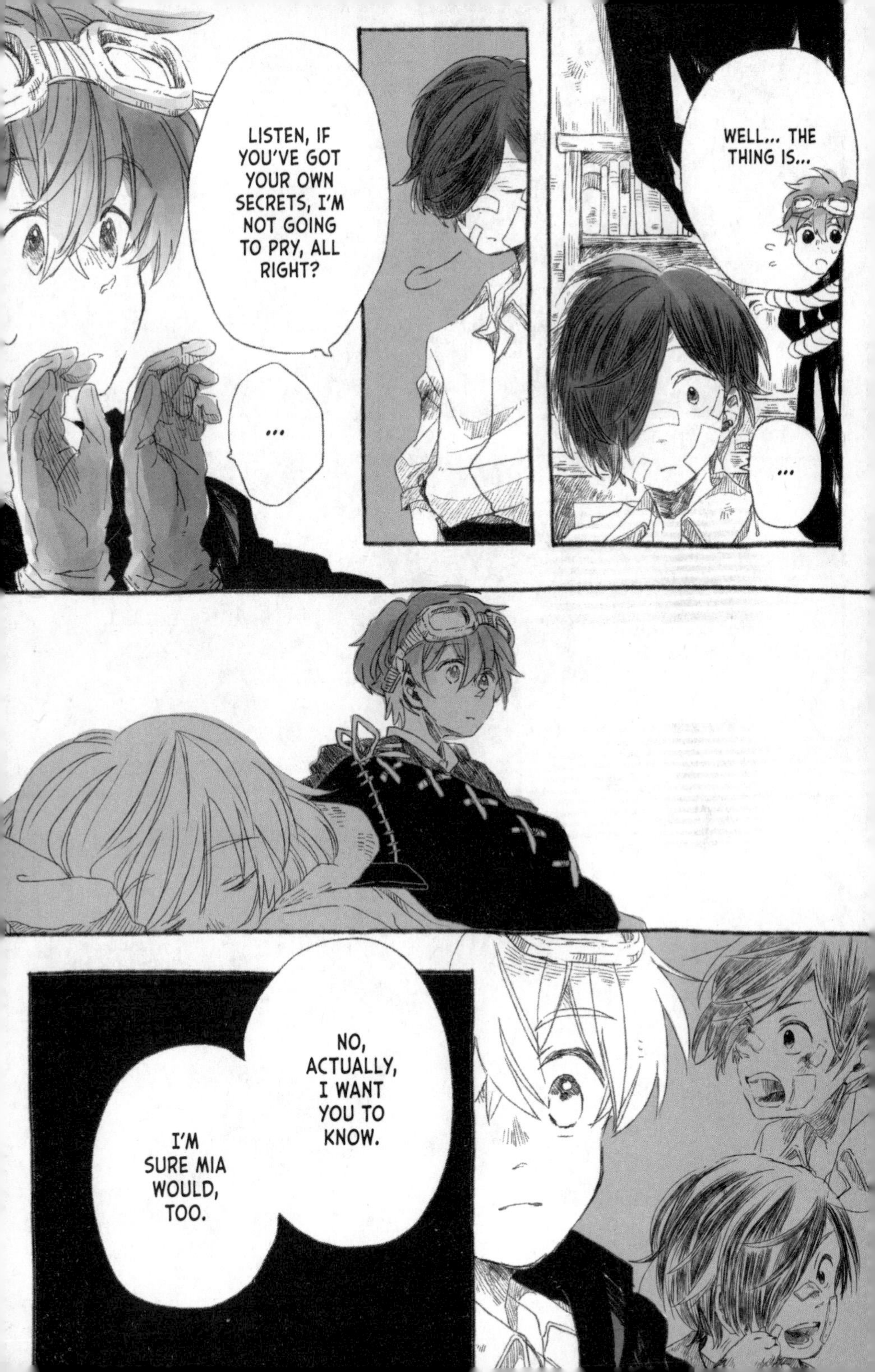
WELL... THE THING IS...
...
LISTEN, IF YOU'VE GOT YOUR OWN SECRETS, I'M NOT GOING TO PRY, ALL RIGHT?
...
NO, ACTUALLY, I WANT YOU TO KNOW.
I'M SURE MIA WOULD, TOO.

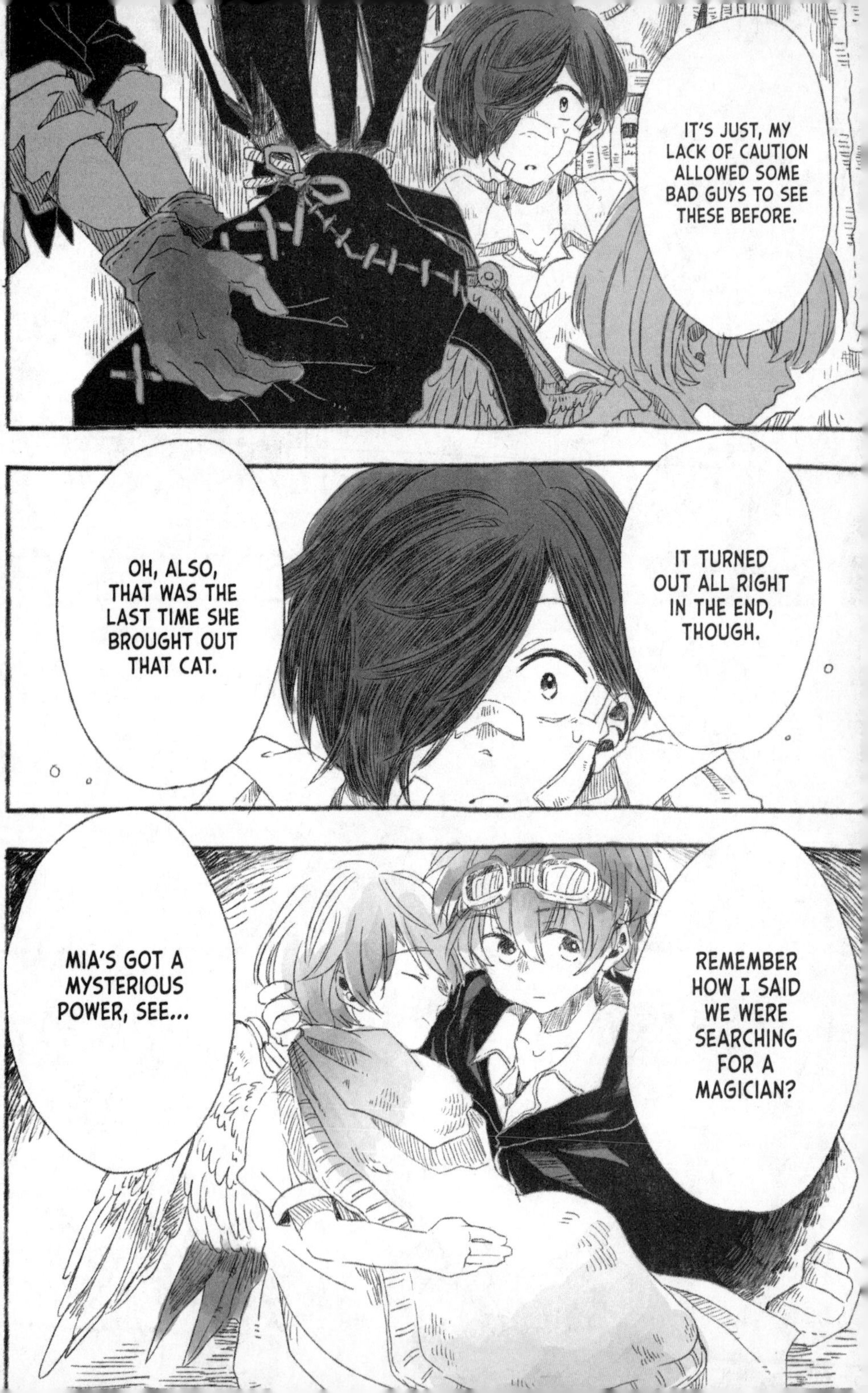
IT'S JUST, MY LACK OF CAUTION ALLOWED SOME BAD GUYS TO SEE THESE BEFORE.
IT TURNED OUT ALL RIGHT IN THE END, THOUGH.
OH, ALSO, THAT WAS THE LAST TIME SHE BROUGHT OUT THAT CAT.
REMEMBER HOW I SAID WE WERE SEARCHING FOR A MAGICIAN?
MIA'S GOT A MYSTERIOUS POWER, SEE...

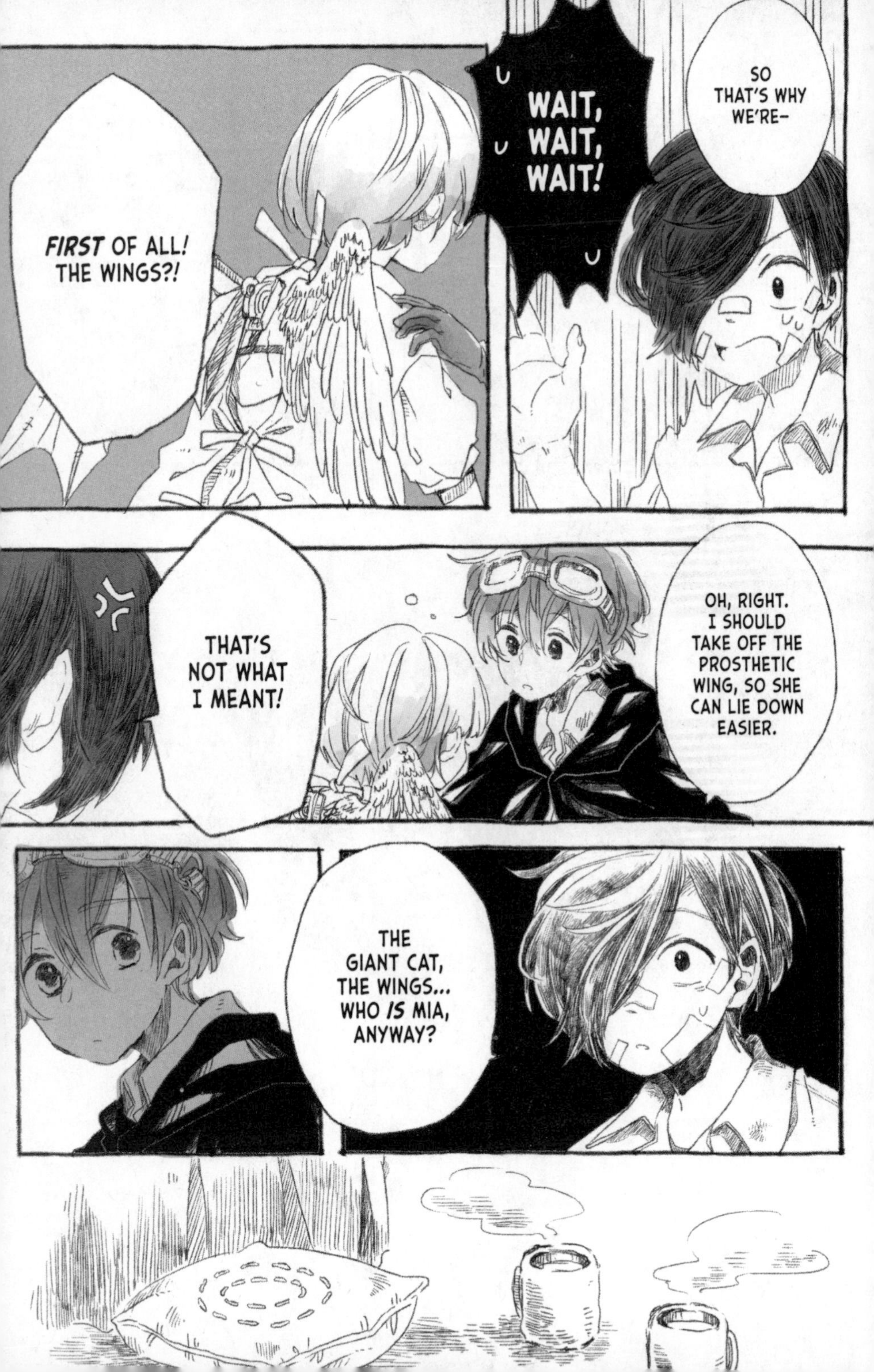
SO THAT'S WHY WE'RE–
WAIT, WAIT, WAIT!
FIRST OF ALL! THE WINGS?!
OH, RIGHT. I SHOULD TAKE OFF THE PROSTHETIC WING, SO SHE CAN LIE DOWN EASIER.
THAT'S NOT WHAT I MEANT!
THE GIANT CAT, THE WINGS... WHO IS MIA, ANYWAY?

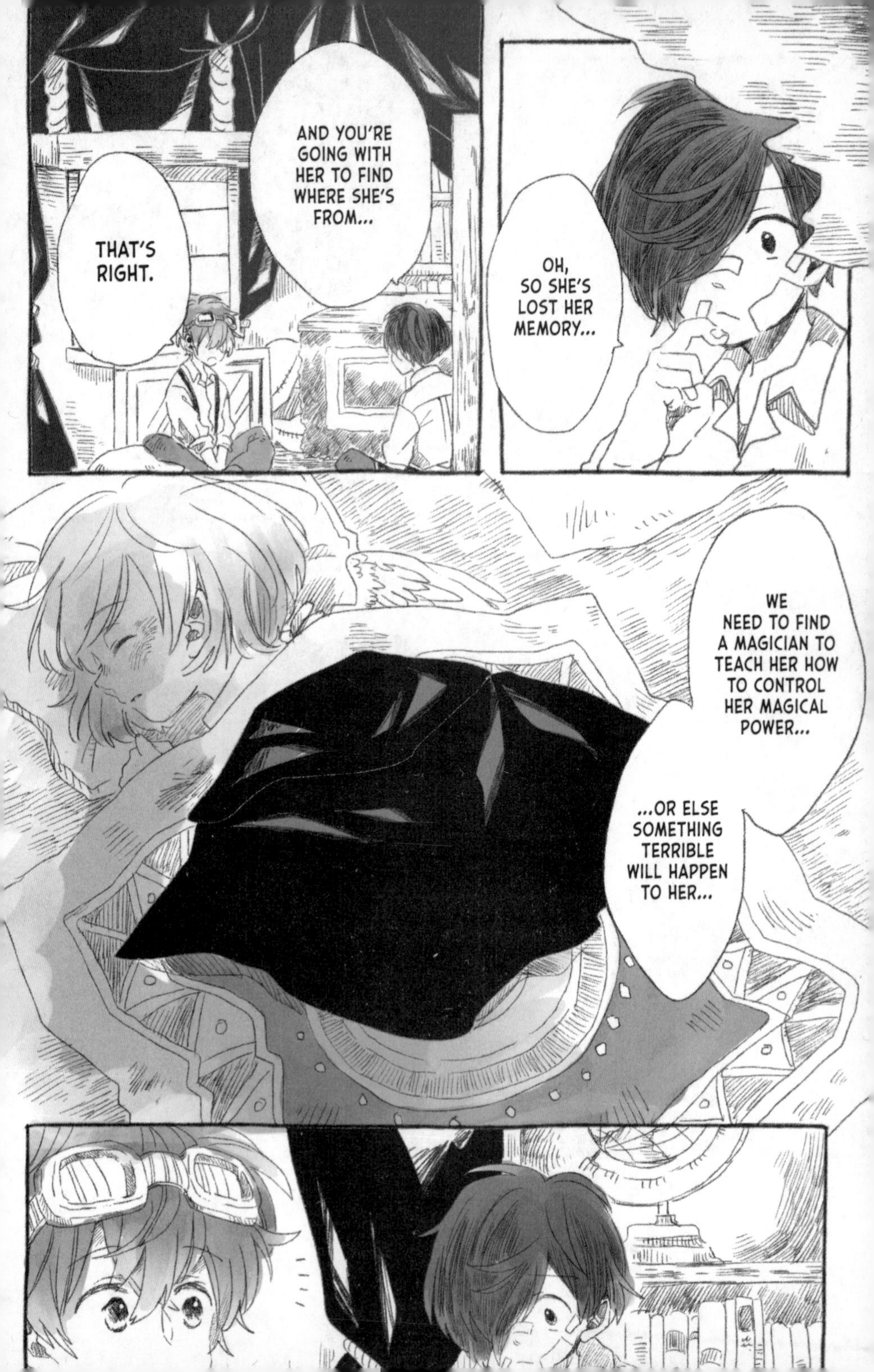
OH, SO SHE'S LOST HER MEMORY...
AND YOU'RE GOING WITH HER TO FIND WHERE SHE'S FROM...
THAT'S RIGHT.
WE NEED TO FIND A MAGICIAN TO TEACH HER HOW TO CONTROL HER MAGICAL POWER...
...OR ELSE SOMETHING TERRIBLE WILL HAPPEN TO HER...

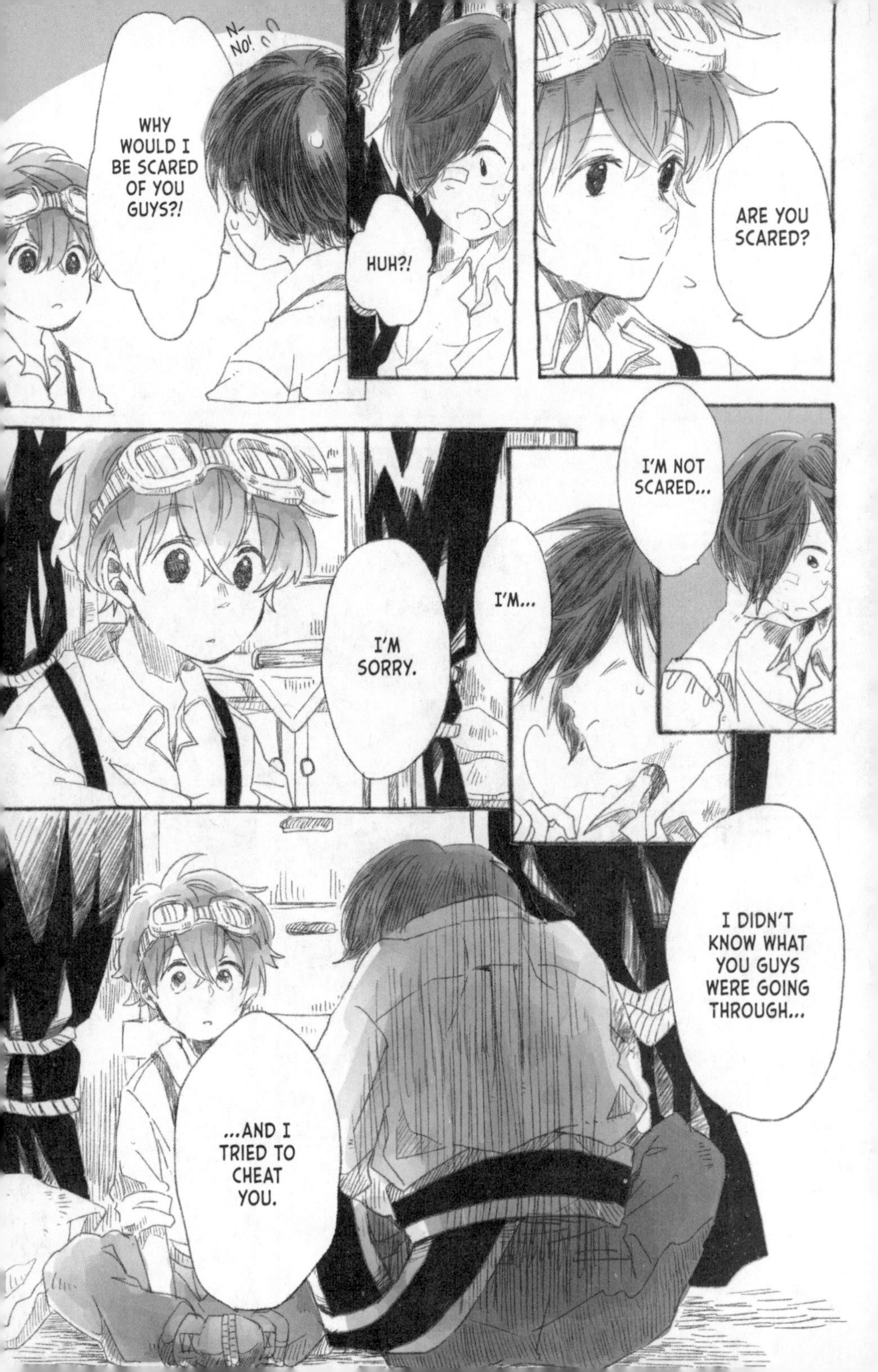
ARE YOU SCARED?
HUH?!
N- NO!
WHY WOULD I BE SCARED OF YOU GUYS?!
I'M NOT SCARED...
I'M...
I'M SORRY.
I DIDN'T KNOW WHAT YOU GUYS WERE GOING THROUGH...
...AND I TRIED TO CHEAT YOU.

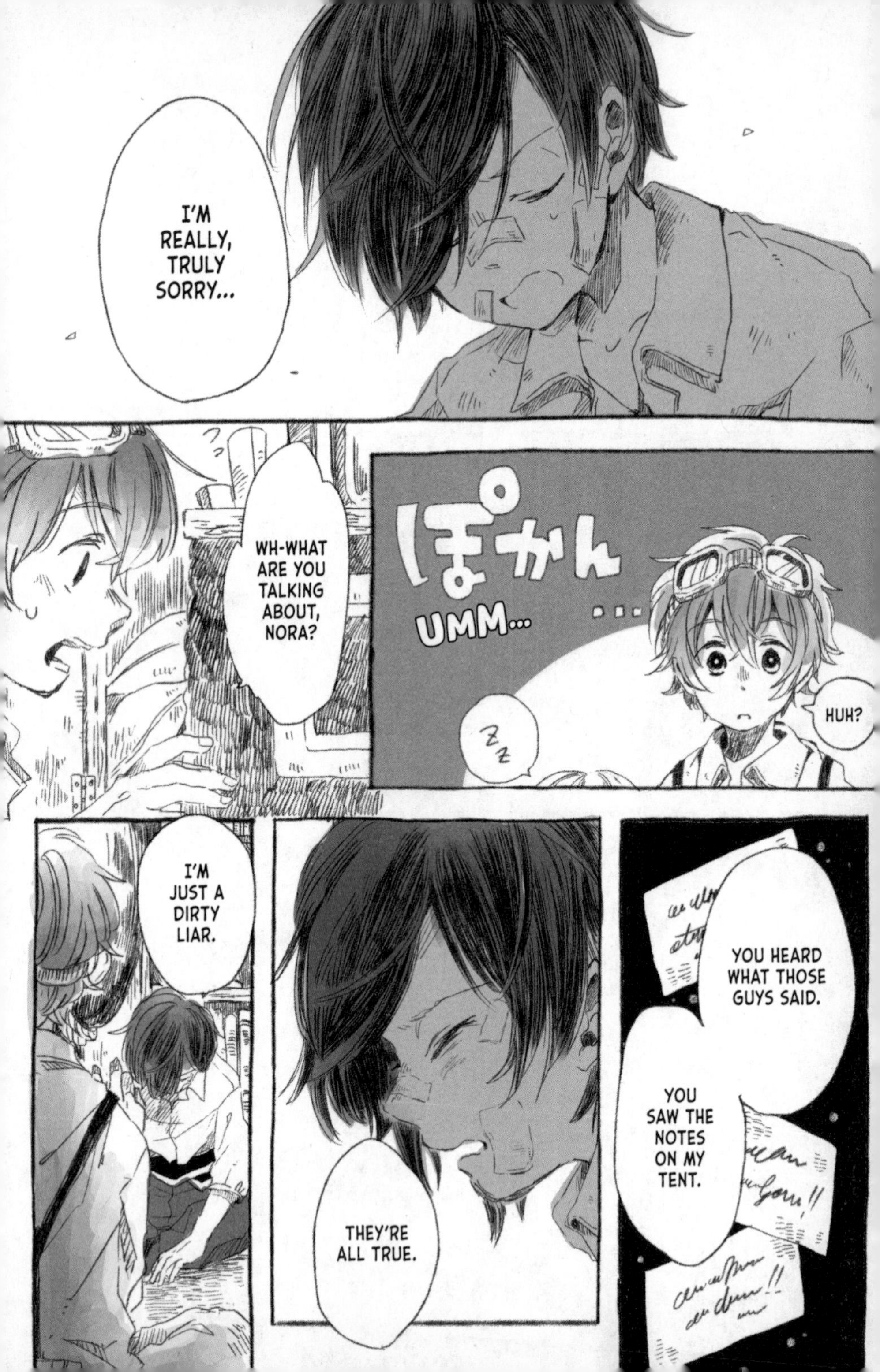
I'M REALLY, TRULY SORRY...
ぽかん
UMM...
...
HUH?
ZZ
WH-WHAT ARE YOU TALKING ABOUT, NORA?
YOU HEARD WHAT THOSE GUYS SAID.
YOU SAW THE NOTES ON MY TENT.
THEY'RE ALL TRUE.
I'M JUST A DIRTY LIAR.

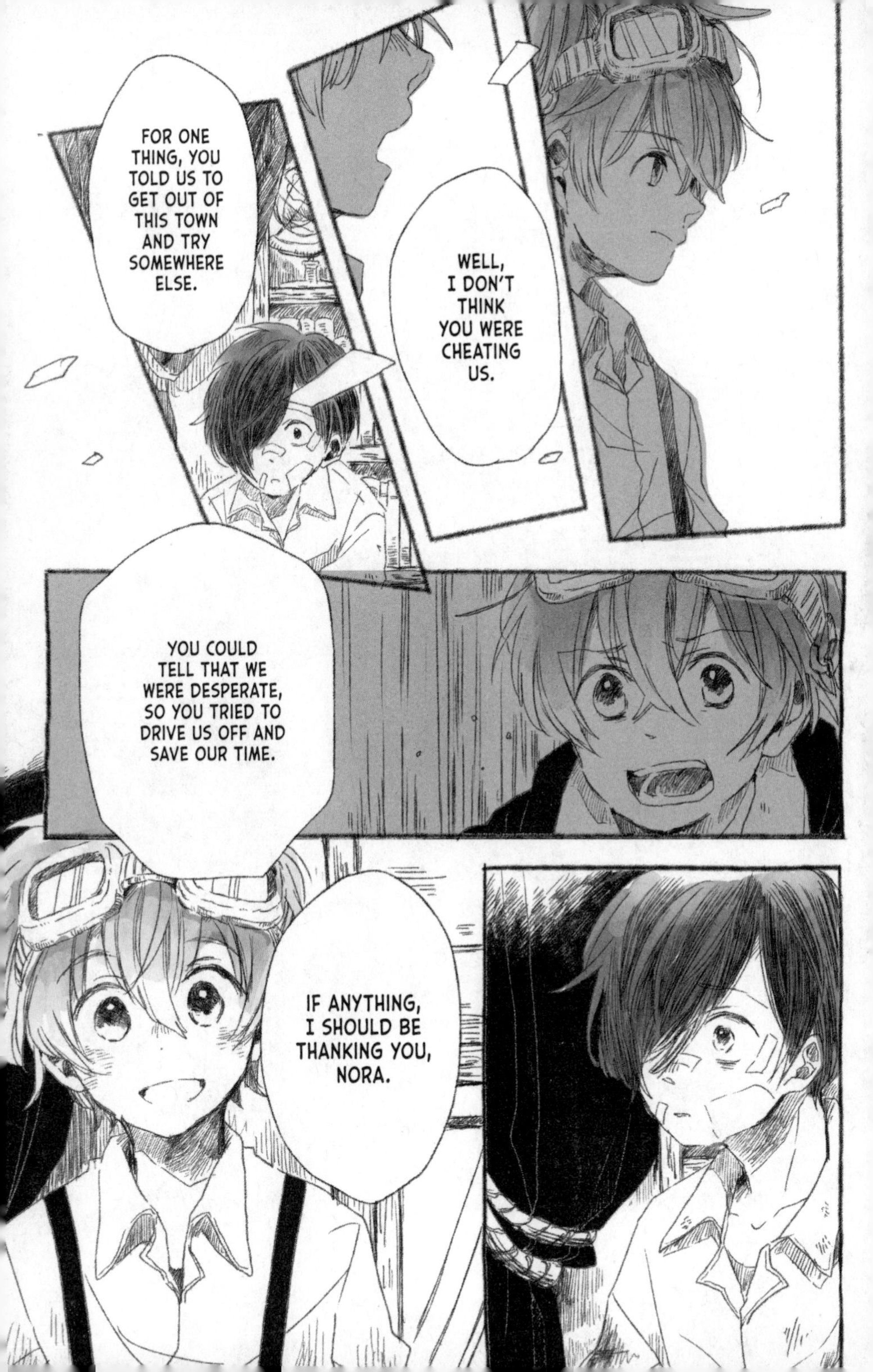
WELL, I DON'T THINK YOU WERE CHEATING US.
FOR ONE THING, YOU TOLD US TO GET OUT OF THIS TOWN AND TRY SOMEWHERE ELSE.
YOU COULD TELL THAT WE WERE DESPERATE, SO YOU TRIED TO DRIVE US OFF AND SAVE OUR TIME.
IF ANYTHING, I SHOULD BE THANKING YOU, NORA.

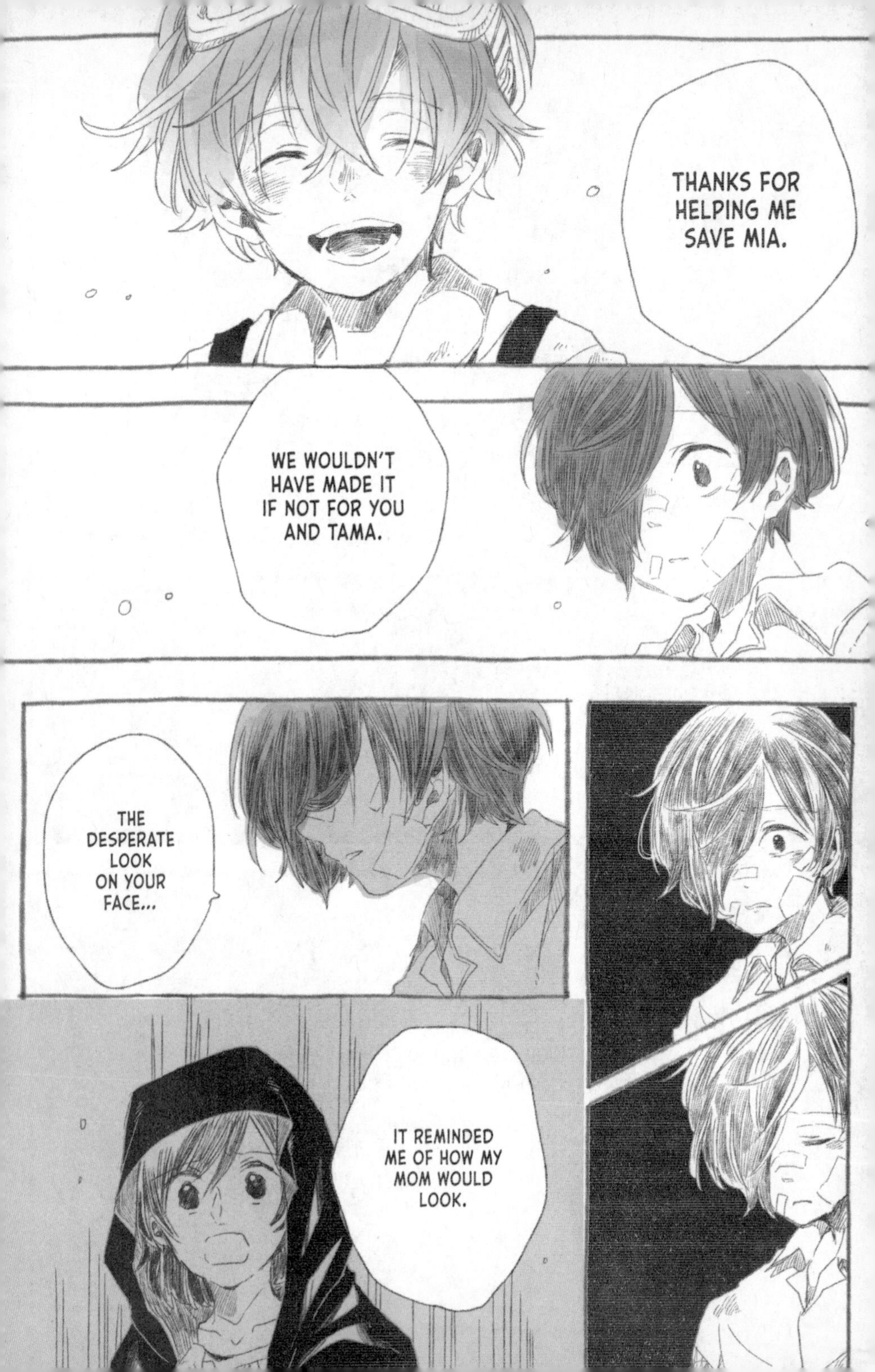
THANKS FOR HELPING ME SAVE MIA.
WE WOULDN'T HAVE MADE IT IF NOT FOR YOU AND TAMA.
THE DESPERATE LOOK ON YOUR FACE...
IT REMINDED ME OF HOW MY MOM WOULD LOOK.

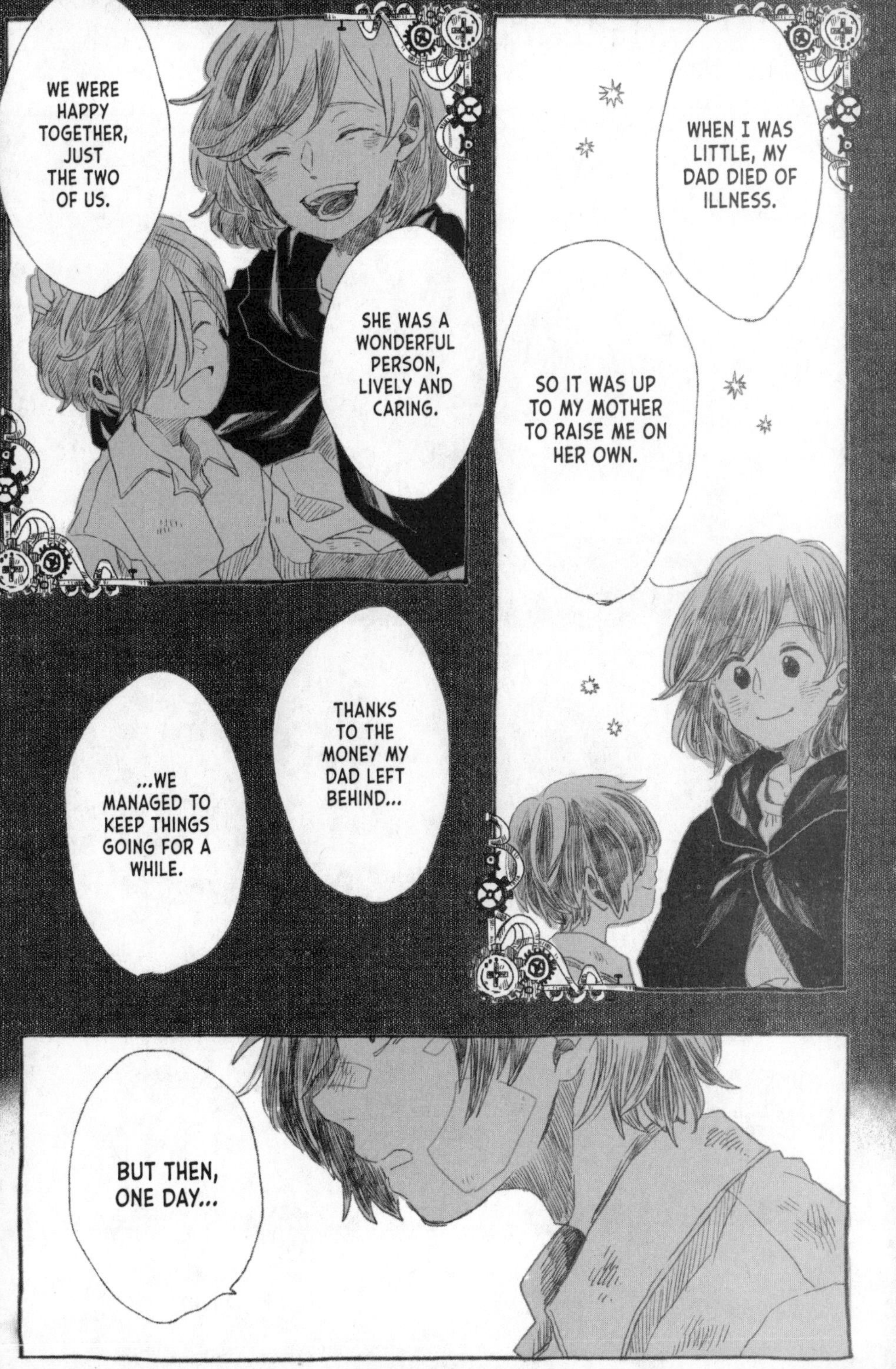
WHEN I WAS LITTLE, MY DAD DIED OF ILLNESS.
SO IT WAS UP TO MY MOTHER TO RAISE ME ON HER OWN.
SHE WAS A WONDERFUL PERSON, LIVELY AND CARING.
WE WERE HAPPY TOGETHER, JUST THE TWO OF US.
THANKS TO THE MONEY MY DAD LEFT BEHIND...
...WE MANAGED TO KEEP THINGS GOING FOR A WHILE.
BUT THEN, ONE DAY...

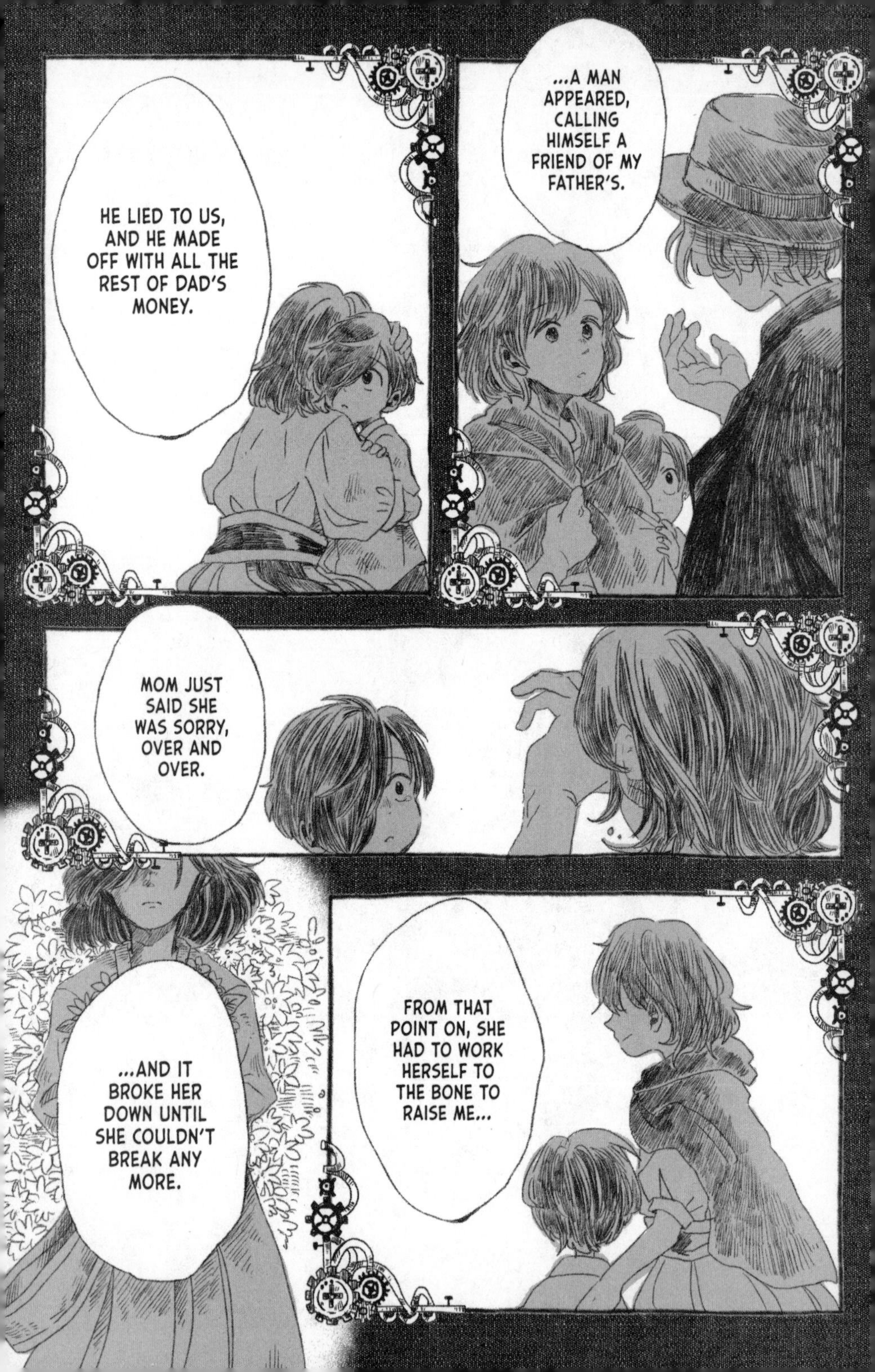
...A MAN APPEARED, CALLING HIMSELF A FRIEND OF MY FATHER'S.
HE LIED TO US, AND HE MADE OFF WITH ALL THE REST OF DAD'S MONEY.
MOM JUST SAID SHE WAS SORRY, OVER AND OVER.
FROM THAT POINT ON, SHE HAD TO WORK HERSELF TO THE BONE TO RAISE ME...
...AND IT BROKE HER DOWN UNTIL SHE COULDN'T BREAK ANY MORE.

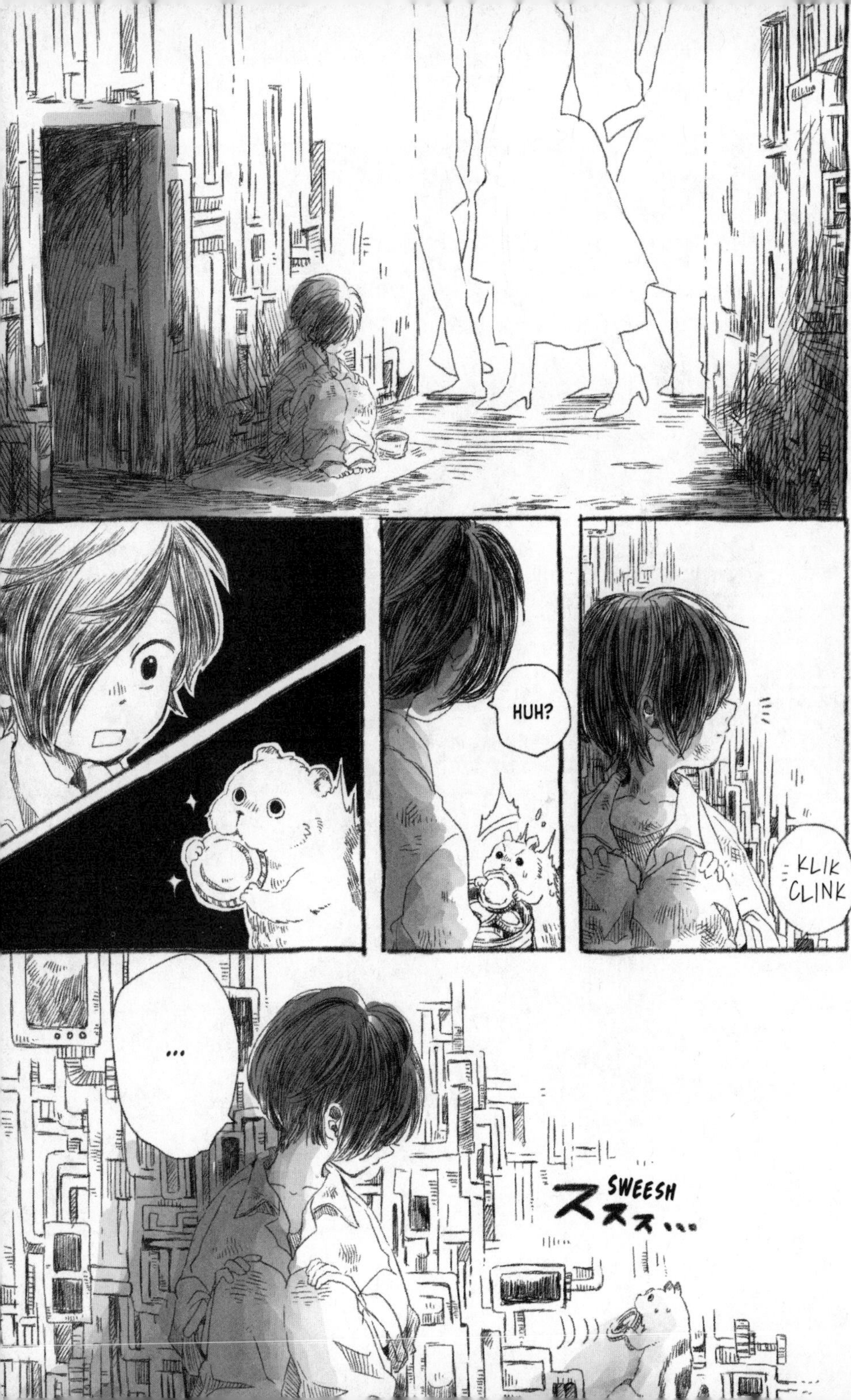
KLIK
CLINK
HUH?
...
SWEESH
ススス...

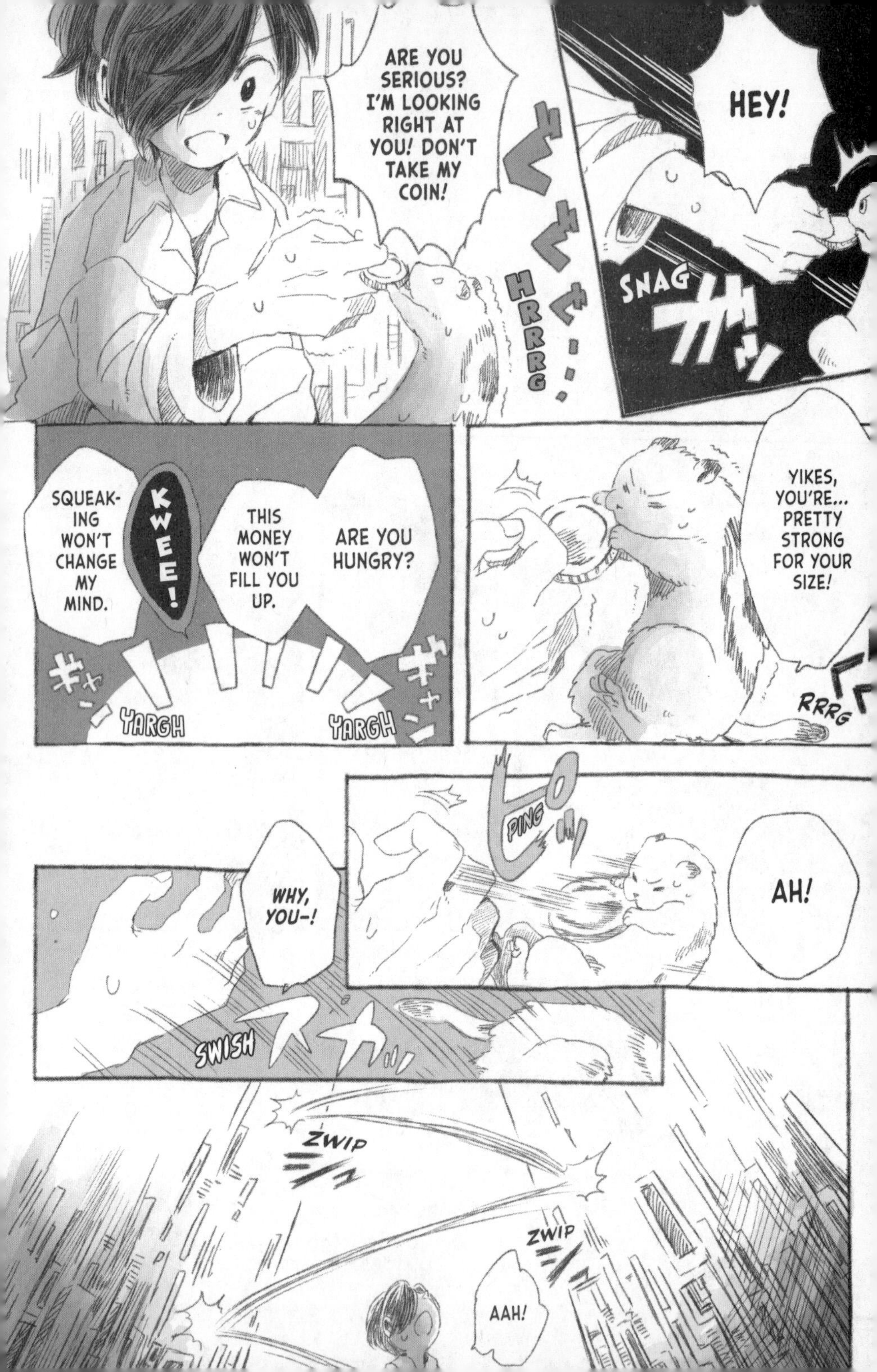
HEY!
SNAG
ARE YOU SERIOUS? I'M LOOKING RIGHT AT YOU! DON'T TAKE MY COIN!
HRRRG
YIKES, YOU'RE... PRETTY STRONG FOR YOUR SIZE!
RRRG
ARE YOU HUNGRY?
THIS MONEY WON'T FILL YOU UP.
KWEE!
SQUEAK-ING WON'T CHANGE MY MIND.
YARGH
YARGH
AH!
PING
WHY, YOU-!
SWISH
ZWIP
ZWIP
AAH!

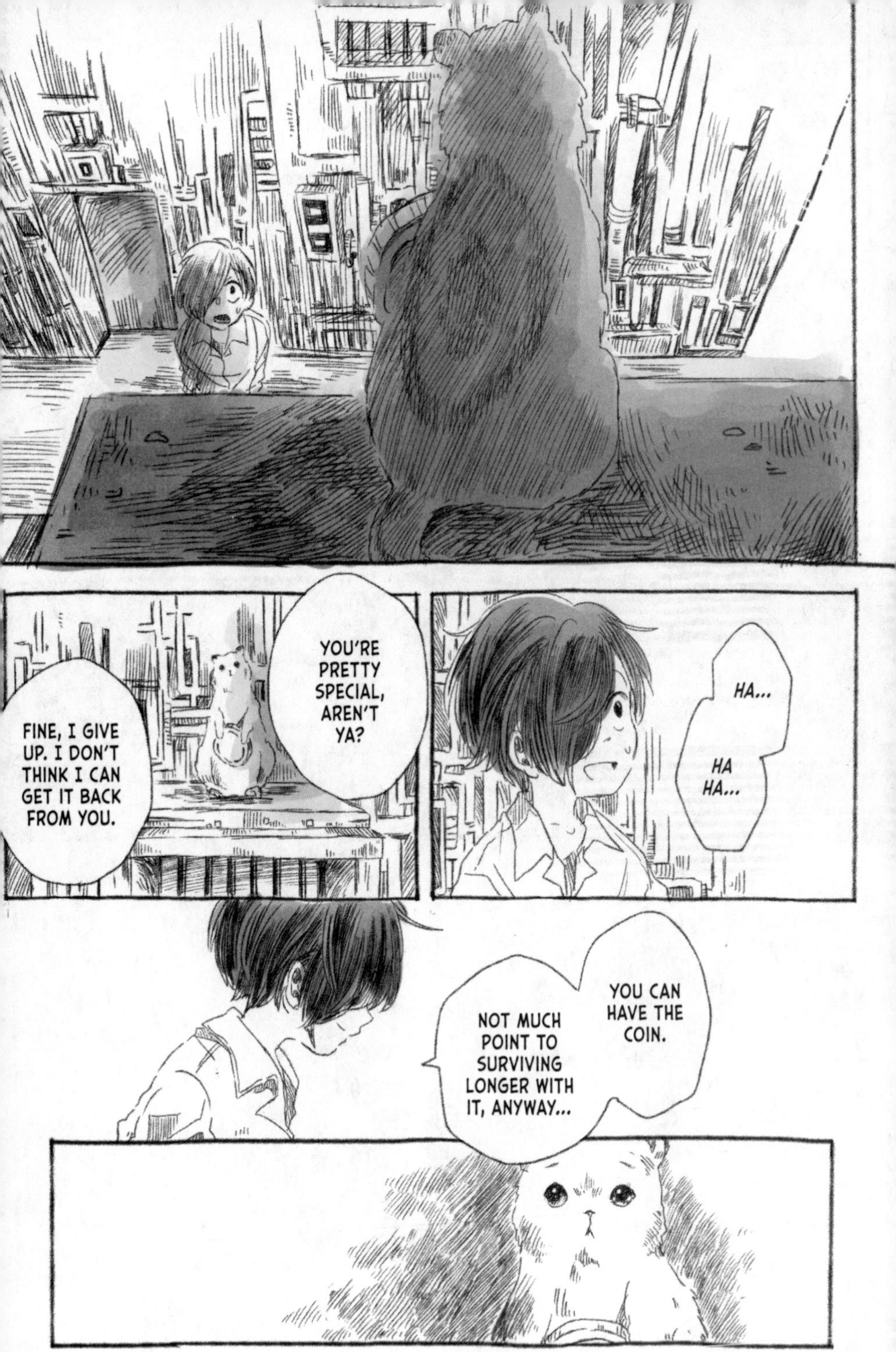
HA... HA HA...
YOU'RE PRETTY SPECIAL, AREN'T YA?
FINE, I GIVE UP. I DON'T THINK I CAN GET IT BACK FROM YOU.
YOU CAN HAVE THE COIN.
NOT MUCH POINT TO SURVIVING LONGER WITH IT, ANYWAY...

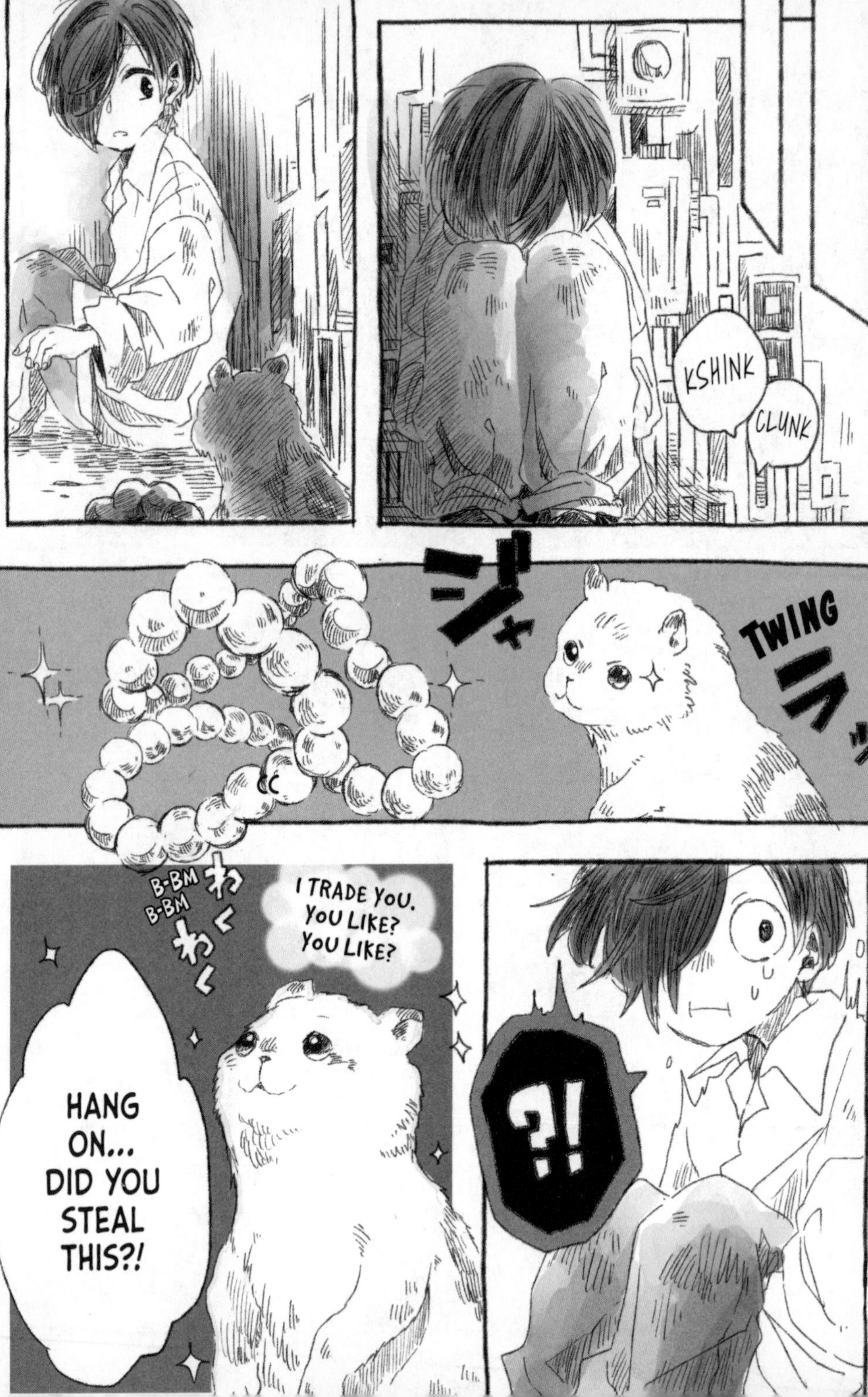
KSHINK
CLUNK
ジャラッ
TWING
?!
I TRADE YOU. YOU LIKE? YOU LIKE?
B-BM B-BM
わくわく
HANG ON... DID YOU STEAL THIS?!

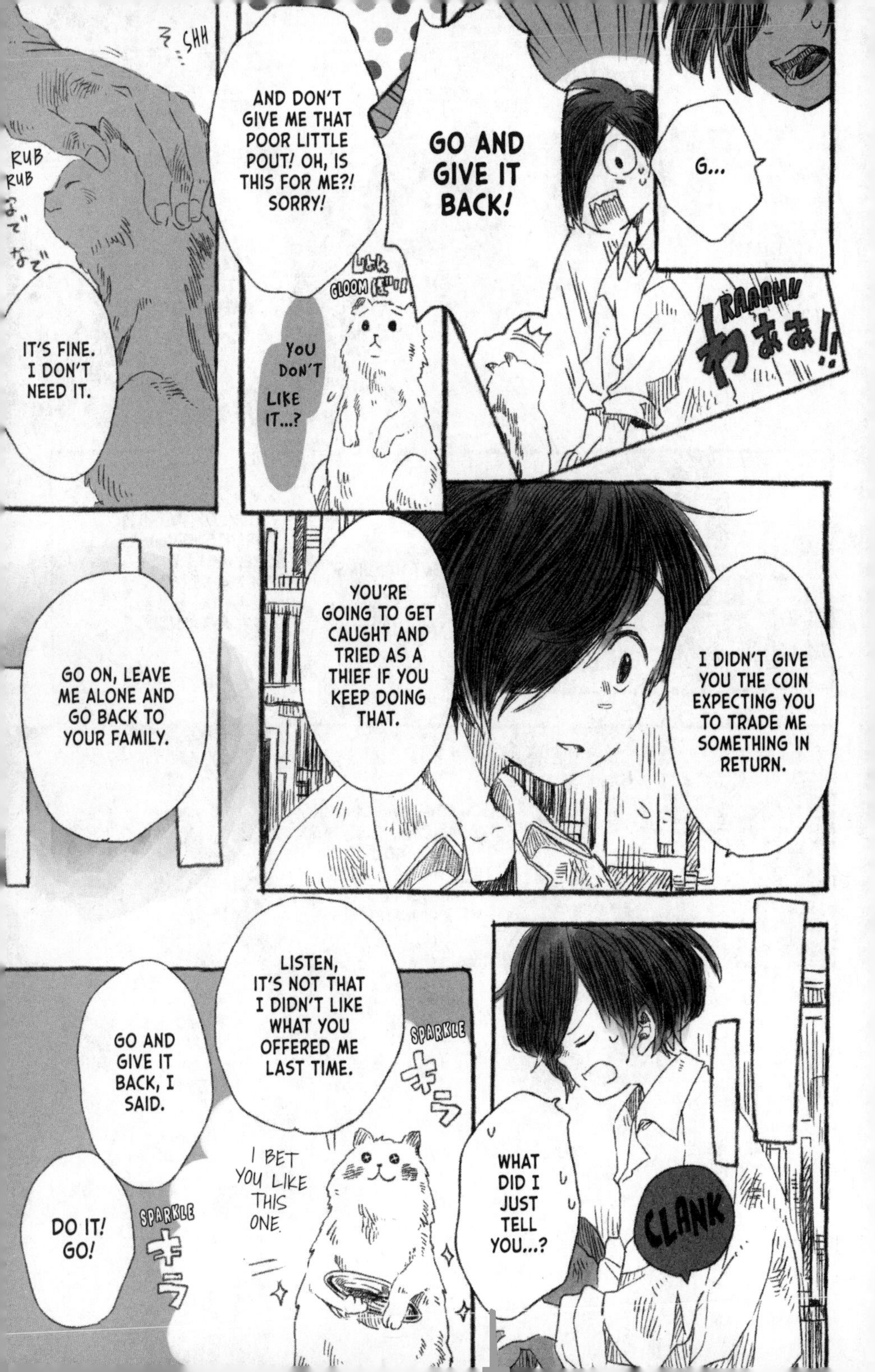
G...
GO AND GIVE IT BACK!
RAAAH!!
わぁぁ!!
AND DON'T GIVE ME THAT POOR LITTLE POUT! OH, IS THIS FOR ME?! SORRY!
GLOOM
YOU DON'T LIKE IT...?
SHH
RUB RUB
なでなで
IT'S FINE. I DON'T NEED IT.
I DIDN'T GIVE YOU THE COIN EXPECTING YOU TO TRADE ME SOMETHING IN RETURN.
YOU'RE GOING TO GET CAUGHT AND TRIED AS A THIEF IF YOU KEEP DOING THAT.
GO ON, LEAVE ME ALONE AND GO BACK TO YOUR FAMILY.
CLANK
WHAT DID I JUST TELL YOU...?
LISTEN, IT'S NOT THAT I DIDN'T LIKE WHAT YOU OFFERED ME LAST TIME.
SPARKLE
キラ
I BET YOU LIKE THIS ONE.
GO AND GIVE IT BACK, I SAID.
SPARKLE
キラ
DO IT! GO!

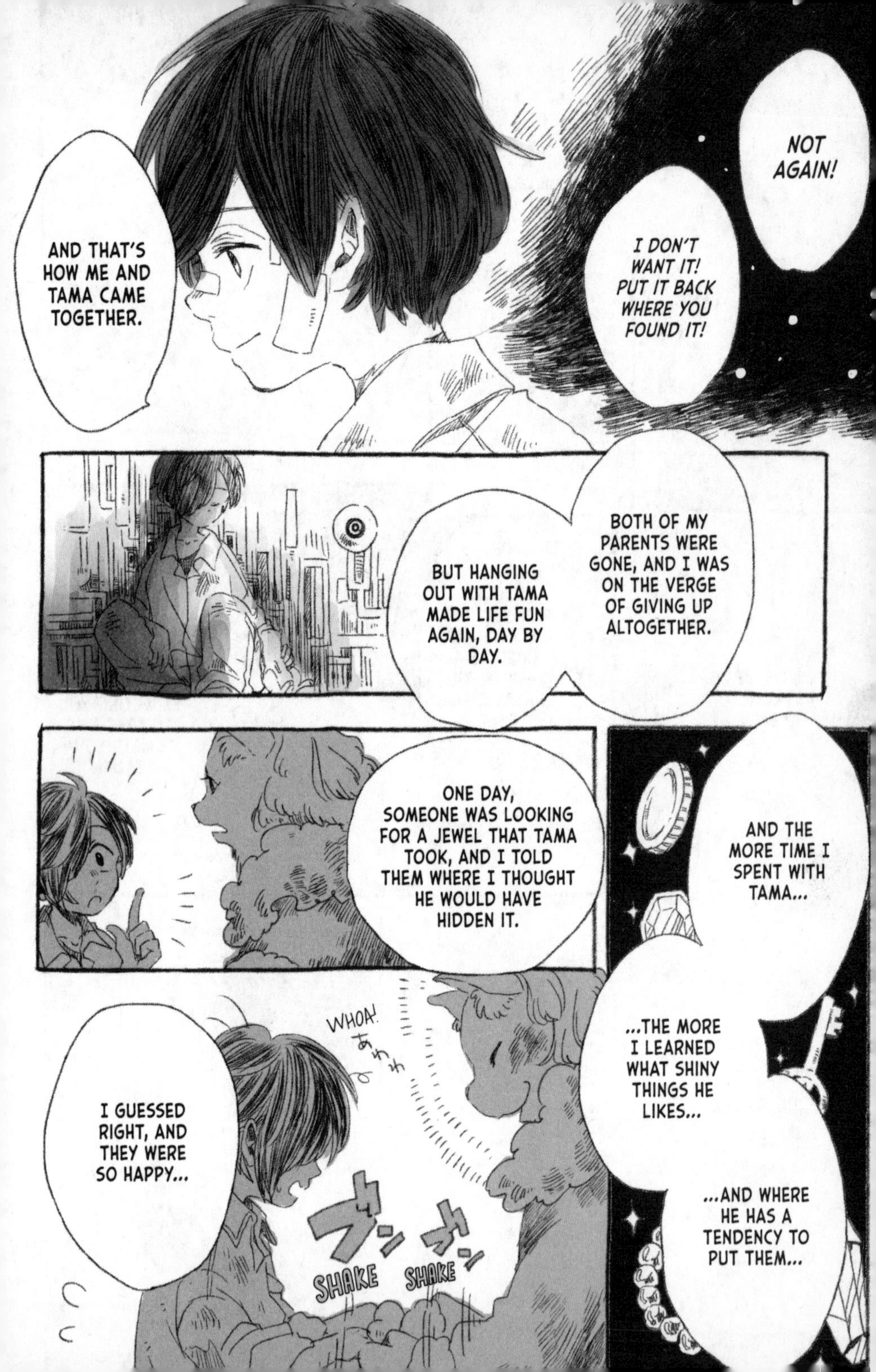
NOT AGAIN!
I DON'T WANT IT! PUT IT BACK WHERE YOU FOUND IT!
AND THAT'S HOW ME AND TAMA CAME TOGETHER.
BOTH OF MY PARENTS WERE GONE, AND I WAS ON THE VERGE OF GIVING UP ALTOGETHER.
BUT HANGING OUT WITH TAMA MADE LIFE FUN AGAIN, DAY BY DAY.
AND THE MORE TIME I SPENT WITH TAMA...
...THE MORE I LEARNED WHAT SHINY THINGS HE LIKES...
...AND WHERE HE HAS A TENDENCY TO PUT THEM...
ONE DAY, SOMEONE WAS LOOKING FOR A JEWEL THAT TAMA TOOK, AND I TOLD THEM WHERE I THOUGHT HE WOULD HAVE HIDDEN IT.
WHOA!
I GUESSED RIGHT, AND THEY WERE SO HAPPY...
SHAKE SHAKE

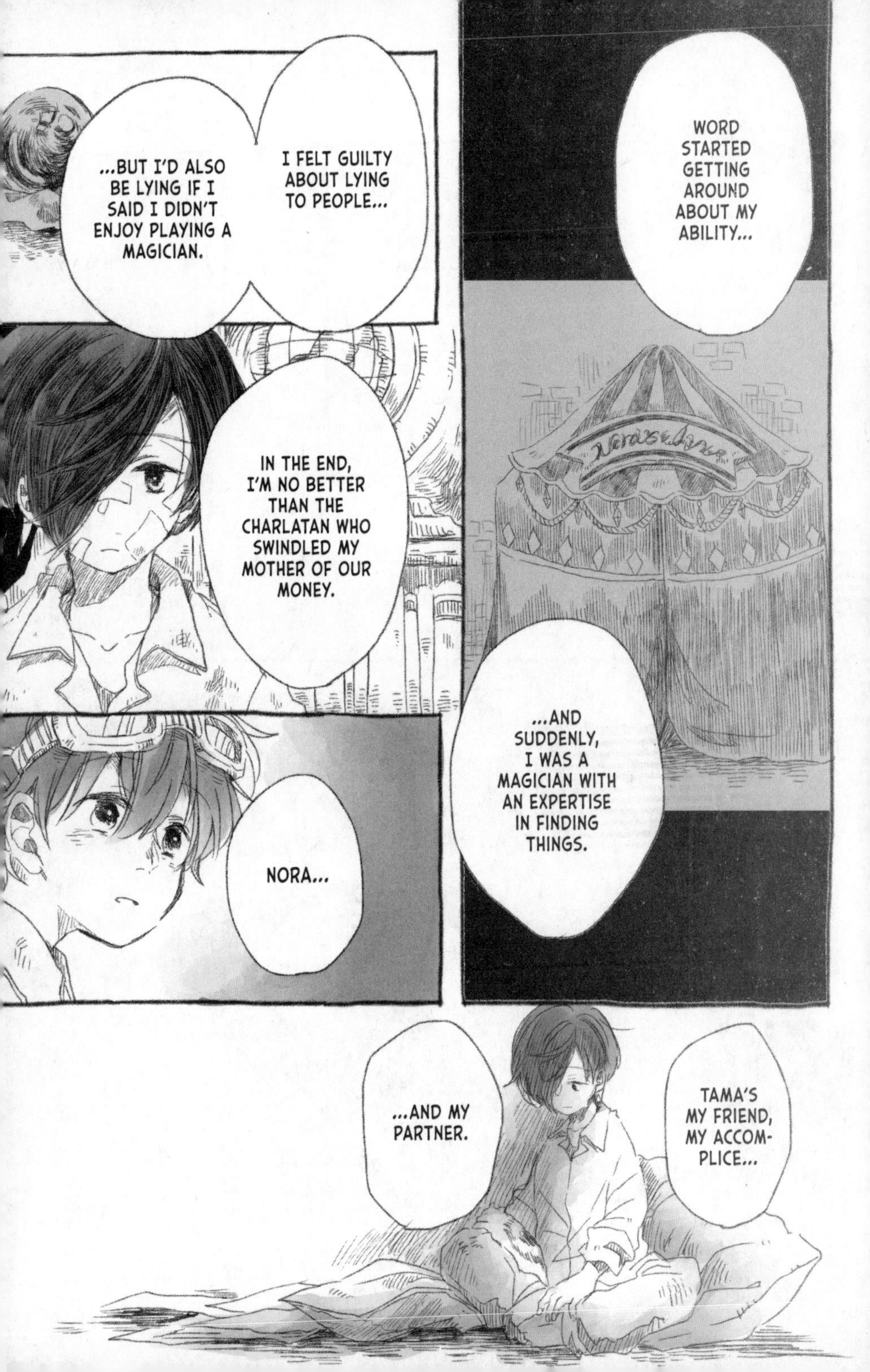
WORD STARTED GETTING AROUND ABOUT MY ABILITY...
...AND SUDDENLY, I WAS A MAGICIAN WITH AN EXPERTISE IN FINDING THINGS.
I FELT GUILTY ABOUT LYING TO PEOPLE...
...BUT I'D ALSO BE LYING IF I SAID I DIDN'T ENJOY PLAYING A MAGICIAN.
IN THE END, I'M NO BETTER THAN THE CHARLATAN WHO SWINDLED MY MOTHER OF OUR MONEY.
NORA...
TAMA'S MY FRIEND, MY ACCOM-PLICE...
...AND MY PARTNER.

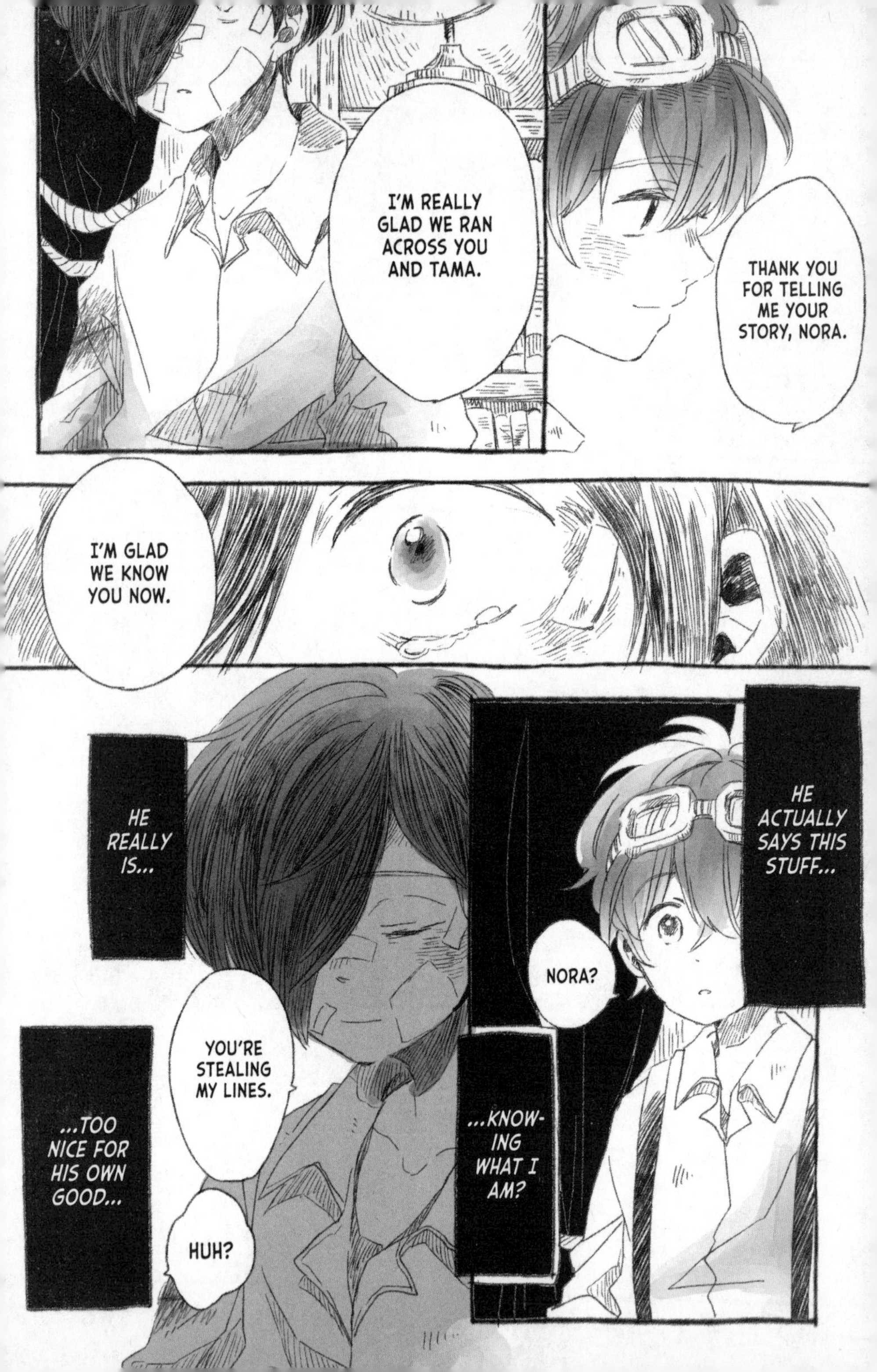
THANK YOU FOR TELLING ME YOUR STORY, NORA.
I'M REALLY GLAD WE RAN ACROSS YOU AND TAMA.
I'M GLAD WE KNOW YOU NOW.
HE ACTUALLY SAYS THIS STUFF...
NORA?
...KNOWING-ING WHAT I AM?
HE REALLY IS...
YOU'RE STEALING MY LINES.
...TOO NICE FOR HIS OWN GOOD...
HUH?

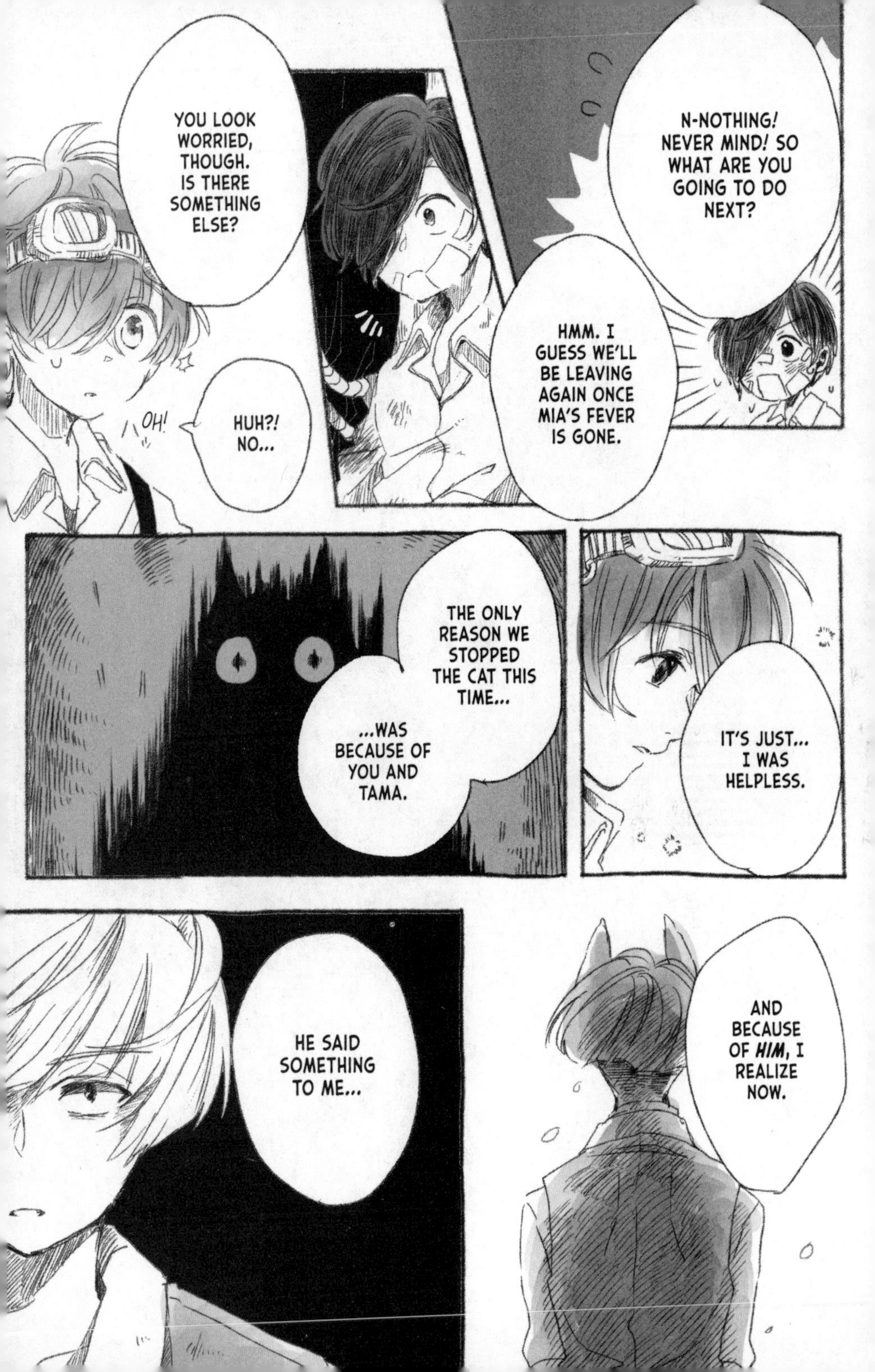
N-NOTHING! NEVER MIND! SO WHAT ARE YOU GOING TO DO NEXT?
HMM. I GUESS WE'LL BE LEAVING AGAIN ONCE MIA'S FEVER IS GONE.
YOU LOOK WORRIED, THOUGH. IS THERE SOMETHING ELSE?
HUH?! NO...
OH!
IT'S JUST... I WAS HELPLESS.
THE ONLY REASON WE STOPPED THE CAT THIS TIME...
...WAS BECAUSE OF YOU AND TAMA.
AND BECAUSE OF *HIM*, I REALIZE NOW.
HE SAID SOMETHING TO ME...

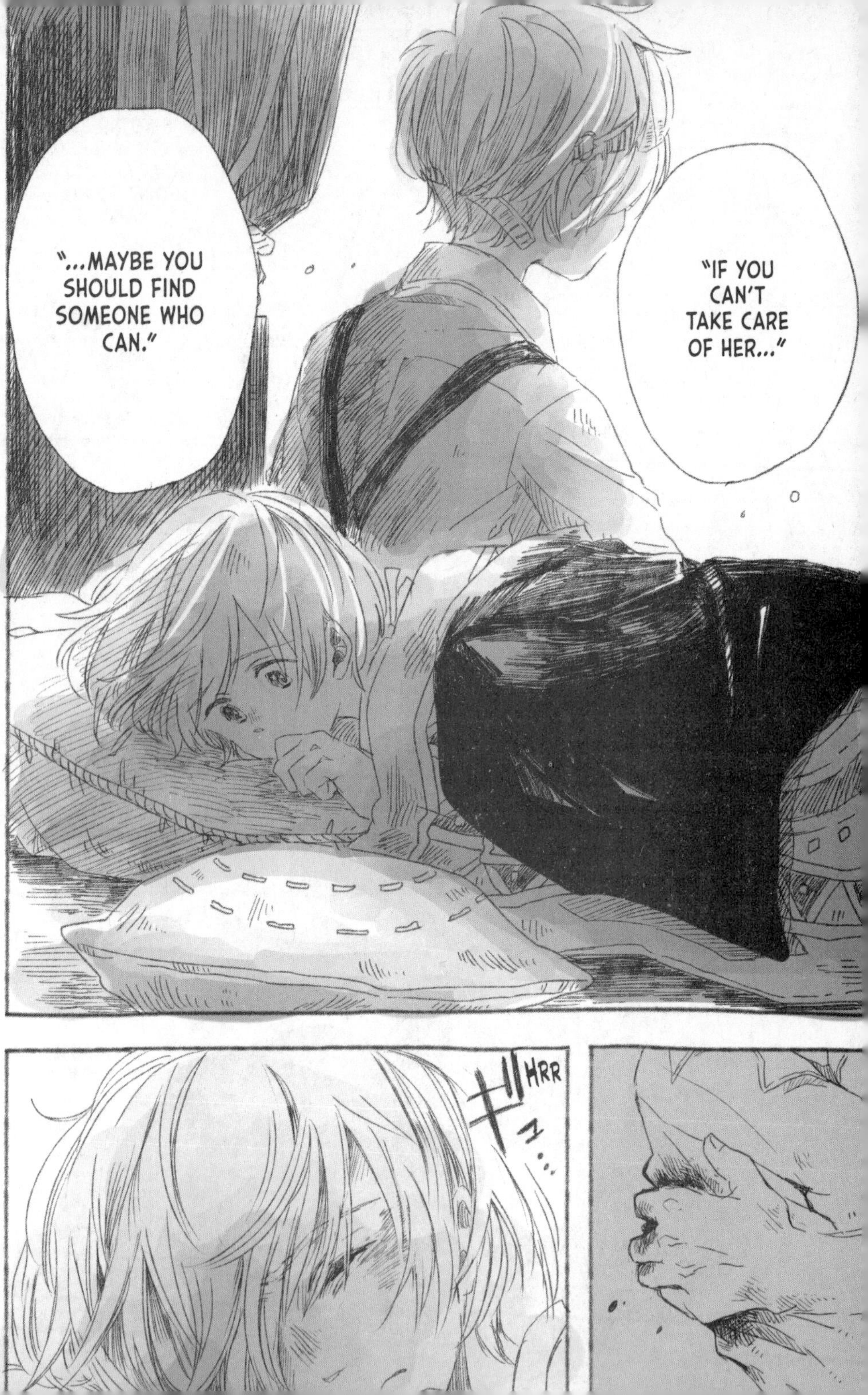
"IF YOU CAN'T TAKE CARE OF HER..."
"...MAYBE YOU SHOULD FIND SOMEONE WHO CAN."
HRR

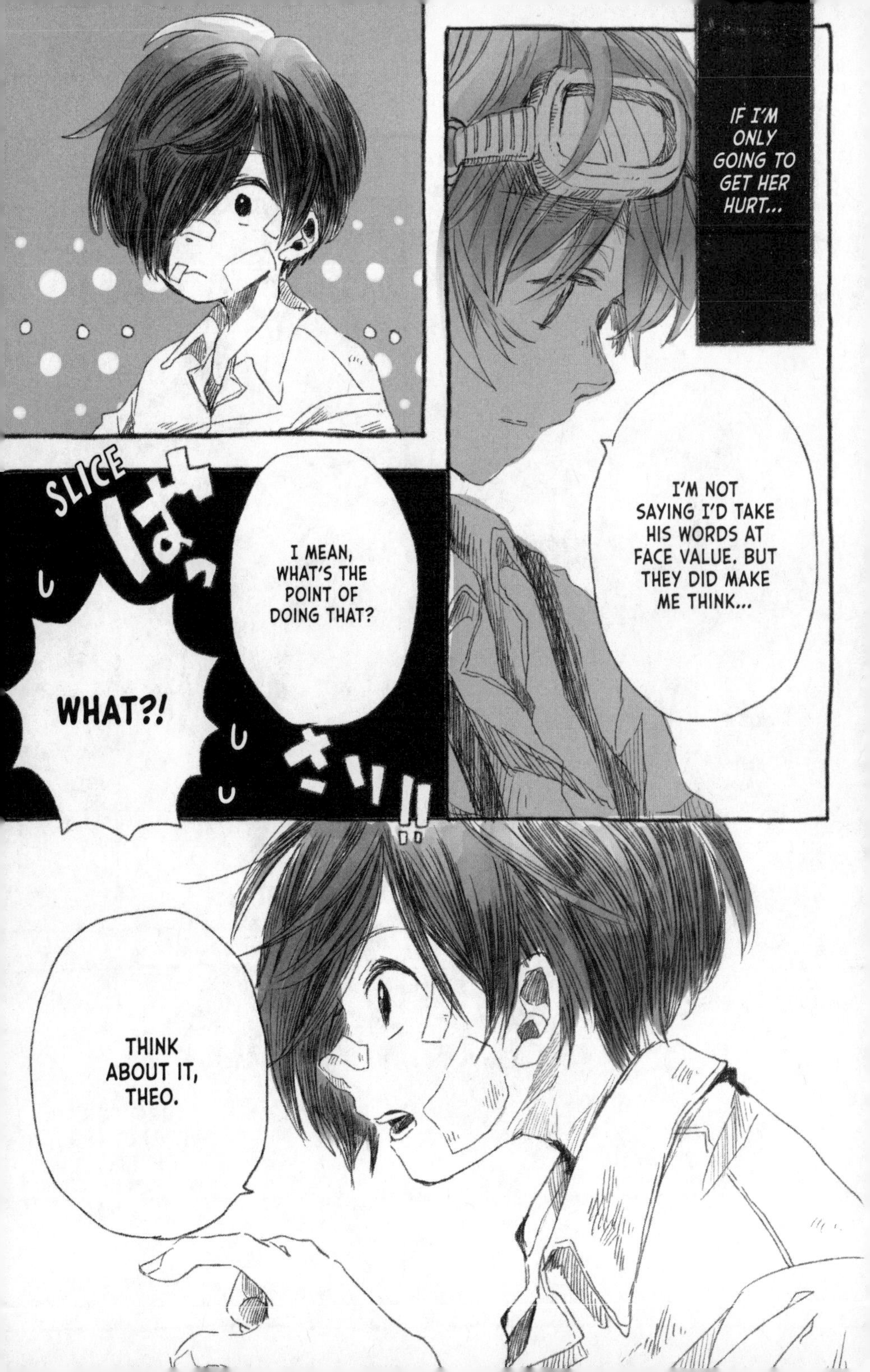
IF I'M ONLY GOING TO GET HER HURT...
I'M NOT SAYING I'D TAKE HIS WORDS AT FACE VALUE. BUT THEY DID MAKE ME THINK...
I MEAN, WHAT'S THE POINT OF DOING THAT?
SLICE
ばっ
WHAT?!
さッ!!
THINK ABOUT IT, THEO.

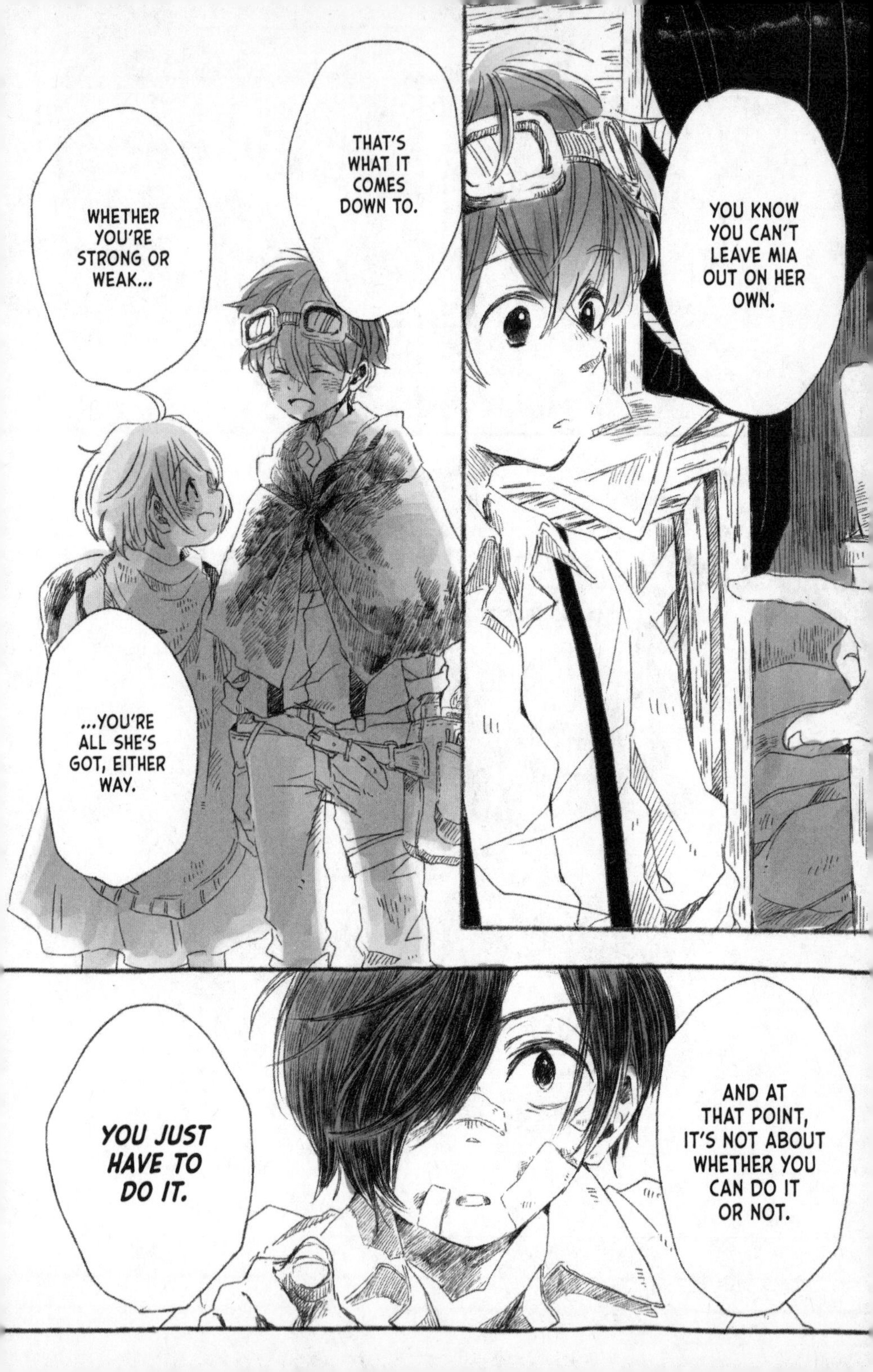
YOU KNOW YOU CAN'T LEAVE MIA OUT ON HER OWN.
THAT'S WHAT IT COMES DOWN TO.
WHETHER YOU'RE STRONG OR WEAK...
...YOU'RE ALL SHE'S GOT, EITHER WAY.
AND AT THAT POINT, IT'S NOT ABOUT WHETHER YOU CAN DO IT OR NOT.
YOU JUST HAVE TO DO IT.

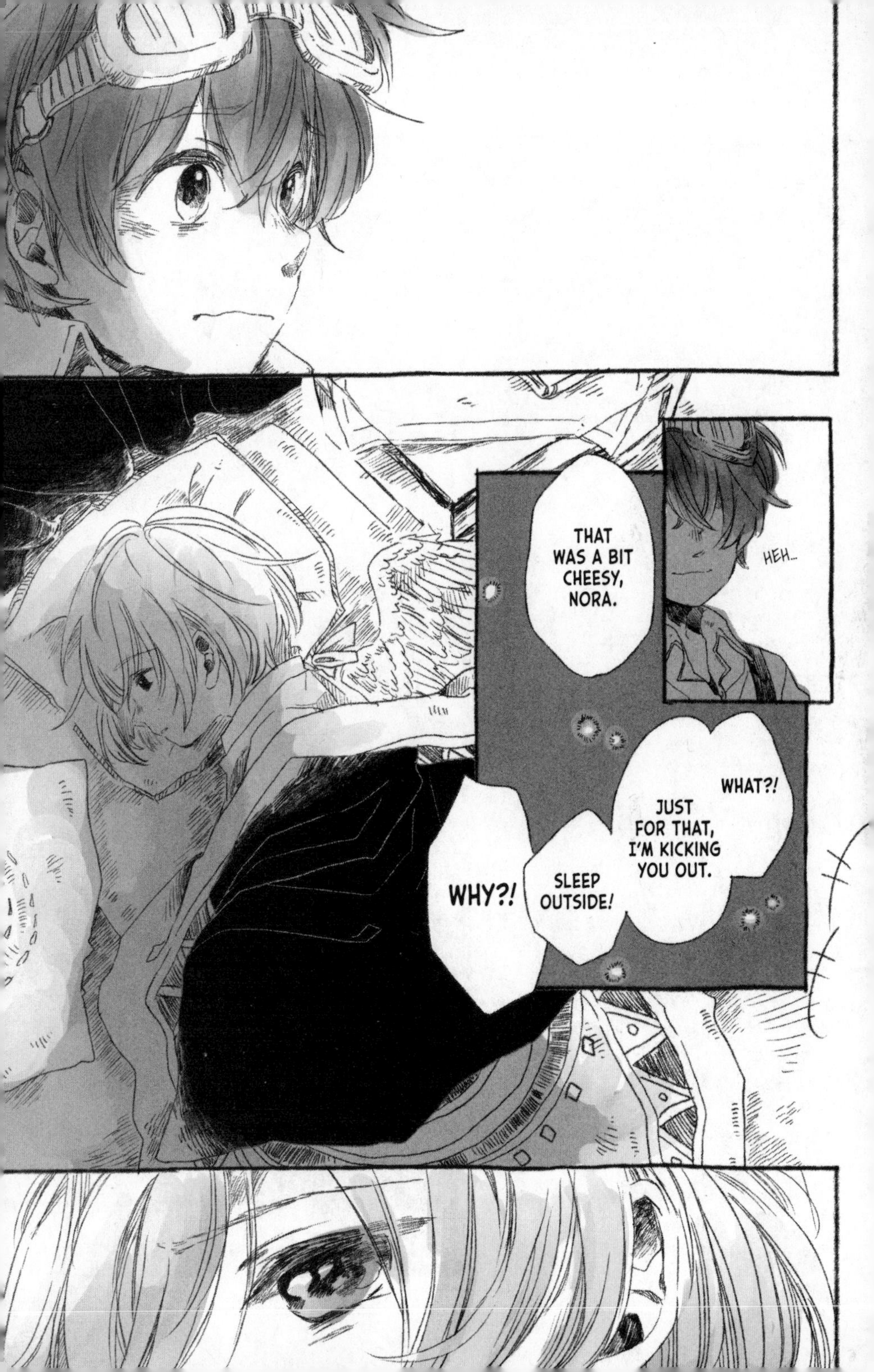
HEH...
THAT WAS A BIT CHEESY, NORA.
WHAT?!
JUST FOR THAT, I'M KICKING YOU OUT.
SLEEP OUTSIDE!
WHY?!

Chapter 17: Like a Distant Melody

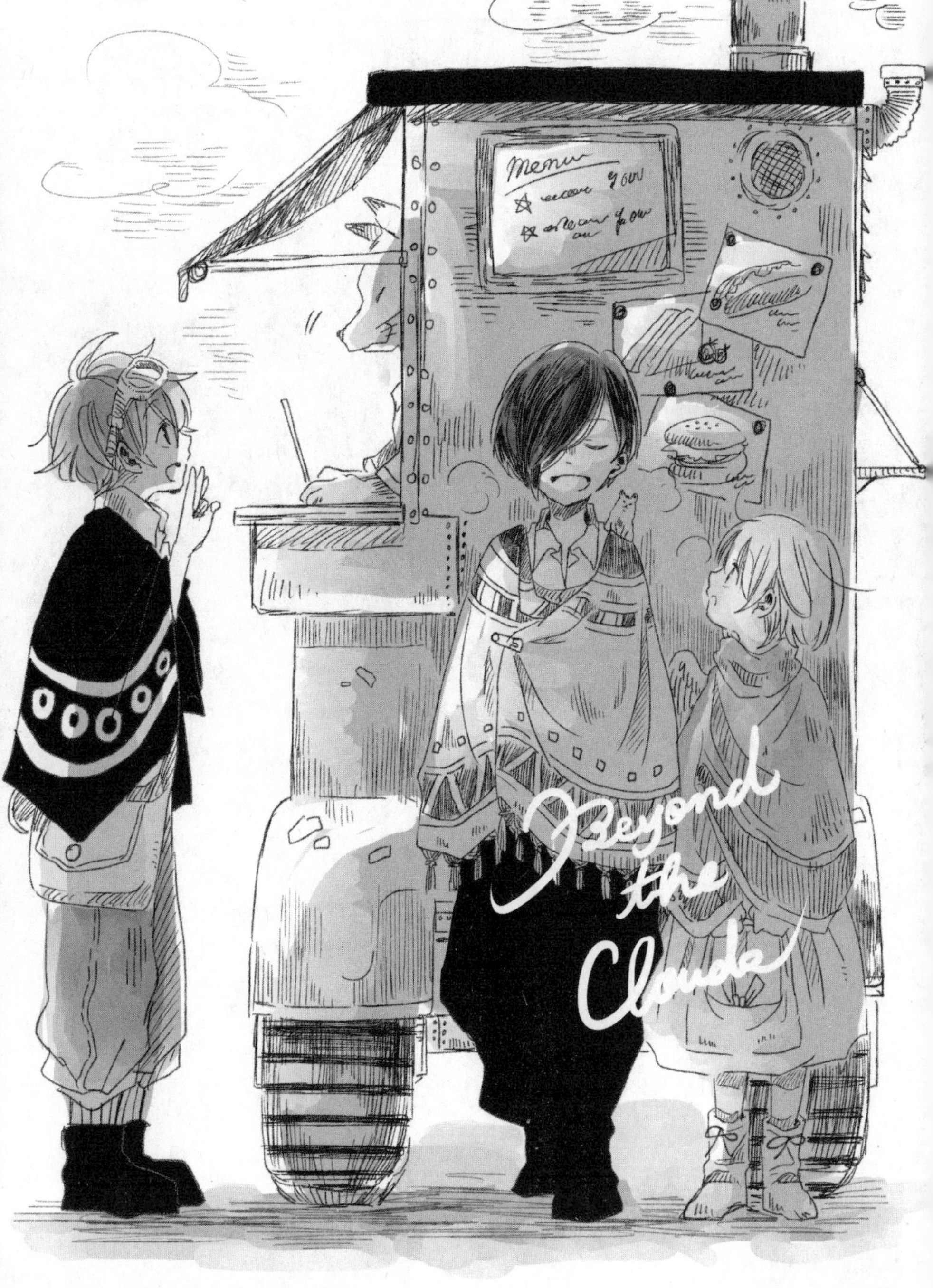
Menu
Beyond the Clouds

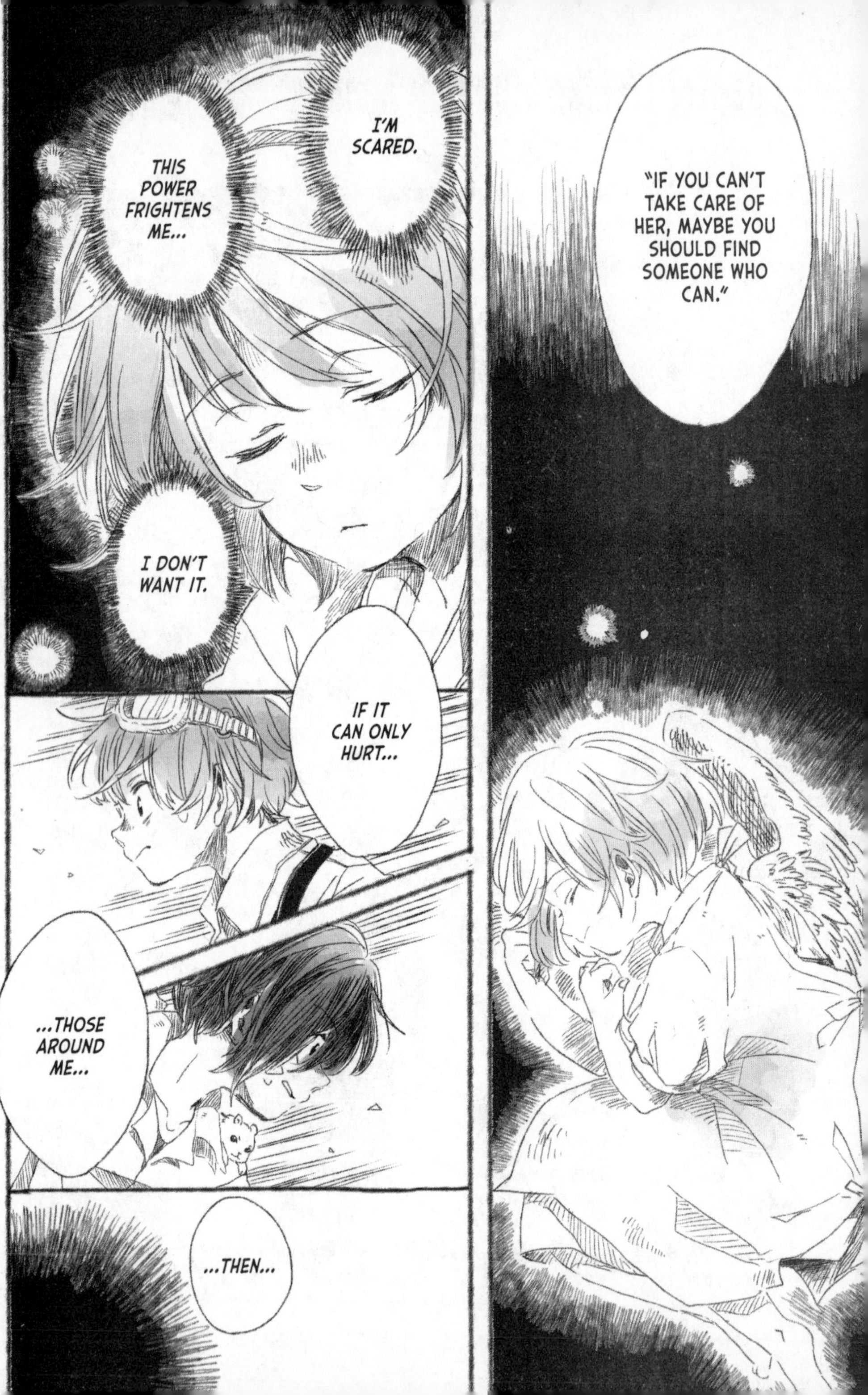
"IF YOU CAN'T TAKE CARE OF HER, MAYBE YOU SHOULD FIND SOMEONE WHO CAN."
I'M SCARED.
THIS POWER FRIGHTENS ME...
I DON'T WANT IT.
IF IT CAN ONLY HURT...
...THOSE AROUND ME...
...THEN...

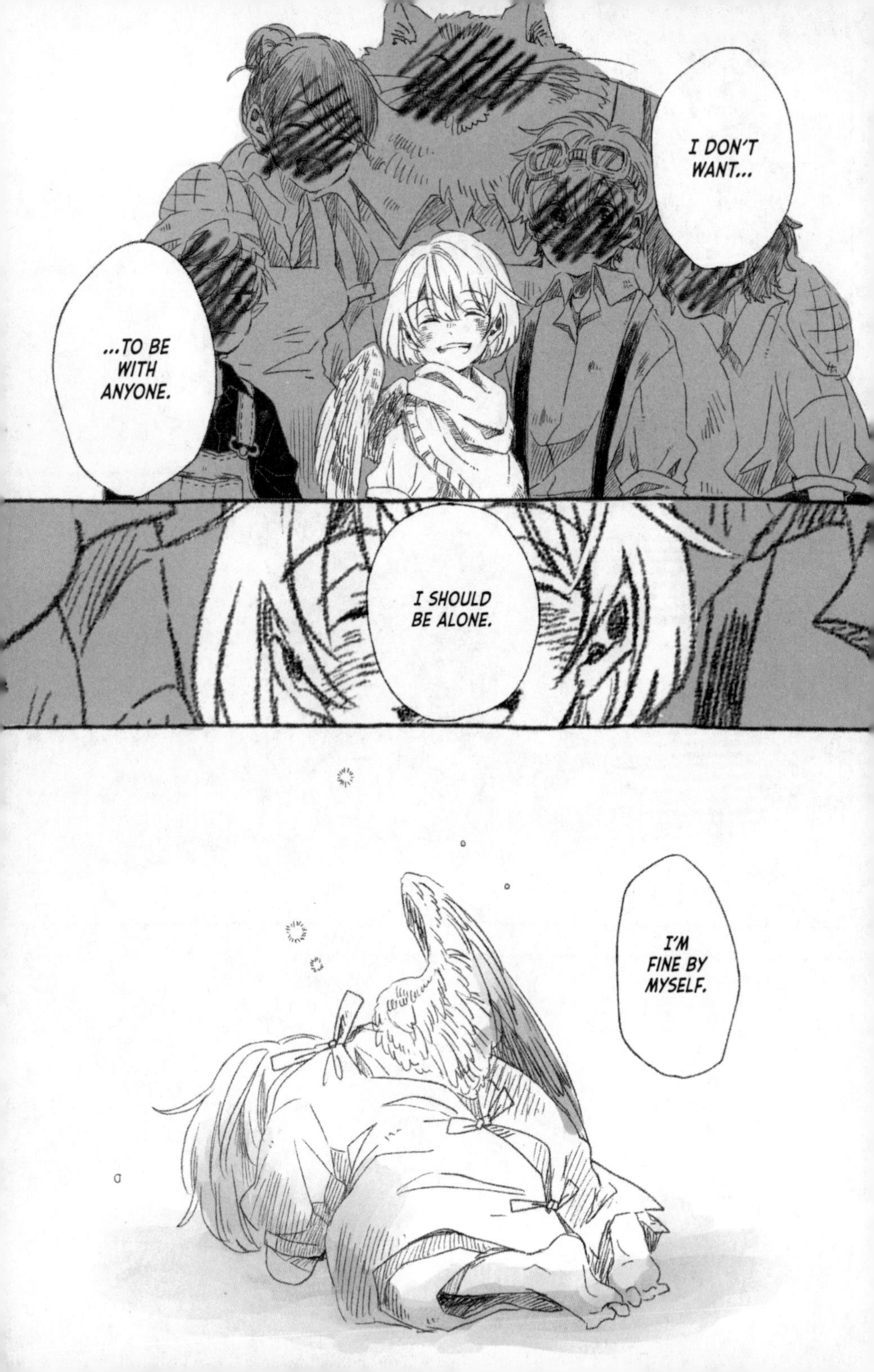
I DON'T WANT...
...TO BE WITH ANYONE.
I SHOULD BE ALONE.
I'M FINE BY MYSELF.

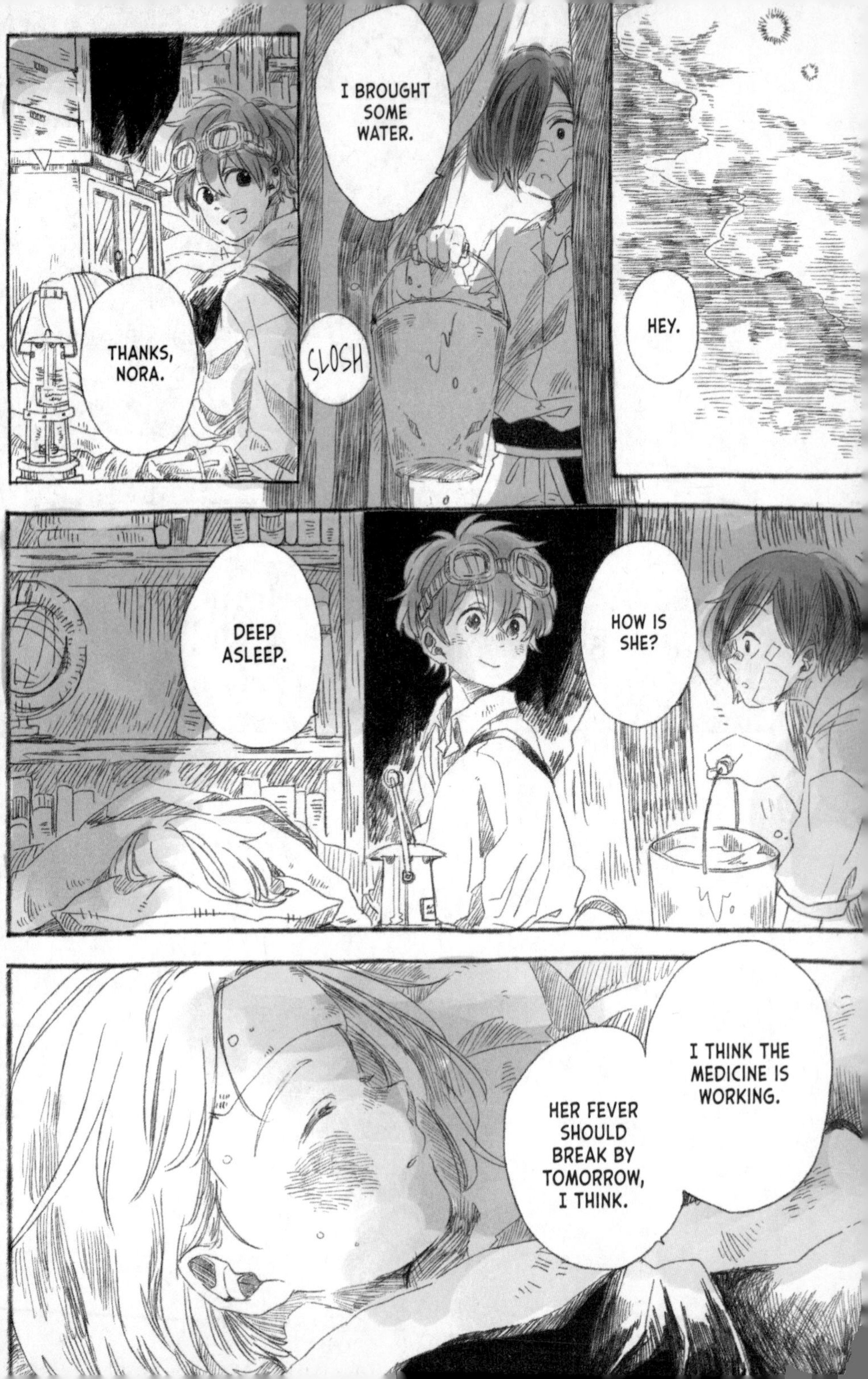
HEY.
I BROUGHT SOME WATER.
SLOSH
THANKS, NORA.
HOW IS SHE?
DEEP ASLEEP.
I THINK THE MEDICINE IS WORKING.
HER FEVER SHOULD BREAK BY TOMORROW, I THINK.

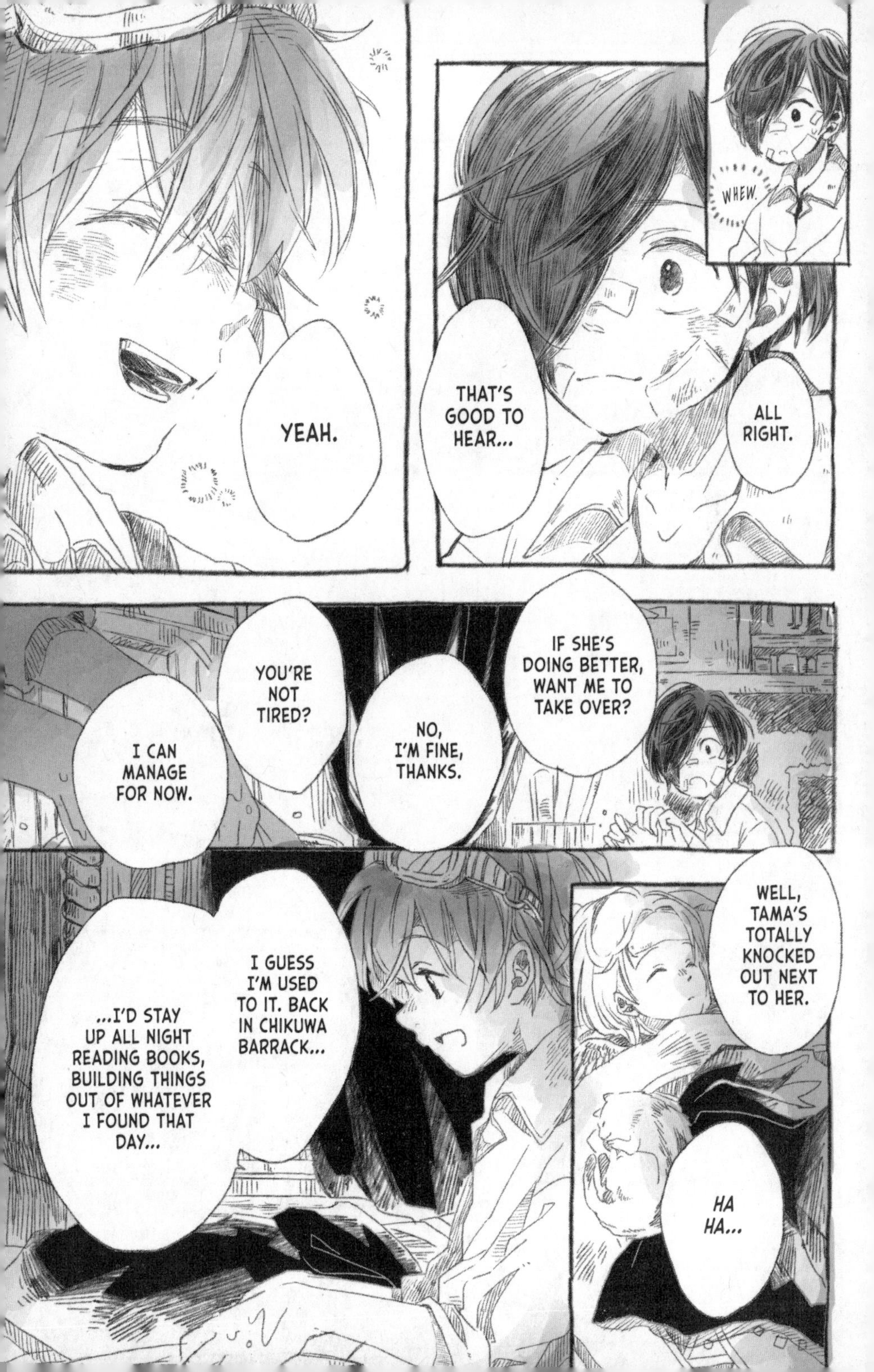
WHEW.
ALL RIGHT.
THAT'S GOOD TO HEAR...
YEAH.
IF SHE'S DOING BETTER, WANT ME TO TAKE OVER?
NO, I'M FINE, THANKS.
YOU'RE NOT TIRED?
I CAN MANAGE FOR NOW.
WELL, TAMA'S TOTALLY KNOCKED OUT NEXT TO HER.
HA HA...
I GUESS I'M USED TO IT. BACK IN CHIKUWA BARRACK...
...I'D STAY UP ALL NIGHT READING BOOKS, BUILDING THINGS OUT OF WHATEVER I FOUND THAT DAY...

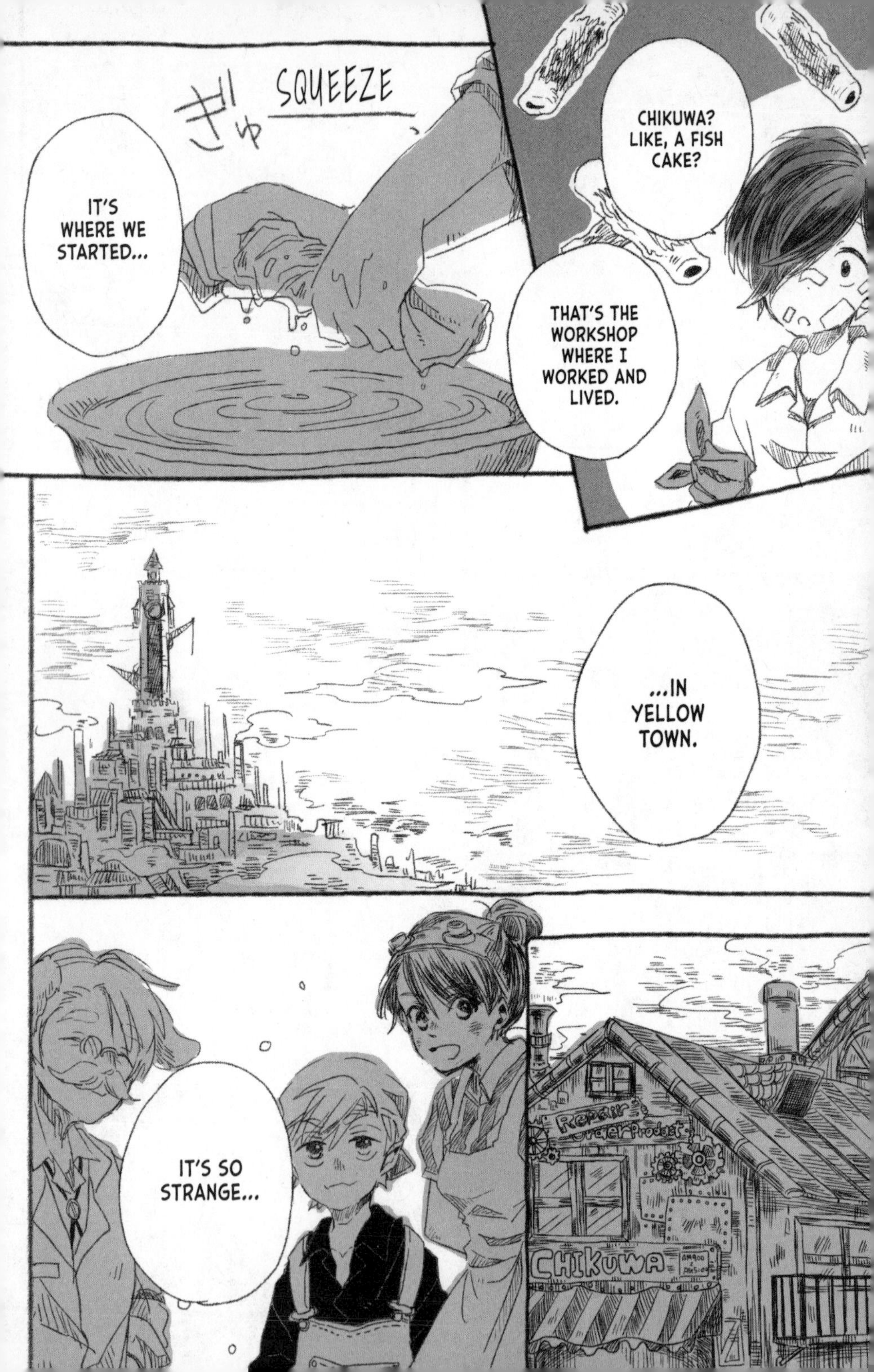
CHIKUWA? LIKE, A FISH CAKE?
THAT'S THE WORKSHOP WHERE I WORKED AND LIVED.
ぎゅ
SQUEEZE
IT'S WHERE WE STARTED...
...IN YELLOW TOWN.
Repair
Order Product
CHIKUWA
IT'S SO STRANGE...

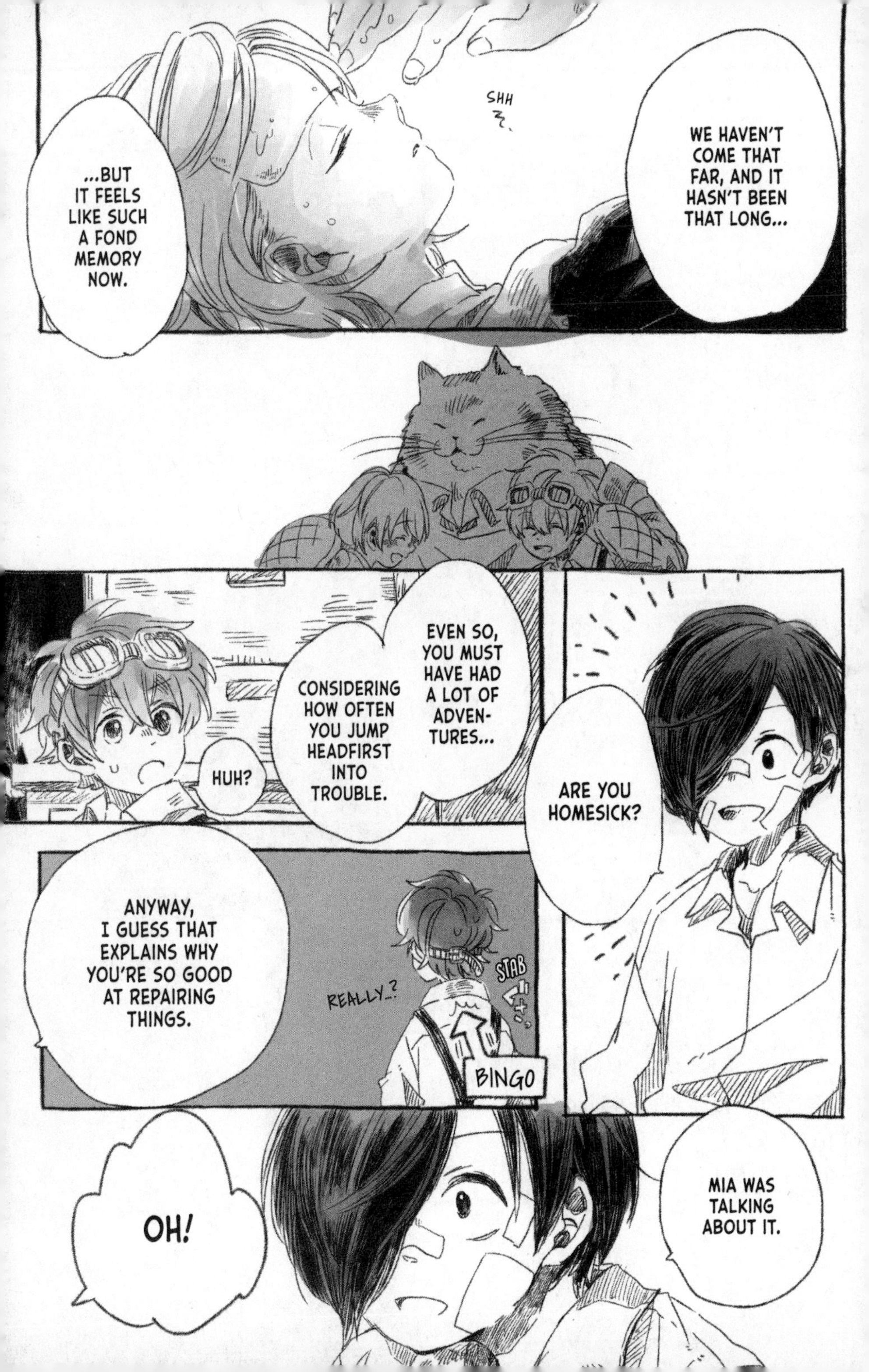
WE HAVEN'T COME THAT FAR, AND IT HASN'T BEEN THAT LONG...
SHH
...BUT IT FEELS LIKE SUCH A FOND MEMORY NOW.
ARE YOU HOMESICK?
EVEN SO, YOU MUST HAVE HAD A LOT OF ADVENTURES...
CONSIDERING HOW OFTEN YOU JUMP HEADFIRST INTO TROUBLE.
HUH?
STAB
BINGO
REALLY...?
ANYWAY, I GUESS THAT EXPLAINS WHY YOU'RE SO GOOD AT REPAIRING THINGS.
MIA WAS TALKING ABOUT IT.
OH!

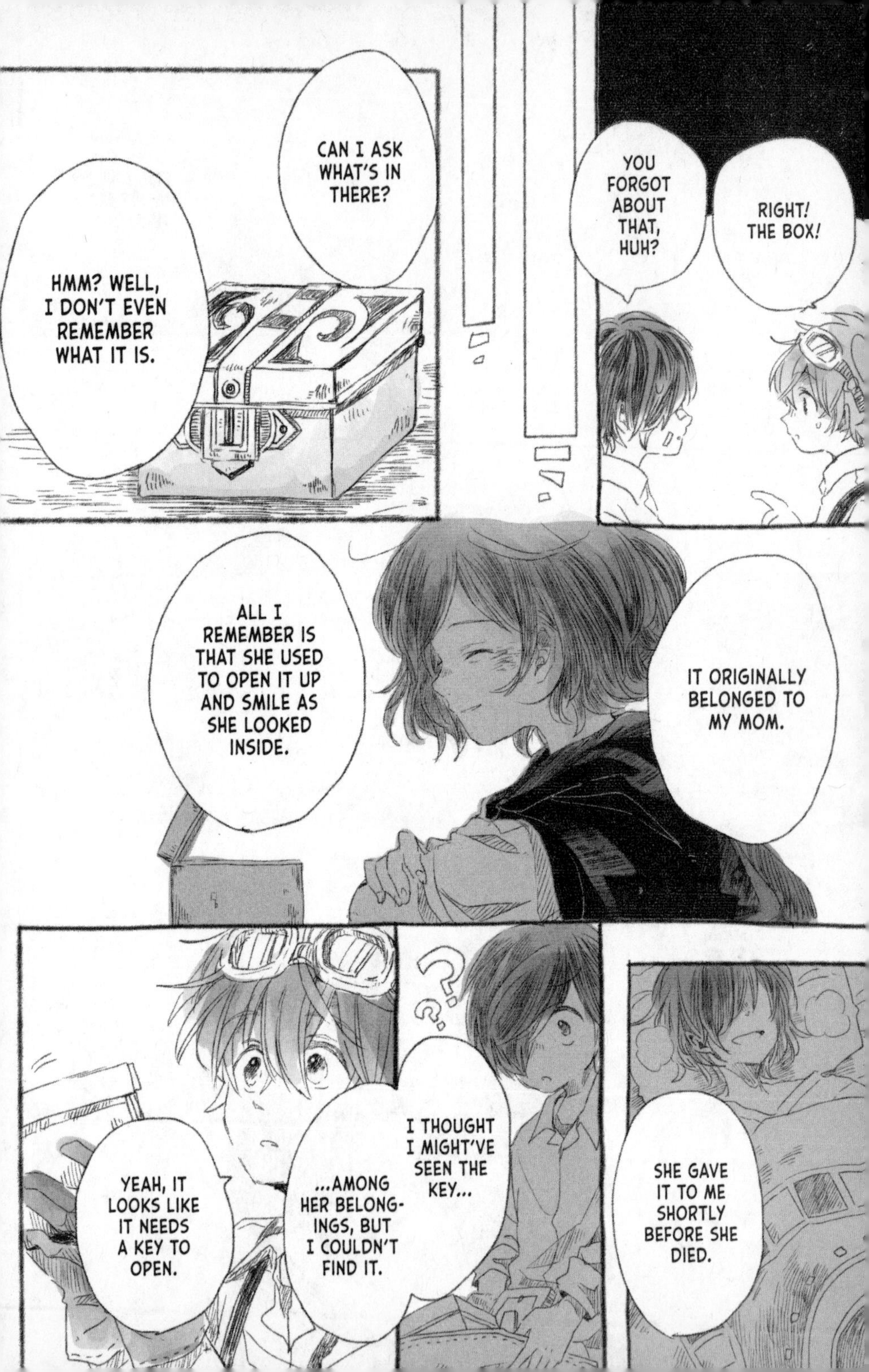
RIGHT! THE BOX!
YOU FORGOT ABOUT THAT, HUH?
CAN I ASK WHAT'S IN THERE?
HMM? WELL, I DON'T EVEN REMEMBER WHAT IT IS.
IT ORIGINALLY BELONGED TO MY MOM.
ALL I REMEMBER IS THAT SHE USED TO OPEN IT UP AND SMILE AS SHE LOOKED INSIDE.
SHE GAVE IT TO ME SHORTLY BEFORE SHE DIED.
I THOUGHT I MIGHT'VE SEEN THE KEY...
...AMONG HER BELONG-INGS, BUT I COULDN'T FIND IT.
YEAH, IT LOOKS LIKE IT NEEDS A KEY TO OPEN.

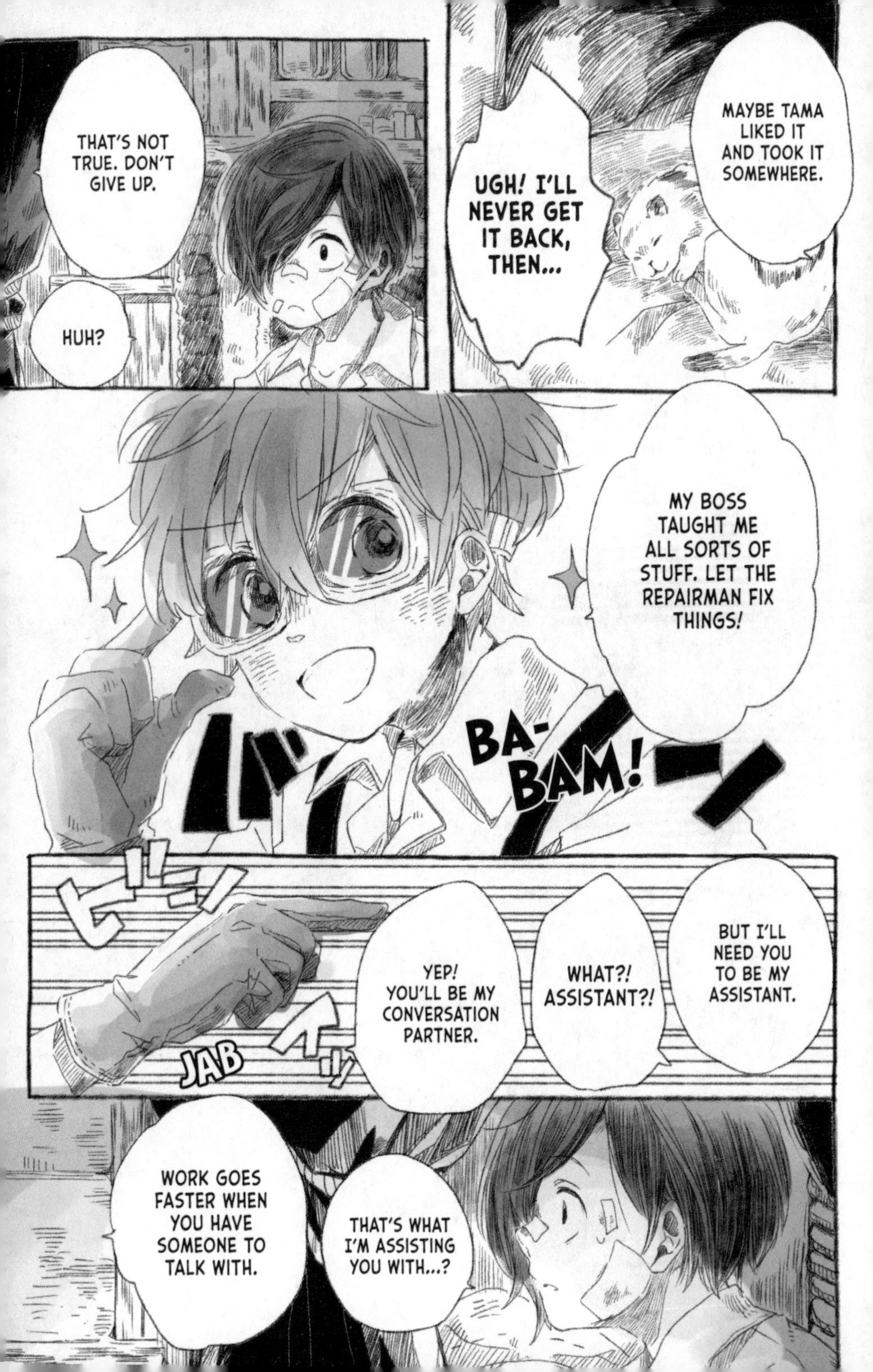
MAYBE TAMA LIKED IT AND TOOK IT SOMEWHERE.
UGH! I'LL NEVER GET IT BACK, THEN...
THAT'S NOT TRUE. DON'T GIVE UP.
HUH?
MY BOSS TAUGHT ME ALL SORTS OF STUFF. LET THE REPAIRMAN FIX THINGS!
BA-BAM!
BUT I'LL NEED YOU TO BE MY ASSISTANT.
WHAT?! ASSISTANT?!
YEP! YOU'LL BE MY CONVERSATION PARTNER.
JAB
WORK GOES FASTER WHEN YOU HAVE SOMEONE TO TALK WITH.
THAT'S WHAT I'M ASSISTING YOU WITH...?

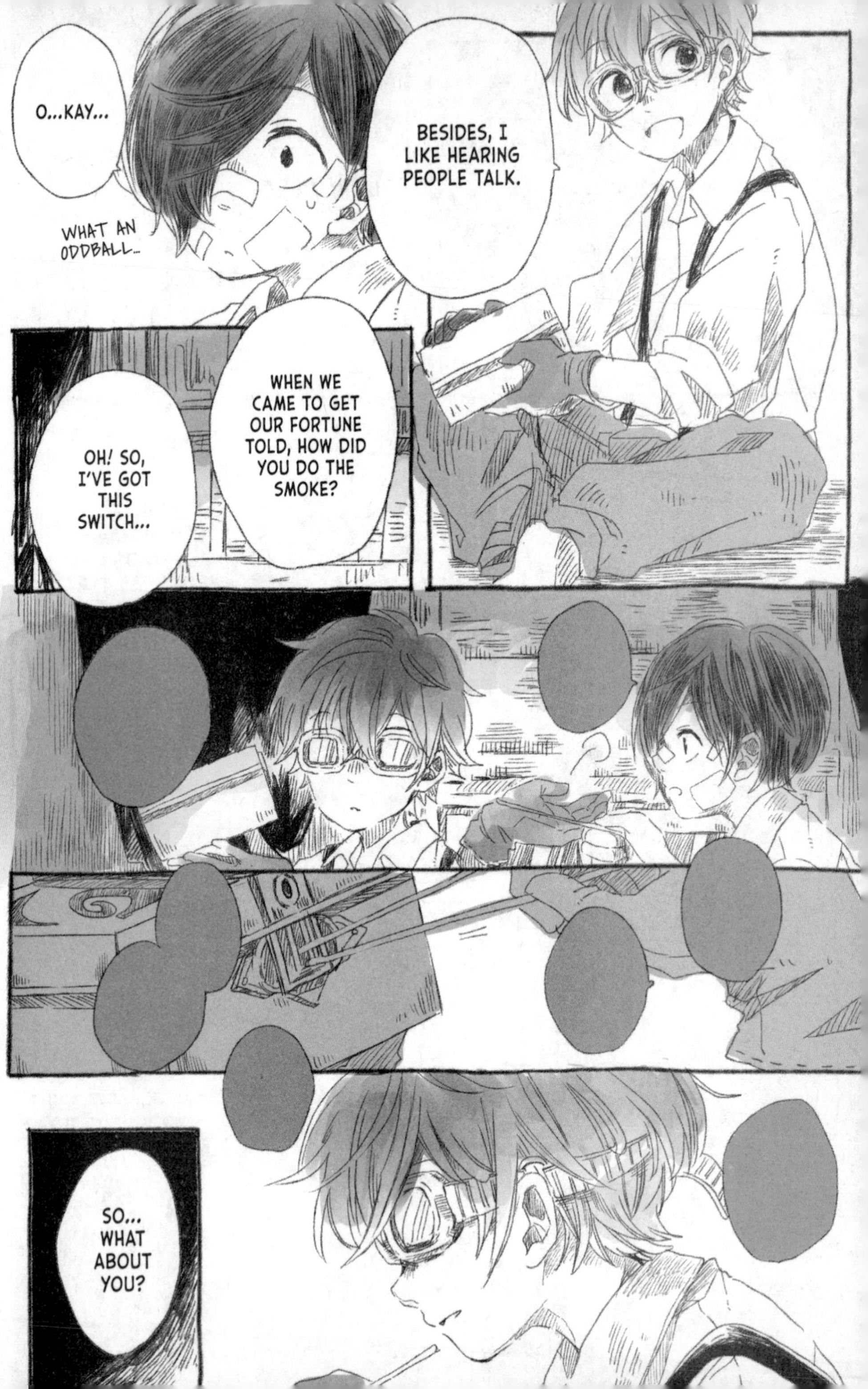
BESIDES, I LIKE HEARING PEOPLE TALK.
O...KAY...
WHAT AN ODDBALL...
WHEN WE CAME TO GET OUR FORTUNE TOLD, HOW DID YOU DO THE SMOKE?
OH! SO, I'VE GOT THIS SWITCH...
SO... WHAT ABOUT YOU?

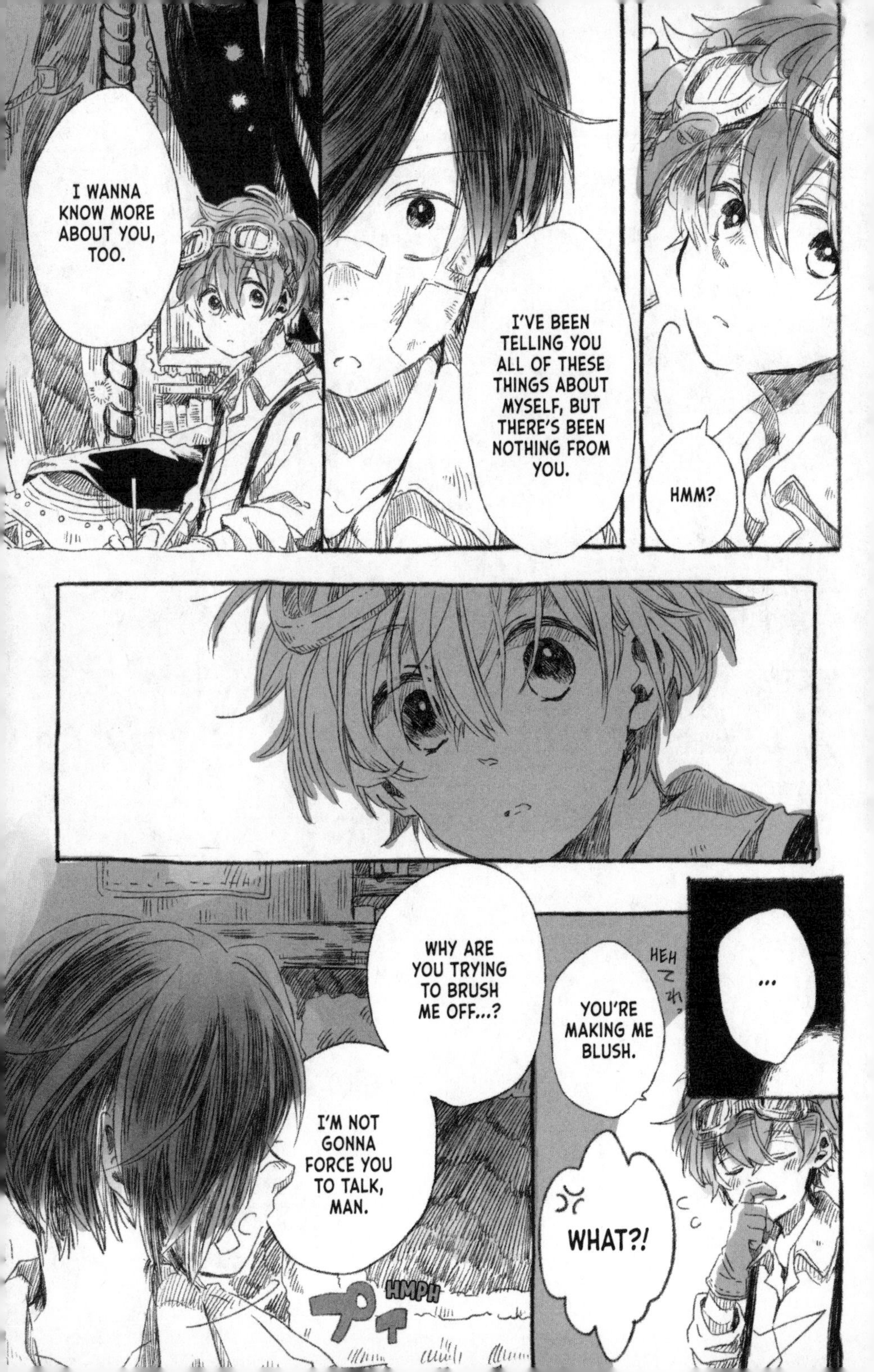
HMM?
I'VE BEEN TELLING YOU ALL OF THESE THINGS ABOUT MYSELF, BUT THERE'S BEEN NOTHING FROM YOU.
I WANNA KNOW MORE ABOUT YOU, TOO.
...
HEH
YOU'RE MAKING ME BLUSH.
WHAT?!
WHY ARE YOU TRYING TO BRUSH ME OFF...?
I'M NOT GONNA FORCE YOU TO TALK, MAN.
HMPH

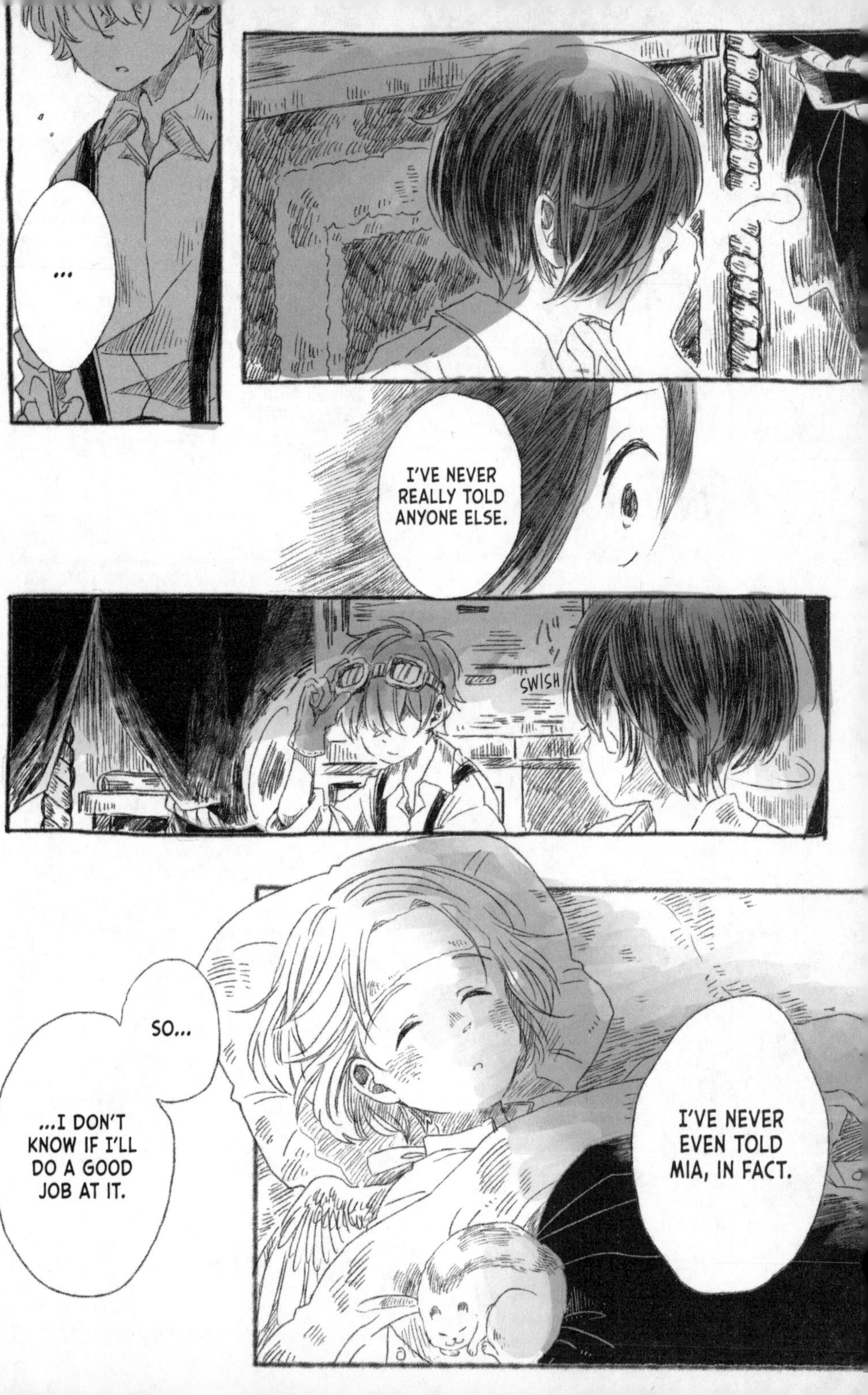
I'VE NEVER REALLY TOLD ANYONE ELSE.
...
SWISH
I'VE NEVER EVEN TOLD MIA, IN FACT.
SO...
...I DON'T KNOW IF I'LL DO A GOOD JOB AT IT.

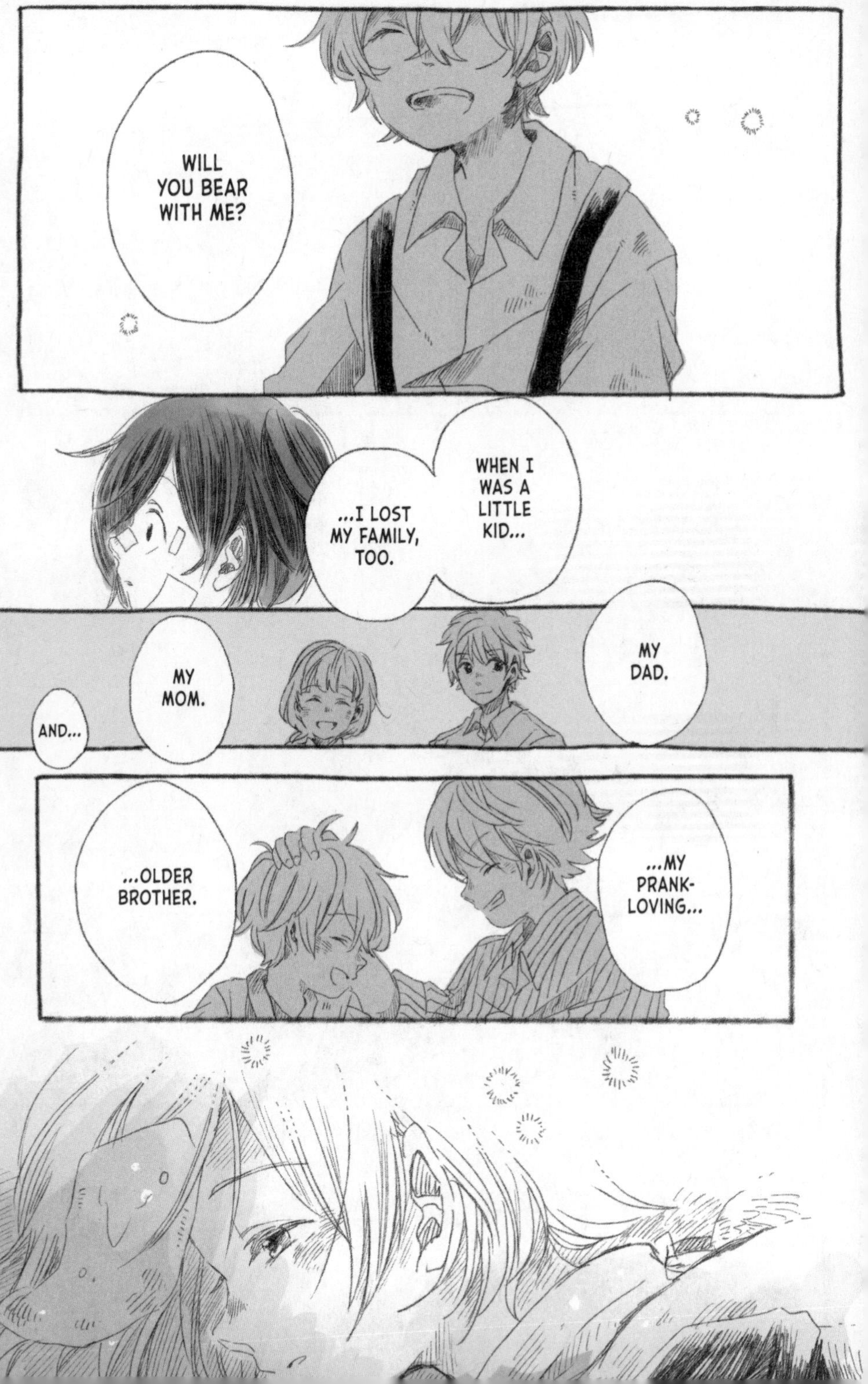
WILL YOU BEAR WITH ME?
WHEN I WAS A LITTLE KID...
...I LOST MY FAMILY, TOO.
MY DAD.
MY MOM.
AND...
...MY PRANK-LOVING...
...OLDER BROTHER.

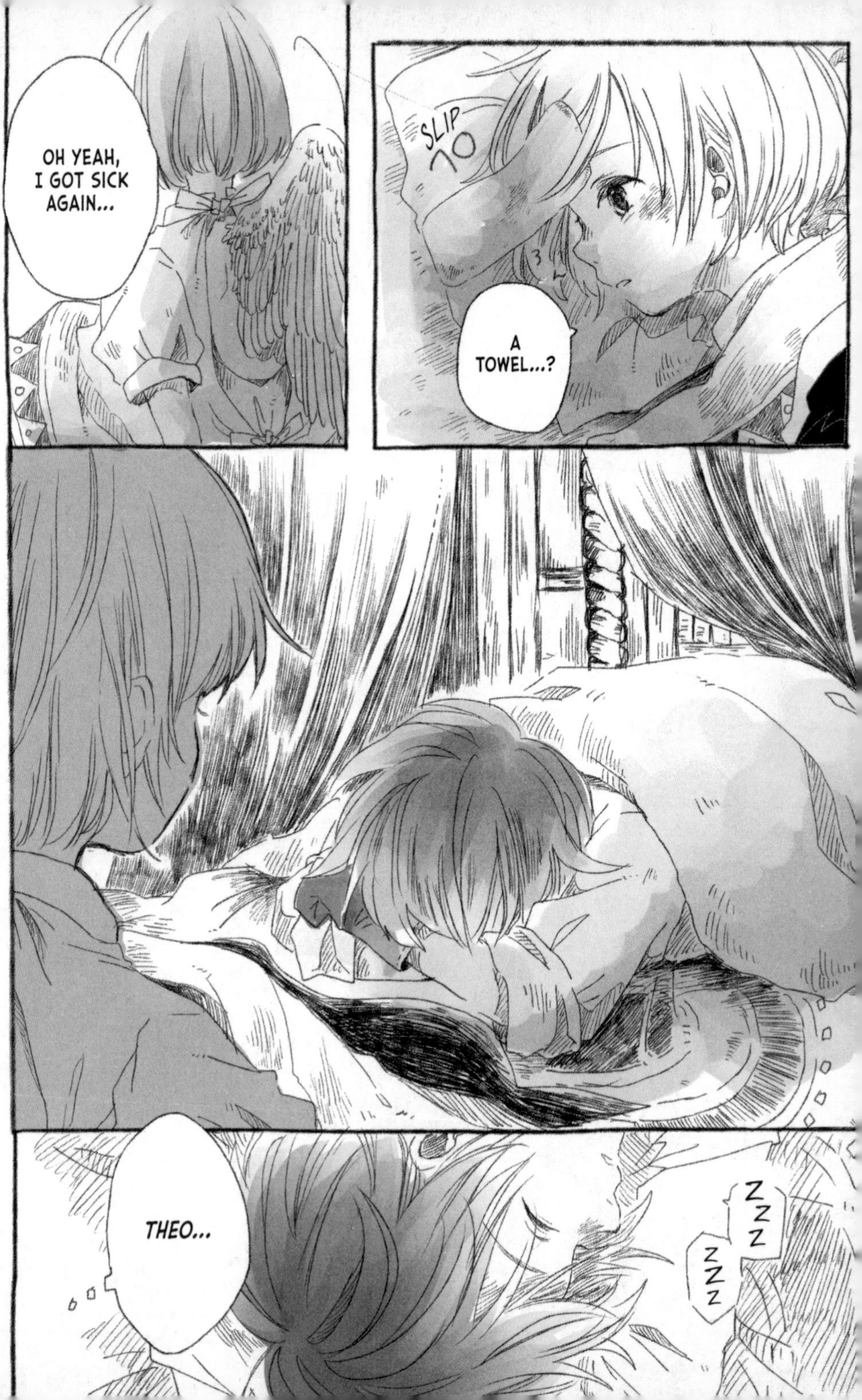
SLIP
A TOWEL...?
OH YEAH, I GOT SICK AGAIN...
ZZZ
ZZZ
THEO...

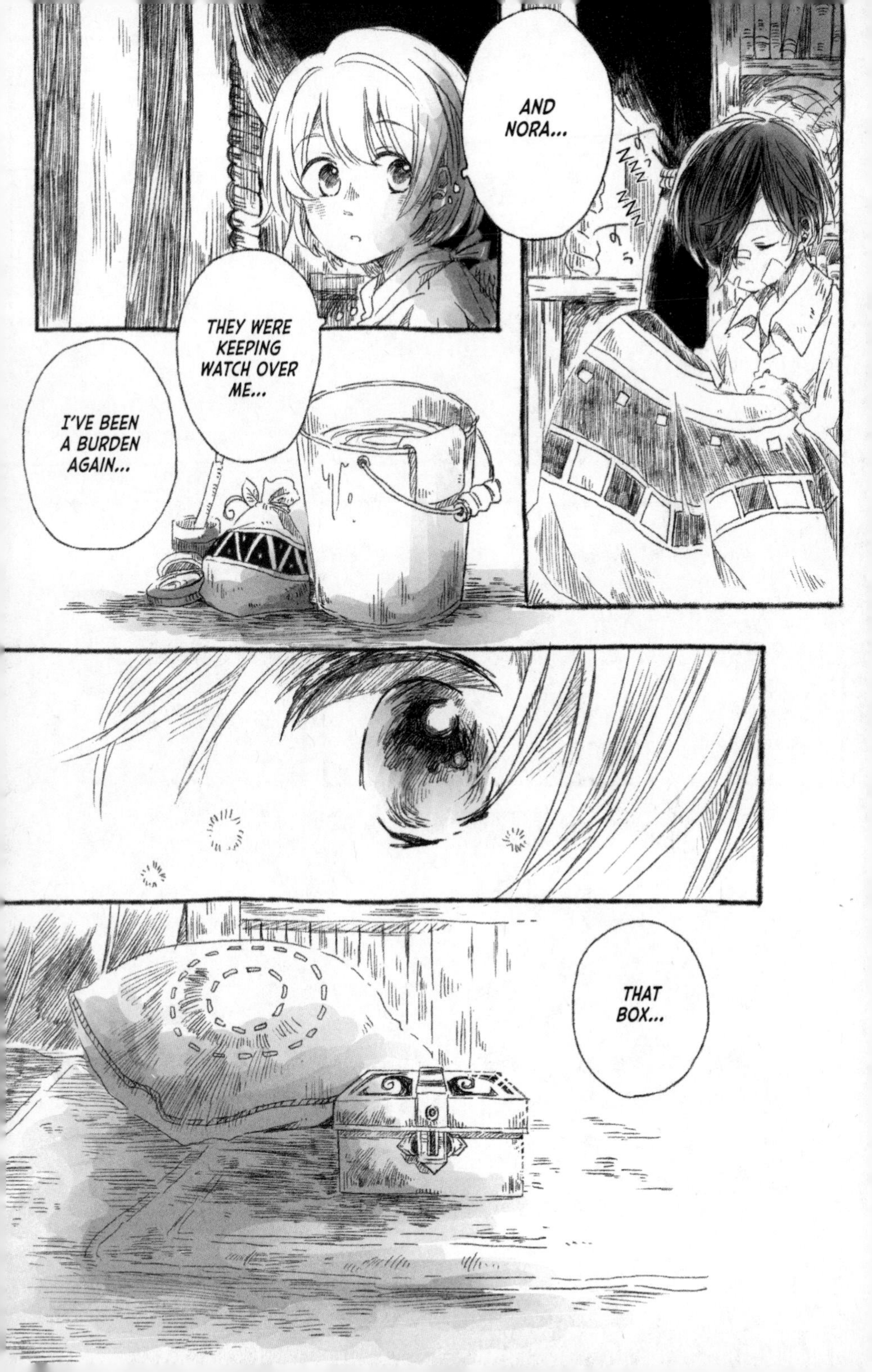
AND NORA...
THEY WERE KEEPING WATCH OVER ME...
I'VE BEEN A BURDEN AGAIN...
THAT BOX...

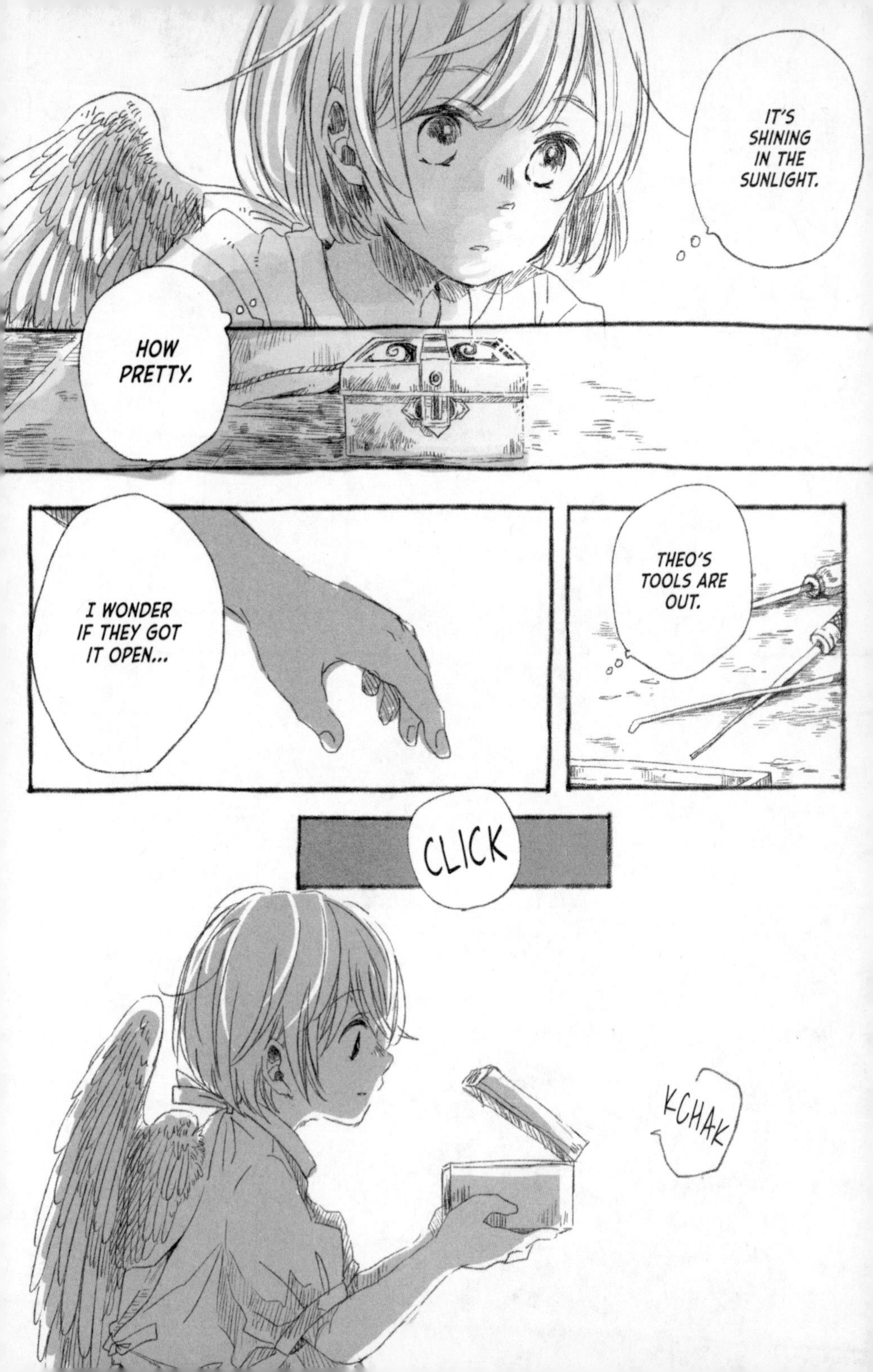
IT'S SHINING IN THE SUNLIGHT.
HOW PRETTY.
THEO'S TOOLS ARE OUT.
I WONDER IF THEY GOT IT OPEN...
CLICK
KCHAK

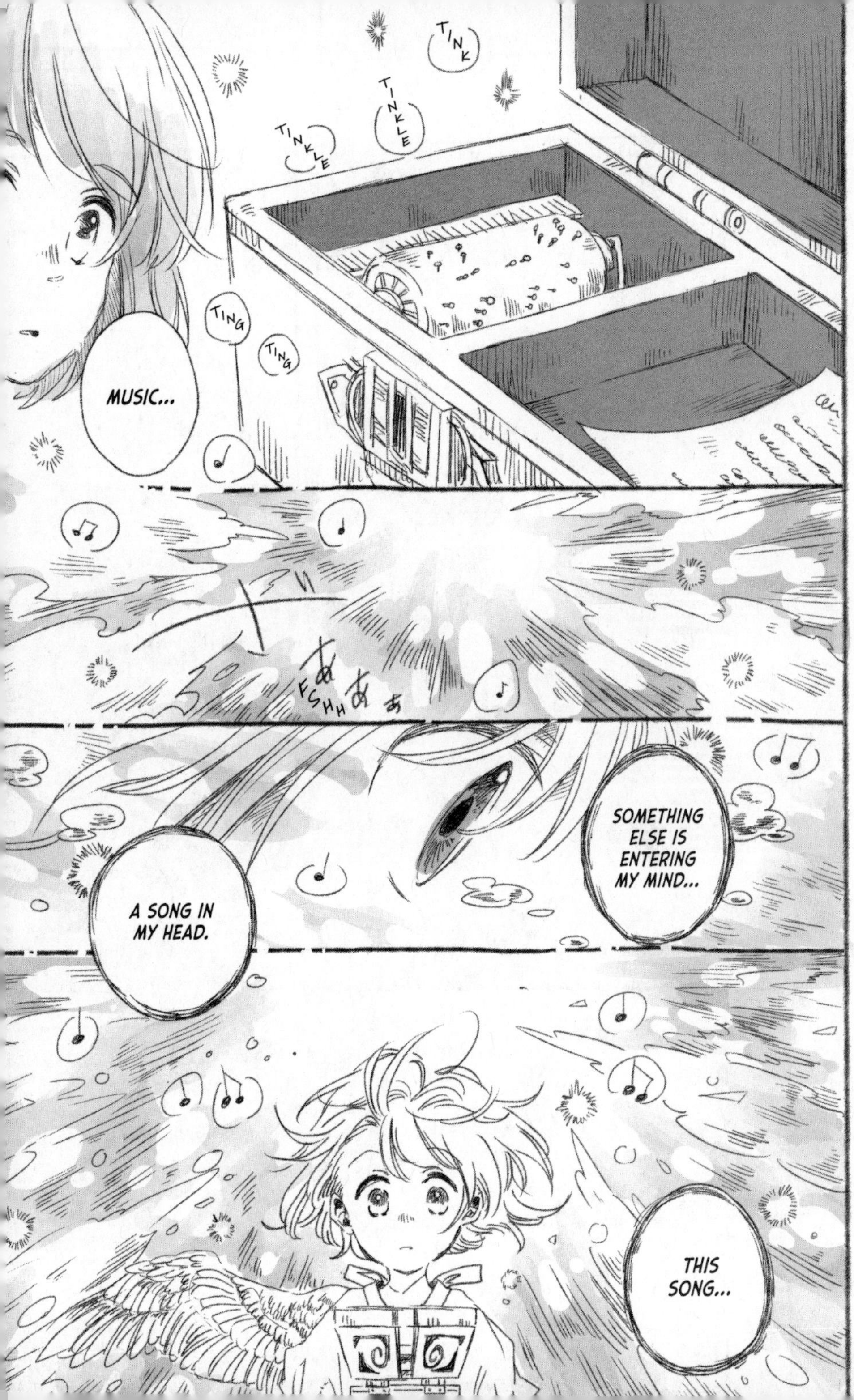
TINK
TINKLE
TINKLE
TING
TING
MUSIC...
FSHH
SOMETHING ELSE IS ENTERING MY MIND...
A SONG IN MY HEAD.
THIS SONG...

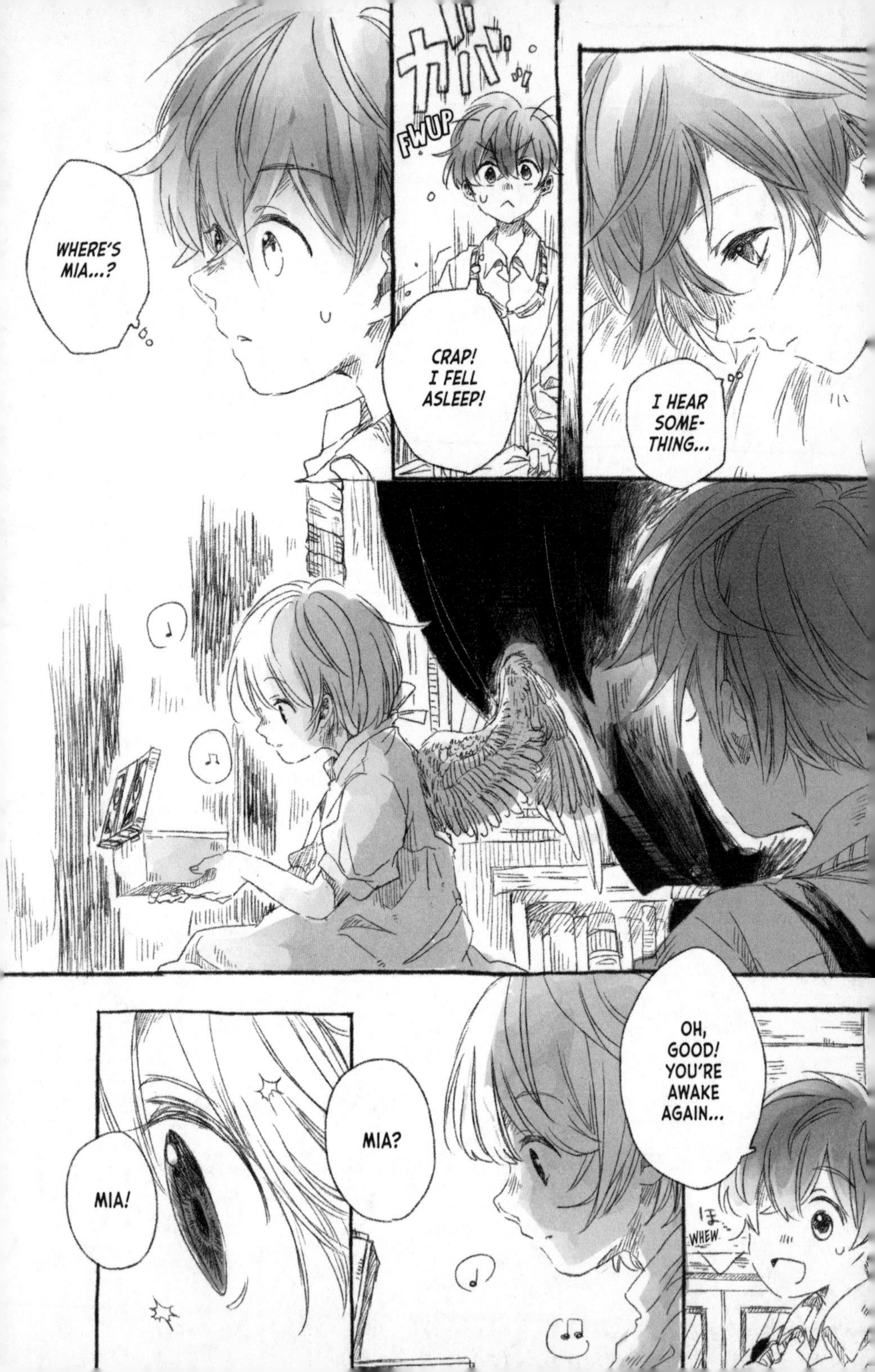
I HEAR SOME-THING...
カバッ
FWUP
CRAP! I FELL ASLEEP!
WHERE'S MIA...?
OH, GOOD! YOU'RE AWAKE AGAIN...
ほ…
WHEW
MIA?
MIA!

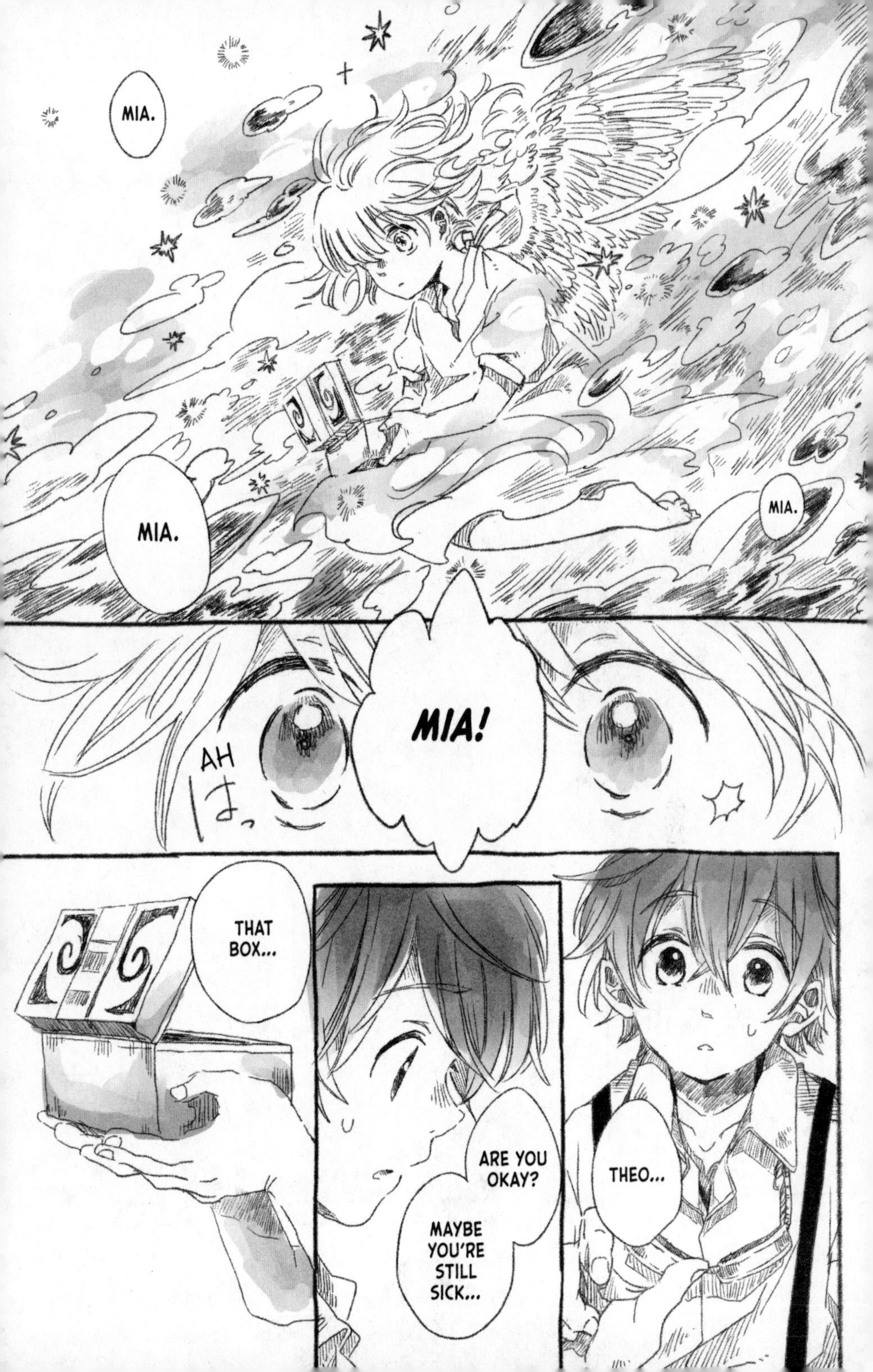
MIA.
MIA.
MIA.
MIA!
AH
は
THEO...
ARE YOU OKAY?
MAYBE YOU'RE STILL SICK...
THAT BOX...

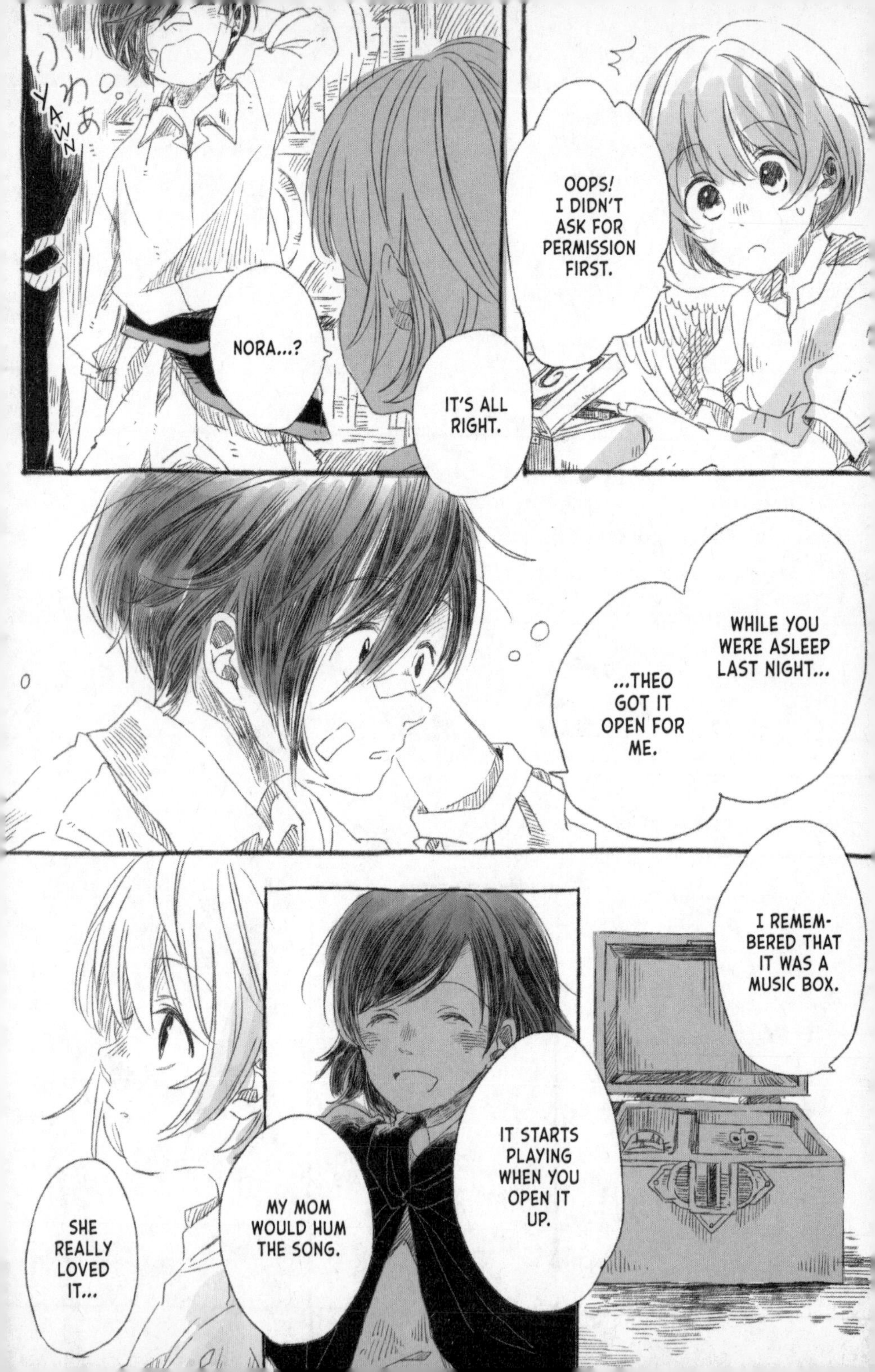
OOPS! I DIDN'T ASK FOR PERMISSION FIRST.
ふわあ
YAWN
NORA...?
IT'S ALL RIGHT.
WHILE YOU WERE ASLEEP LAST NIGHT...
...THEO GOT IT OPEN FOR ME.
I REMEM-BERED THAT IT WAS A MUSIC BOX.
IT STARTS PLAYING WHEN YOU OPEN IT UP.
MY MOM WOULD HUM THE SONG.
SHE REALLY LOVED IT...

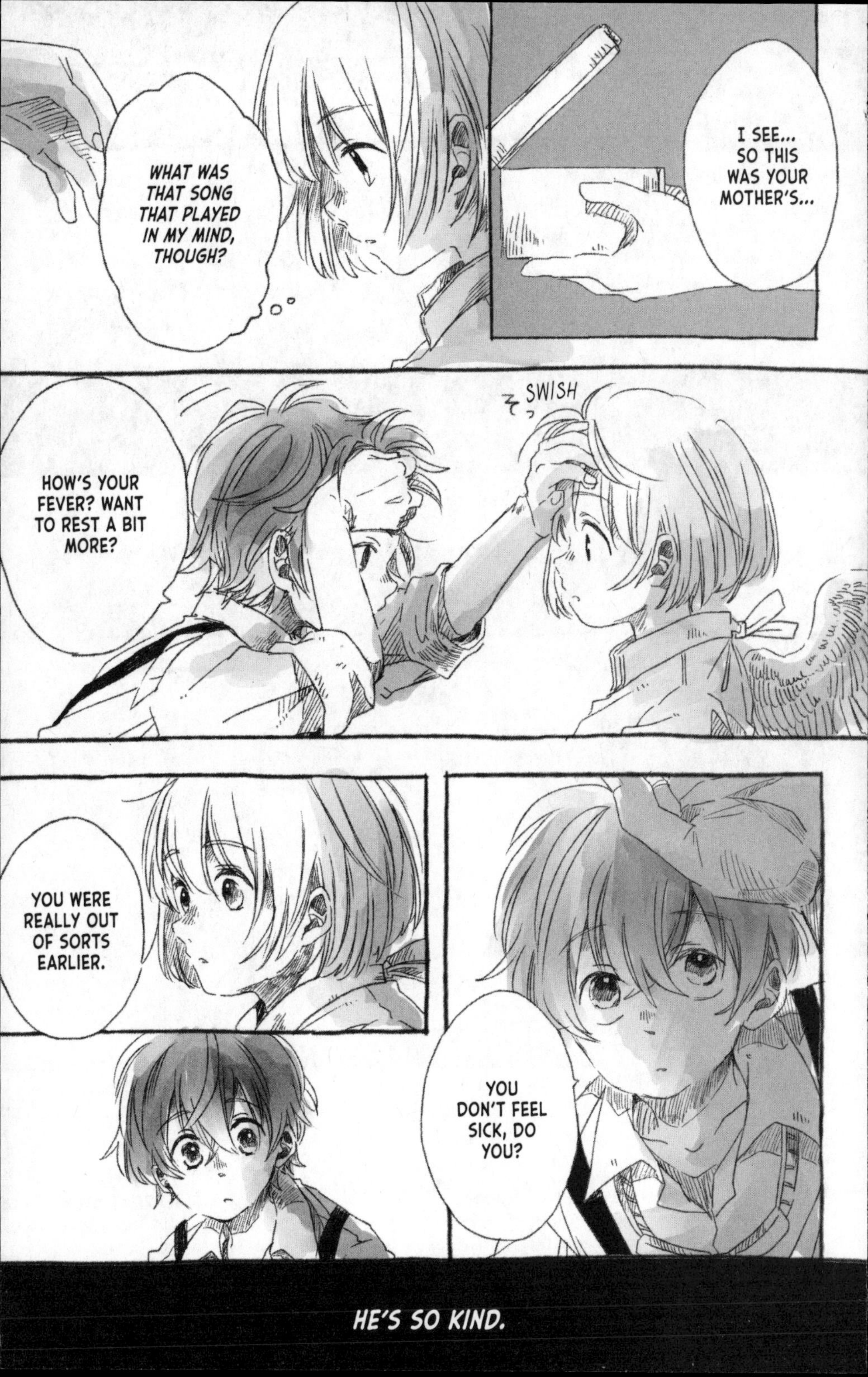
I SEE... SO THIS WAS YOUR MOTHER'S...
WHAT WAS THAT SONG THAT PLAYED IN MY MIND, THOUGH?
SWISH
HOW'S YOUR FEVER? WANT TO REST A BIT MORE?
YOU DON'T FEEL SICK, DO YOU?
YOU WERE REALLY OUT OF SORTS EARLIER.
HE'S SO KIND.

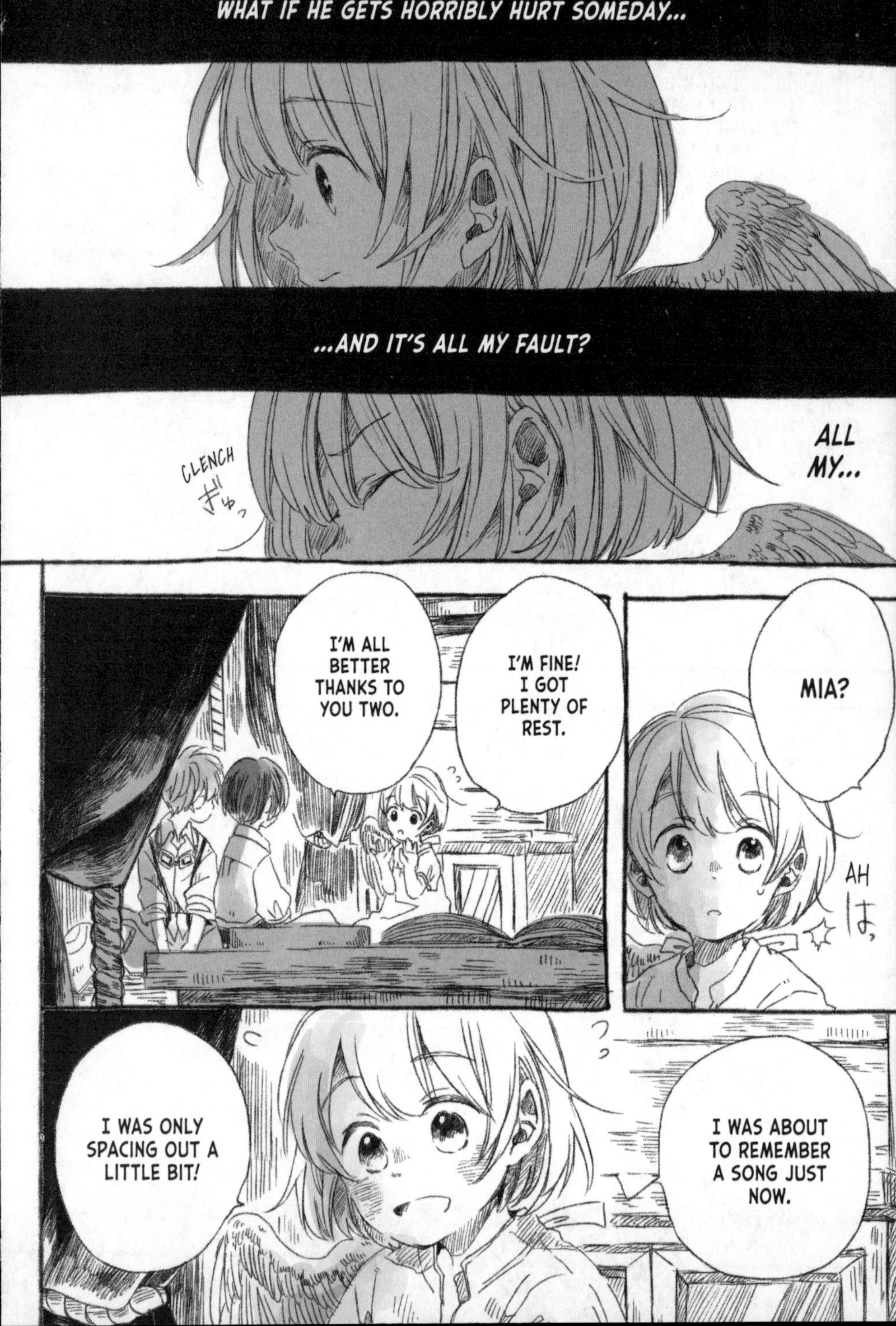
WHAT IF HE GETS HORRIBLY HURT SOMEDAY...
...AND IT'S ALL MY FAULT?
ALL MY...
CLENCH
ぎゅっ
MIA?
AH
は,
I'M FINE! I GOT PLENTY OF REST.
I'M ALL BETTER THANKS TO YOU TWO.
I WAS ABOUT TO REMEMBER A SONG JUST NOW.
I WAS ONLY SPACING OUT A LITTLE BIT!

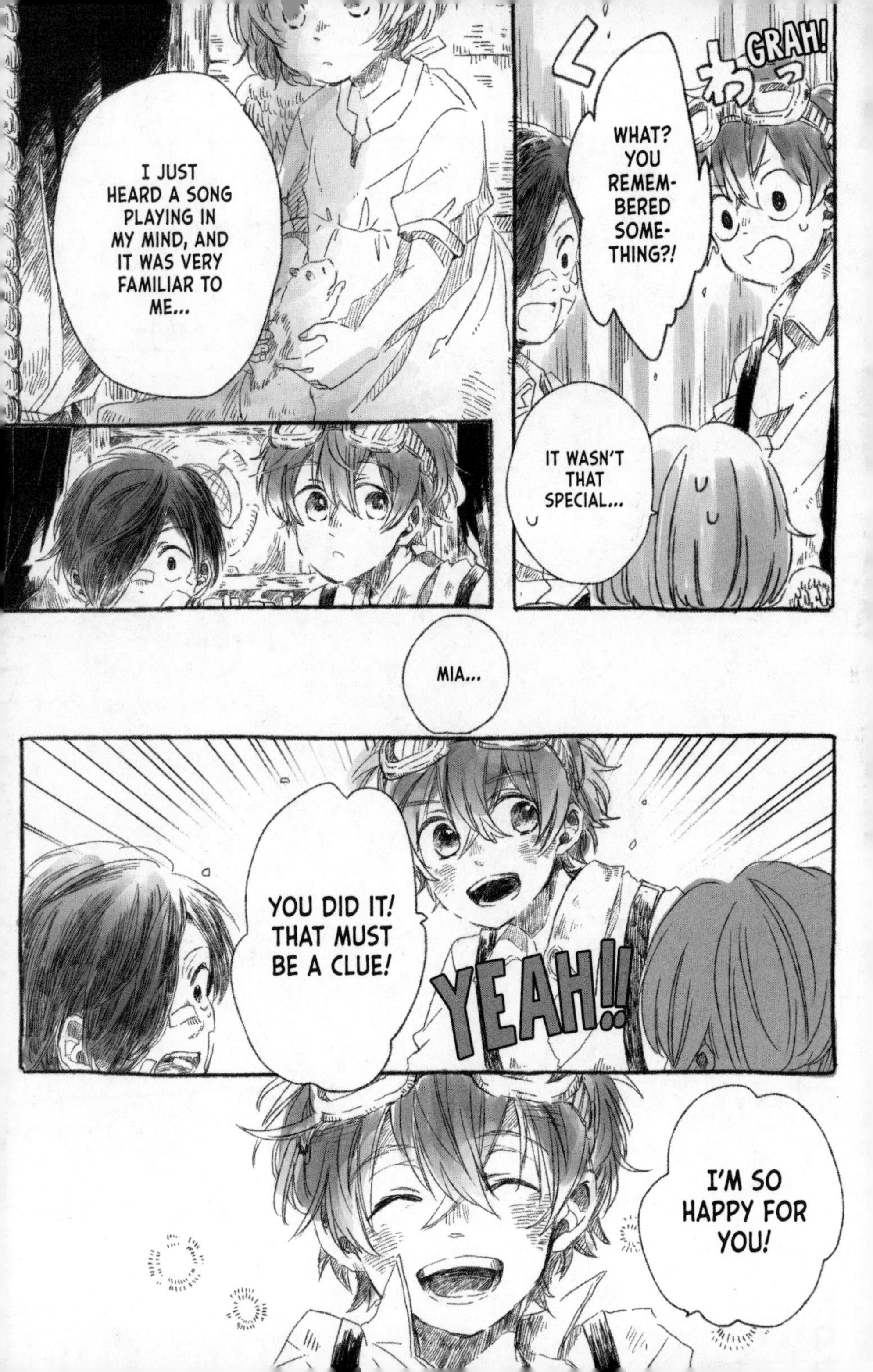

くわっ
GRAH!
WHAT? YOU REMEMBERED SOMETHING?!
IT WASN'T THAT SPECIAL...
I JUST HEARD A SONG PLAYING IN MY MIND, AND IT WAS VERY FAMILIAR TO ME...
MIA...
YOU DID IT! THAT MUST BE A CLUE!
YEAH!!
I'M SO HAPPY FOR YOU!

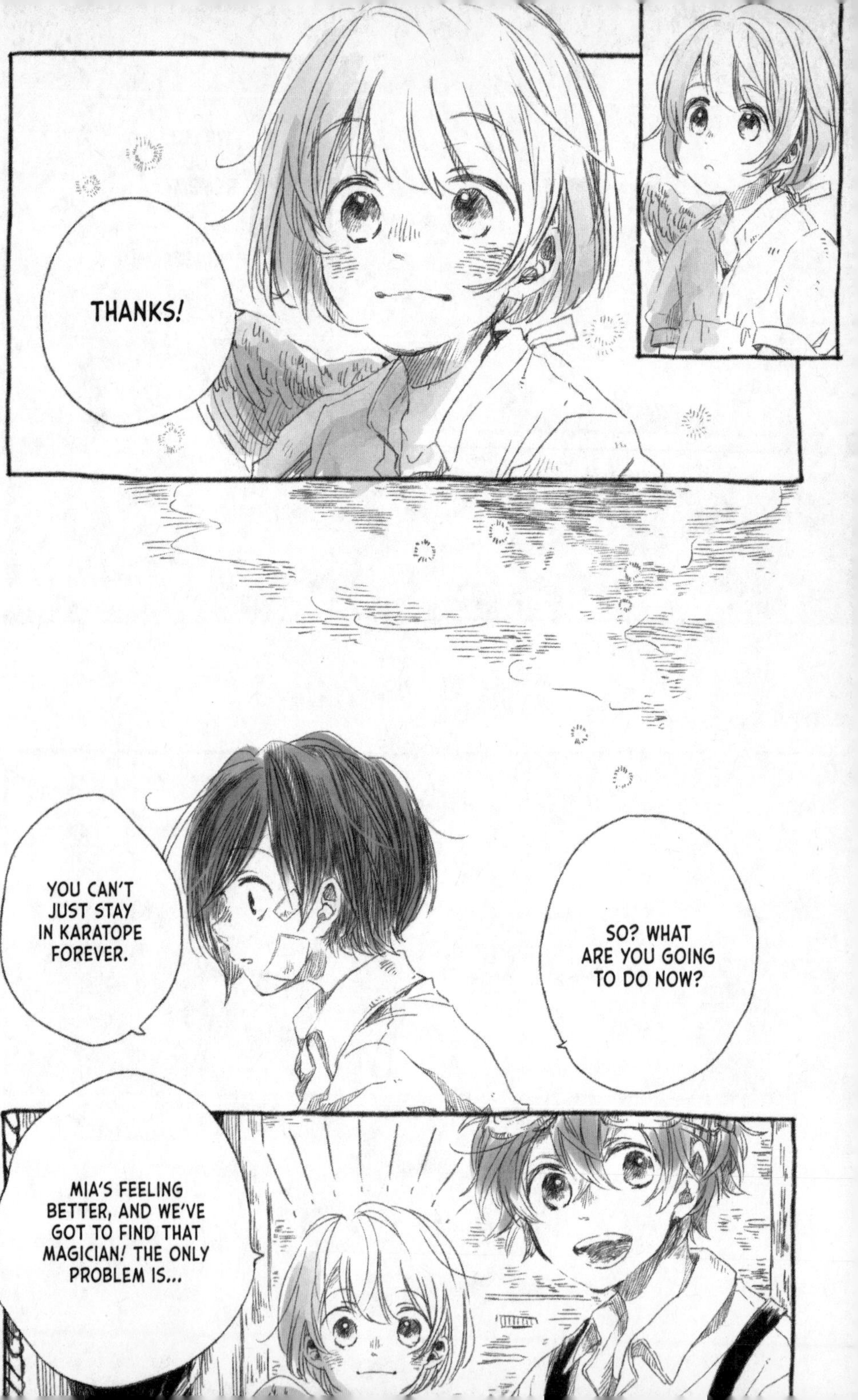
THANKS!
SO? WHAT ARE YOU GOING TO DO NOW?
YOU CAN'T JUST STAY IN KARATOPE FOREVER.
MIA'S FEELING BETTER, AND WE'VE GOT TO FIND THAT MAGICIAN! THE ONLY PROBLEM IS...

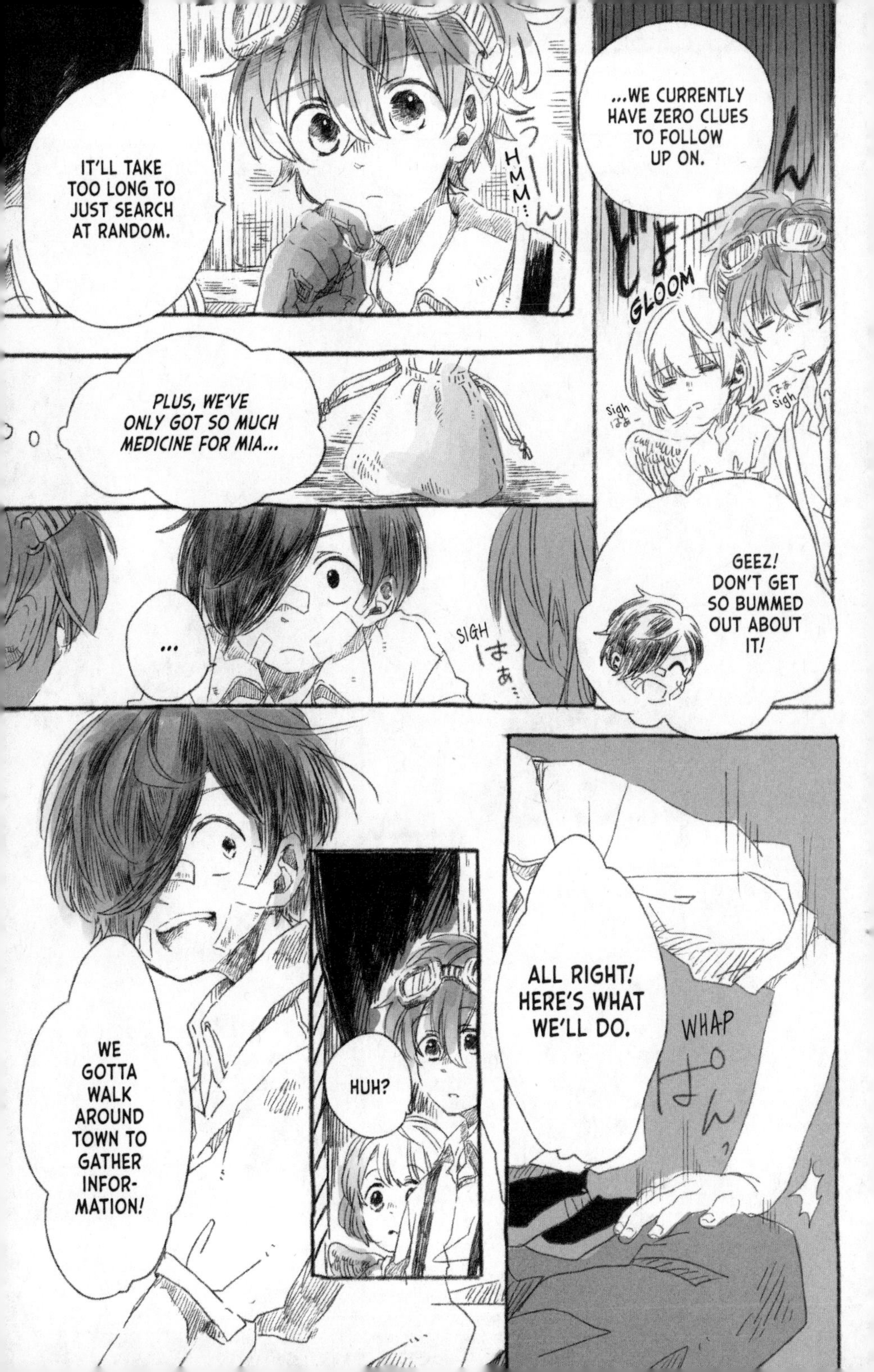
...WE CURRENTLY HAVE ZERO CLUES TO FOLLOW UP ON.
GLOOM
sigh
sigh
GEEZ! DON'T GET SO BUMMED OUT ABOUT IT!
HMM...
IT'LL TAKE TOO LONG TO JUST SEARCH AT RANDOM.
PLUS, WE'VE ONLY GOT SO MUCH MEDICINE FOR MIA...
SIGH
...
ALL RIGHT! HERE'S WHAT WE'LL DO.
WHAP
HUH?
WE GOTTA WALK AROUND TOWN TO GATHER INFOR-MATION!

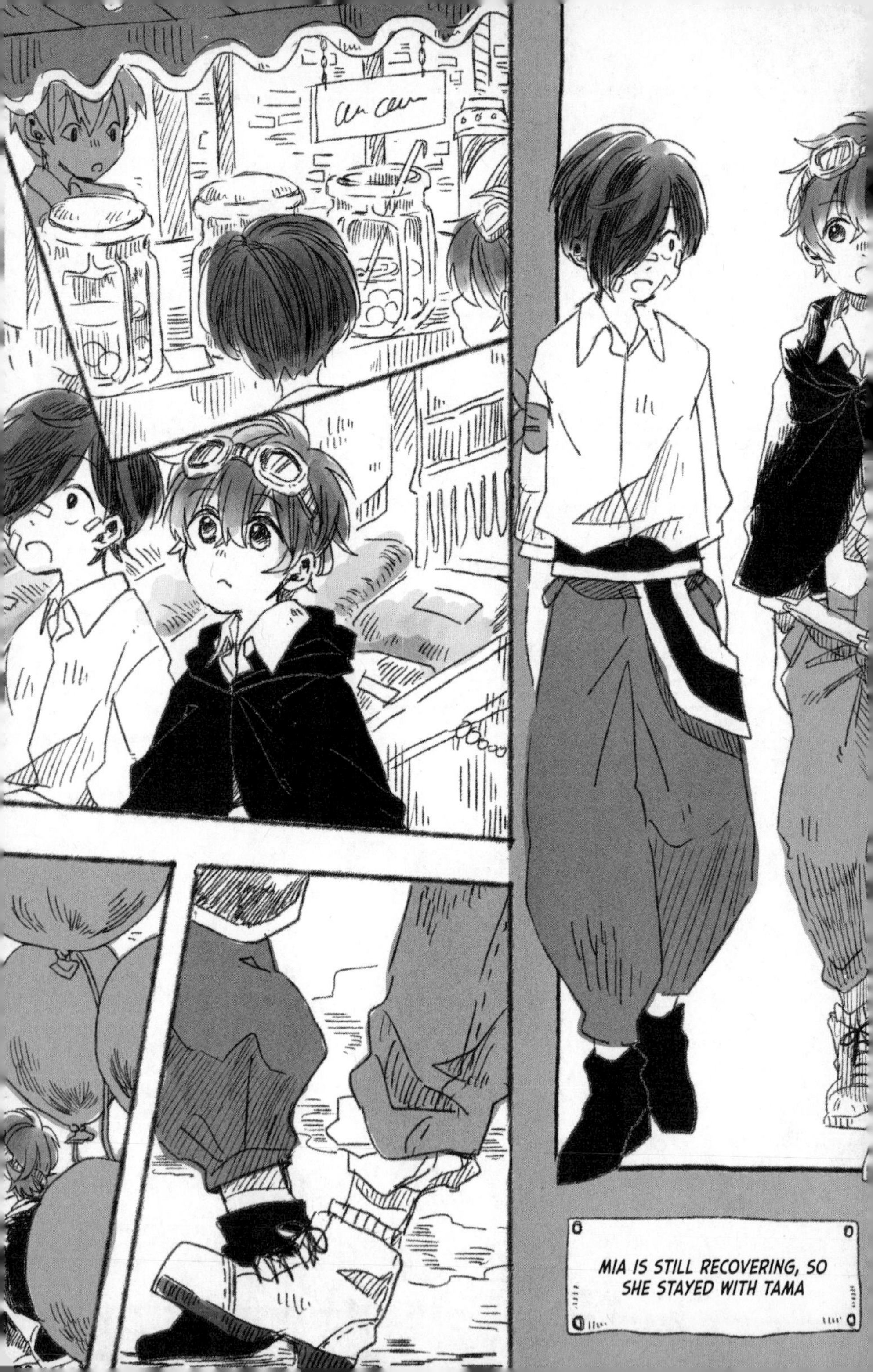
MIA IS STILL RECOVERING, SO
SHE STAYED WITH TAMA

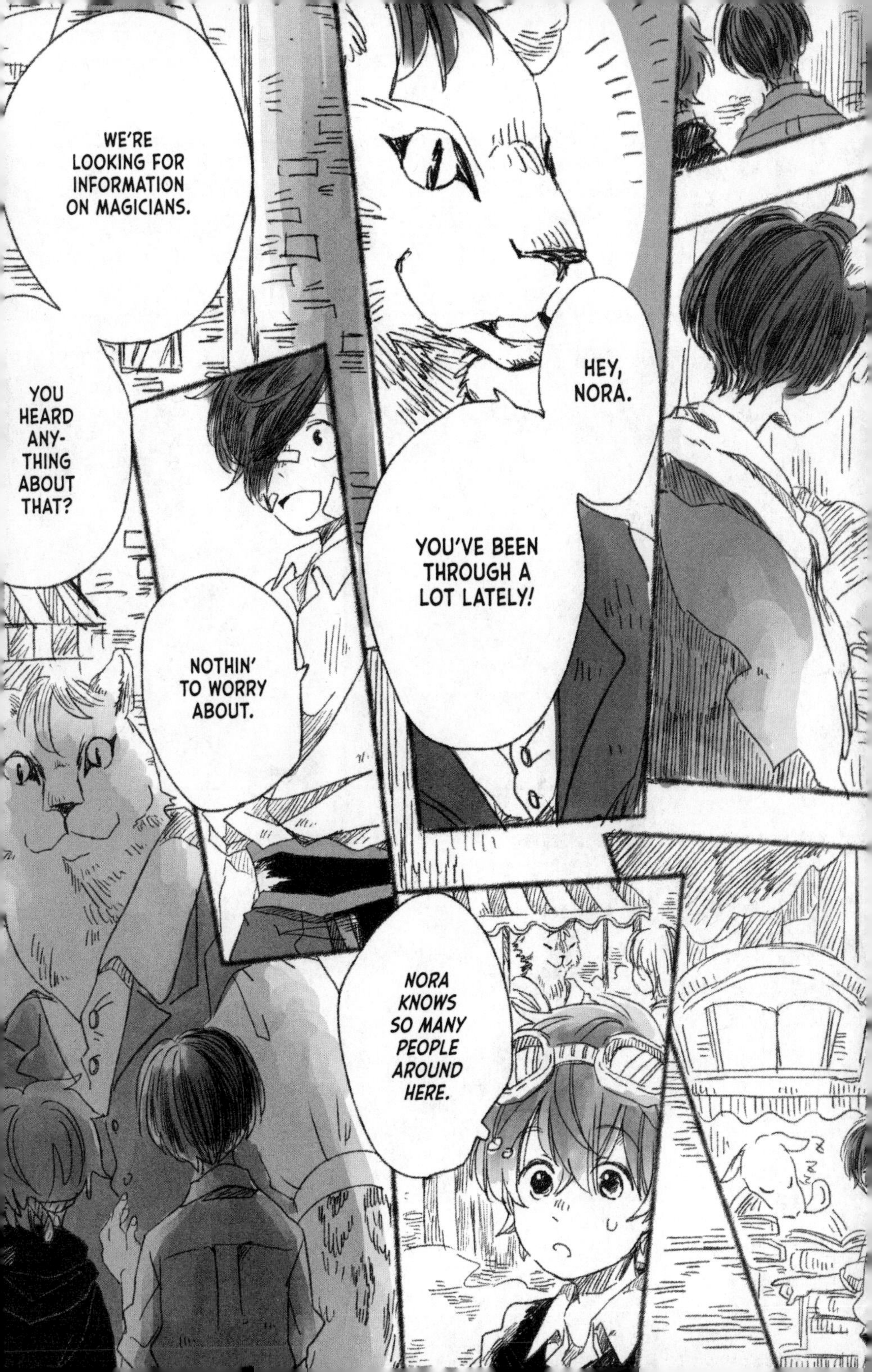
HEY, NORA.
YOU'VE BEEN THROUGH A LOT LATELY!
WE'RE LOOKING FOR INFORMATION ON MAGICIANS.
YOU HEARD ANY-THING ABOUT THAT?
NOTHIN' TO WORRY ABOUT.
NORA KNOWS SO MANY PEOPLE AROUND HERE.

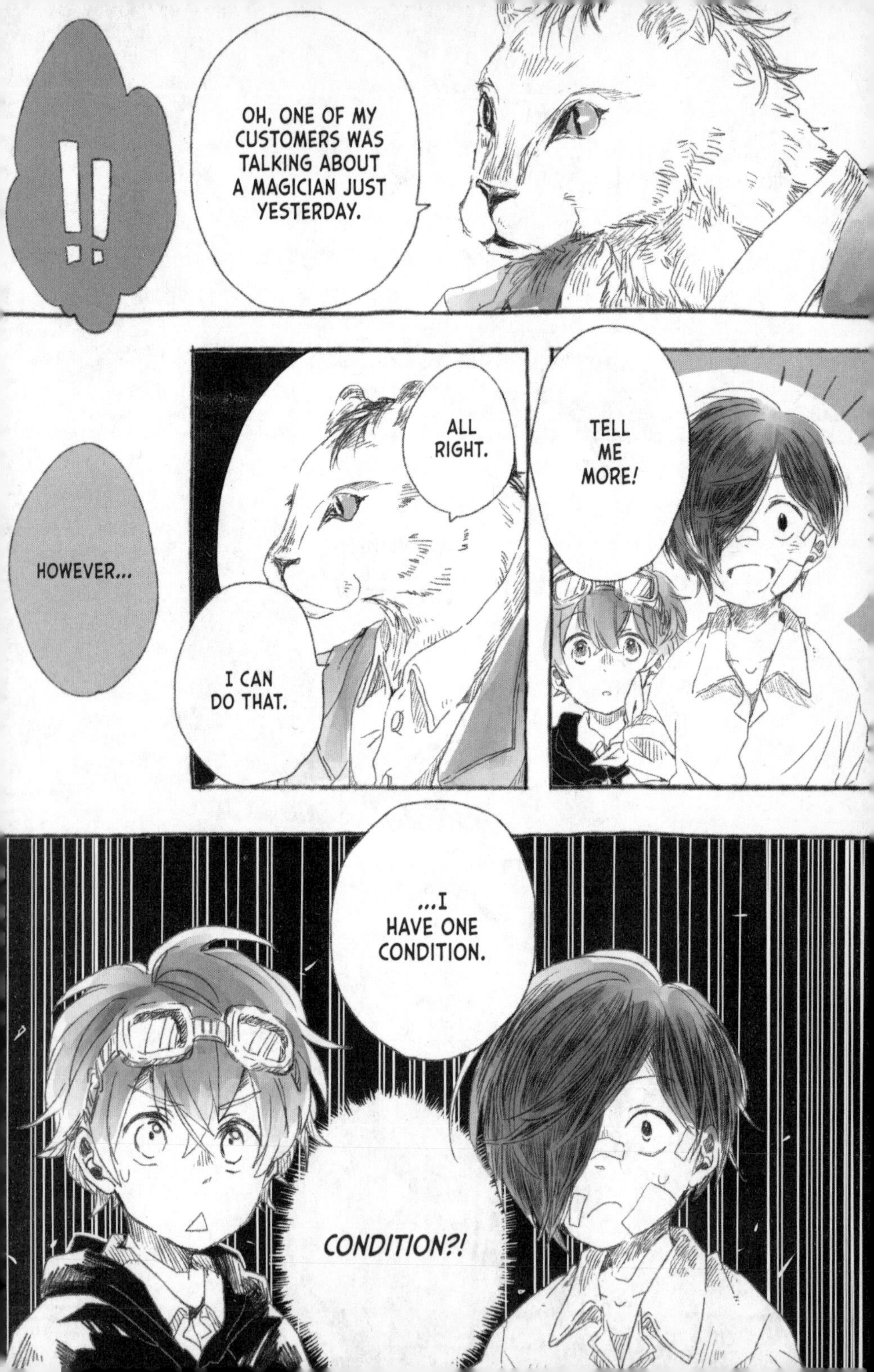
OH, ONE OF MY CUSTOMERS WAS TALKING ABOUT A MAGICIAN JUST YESTERDAY.
!!
TELL ME MORE!
ALL RIGHT.
I CAN DO THAT.
HOWEVER...
...I HAVE ONE CONDITION.
CONDITION?!

Beyond *the* Clouds

The Girl Who Fell From the Sky

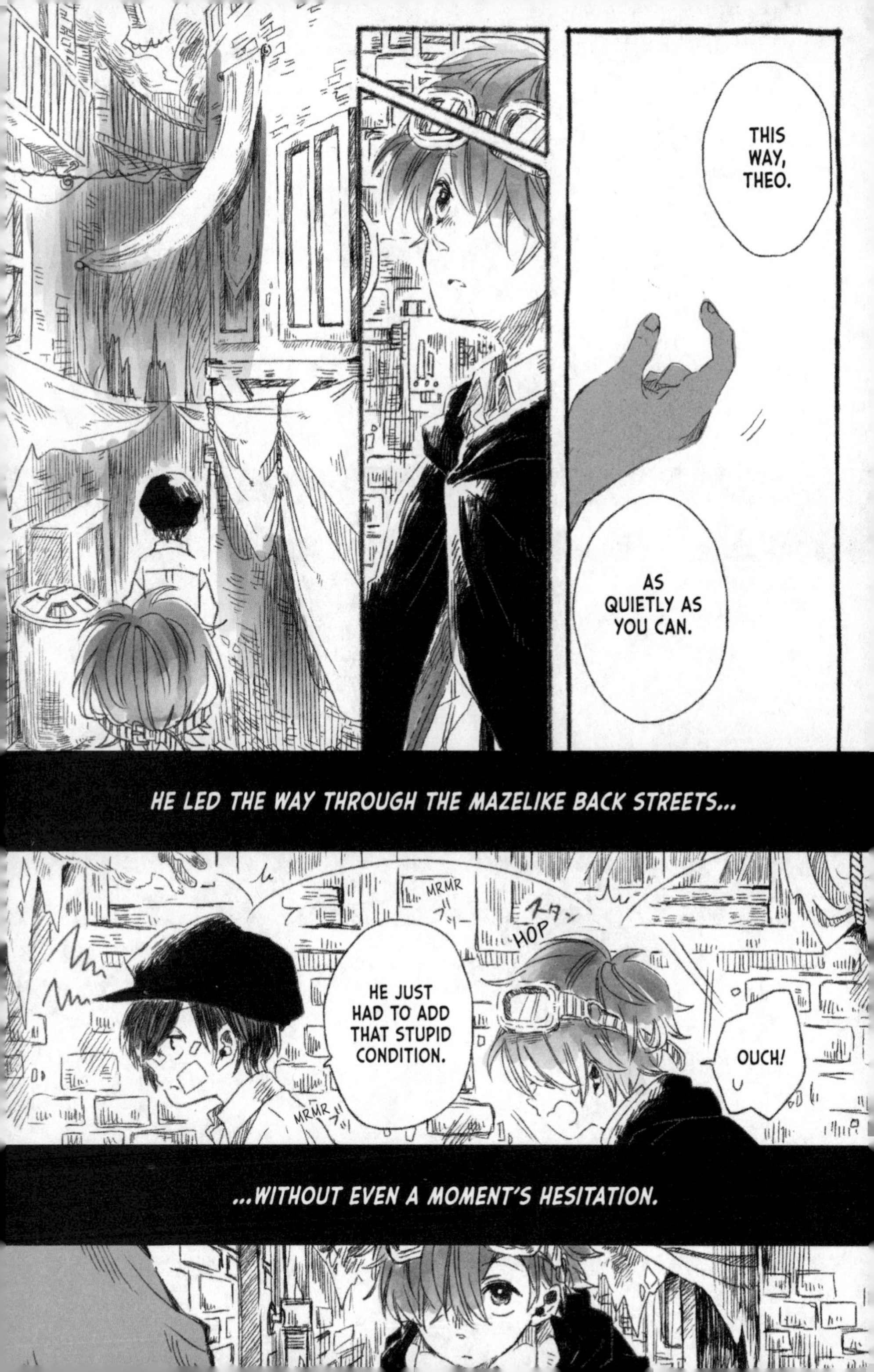
THIS WAY, THEO.
AS QUIETLY AS YOU CAN.
HE LED THE WAY THROUGH THE MAZELIKE BACK STREETS...
OUCH!
HOP
MRMR
HE JUST HAD TO ADD THAT STUPID CONDITION.
MRMR
...WITHOUT EVEN A MOMENT'S HESITATION.

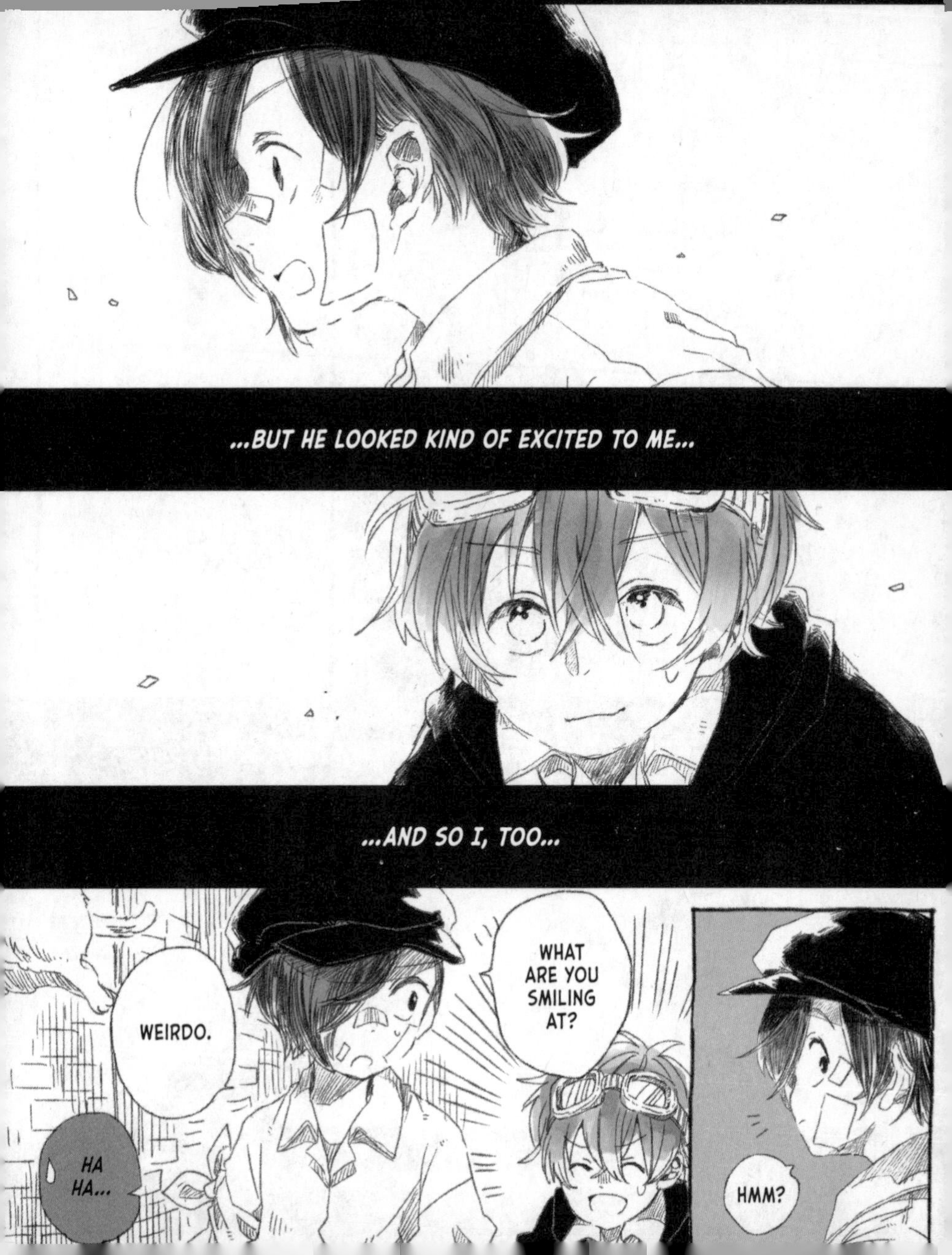
...BUT HE LOOKED KIND OF EXCITED TO ME...
...AND SO I, TOO...
HMM?
WHAT ARE YOU SMILING AT?
WEIRDO.
HA HA...

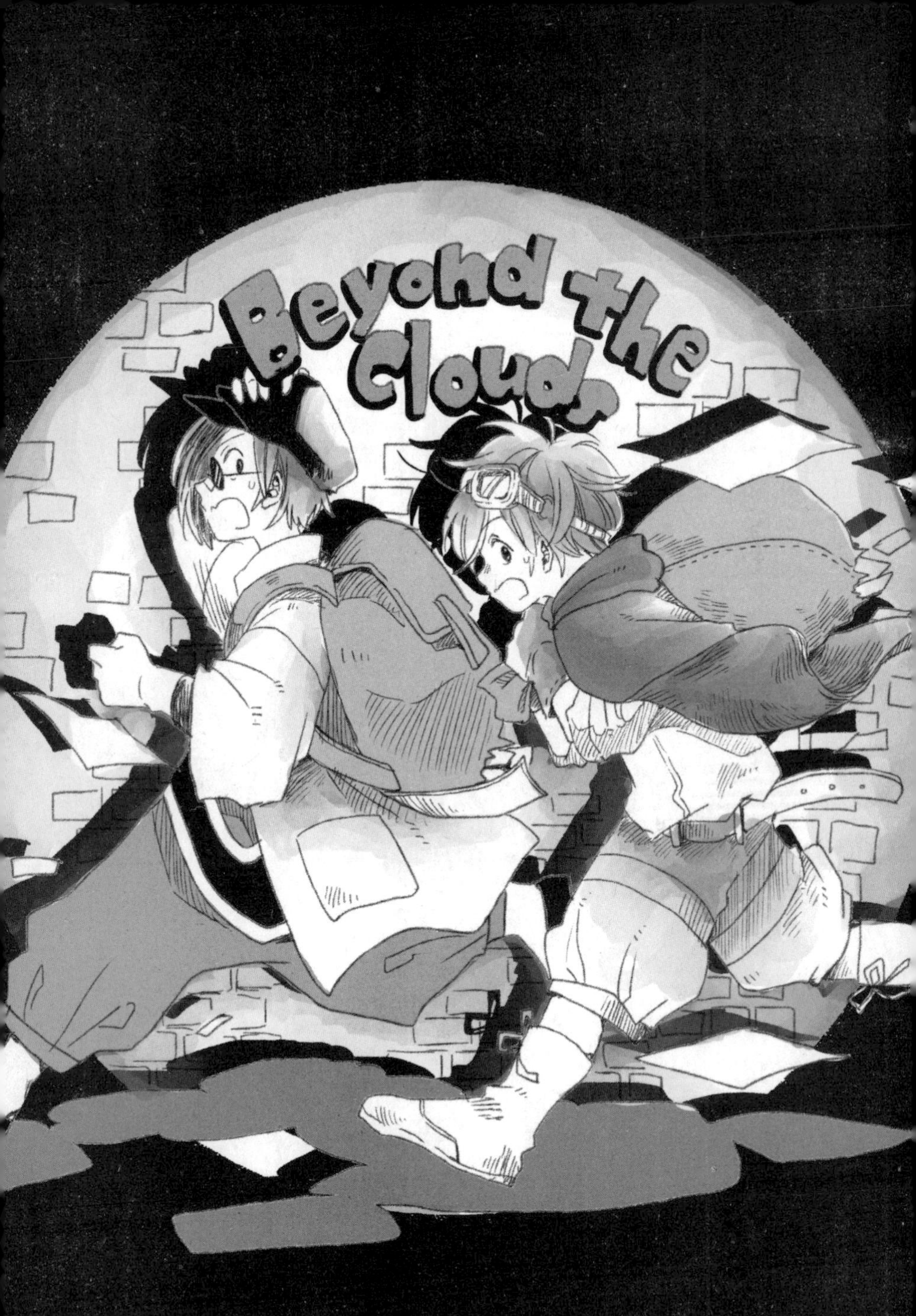
Beyond the Clouds

Chapter 18: Budding Detectives

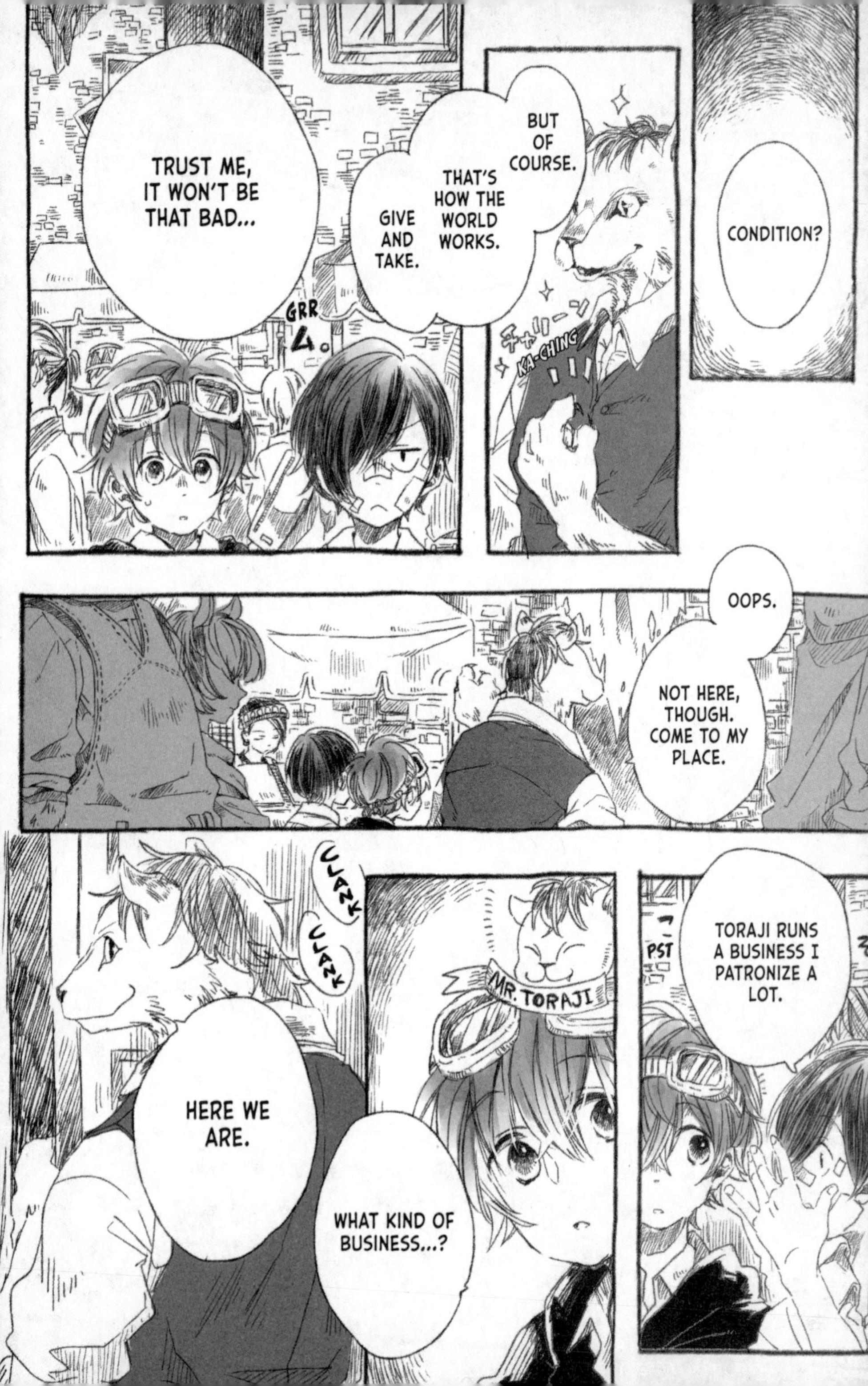
CONDITION?
BUT OF COURSE.
THAT'S HOW THE WORLD WORKS.
GIVE AND TAKE.
KA-CHING
TRUST ME, IT WON'T BE THAT BAD...
GRR
OOPS.
NOT HERE, THOUGH. COME TO MY PLACE.
PST
TORAJI RUNS A BUSINESS I PATRONIZE A LOT.
MR. TORAJI
WHAT KIND OF BUSINESS...?
CLANK
CLANK
HERE WE ARE.

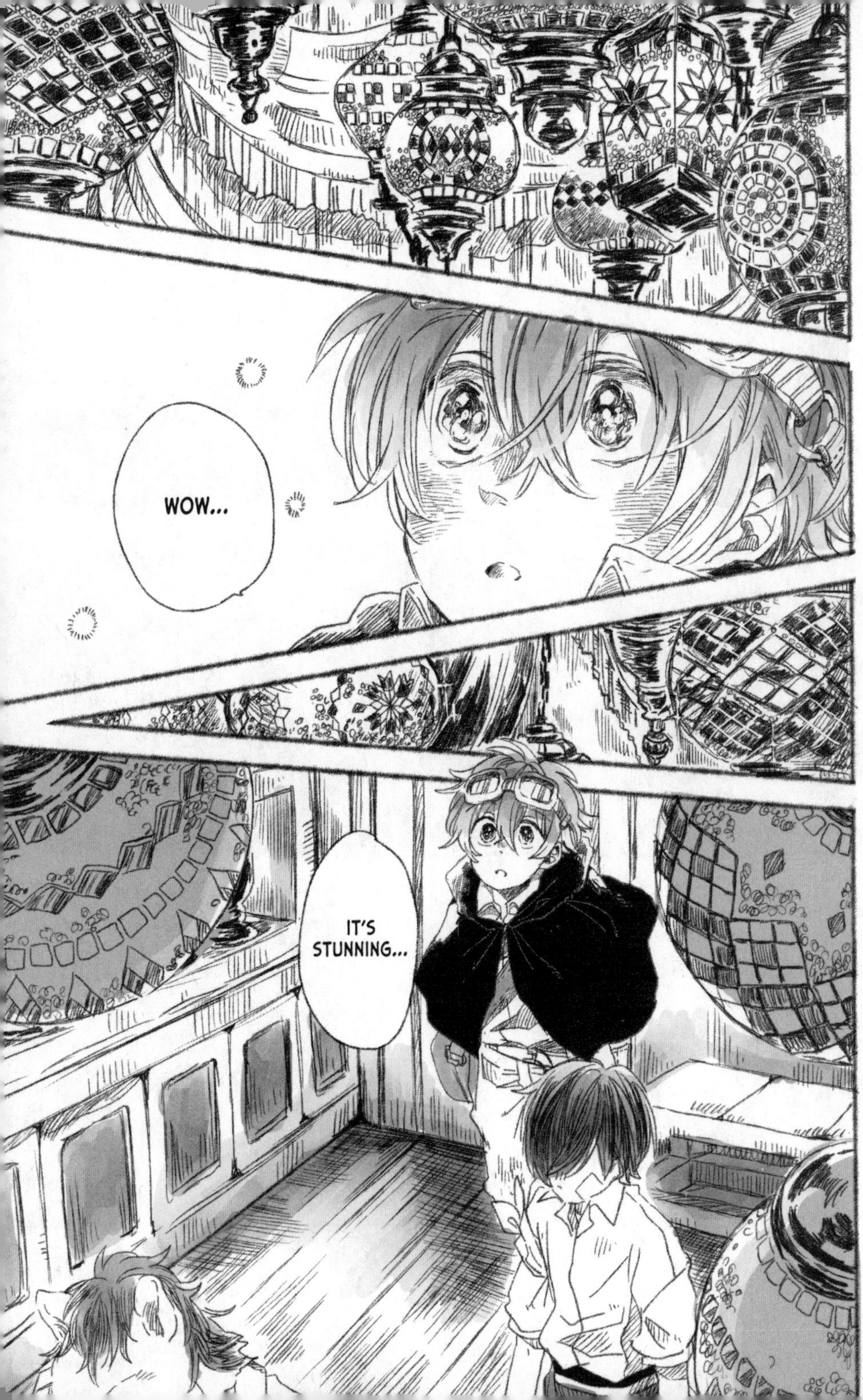
WOW...
IT'S STUNNING...

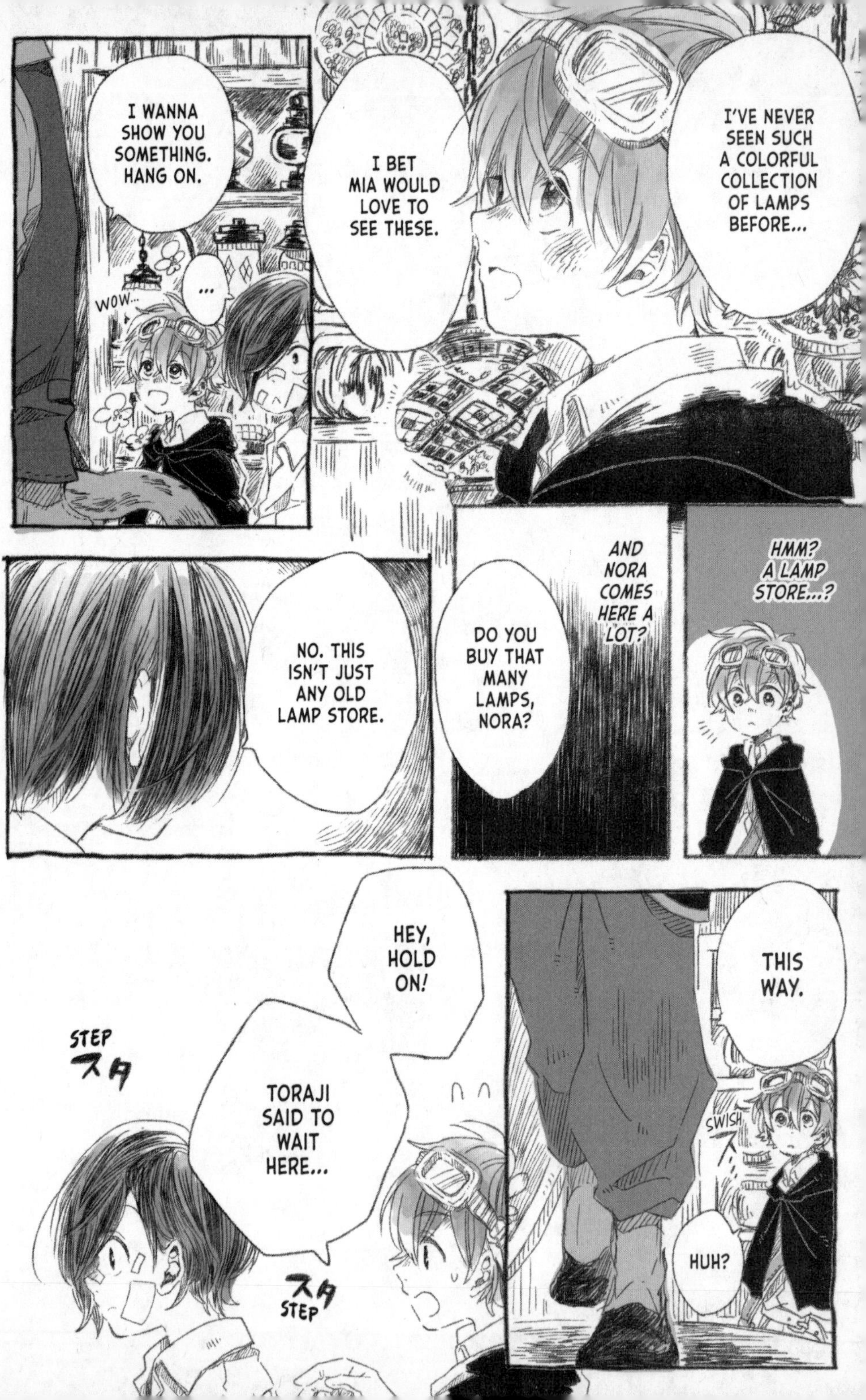
I'VE NEVER SEEN SUCH A COLORFUL COLLECTION OF LAMPS BEFORE...
I BET MIA WOULD LOVE TO SEE THESE.
WOW...
...
I WANNA SHOW YOU SOMETHING. HANG ON.
HMM? A LAMP STORE...?
AND NORA COMES HERE A LOT?
DO YOU BUY THAT MANY LAMPS, NORA?
NO. THIS ISN'T JUST ANY OLD LAMP STORE.
THIS WAY.
SWISH
HUH?
HEY, HOLD ON!
TORAJI SAID TO WAIT HERE...
STEP
スタ
スタ
STEP

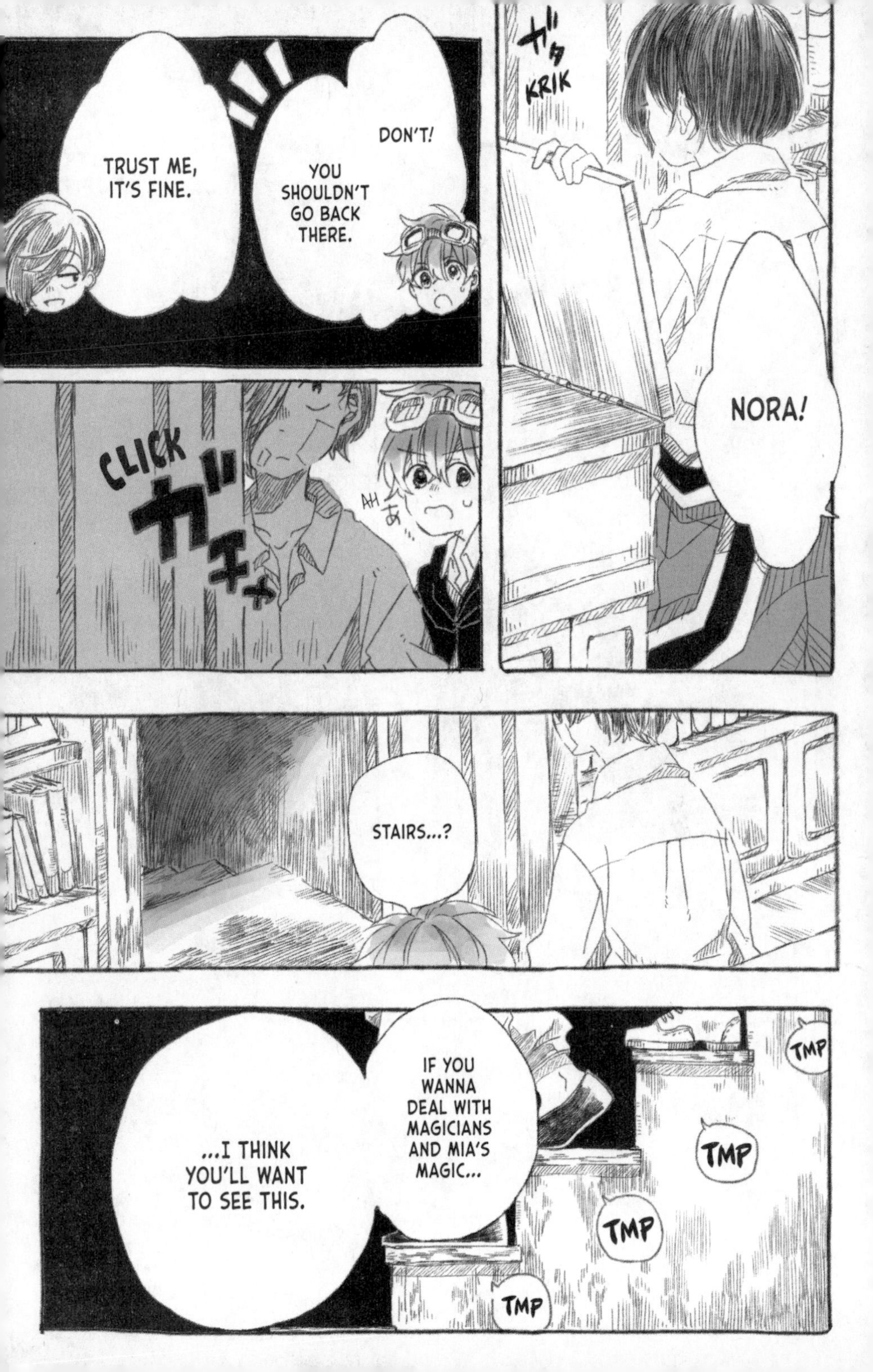
ガタ
KRIK
NORA!
DON'T!
YOU SHOULDN'T GO BACK THERE.
TRUST ME, IT'S FINE.
CLICK
ガチャ
AH
あ
STAIRS...?
TMP
IF YOU WANNA DEAL WITH MAGICIANS AND MIA'S MAGIC...
TMP
TMP
...I THINK YOU'LL WANT TO SEE THIS.
TMP

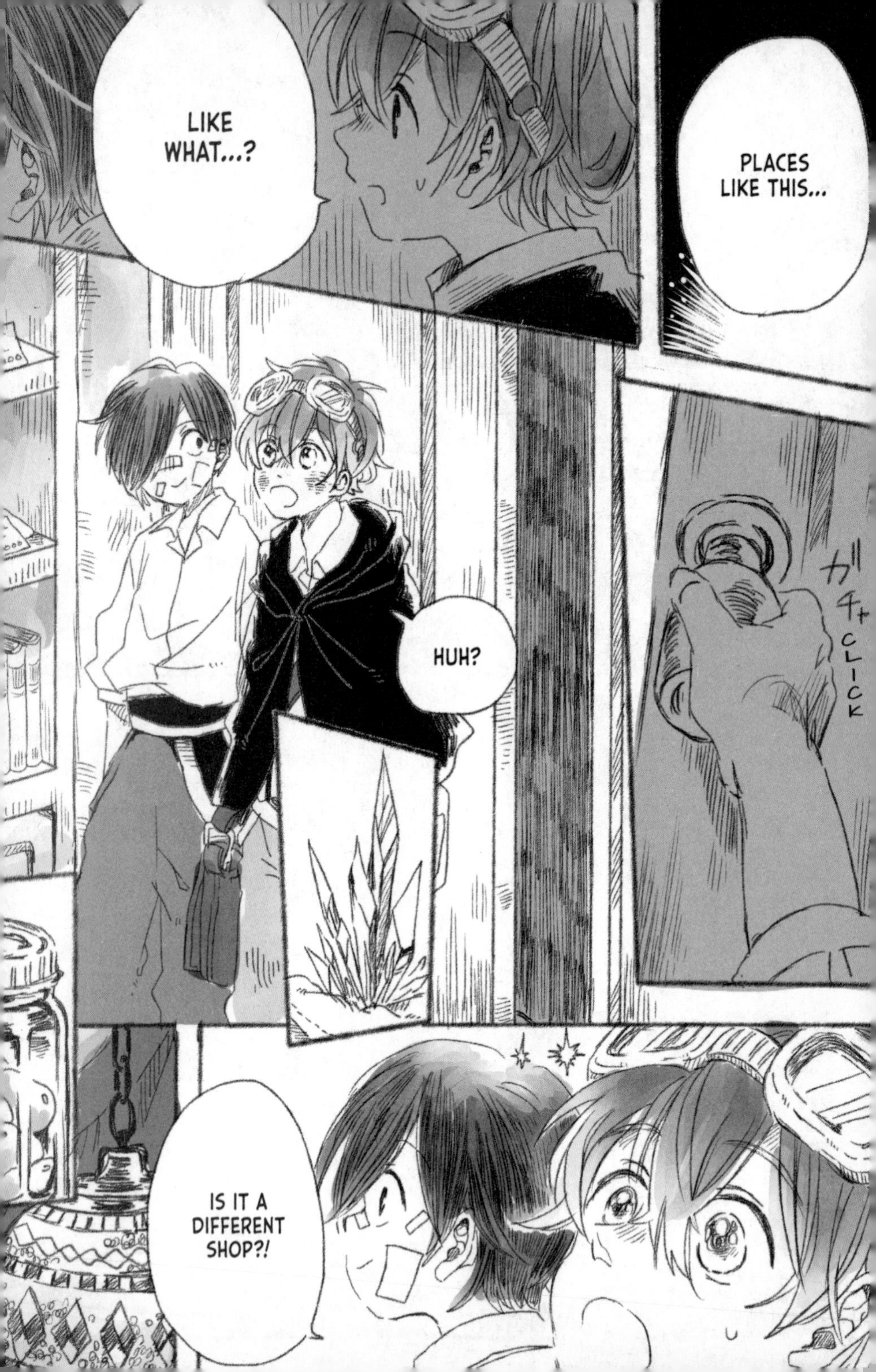
PLACES LIKE THIS...
LIKE WHAT...?
ガチャ
CLICK
HUH?
IS IT A DIFFERENT SHOP?!

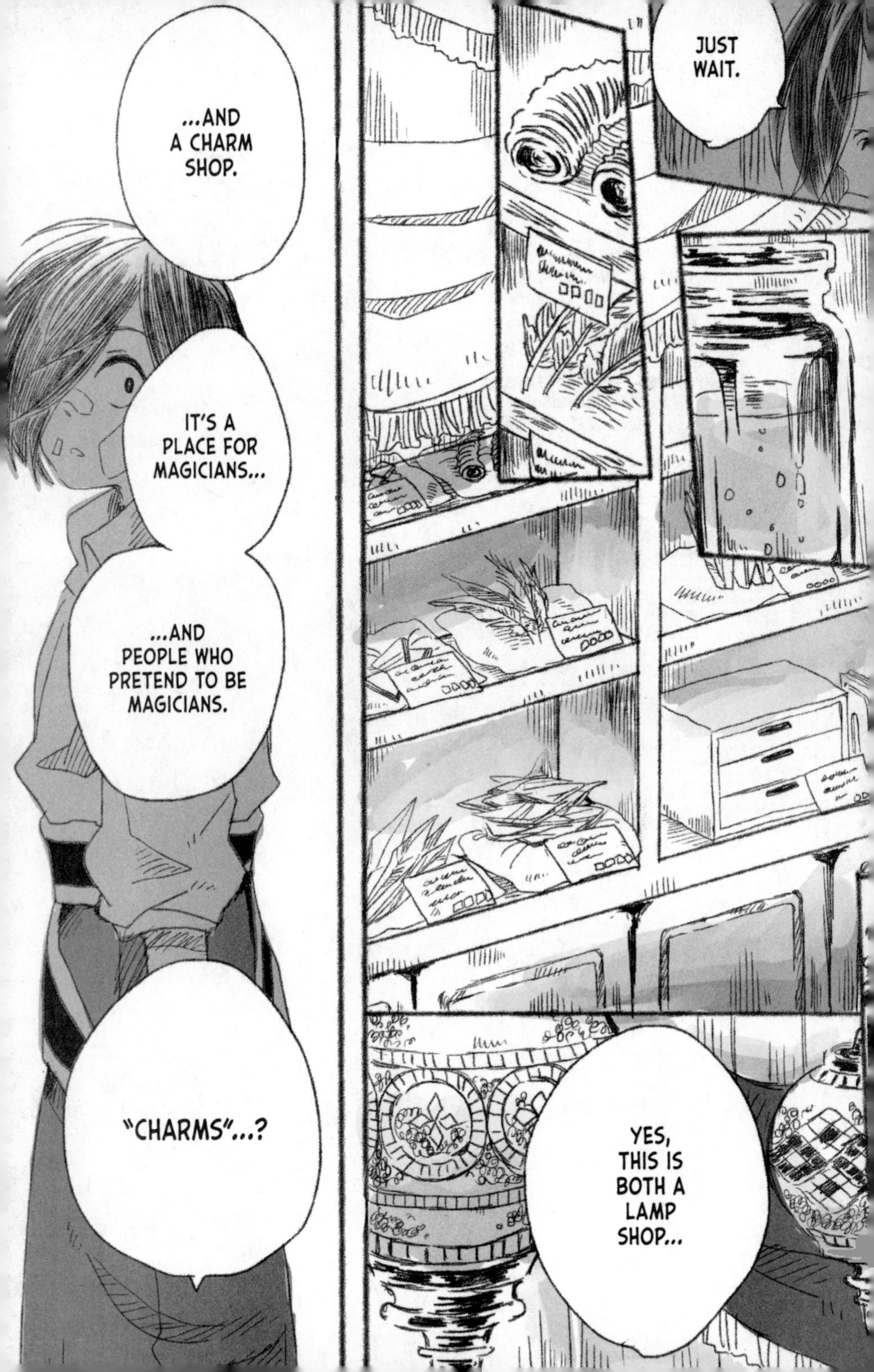
JUST WAIT.
YES, THIS IS BOTH A LAMP SHOP...
...AND A CHARM SHOP.
IT'S A PLACE FOR MAGICIANS...
...AND PEOPLE WHO PRETEND TO BE MAGICIANS.
"CHARMS"...?

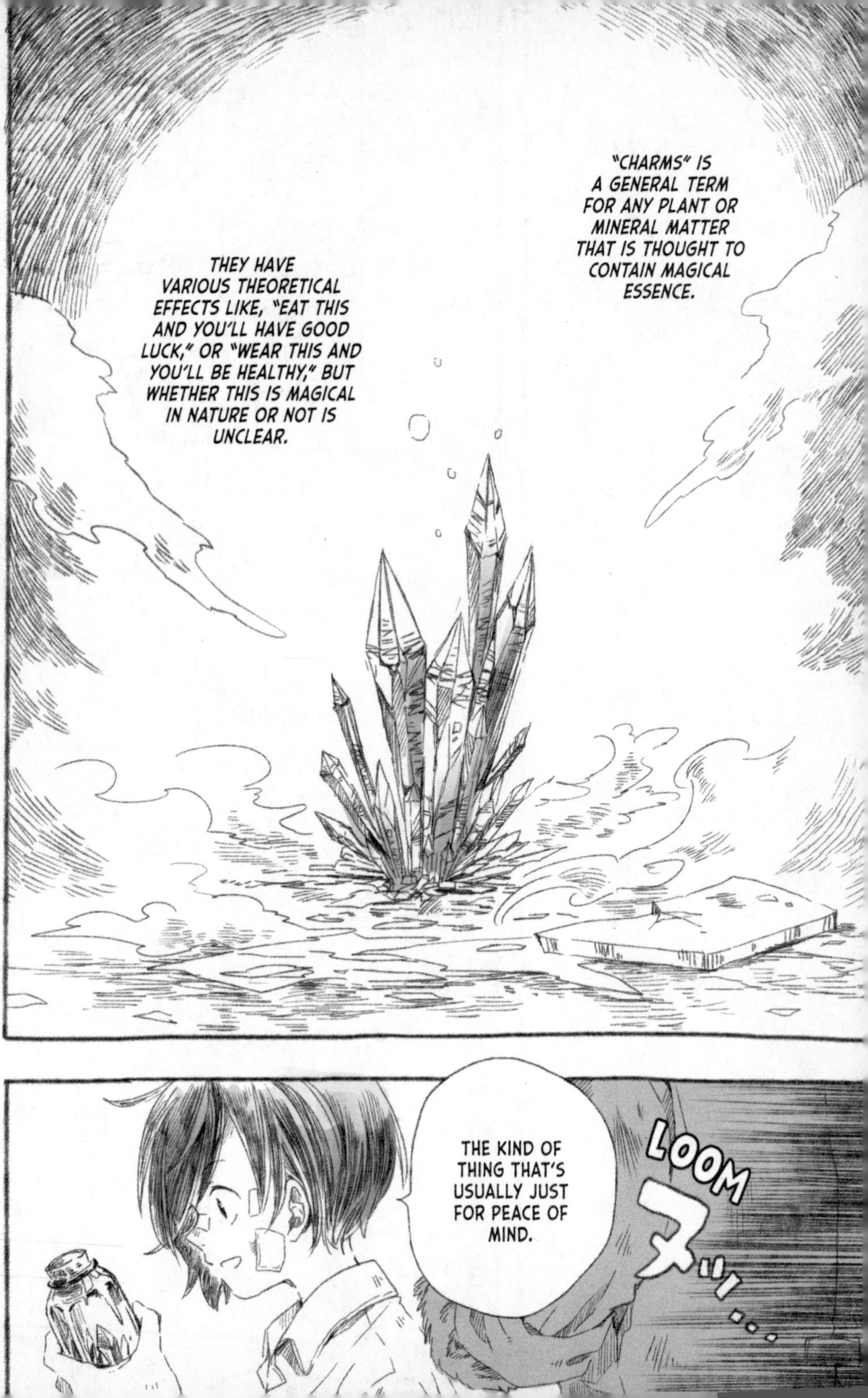
"CHARMS" IS A GENERAL TERM FOR ANY PLANT OR MINERAL MATTER THAT IS THOUGHT TO CONTAIN MAGICAL ESSENCE.
THEY HAVE VARIOUS THEORETICAL EFFECTS LIKE, "EAT THIS AND YOU'LL HAVE GOOD LUCK," OR "WEAR THIS AND YOU'LL BE HEALTHY," BUT WHETHER THIS IS MAGICAL IN NATURE OR NOT IS UNCLEAR.
LOOM
THE KIND OF THING THAT'S USUALLY JUST FOR PEACE OF MIND.

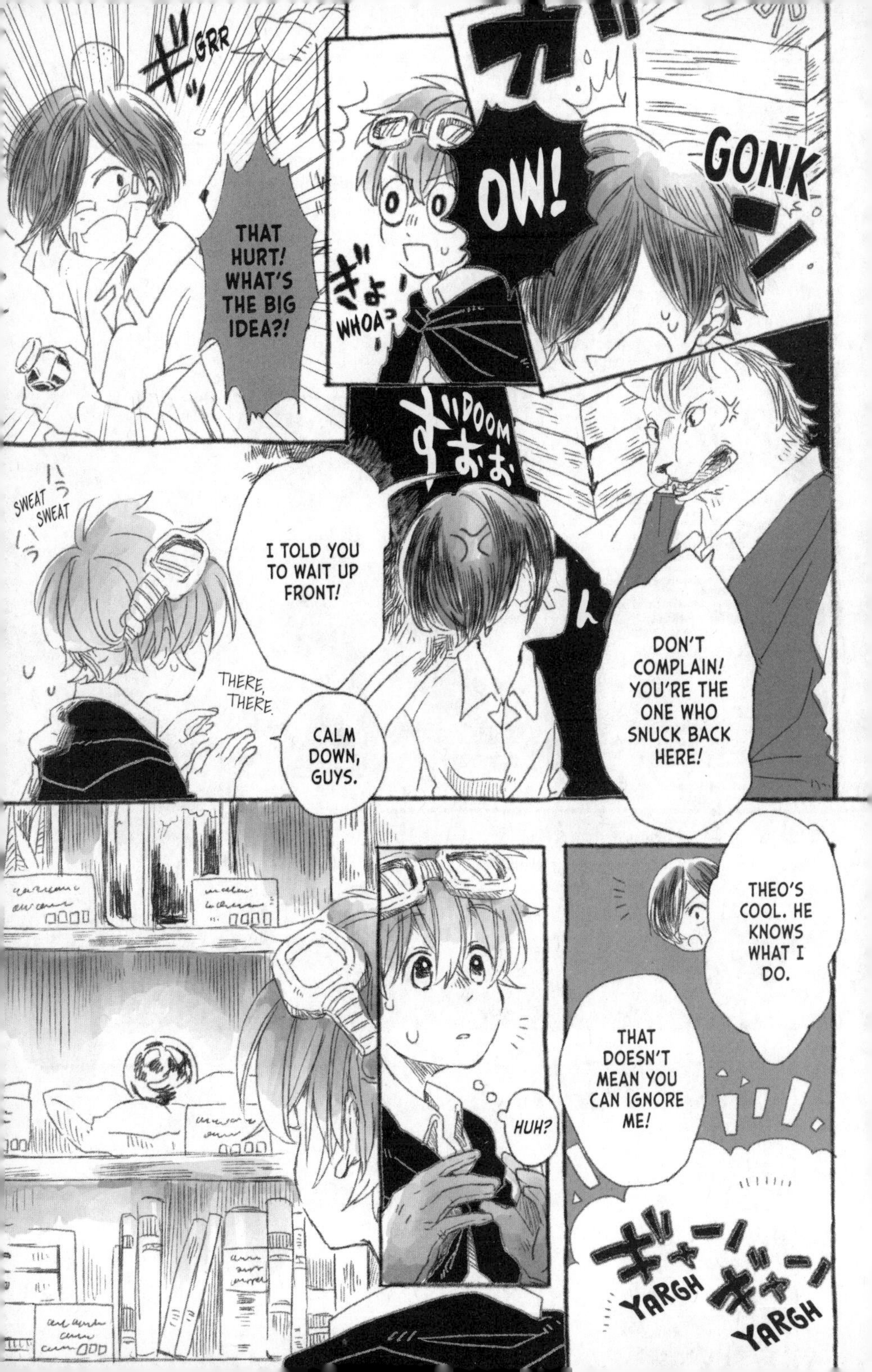
GONK
OW!
WHOA
GRR
THAT HURT! WHAT'S THE BIG IDEA?!
DOOM
DON'T COMPLAIN! YOU'RE THE ONE WHO SNUCK BACK HERE!
I TOLD YOU TO WAIT UP FRONT!
SWEAT SWEAT
THERE, THERE.
CALM DOWN, GUYS.
THEO'S COOL. HE KNOWS WHAT I DO.
THAT DOESN'T MEAN YOU CAN IGNORE ME!
YARGH
YARGH
HUH?

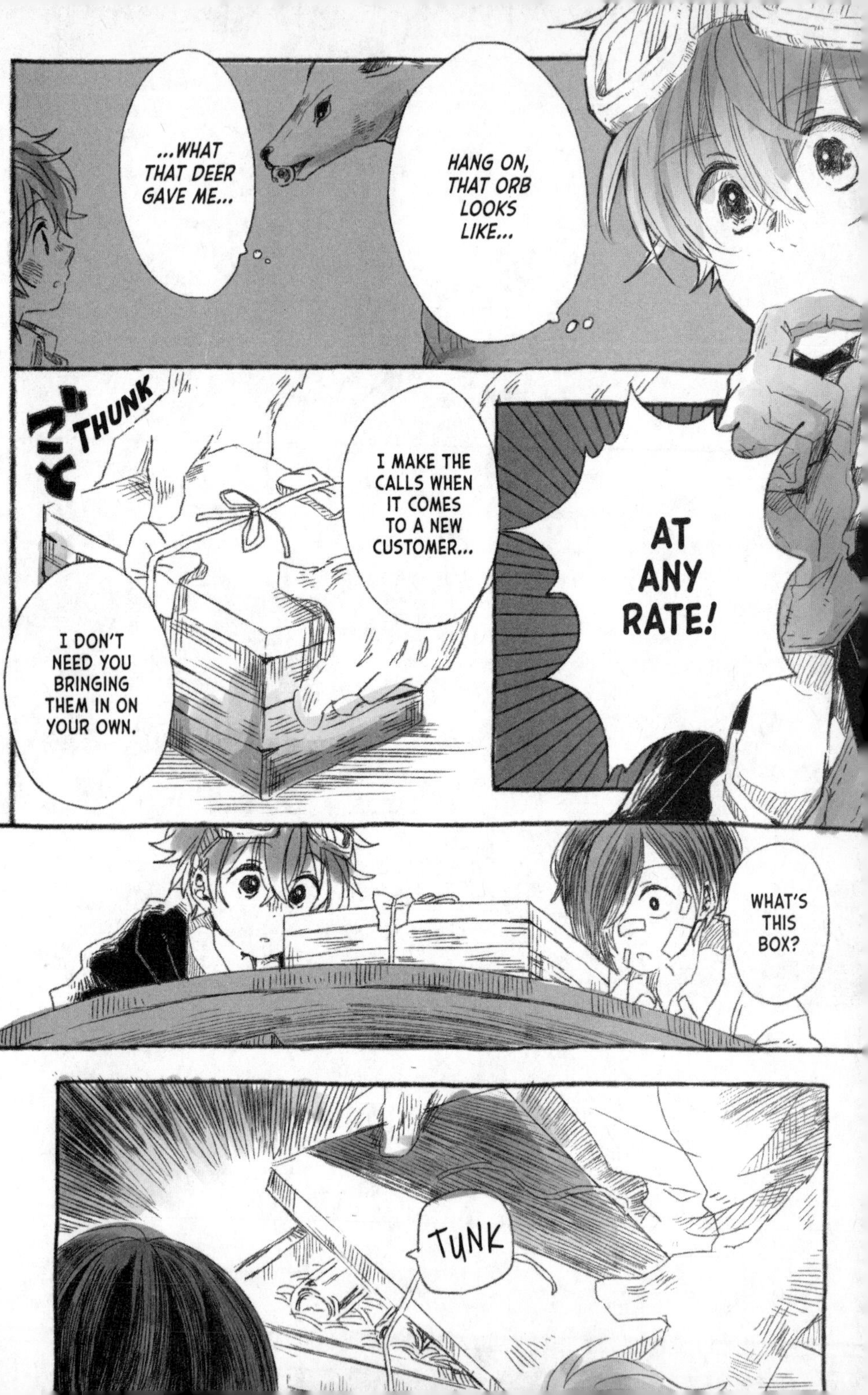
HANG ON, THAT ORB LOOKS LIKE...
...WHAT THAT DEER GAVE ME...
AT ANY RATE!
I MAKE THE CALLS WHEN IT COMES TO A NEW CUSTOMER...
THUNK
I DON'T NEED YOU BRINGING THEM IN ON YOUR OWN.
WHAT'S THIS BOX?
TUNK

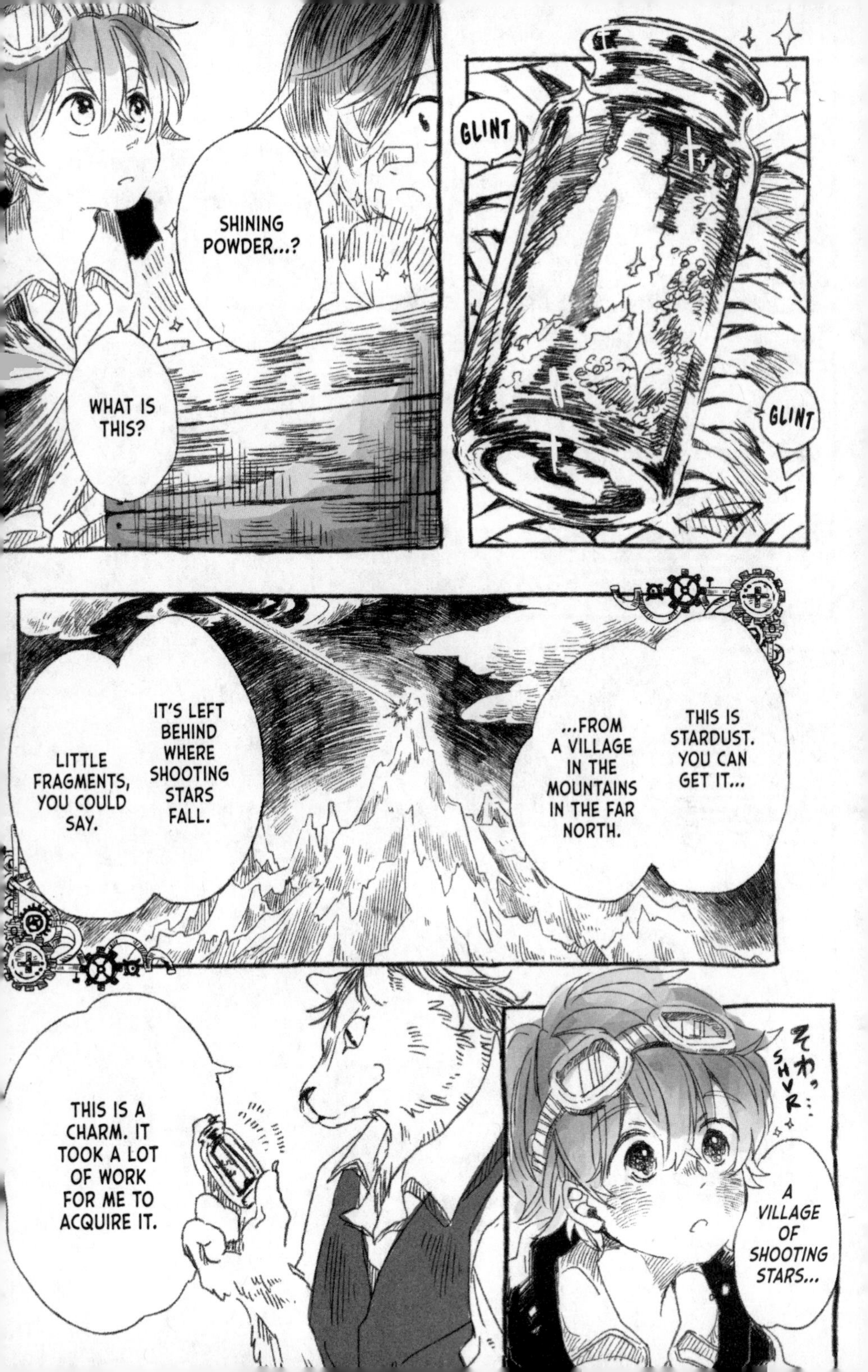
GLINT
GLINT
SHINING POWDER...?
WHAT IS THIS?
THIS IS STARDUST. YOU CAN GET IT...
...FROM A VILLAGE IN THE MOUNTAINS IN THE FAR NORTH.
IT'S LEFT BEHIND WHERE SHOOTING STARS FALL.
LITTLE FRAGMENTS, YOU COULD SAY.
そわっ
SHVR
A VILLAGE OF SHOOTING STARS...
THIS IS A CHARM. IT TOOK A LOT OF WORK FOR ME TO ACQUIRE IT.

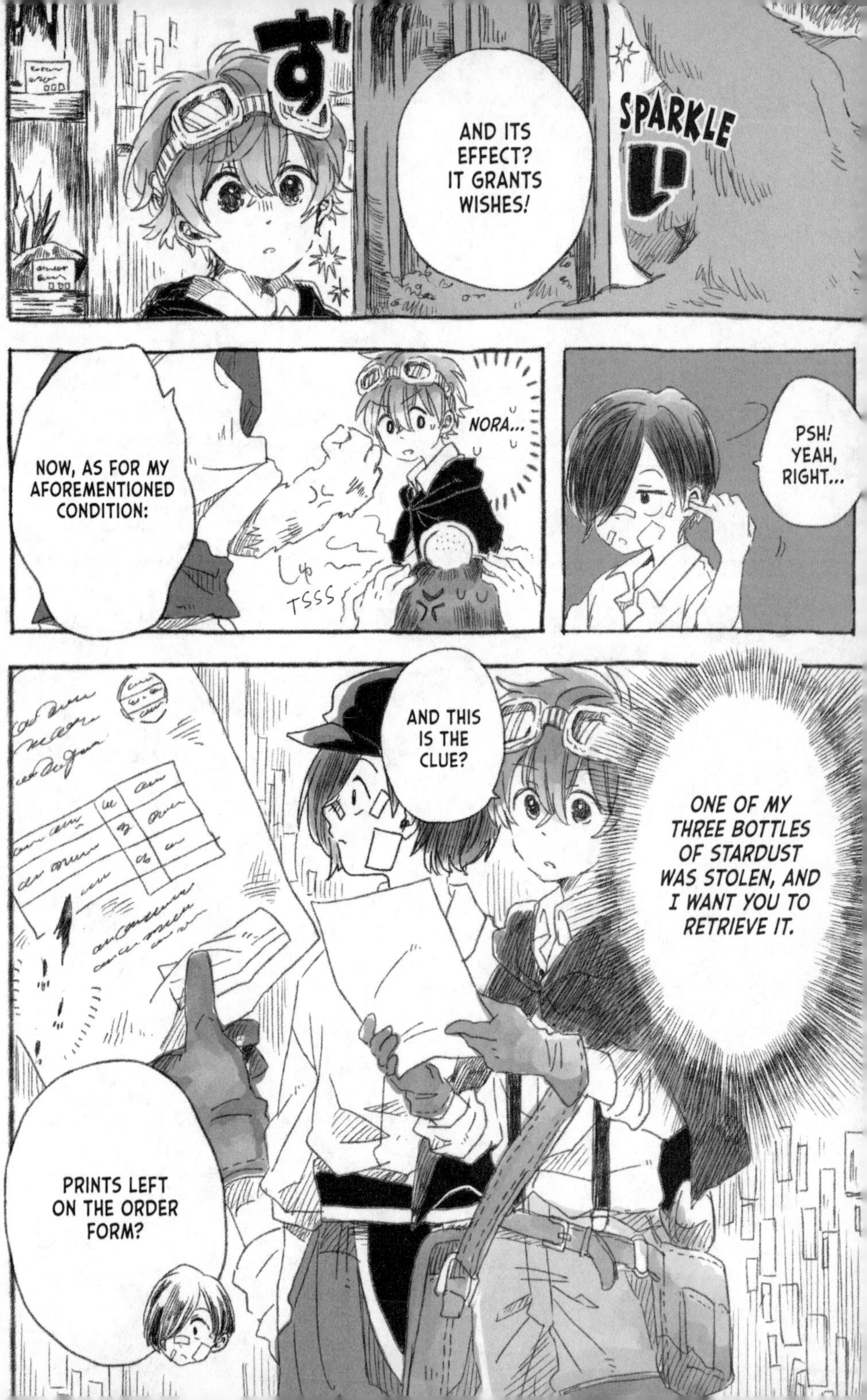
SPARKLE
AND ITS EFFECT? IT GRANTS WISHES!
ず
PSH! YEAH, RIGHT...
NORA...
NOW, AS FOR MY AFOREMENTIONED CONDITION:
しゅ
TSSS
ONE OF MY THREE BOTTLES OF STARDUST WAS STOLEN, AND I WANT YOU TO RETRIEVE IT.
AND THIS IS THE CLUE?
PRINTS LEFT ON THE ORDER FORM?

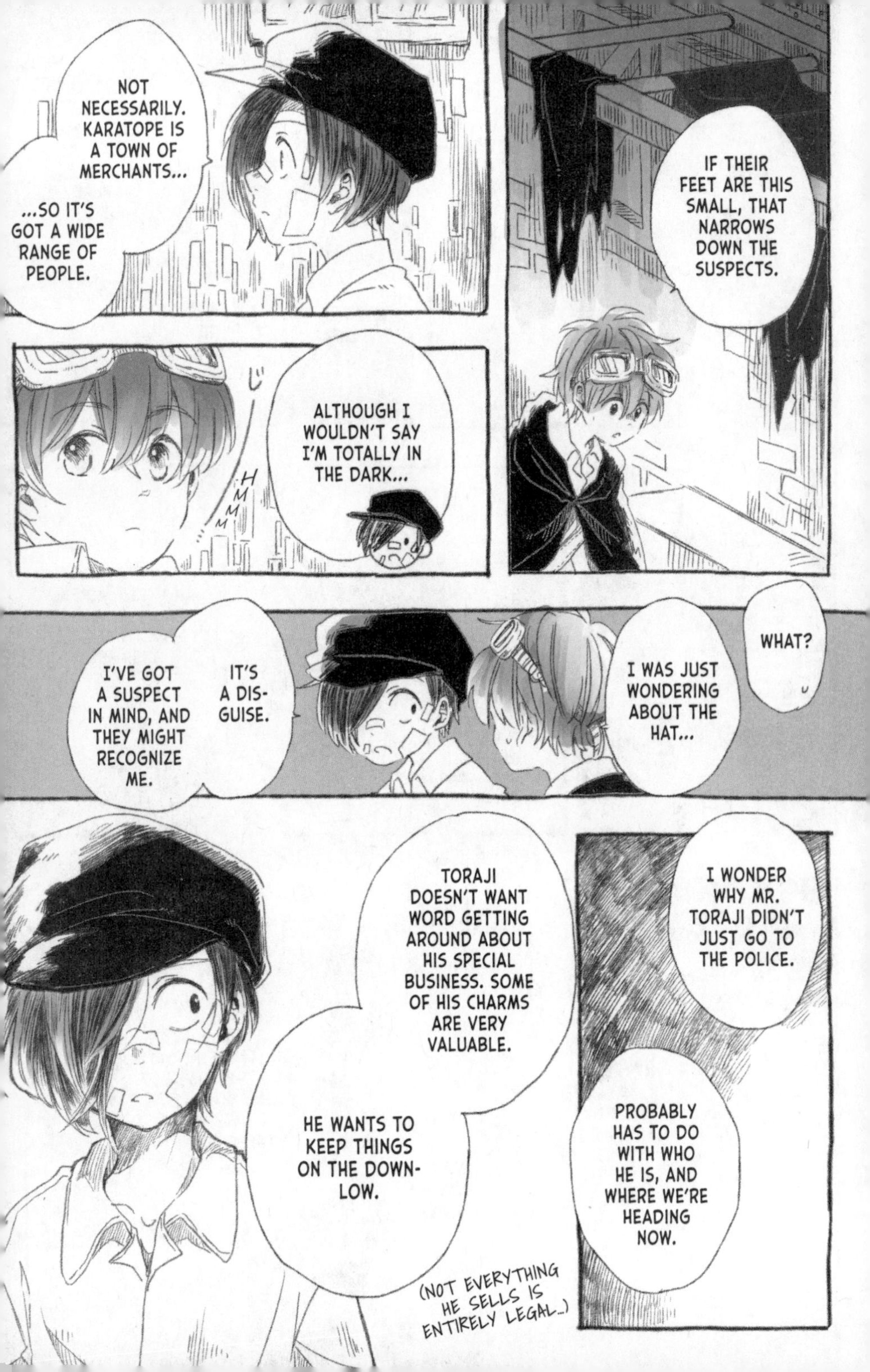
IF THEIR FEET ARE THIS SMALL, THAT NARROWS DOWN THE SUSPECTS.
NOT NECESSARILY. KARATOPE IS A TOWN OF MERCHANTS...
...SO IT'S GOT A WIDE RANGE OF PEOPLE.
じ
HMMM
ALTHOUGH I WOULDN'T SAY I'M TOTALLY IN THE DARK...
WHAT?
I WAS JUST WONDERING ABOUT THE HAT...
IT'S A DISGUISE.
I'VE GOT A SUSPECT IN MIND, AND THEY MIGHT RECOGNIZE ME.
I WONDER WHY MR. TORAJI DIDN'T JUST GO TO THE POLICE.
PROBABLY HAS TO DO WITH WHO HE IS, AND WHERE WE'RE HEADING NOW.
TORAJI DOESN'T WANT WORD GETTING AROUND ABOUT HIS SPECIAL BUSINESS. SOME OF HIS CHARMS ARE VERY VALUABLE.
HE WANTS TO KEEP THINGS ON THE DOWN-LOW.
(NOT EVERYTHING HE SELLS IS ENTIRELY LEGAL...)

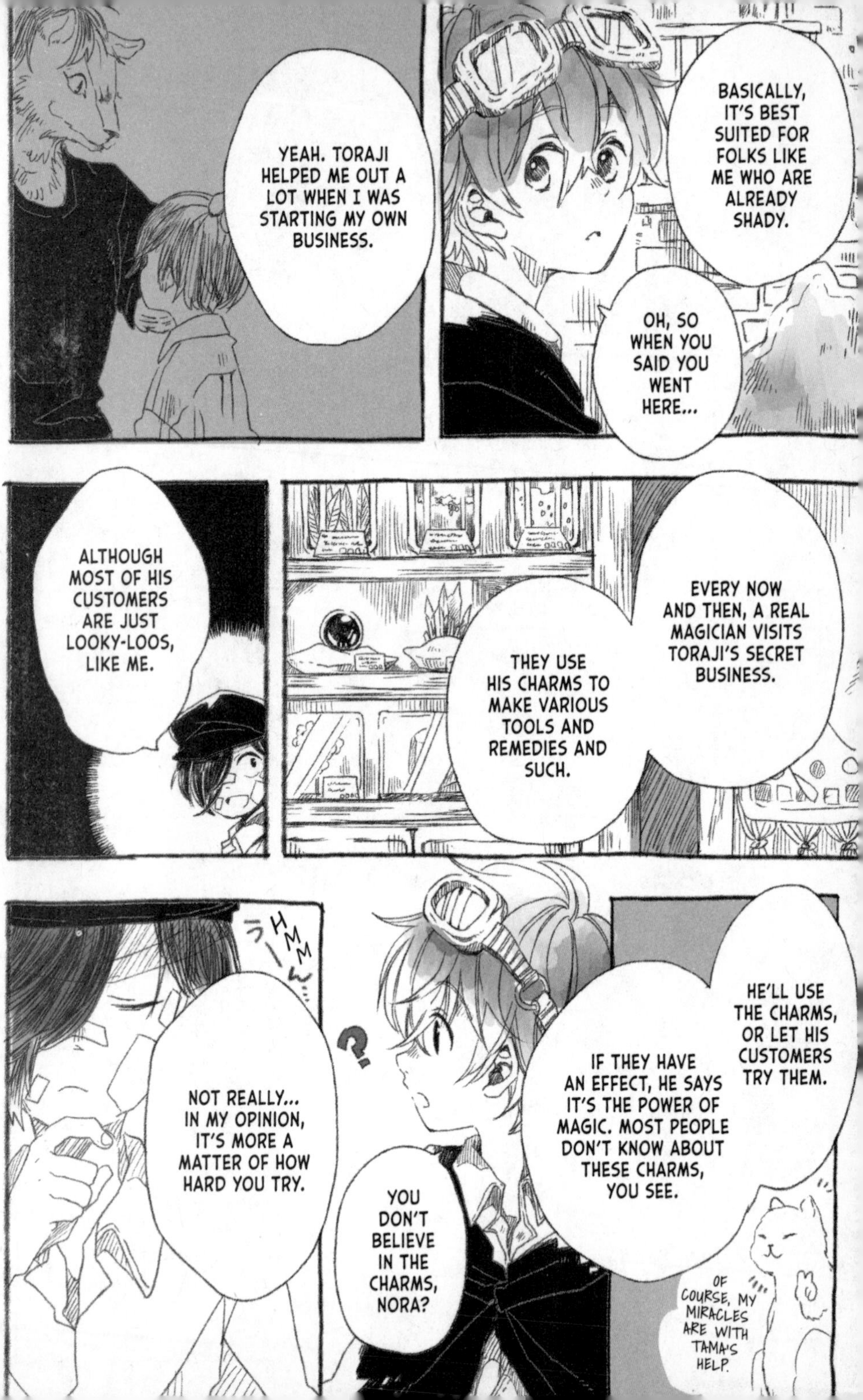
BASICALLY, IT'S BEST SUITED FOR FOLKS LIKE ME WHO ARE ALREADY SHADY.
OH, SO WHEN YOU SAID YOU WENT HERE...
YEAH. TORAJI HELPED ME OUT A LOT WHEN I WAS STARTING MY OWN BUSINESS.
EVERY NOW AND THEN, A REAL MAGICIAN VISITS TORAJI'S SECRET BUSINESS.
THEY USE HIS CHARMS TO MAKE VARIOUS TOOLS AND REMEDIES AND SUCH.
ALTHOUGH MOST OF HIS CUSTOMERS ARE JUST LOOKY-LOOS, LIKE ME.
HE'LL USE THE CHARMS, OR LET HIS CUSTOMERS TRY THEM.
IF THEY HAVE AN EFFECT, HE SAYS IT'S THE POWER OF MAGIC. MOST PEOPLE DON'T KNOW ABOUT THESE CHARMS, YOU SEE.
OF COURSE, MY MIRACLES ARE WITH TAMA'S HELP.
YOU DON'T BELIEVE IN THE CHARMS, NORA?
?
HMM
NOT REALLY... IN MY OPINION, IT'S MORE A MATTER OF HOW HARD YOU TRY.

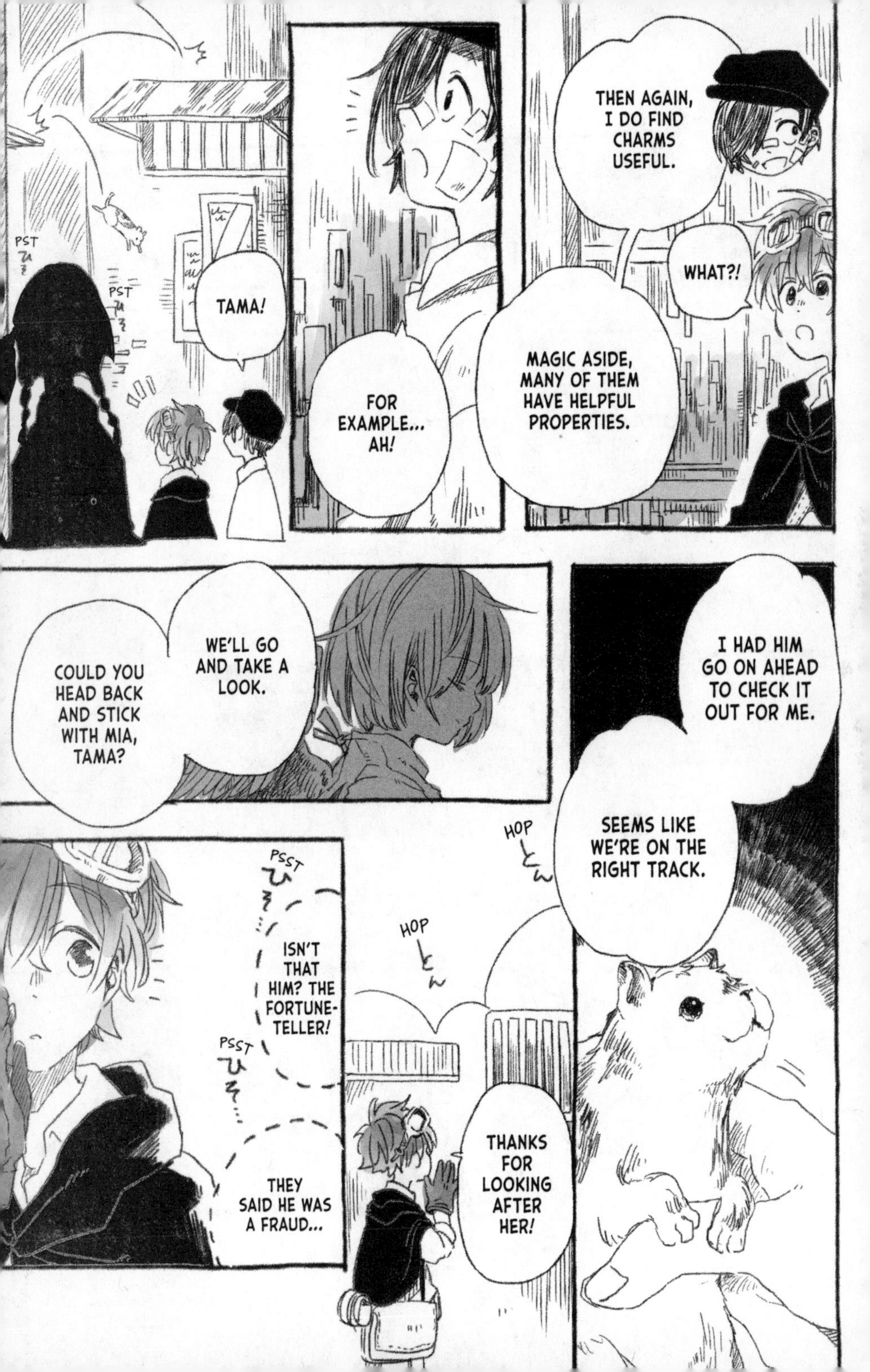
THEN AGAIN, I DO FIND CHARMS USEFUL.
WHAT?!
MAGIC ASIDE, MANY OF THEM HAVE HELPFUL PROPERTIES.
FOR EXAMPLE... AH!
PST
PST
TAMA!
I HAD HIM GO ON AHEAD TO CHECK IT OUT FOR ME.
SEEMS LIKE WE'RE ON THE RIGHT TRACK.
WE'LL GO AND TAKE A LOOK.
COULD YOU HEAD BACK AND STICK WITH MIA, TAMA?
HOP
HOP
THANKS FOR LOOKING AFTER HER!
PSST
ISN'T THAT HIM? THE FORTUNE-TELLER!
PSST
THEY SAID HE WAS A FRAUD...

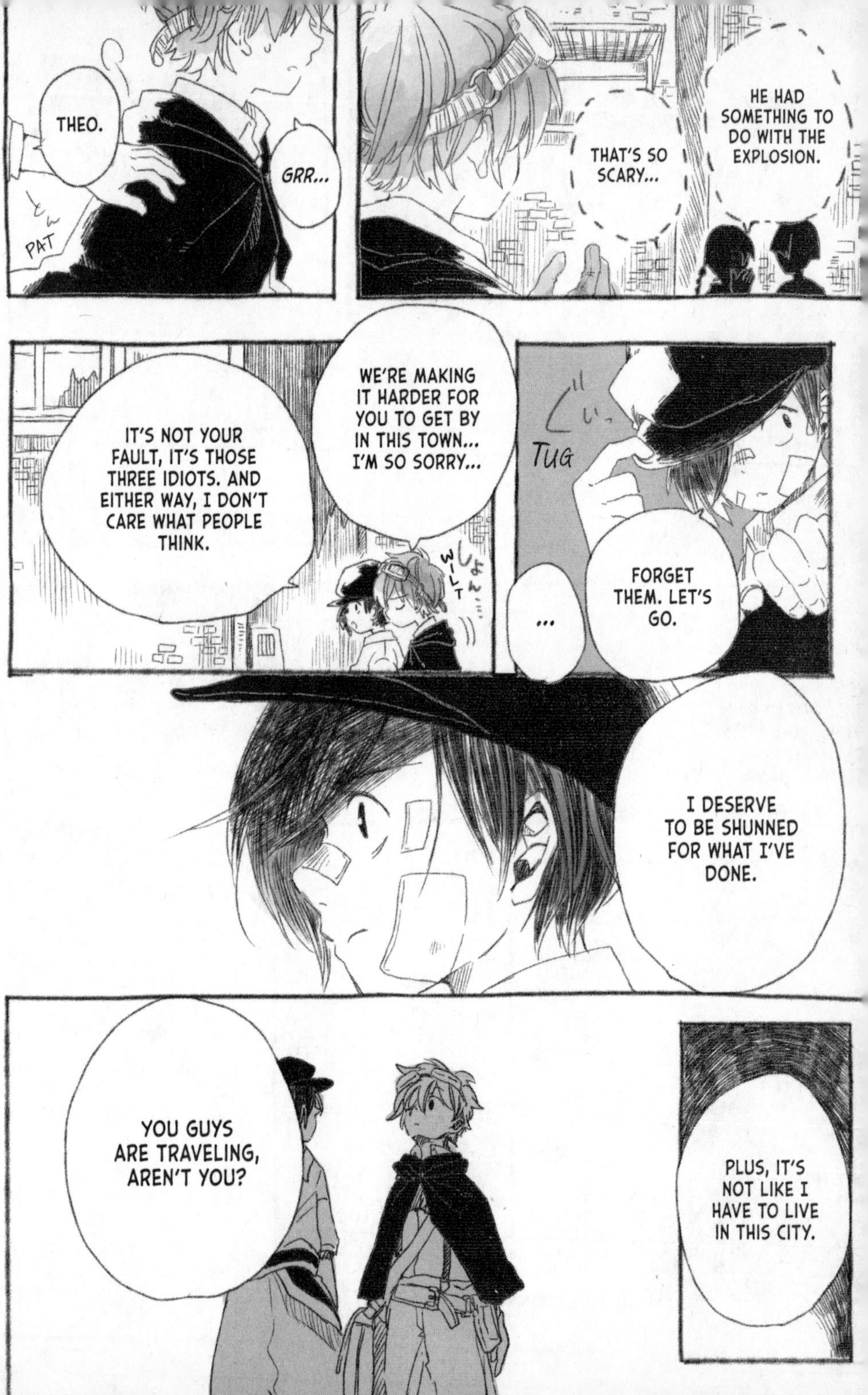
HE HAD SOMETHING TO DO WITH THE EXPLOSION.
THAT'S SO SCARY...
GRR...
THEO.
PAT
FORGET THEM. LET'S GO.
...
TUG
WE'RE MAKING IT HARDER FOR YOU TO GET BY IN THIS TOWN... I'M SO SORRY...
WILT
IT'S NOT YOUR FAULT, IT'S THOSE THREE IDIOTS. AND EITHER WAY, I DON'T CARE WHAT PEOPLE THINK.
I DESERVE TO BE SHUNNED FOR WHAT I'VE DONE.
PLUS, IT'S NOT LIKE I HAVE TO LIVE IN THIS CITY.
YOU GUYS ARE TRAVELING, AREN'T YOU?

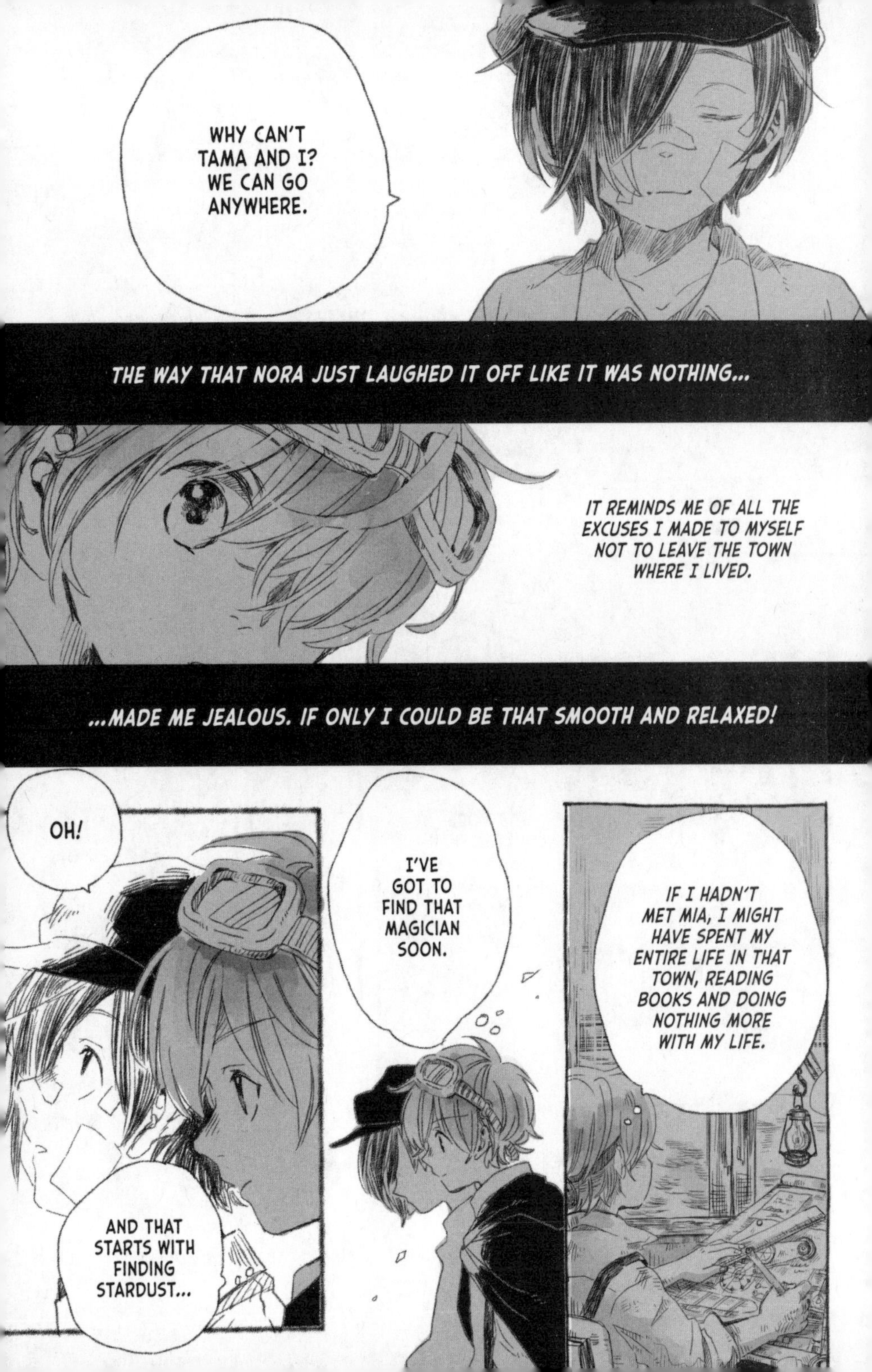
WHY CAN'T TAMA AND I? WE CAN GO ANYWHERE.
THE WAY THAT NORA JUST LAUGHED IT OFF LIKE IT WAS NOTHING...
IT REMINDS ME OF ALL THE EXCUSES I MADE TO MYSELF NOT TO LEAVE THE TOWN WHERE I LIVED.
...MADE ME JEALOUS. IF ONLY I COULD BE THAT SMOOTH AND RELAXED!
IF I HADN'T MET MIA, I MIGHT HAVE SPENT MY ENTIRE LIFE IN THAT TOWN, READING BOOKS AND DOING NOTHING MORE WITH MY LIFE.
I'VE GOT TO FIND THAT MAGICIAN SOON.
OH!
AND THAT STARTS WITH FINDING STARDUST...

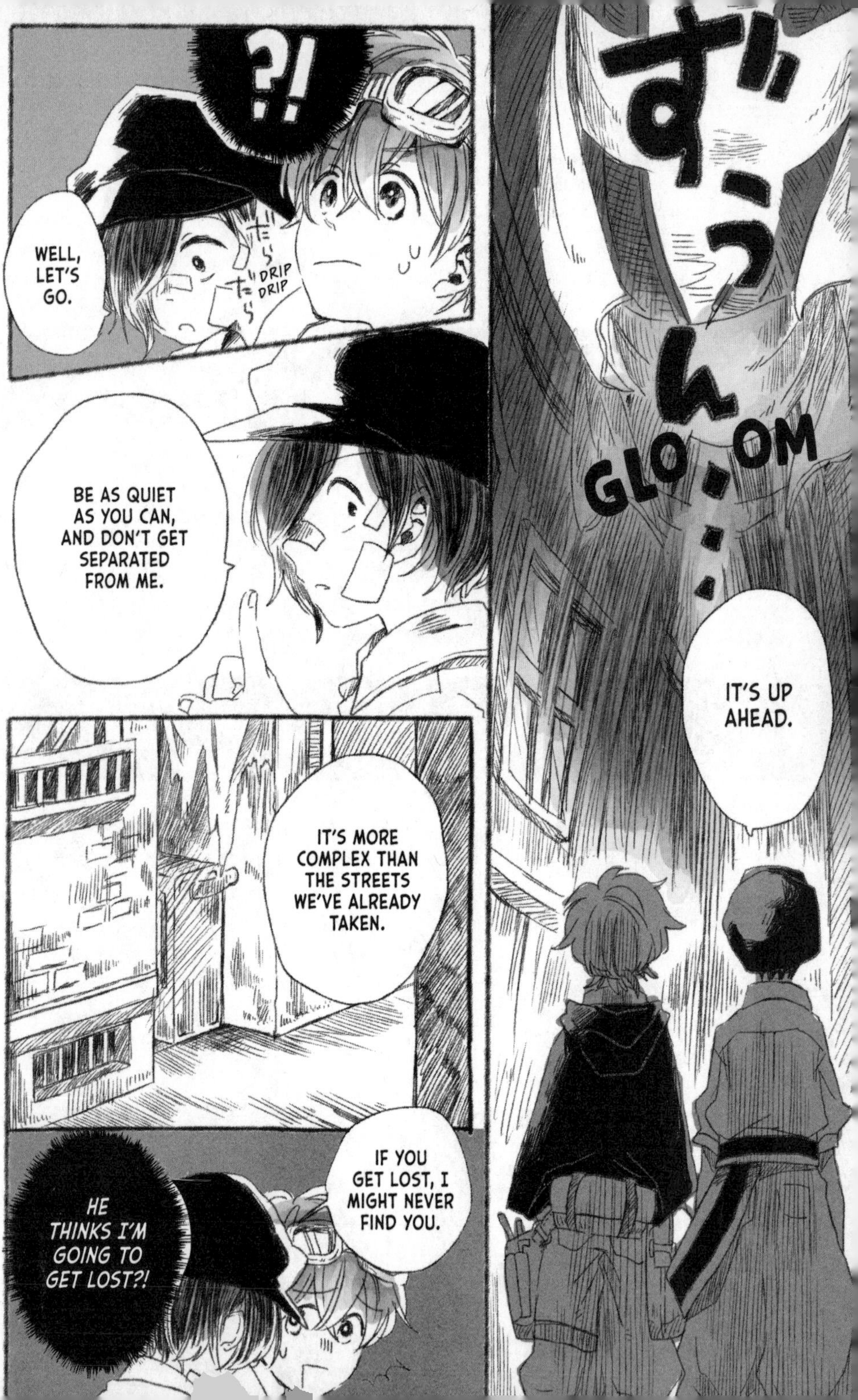
ずぅーん
GLOOM
IT'S UP AHEAD.
?!
WELL, LET'S GO.
DRIP DRIP
BE AS QUIET AS YOU CAN, AND DON'T GET SEPARATED FROM ME.
IT'S MORE COMPLEX THAN THE STREETS WE'VE ALREADY TAKEN.
IF YOU GET LOST, I MIGHT NEVER FIND YOU.
HE THINKS I'M GOING TO GET LOST?!

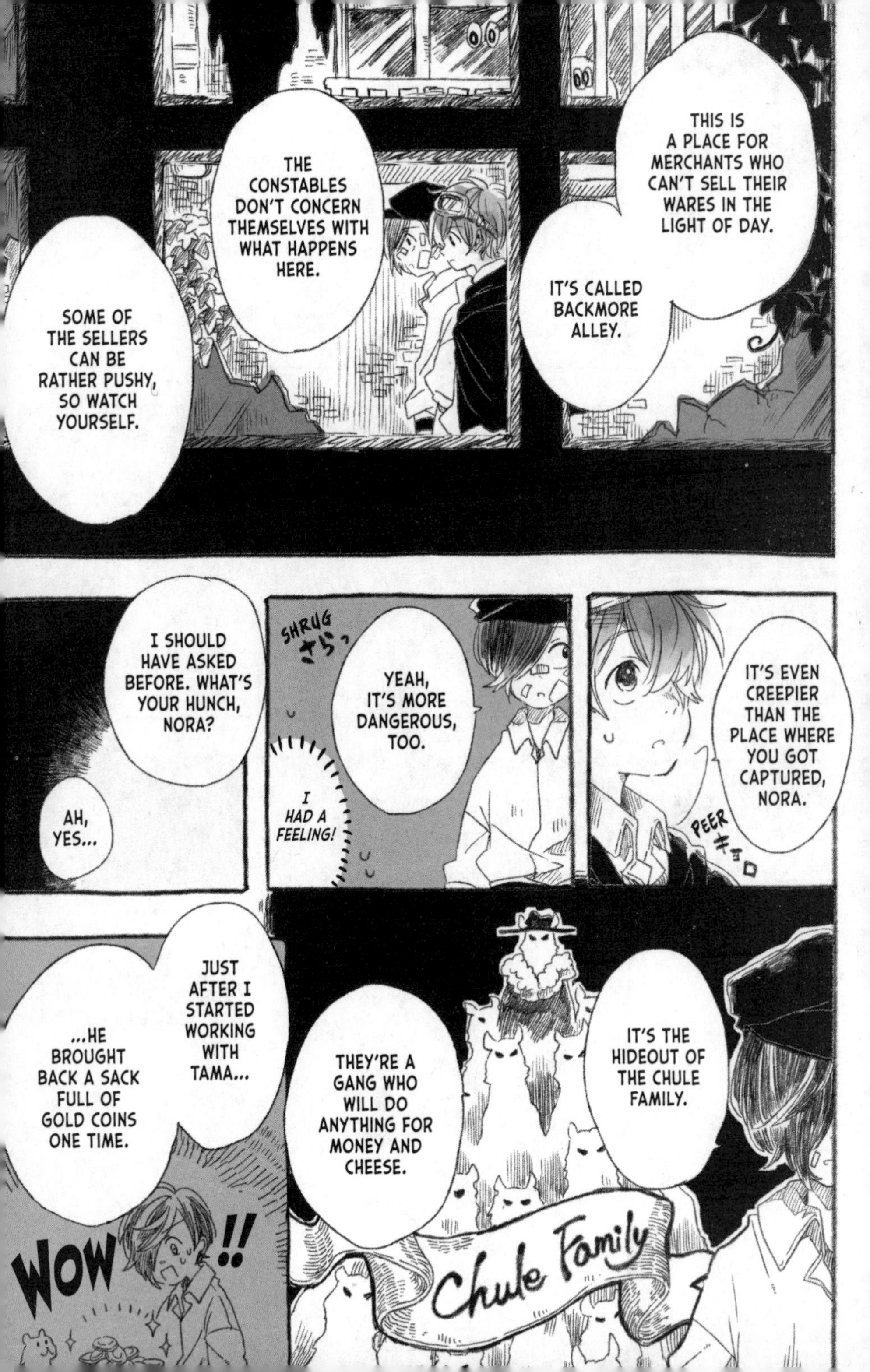
THIS IS A PLACE FOR MERCHANTS WHO CAN'T SELL THEIR WARES IN THE LIGHT OF DAY.
IT'S CALLED BACKMORE ALLEY.
THE CONSTABLES DON'T CONCERN THEMSELVES WITH WHAT HAPPENS HERE.
SOME OF THE SELLERS CAN BE RATHER PUSHY, SO WATCH YOURSELF.
IT'S EVEN CREEPIER THAN THE PLACE WHERE YOU GOT CAPTURED, NORA.
PEER
SHRUG
YEAH, IT'S MORE DANGEROUS, TOO.
I HAD A FEELING!
I SHOULD HAVE ASKED BEFORE. WHAT'S YOUR HUNCH, NORA?
AH, YES...
IT'S THE HIDEOUT OF THE CHULE FAMILY.
THEY'RE A GANG WHO WILL DO ANYTHING FOR MONEY AND CHEESE.
Chule Family
JUST AFTER I STARTED WORKING WITH TAMA...
...HE BROUGHT BACK A SACK FULL OF GOLD COINS ONE TIME.
WOW!!

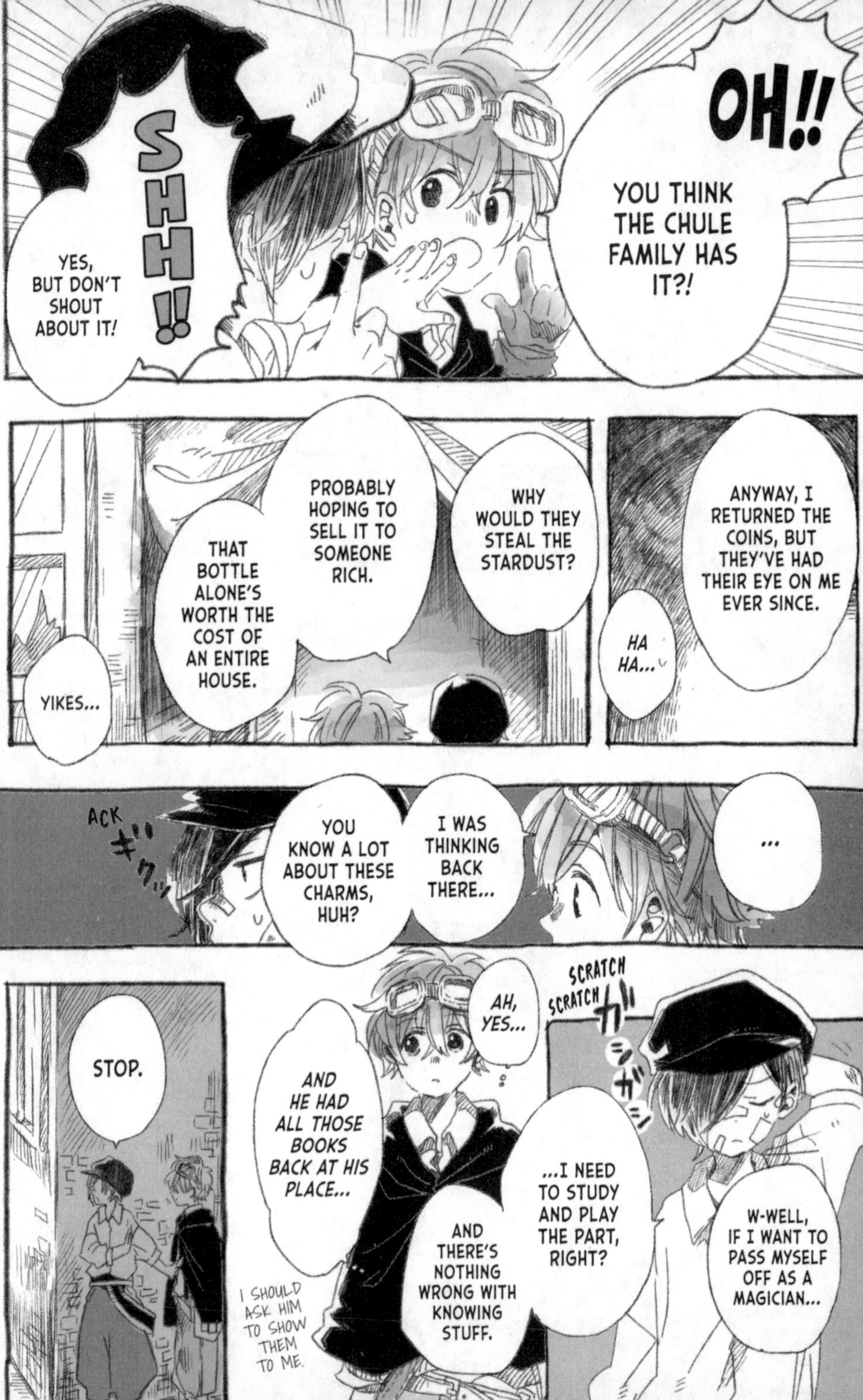
OH!!
YOU THINK THE CHULE FAMILY HAS IT?!
SHH!!
YES, BUT DON'T SHOUT ABOUT IT!
ANYWAY, I RETURNED THE COINS, BUT THEY'VE HAD THEIR EYE ON ME EVER SINCE.
HA HA...
WHY WOULD THEY STEAL THE STARDUST?
PROBABLY HOPING TO SELL IT TO SOMEONE RICH.
THAT BOTTLE ALONE'S WORTH THE COST OF AN ENTIRE HOUSE.
YIKES...
...
I WAS THINKING BACK THERE...
YOU KNOW A LOT ABOUT THESE CHARMS, HUH?
ACK
SCRATCH SCRATCH
W-WELL, IF I WANT TO PASS MYSELF OFF AS A MAGICIAN...
...I NEED TO STUDY AND PLAY THE PART, RIGHT?
AH, YES...
AND HE HAD ALL THOSE BOOKS BACK AT HIS PLACE...
AND THERE'S NOTHING WRONG WITH KNOWING STUFF.
I SHOULD ASK HIM TO SHOW THEM TO ME.
STOP.

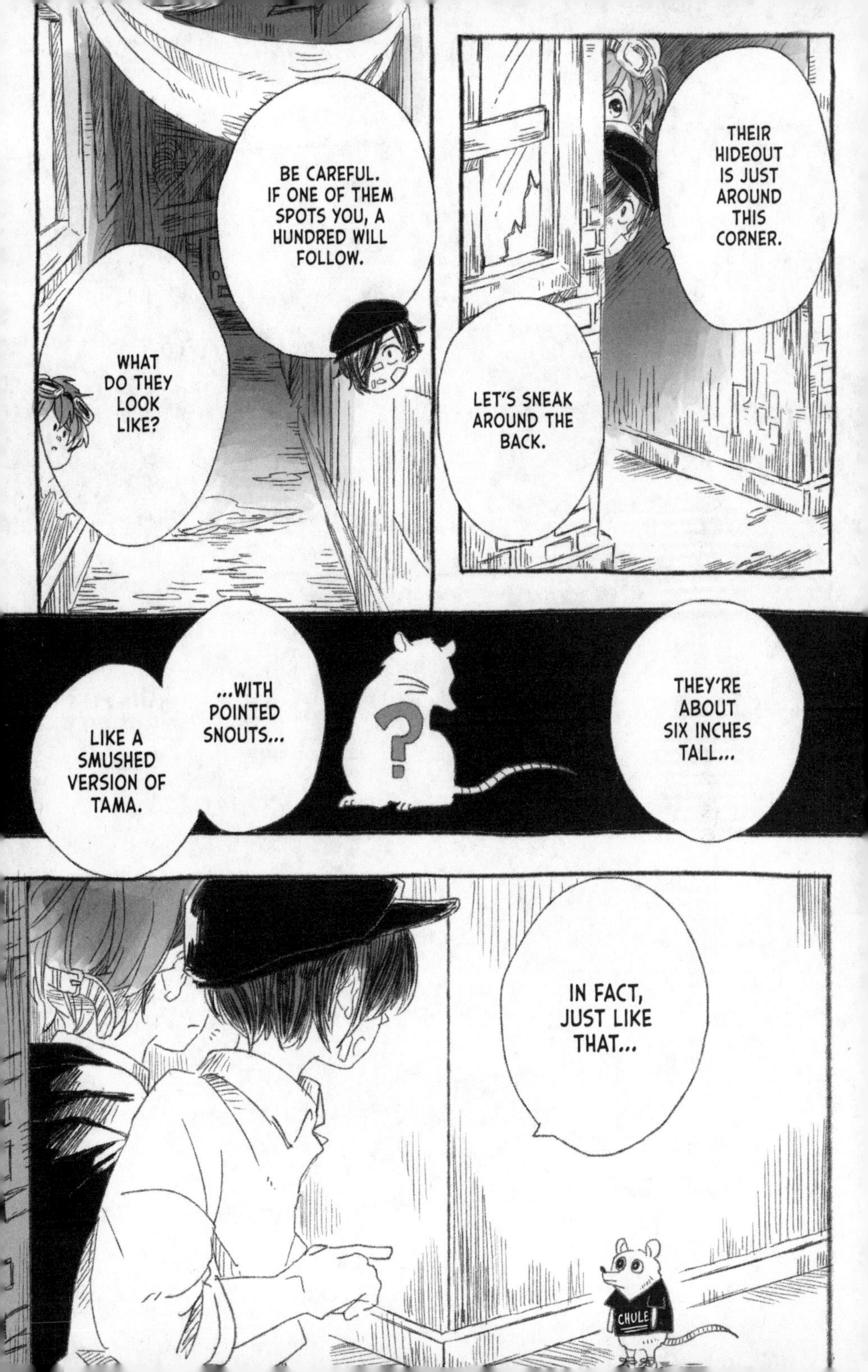
THEIR HIDEOUT IS JUST AROUND THIS CORNER.
LET'S SNEAK AROUND THE BACK.
BE CAREFUL. IF ONE OF THEM SPOTS YOU, A HUNDRED WILL FOLLOW.
WHAT DO THEY LOOK LIKE?
THEY'RE ABOUT SIX INCHES TALL...
...WITH POINTED SNOUTS...
LIKE A SMUSHED VERSION OF TAMA.
IN FACT, JUST LIKE THAT...
CHULE

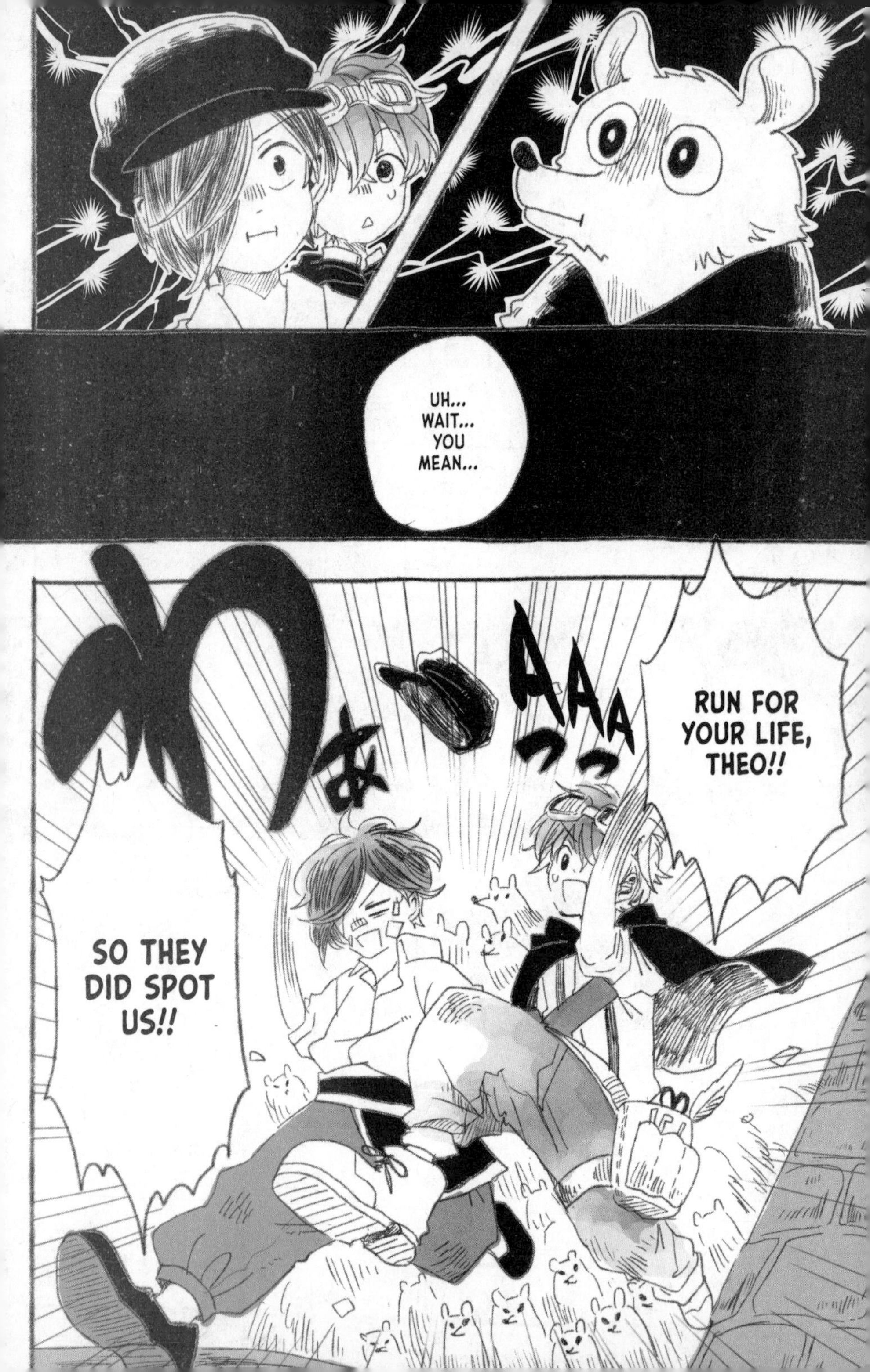
UH... WAIT... YOU MEAN...
AAA
RUN FOR YOUR LIFE, THEO!!
SO THEY DID SPOT US!!

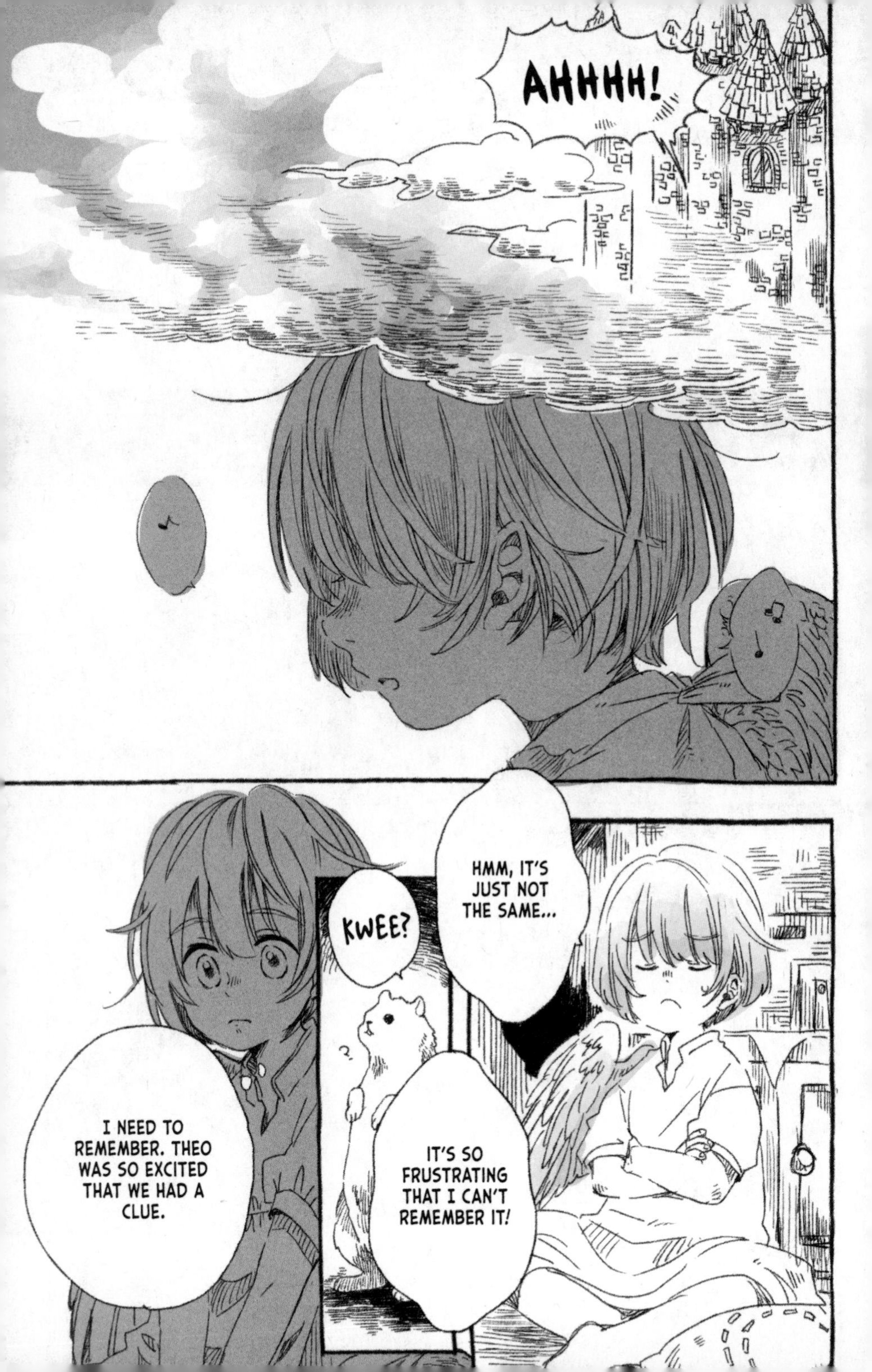
AHHHH!
HMM, IT'S JUST NOT THE SAME...
KWEE?
IT'S SO FRUSTRATING THAT I CAN'T REMEMBER IT!
I NEED TO REMEMBER. THEO WAS SO EXCITED THAT WE HAD A CLUE.

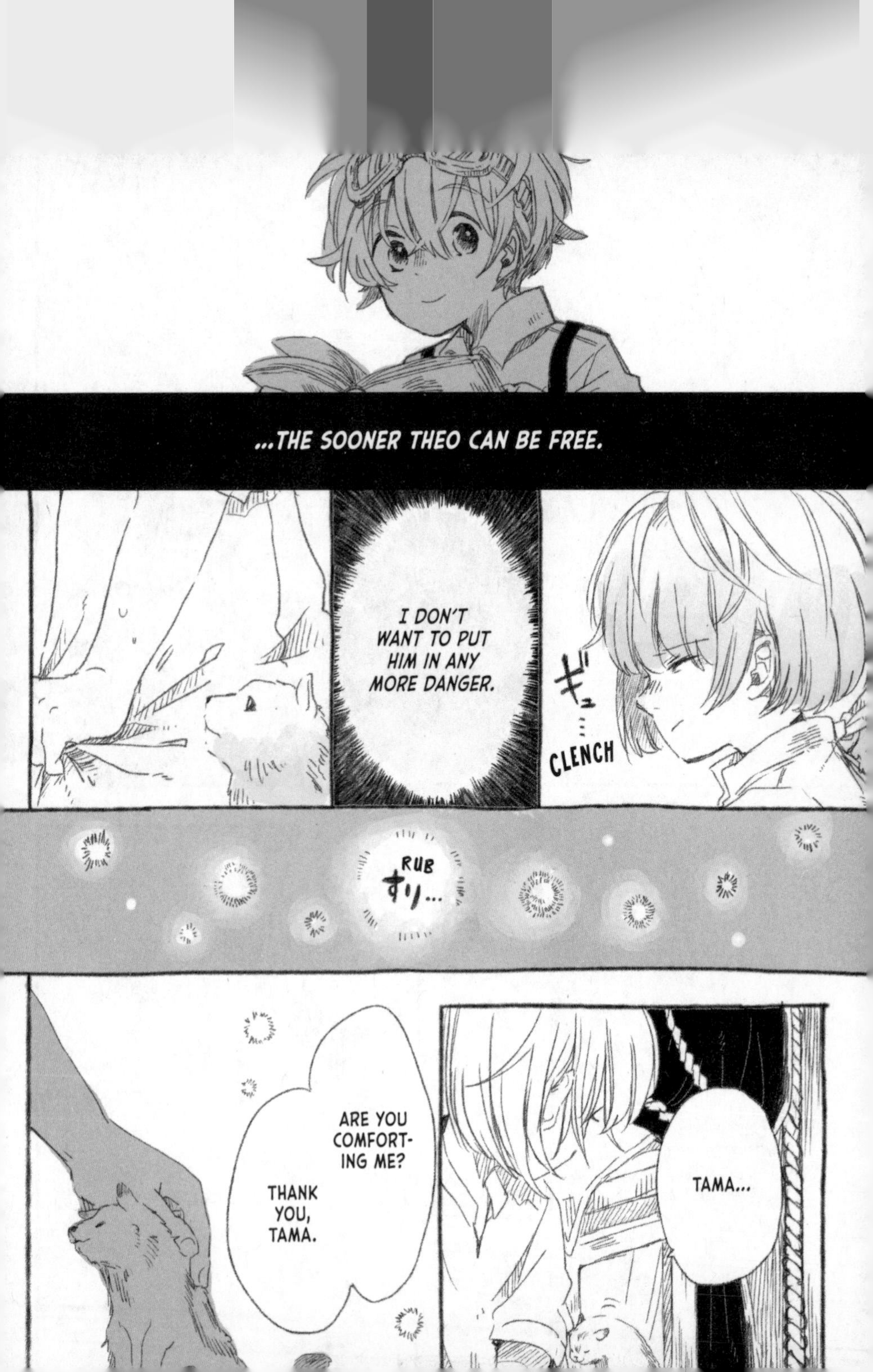
...THE SOONER THEO CAN BE FREE.
CLENCH
I DON'T WANT TO PUT HIM IN ANY MORE DANGER.
RUB すり...
TAMA...
ARE YOU COMFORTING ME?
THANK YOU, TAMA.

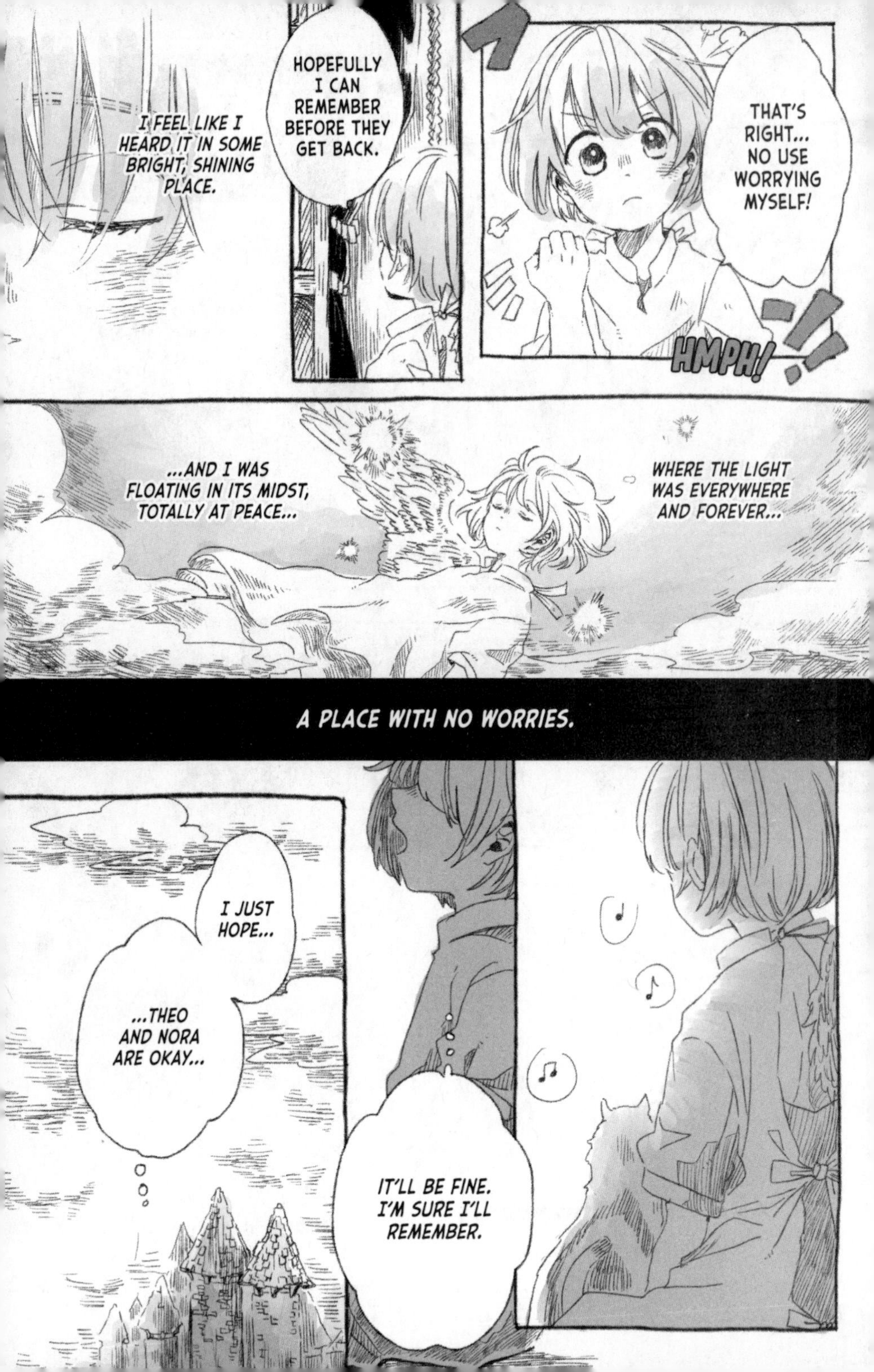
THAT'S RIGHT... NO USE WORRYING MYSELF!
HMPH!
HOPEFULLY I CAN REMEMBER BEFORE THEY GET BACK.
I FEEL LIKE I HEARD IT IN SOME BRIGHT, SHINING PLACE.
WHERE THE LIGHT WAS EVERYWHERE AND FOREVER...
...AND I WAS FLOATING IN ITS MIDST, TOTALLY AT PEACE...
A PLACE WITH NO WORRIES.
IT'LL BE FINE. I'M SURE I'LL REMEMBER.
I JUST HOPE...
...THEO AND NORA ARE OKAY...

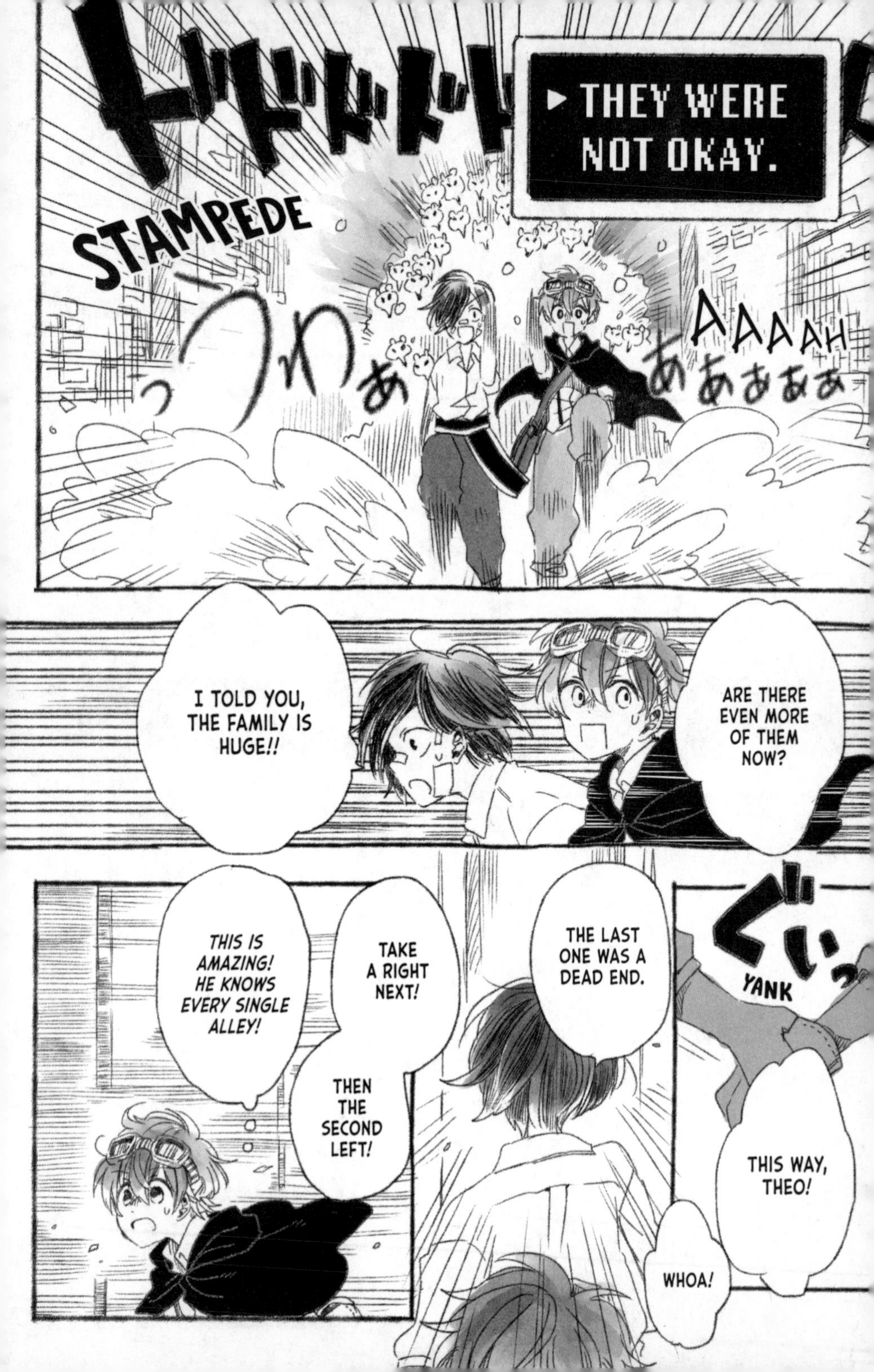
トドドドドド
THEY WERE NOT OKAY.
STAMPEDE
っうわあ
AAAAH
あああああ
ARE THERE EVEN MORE OF THEM NOW?
I TOLD YOU, THE FAMILY IS HUGE!!
ぐいっ
YANK
THIS WAY, THEO!
WHOA!
THE LAST ONE WAS A DEAD END.
TAKE A RIGHT NEXT!
THEN THE SECOND LEFT!
THIS IS AMAZING! HE KNOWS EVERY SINGLE ALLEY!

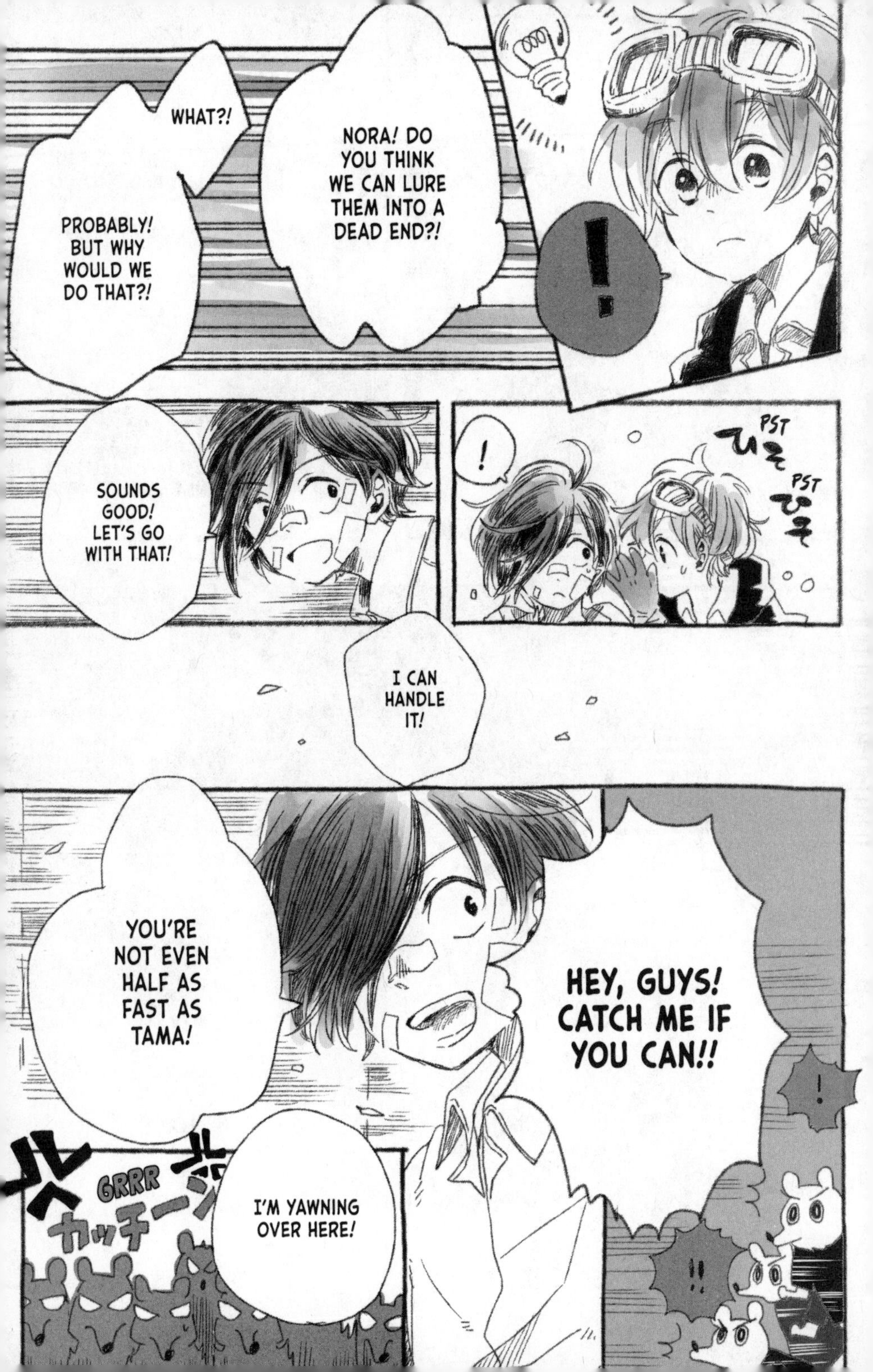
!
NORA! DO YOU THINK WE CAN LURE THEM INTO A DEAD END?!
WHAT?!
PROBABLY! BUT WHY WOULD WE DO THAT?!
PST ひそ
PST ひそ
!
SOUNDS GOOD! LET'S GO WITH THAT!
I CAN HANDLE IT!
HEY, GUYS! CATCH ME IF YOU CAN!!
!
YOU'RE NOT EVEN HALF AS FAST AS TAMA!
!!
GRRR カッチーン
I'M YAWNING OVER HERE!

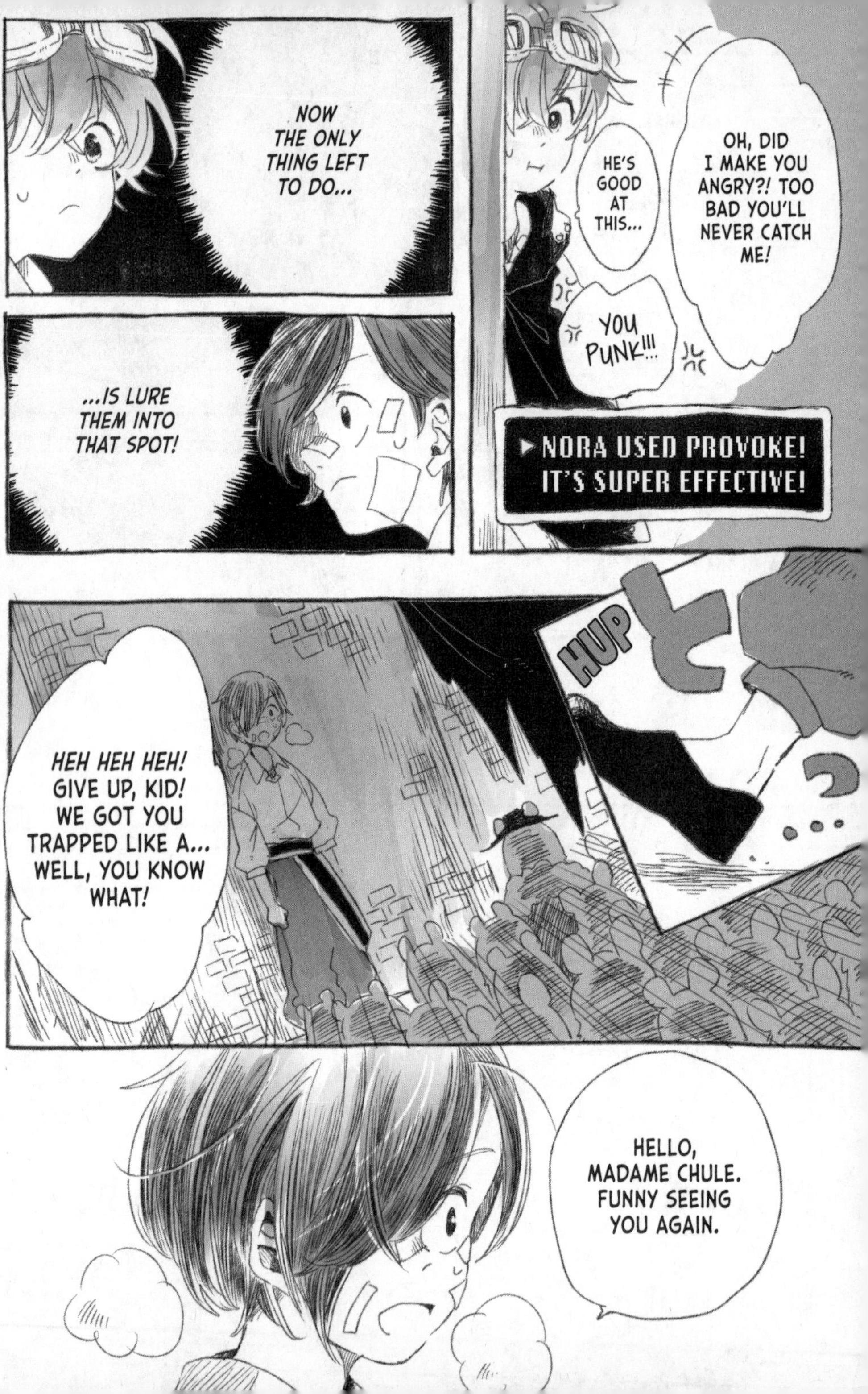

OH, DID I MAKE YOU ANGRY?! TOO BAD YOU'LL NEVER CATCH ME!
HE'S GOOD AT THIS...
YOU PUNK!!!
▸NORA USED PROVOKE! IT'S SUPER EFFECTIVE!
NOW THE ONLY THING LEFT TO DO...
...IS LURE THEM INTO THAT SPOT!
HUP
HEH HEH HEH! GIVE UP, KID! WE GOT YOU TRAPPED LIKE A... WELL, YOU KNOW WHAT!
HELLO, MADAME CHULE. FUNNY SEEING YOU AGAIN.

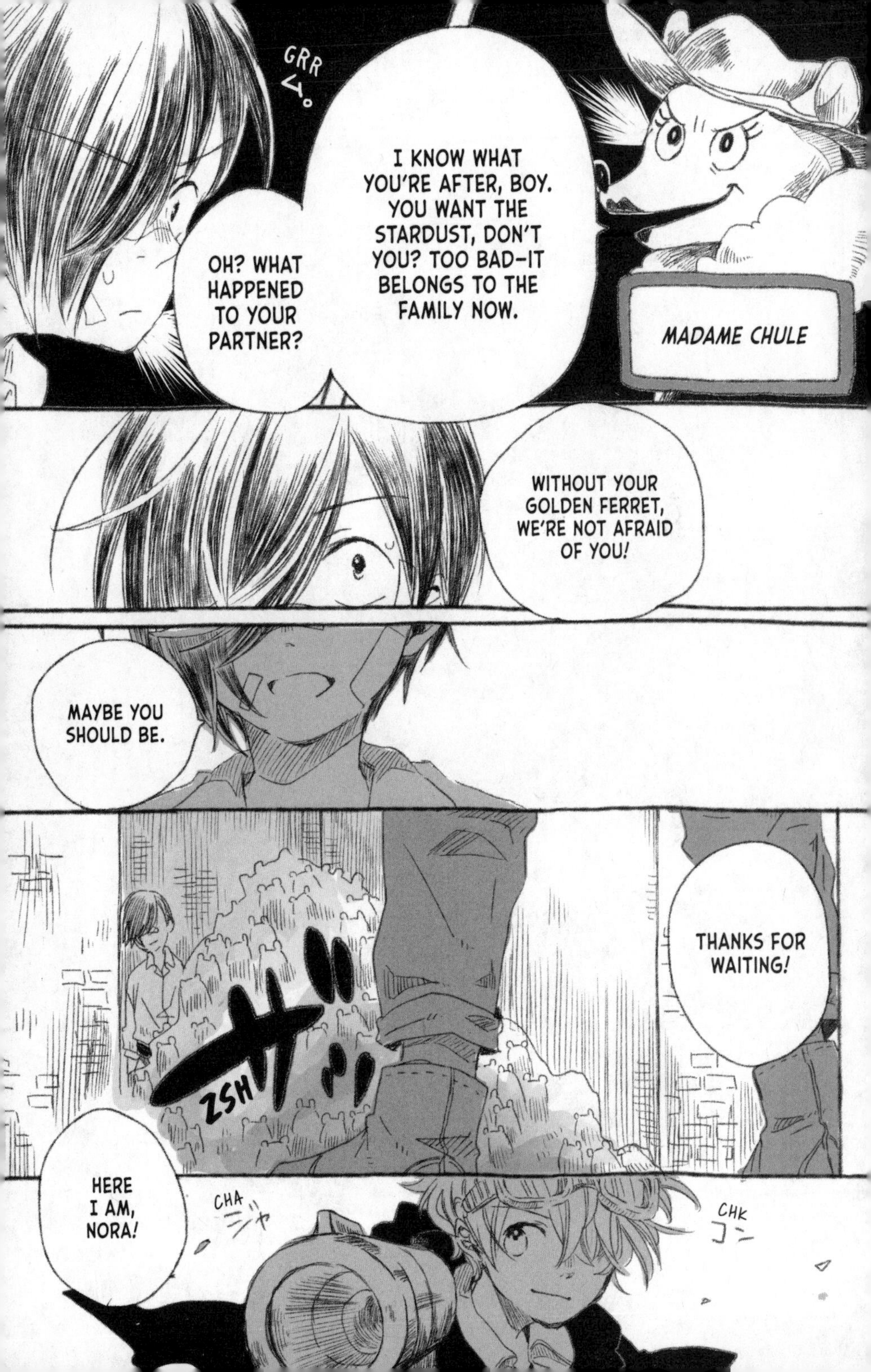
MADAME CHULE
I KNOW WHAT YOU'RE AFTER, BOY. YOU WANT THE STARDUST, DON'T YOU? TOO BAD–IT BELONGS TO THE FAMILY NOW.
GRR
OH? WHAT HAPPENED TO YOUR PARTNER?
WITHOUT YOUR GOLDEN FERRET, WE'RE NOT AFRAID OF YOU!
MAYBE YOU SHOULD BE.
THANKS FOR WAITING!
ZSH
CHK
CHA
HERE I AM, NORA!

Chapter 19: The Legend of the Magician

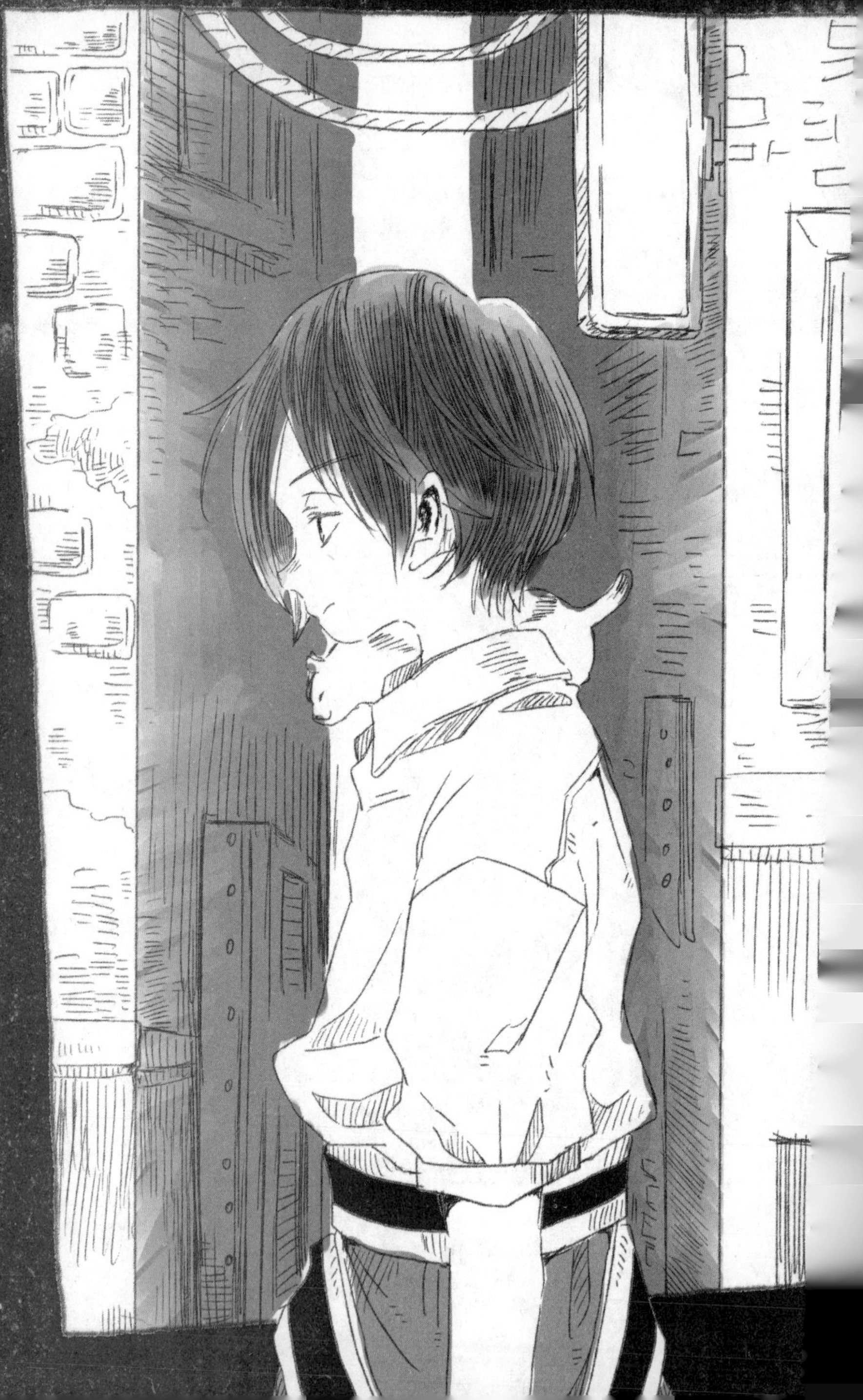

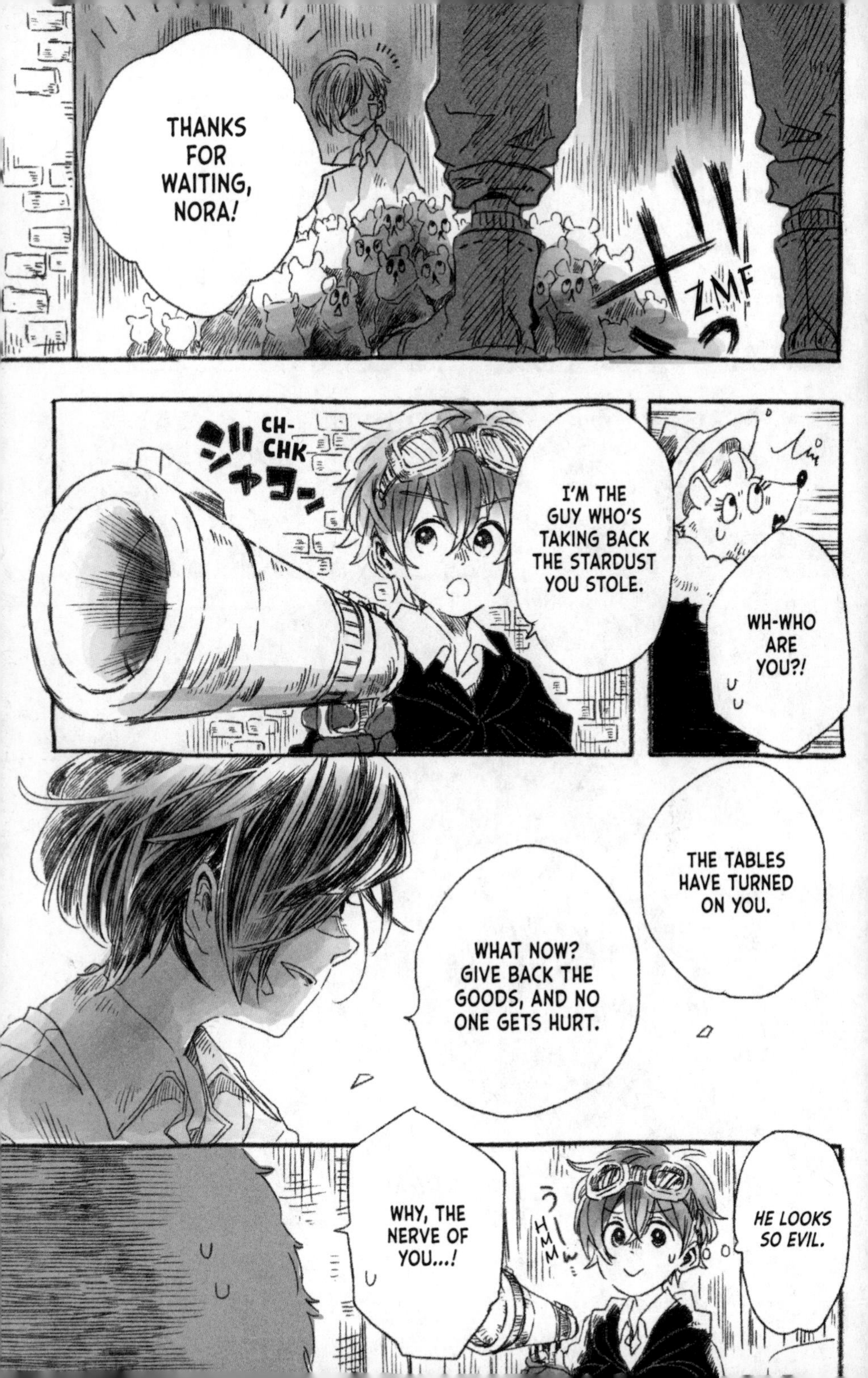
THANKS FOR WAITING, NORA!
ZMF
WH-WHO ARE YOU?!
CH-CHK
I'M THE GUY WHO'S TAKING BACK THE STARDUST YOU STOLE.
THE TABLES HAVE TURNED ON YOU.
WHAT NOW? GIVE BACK THE GOODS, AND NO ONE GETS HURT.
HE LOOKS SO EVIL.
HMM
WHY, THE NERVE OF YOU...!

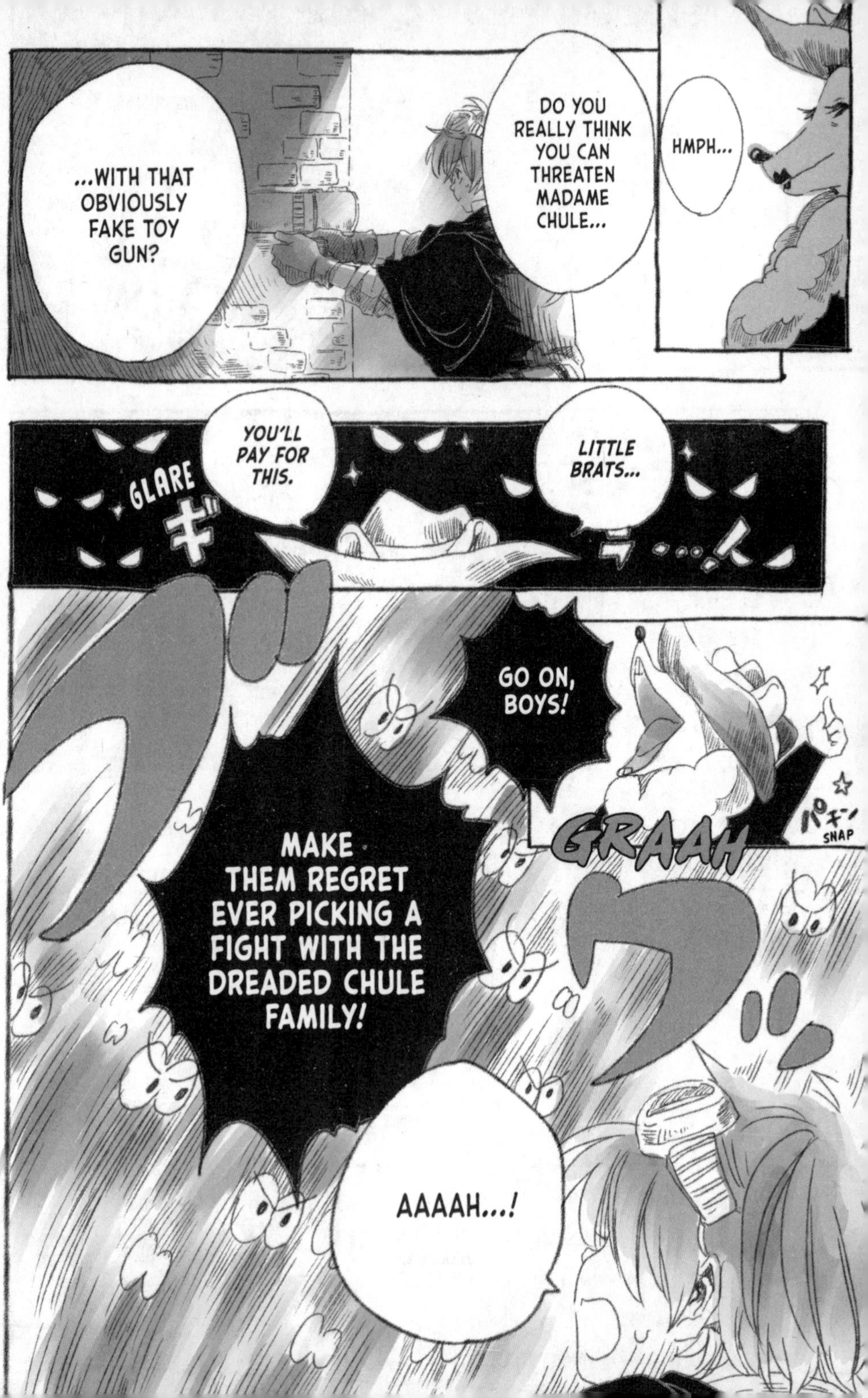
HMPH...
DO YOU REALLY THINK YOU CAN THREATEN MADAME CHULE...
...WITH THAT OBVIOUSLY FAKE TOY GUN?
LITTLE BRATS...
YOU'LL PAY FOR THIS.
GLARE
GO ON, BOYS!
SNAP
GRAAH
MAKE THEM REGRET EVER PICKING A FIGHT WITH THE DREADED CHULE FAMILY!
AAAAH...!

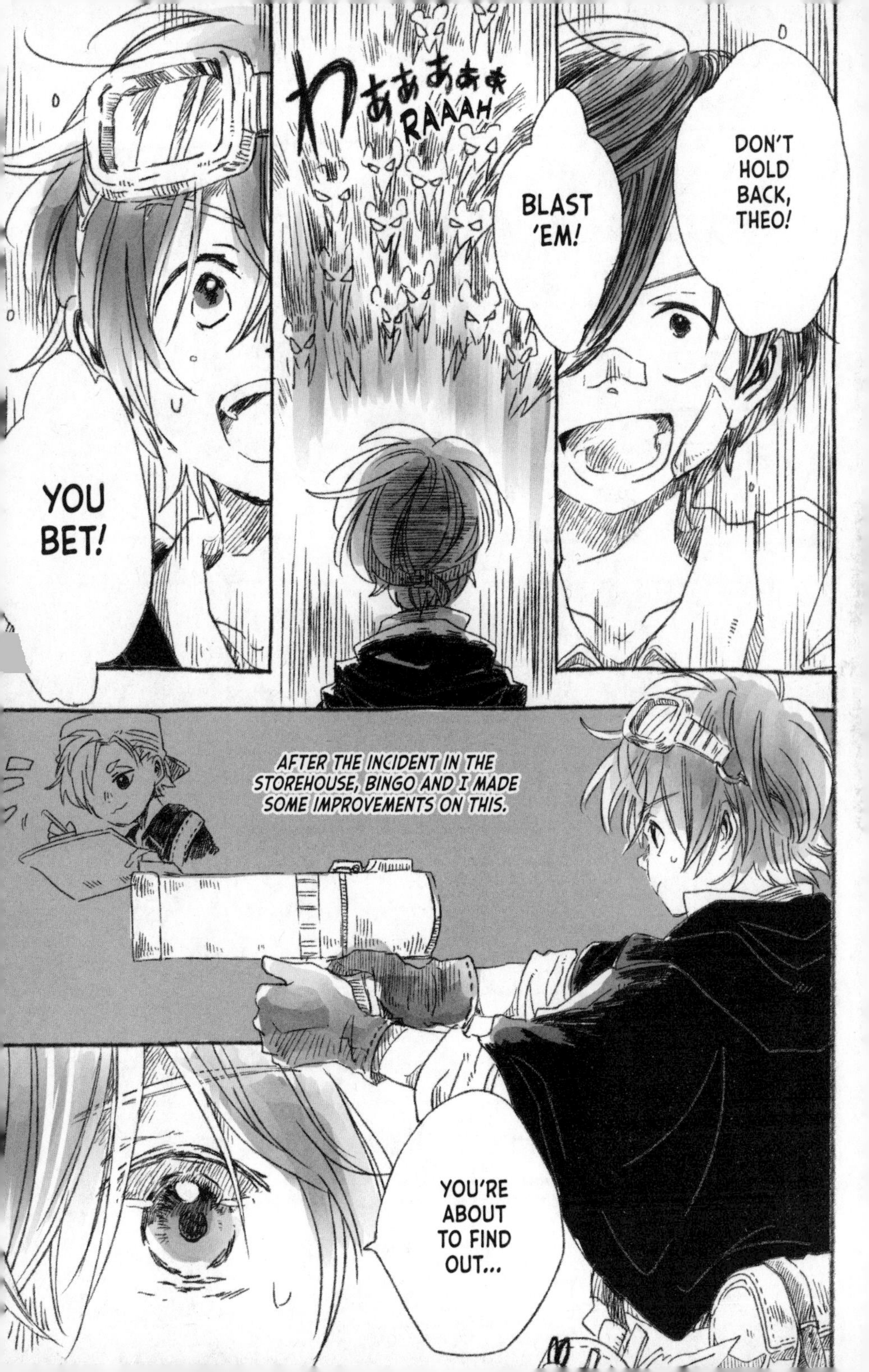
DON'T HOLD BACK, THEO!
BLAST 'EM!
わあああああ
RAAAH
YOU BET!
AFTER THE INCIDENT IN THE STOREHOUSE, BINGO AND I MADE SOME IMPROVEMENTS ON THIS.
YOU'RE ABOUT TO FIND OUT...

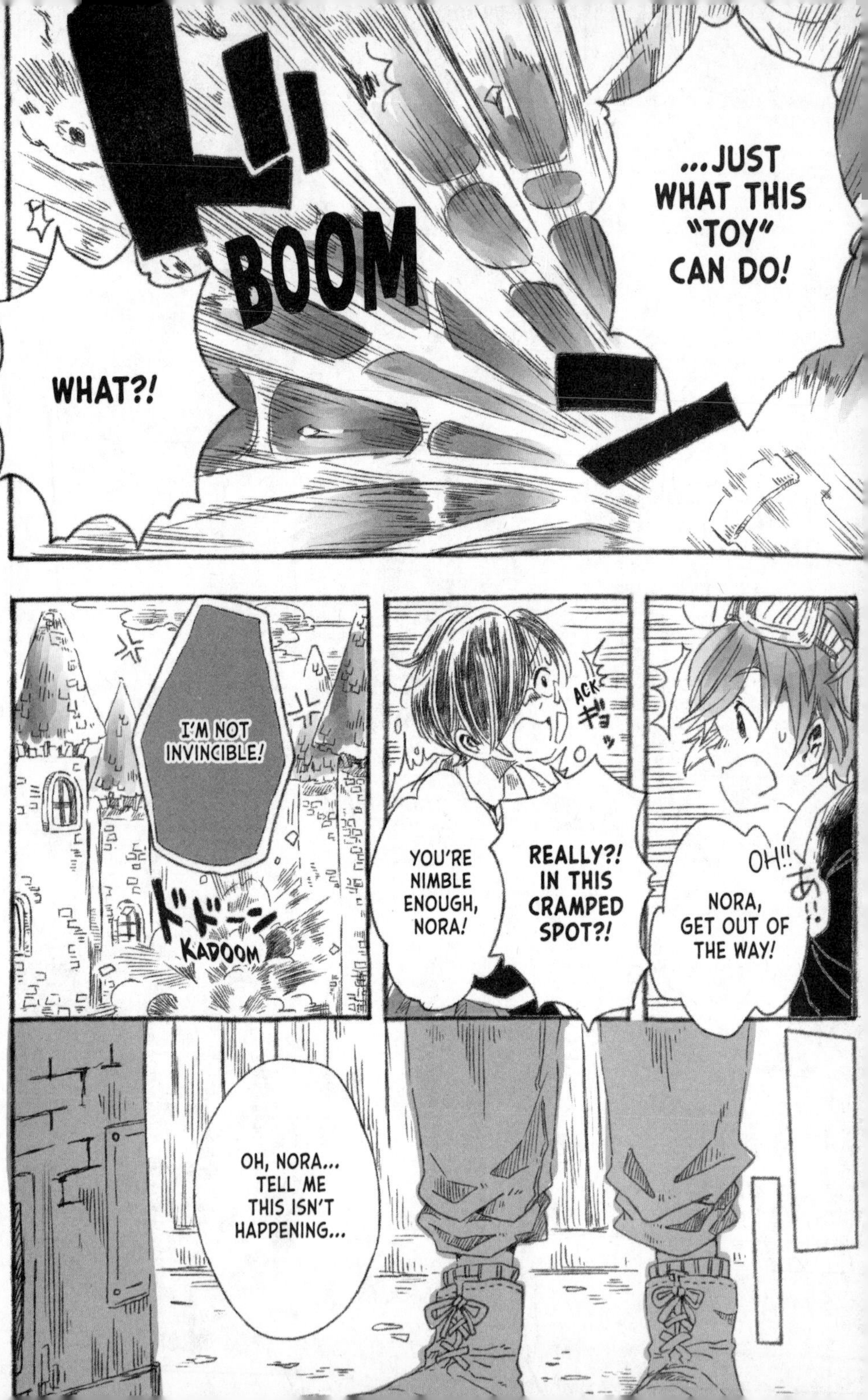
...JUST WHAT THIS "TOY" CAN DO!
BOOM
WHAT?!
OH!! あ!!
NORA, GET OUT OF THE WAY!
ACK ギョッ
REALLY?! IN THIS CRAMPED SPOT?!
YOU'RE NIMBLE ENOUGH, NORA!
I'M NOT INVINCIBLE!
ドドーン
KADOOM
OH, NORA... TELL ME THIS ISN'T HAPPENING...

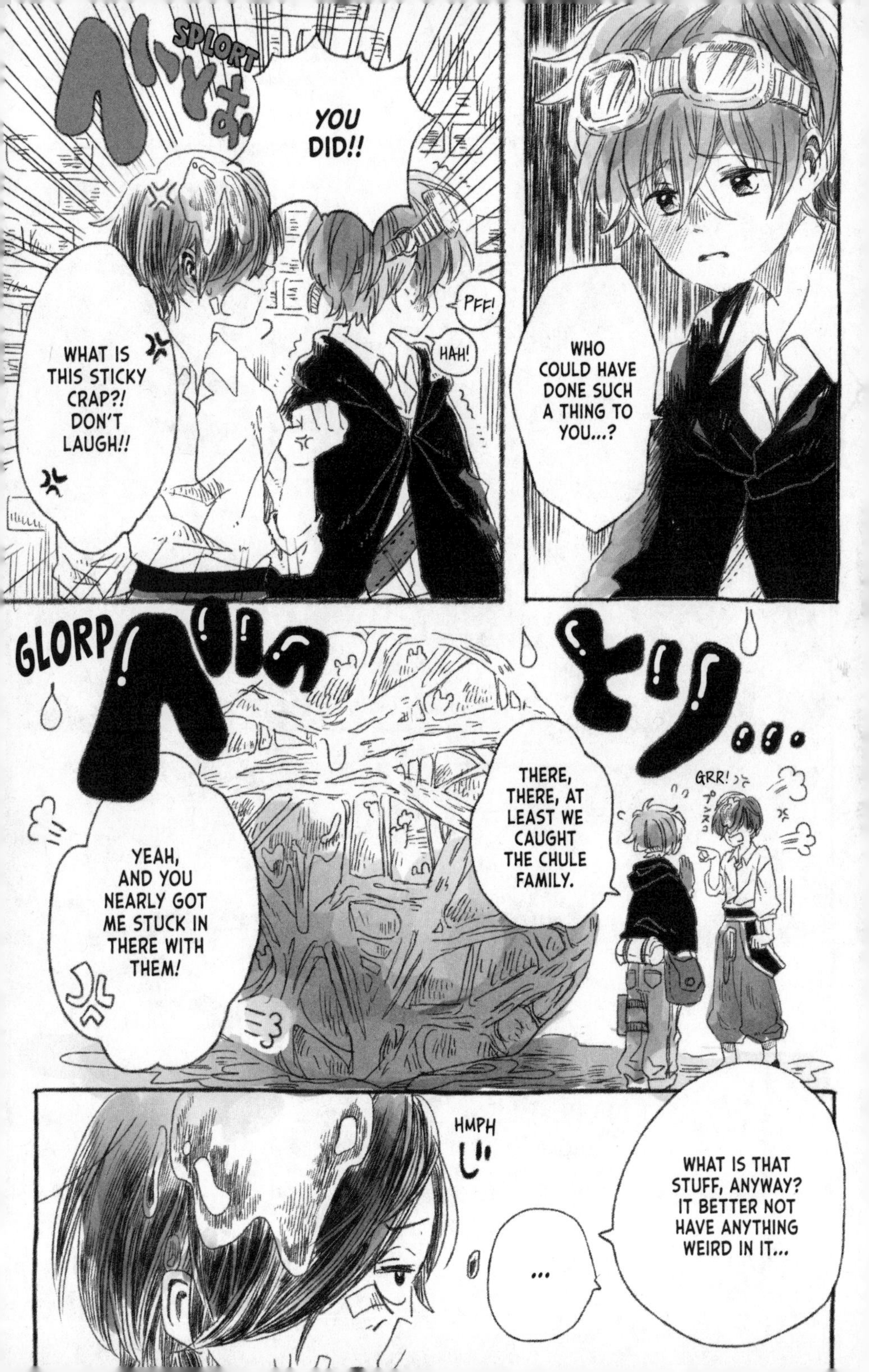
WHO COULD HAVE DONE SUCH A THING TO YOU...?
SPLORT
YOU DID!!
PFF!
HAH!
WHAT IS THIS STICKY CRAP?! DON'T LAUGH!!
GLORP
THERE, THERE, AT LEAST WE CAUGHT THE CHULE FAMILY.
GRR!
YEAH, AND YOU NEARLY GOT ME STUCK IN THERE WITH THEM!
HMPH
WHAT IS THAT STUFF, ANYWAY? IT BETTER NOT HAVE ANYTHING WEIRD IN IT...
...

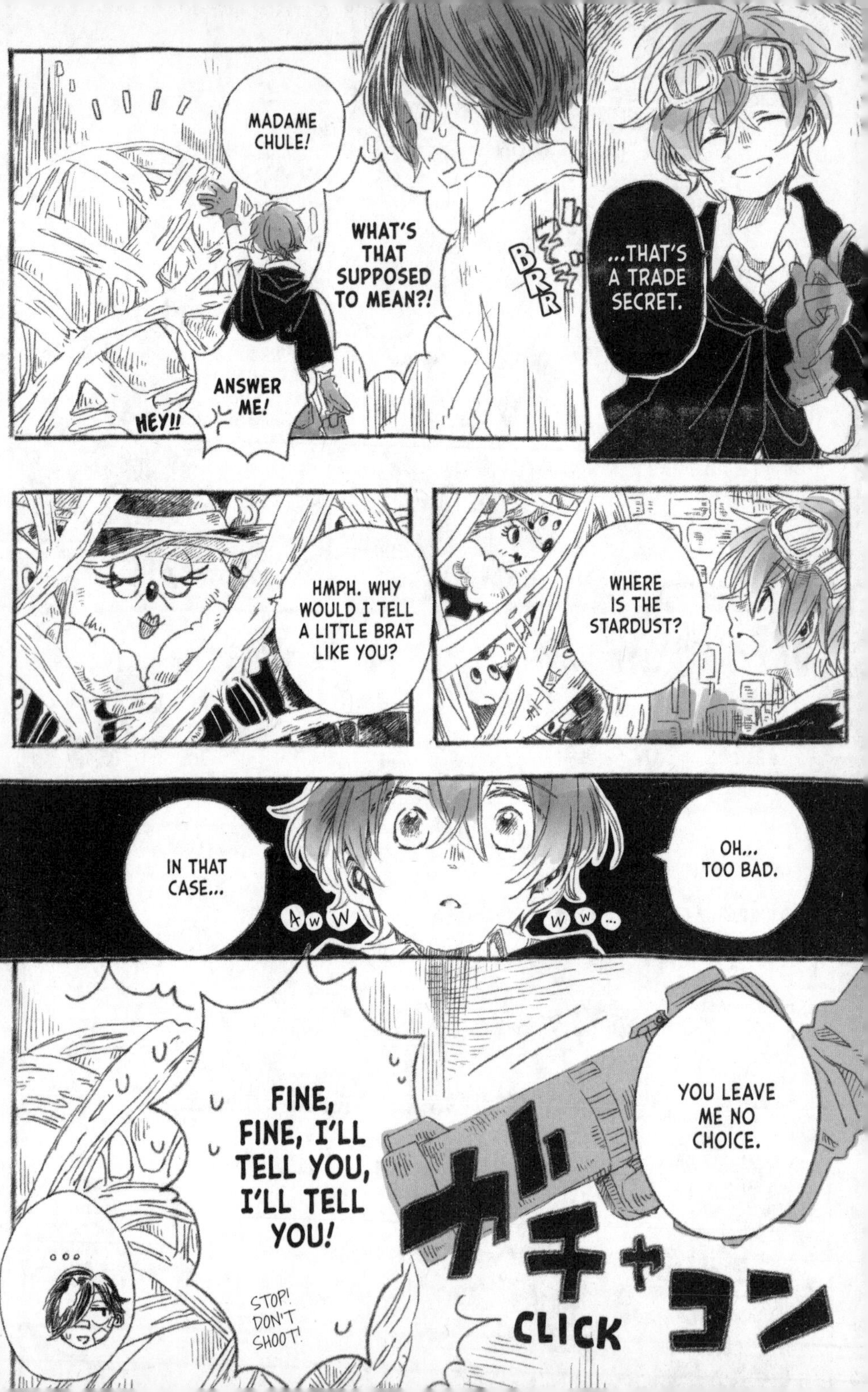
...THAT'S A TRADE SECRET.
MADAME CHULE!
BRR
WHAT'S THAT SUPPOSED TO MEAN?!
ANSWER ME!
HEY!!
WHERE IS THE STARDUST?
HMPH. WHY WOULD I TELL A LITTLE BRAT LIKE YOU?
OH... TOO BAD.
AWW WW...
IN THAT CASE...
YOU LEAVE ME NO CHOICE.
カチャコン
CLICK
FINE, FINE, I'LL TELL YOU, I'LL TELL YOU!
STOP! DON'T SHOOT!
...

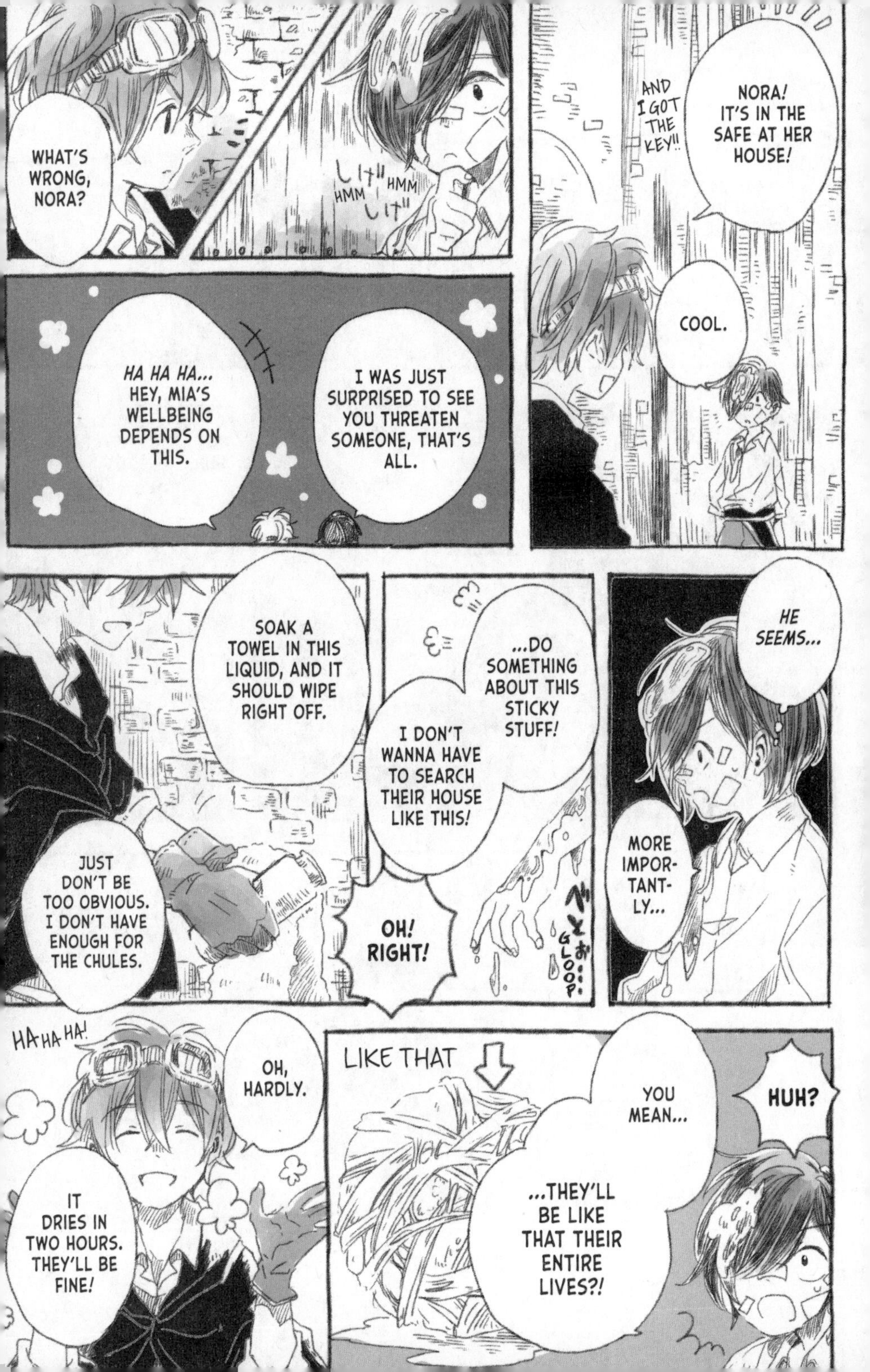
NORA! IT'S IN THE SAFE AT HER HOUSE!
AND I GOT THE KEY!!
COOL.
HMM HMM
WHAT'S WRONG, NORA?
I WAS JUST SURPRISED TO SEE YOU THREATEN SOMEONE, THAT'S ALL.
HA HA HA... HEY, MIA'S WELLBEING DEPENDS ON THIS.
HE SEEMS...
MORE IMPORTANTLY...
...DO SOMETHING ABOUT THIS STICKY STUFF!
I DON'T WANNA HAVE TO SEARCH THEIR HOUSE LIKE THIS!
GLOOP
SOAK A TOWEL IN THIS LIQUID, AND IT SHOULD WIPE RIGHT OFF.
OH! RIGHT!
JUST DON'T BE TOO OBVIOUS. I DON'T HAVE ENOUGH FOR THE CHULES.
HUH?
YOU MEAN...
LIKE THAT
...THEY'LL BE LIKE THAT THEIR ENTIRE LIVES?!
OH, HARDLY.
HA HA HA!
IT DRIES IN TWO HOURS. THEY'LL BE FINE!

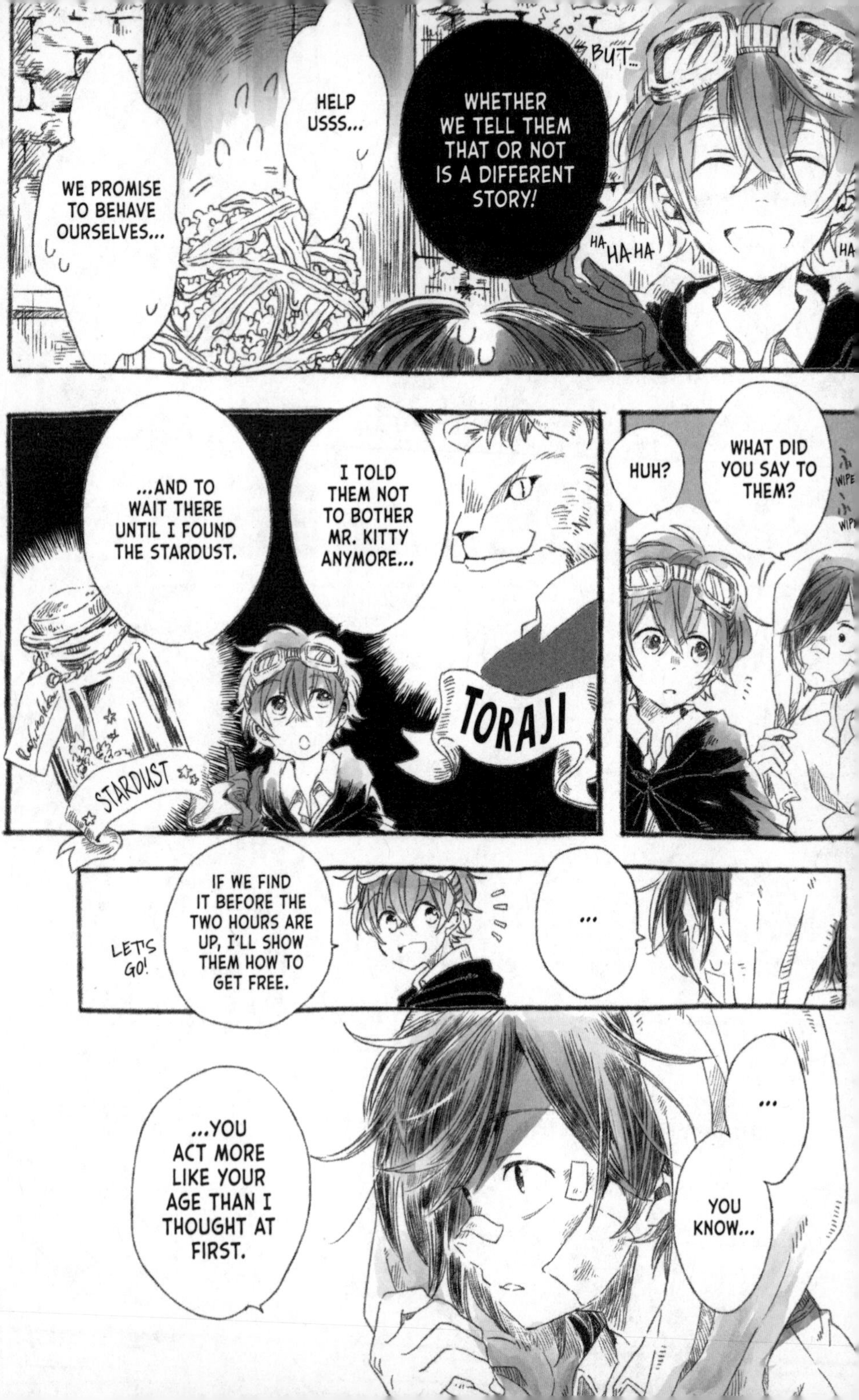
BUT...
HA HA-HA
HA
WHETHER WE TELL THEM THAT OR NOT IS A DIFFERENT STORY!
HELP USSS...
WE PROMISE TO BEHAVE OURSELVES...
WHAT DID YOU SAY TO THEM?
WIPE
WIPE
HUH?
I TOLD THEM NOT TO BOTHER MR. KITTY ANYMORE...
TORAJI
...AND TO WAIT THERE UNTIL I FOUND THE STARDUST.
STARDUST
...
IF WE FIND IT BEFORE THE TWO HOURS ARE UP, I'LL SHOW THEM HOW TO GET FREE.
LET'S GO!
...
YOU KNOW...
...YOU ACT MORE LIKE YOUR AGE THAN I THOUGHT AT FIRST.

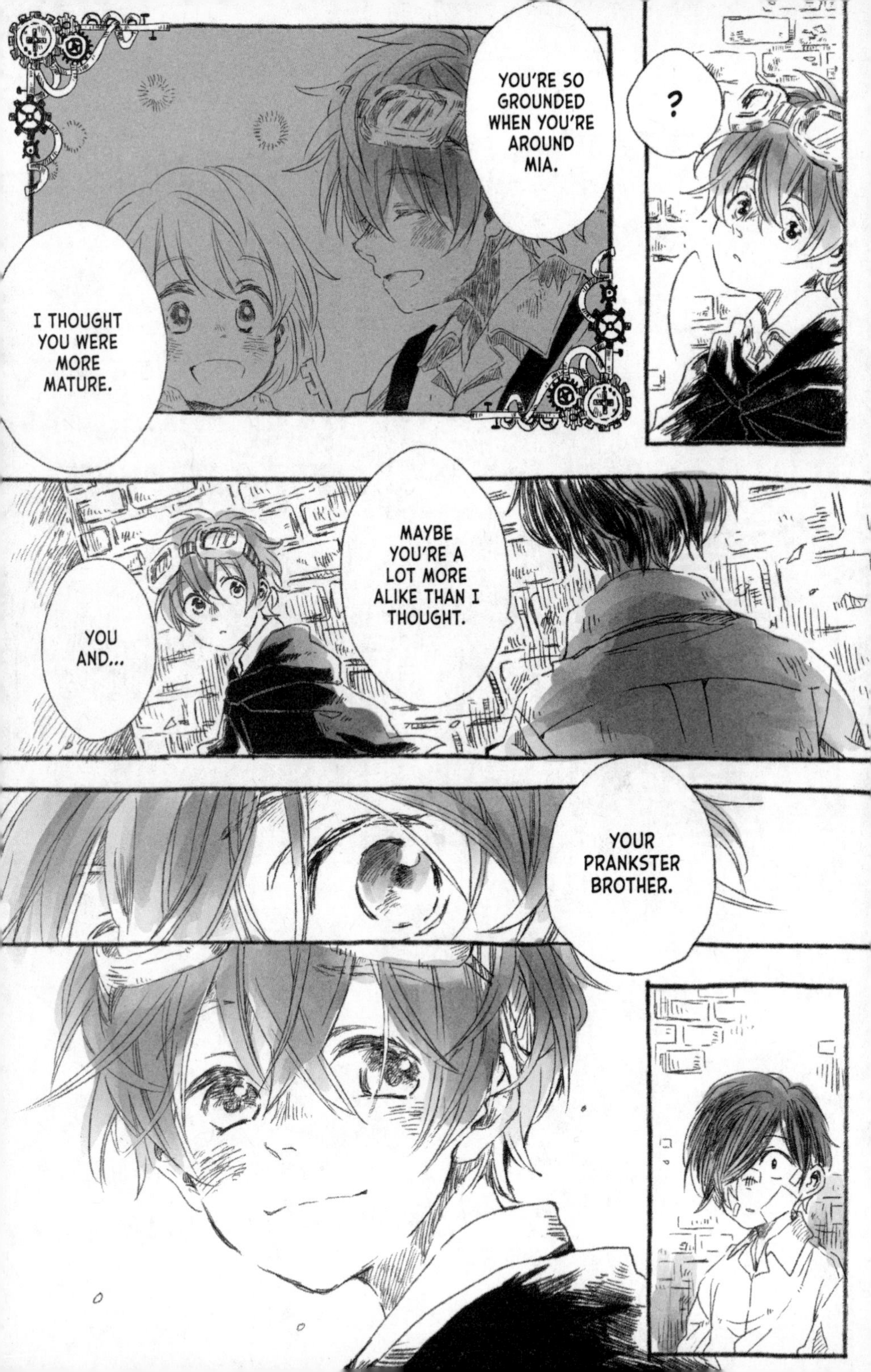
?
YOU'RE SO GROUNDED WHEN YOU'RE AROUND MIA.
I THOUGHT YOU WERE MORE MATURE.
MAYBE YOU'RE A LOT MORE ALIKE THAN I THOUGHT.
YOU AND...
YOUR PRANKSTER BROTHER.

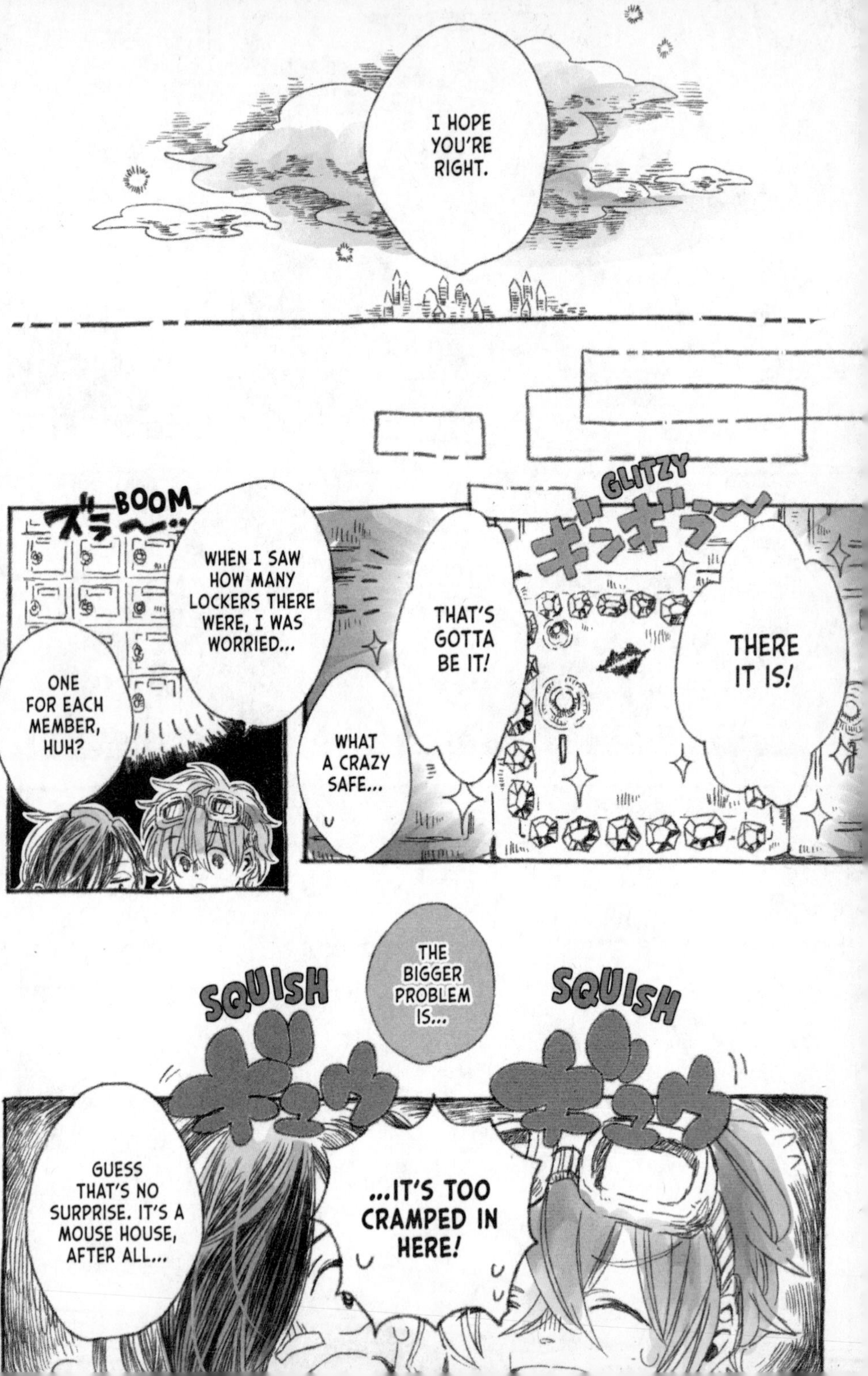
I HOPE YOU'RE RIGHT.
GLITZY
THERE IT IS!
THAT'S GOTTA BE IT!
WHAT A CRAZY SAFE...
BOOM
WHEN I SAW HOW MANY LOCKERS THERE WERE, I WAS WORRIED...
ONE FOR EACH MEMBER, HUH?
THE BIGGER PROBLEM IS...
SQUISH
SQUISH
...IT'S TOO CRAMPED IN HERE!
GUESS THAT'S NO SURPRISE. IT'S A MOUSE HOUSE, AFTER ALL...

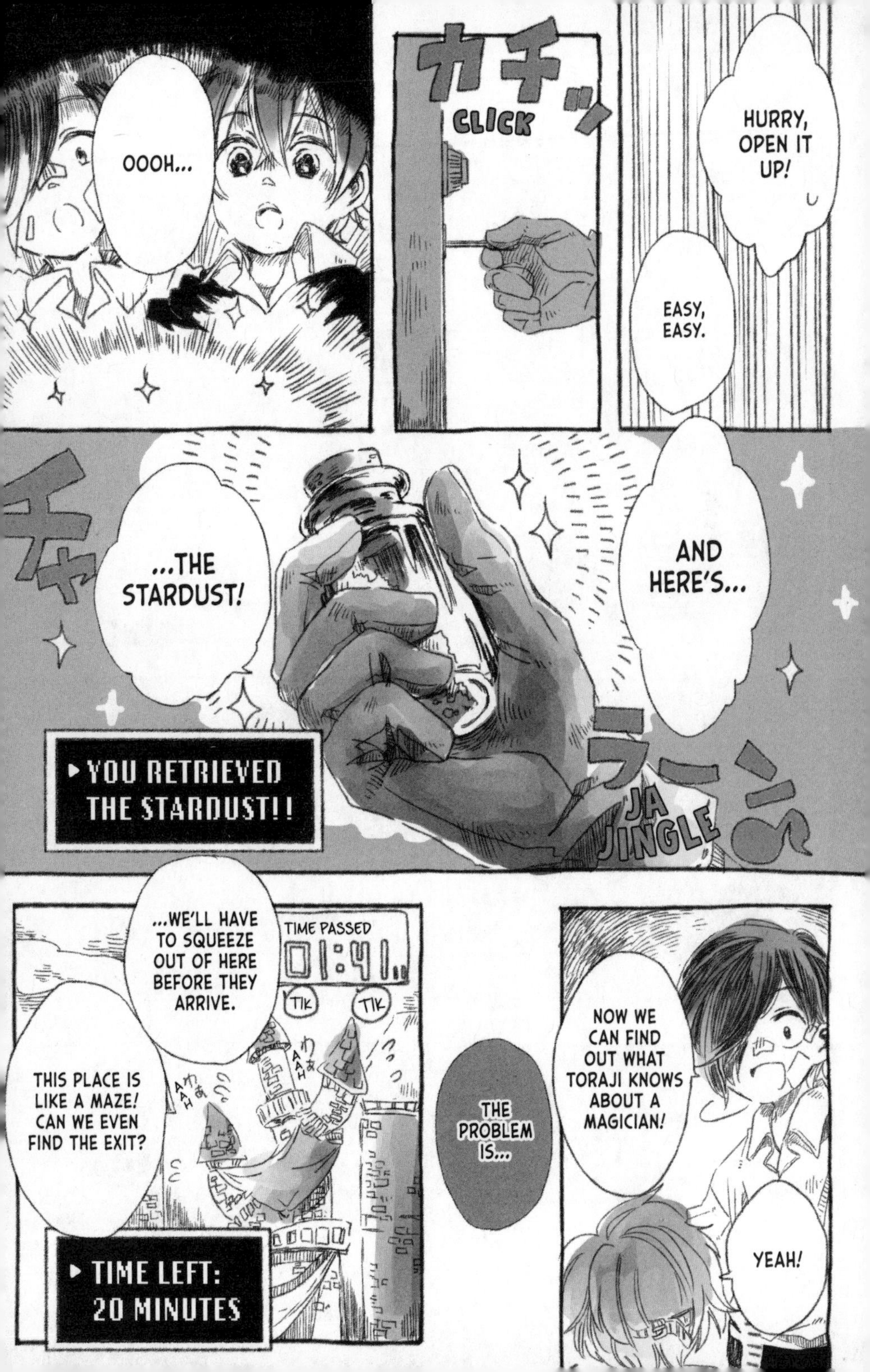
HURRY, OPEN IT UP!
EASY, EASY.
カチッ
CLICK
OOOH...
AND HERE'S...
...THE STARDUST!
チャ
ラーン
JA JINGLE
▸ YOU RETRIEVED THE STARDUST!!
NOW WE CAN FIND OUT WHAT TORAJI KNOWS ABOUT A MAGICIAN!
YEAH!
THE PROBLEM IS...
...WE'LL HAVE TO SQUEEZE OUT OF HERE BEFORE THEY ARRIVE.
TIME PASSED
01:41
TIK
TIK
AAH
AAH
THIS PLACE IS LIKE A MAZE! CAN WE EVEN FIND THE EXIT?
▸ TIME LEFT: 20 MINUTES

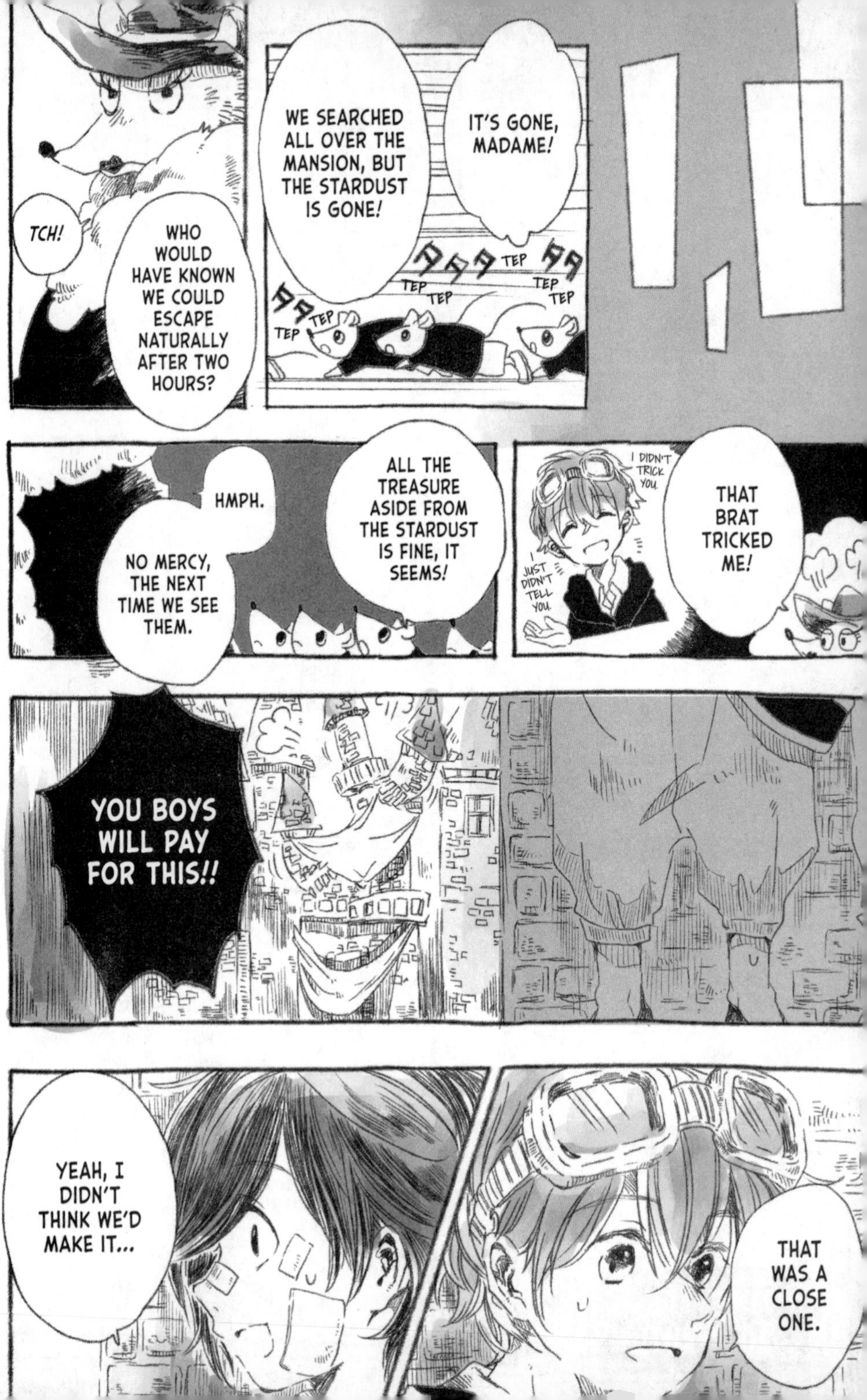
IT'S GONE, MADAME!
WE SEARCHED ALL OVER THE MANSION, BUT THE STARDUST IS GONE!
TEP TEP TEP TEP TEP TEP
WHO WOULD HAVE KNOWN WE COULD ESCAPE NATURALLY AFTER TWO HOURS?
TCH!
THAT BRAT TRICKED ME!
I DIDN'T TRICK YOU.
I JUST DIDN'T TELL YOU.
ALL THE TREASURE ASIDE FROM THE STARDUST IS FINE, IT SEEMS!
HMPH.
NO MERCY, THE NEXT TIME WE SEE THEM.
YOU BOYS WILL PAY FOR THIS!!
THAT WAS A CLOSE ONE.
YEAH, I DIDN'T THINK WE'D MAKE IT...

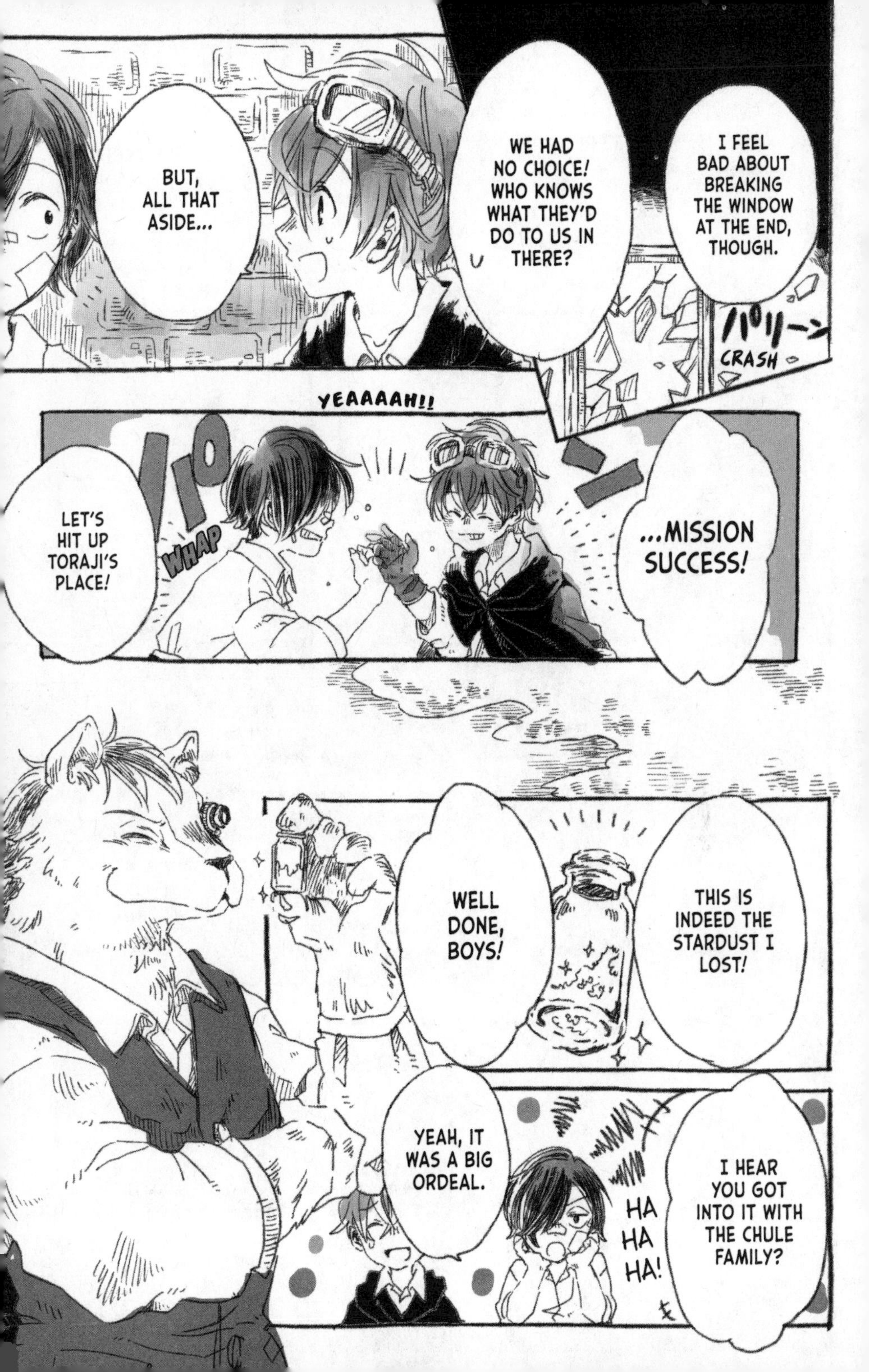
I FEEL BAD ABOUT BREAKING THE WINDOW AT THE END, THOUGH.
CRASH
WE HAD NO CHOICE! WHO KNOWS WHAT THEY'D DO TO US IN THERE?
BUT, ALL THAT ASIDE...
...MISSION SUCCESS!
YEAAAAH!!
WHAP
LET'S HIT UP TORAJI'S PLACE!
THIS IS INDEED THE STARDUST I LOST!
WELL DONE, BOYS!
I HEAR YOU GOT INTO IT WITH THE CHULE FAMILY?
HA HA HA!
YEAH, IT WAS A BIG ORDEAL.

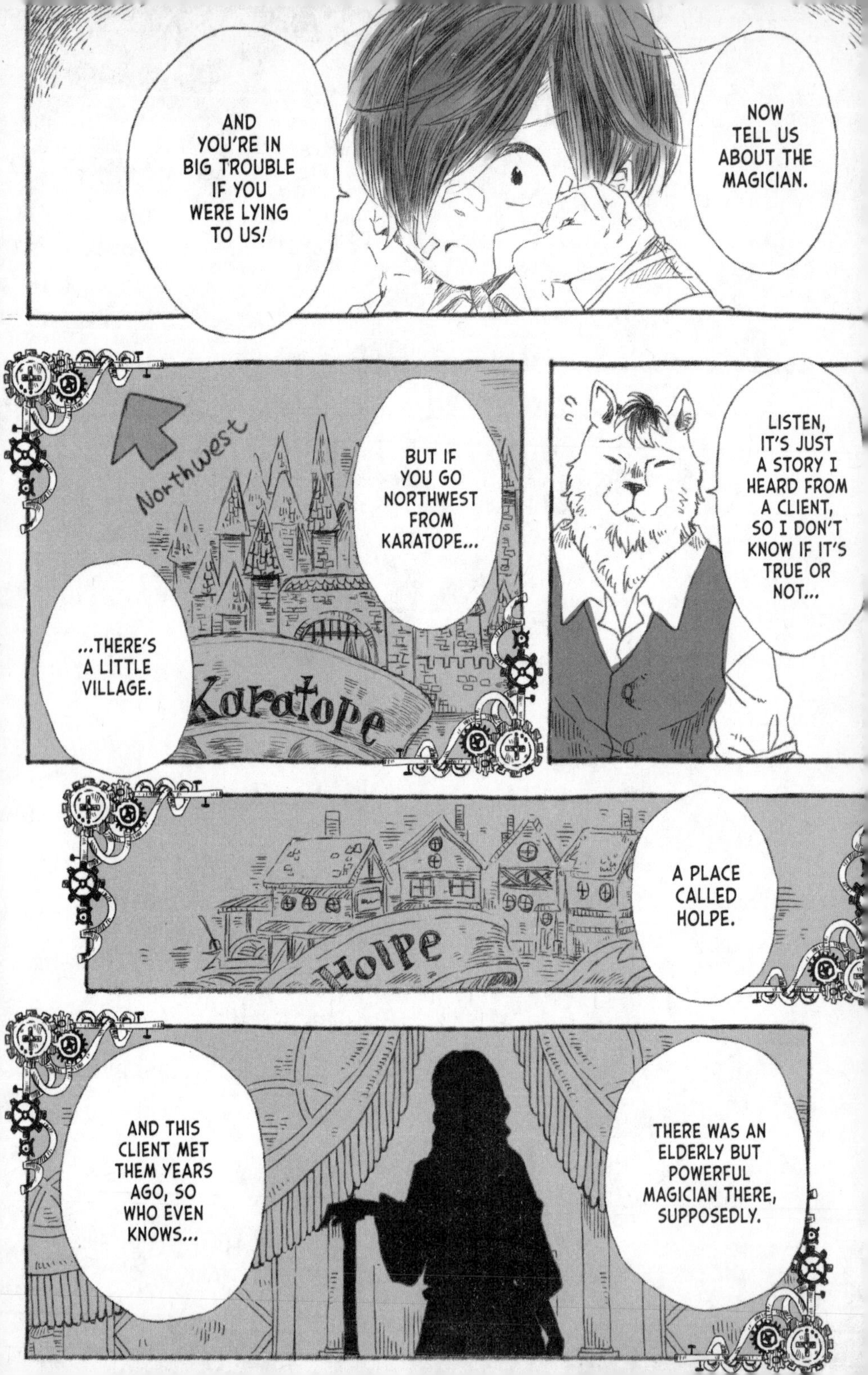
NOW TELL US ABOUT THE MAGICIAN.
AND YOU'RE IN BIG TROUBLE IF YOU WERE LYING TO US!
LISTEN, IT'S JUST A STORY I HEARD FROM A CLIENT, SO I DON'T KNOW IF IT'S TRUE OR NOT...
BUT IF YOU GO NORTHWEST FROM KARATOPE...
Northwest
...THERE'S A LITTLE VILLAGE.
Karatope
A PLACE CALLED HOLPE.
Holpe
THERE WAS AN ELDERLY BUT POWERFUL MAGICIAN THERE, SUPPOSEDLY.
AND THIS CLIENT MET THEM YEARS AGO, SO WHO EVEN KNOWS...

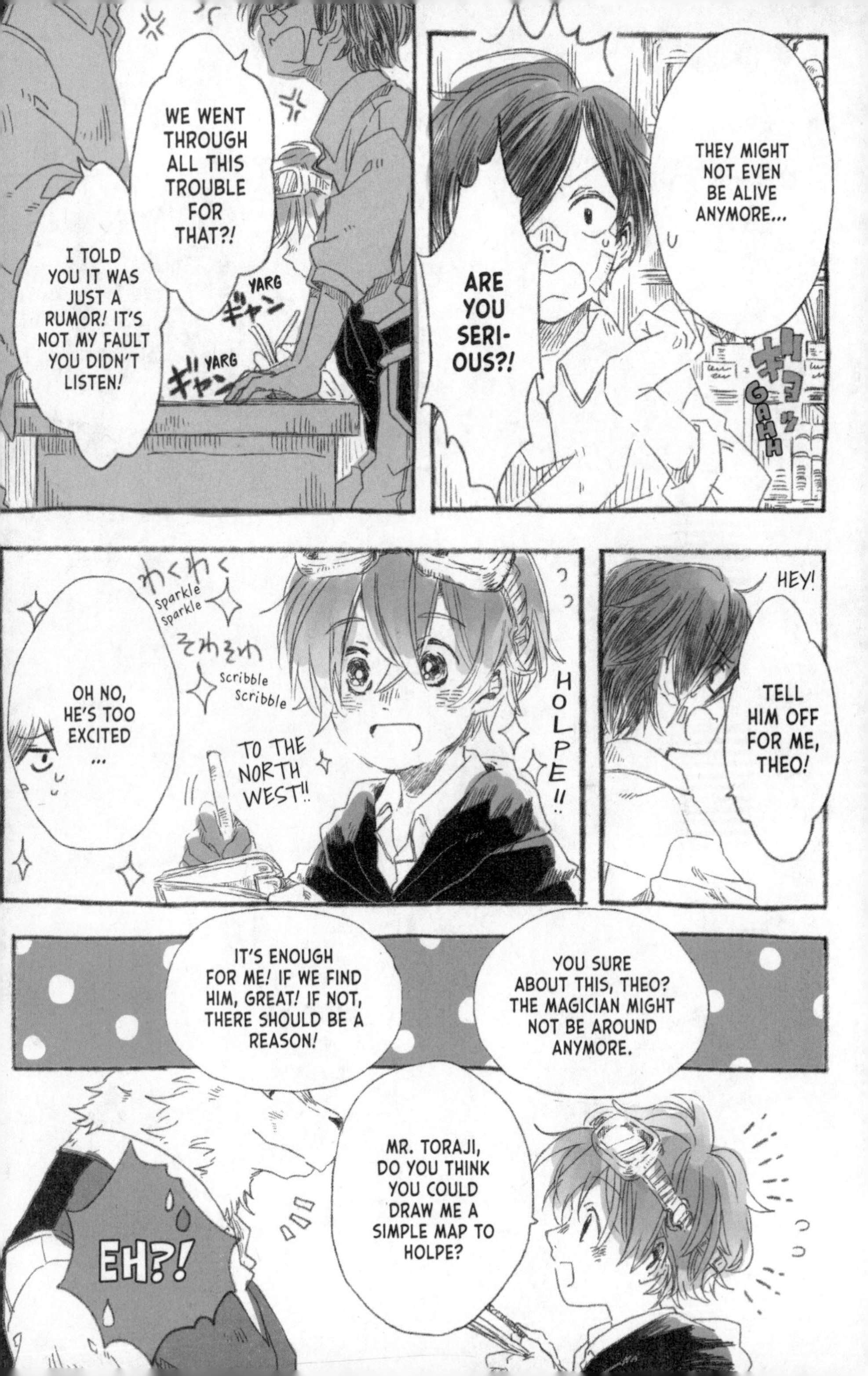
THEY MIGHT NOT EVEN BE ALIVE ANYMORE...
ARE YOU SERI-OUS?!
GAHH
WE WENT THROUGH ALL THIS TROUBLE FOR THAT?!
YARG
YARG
I TOLD YOU IT WAS JUST A RUMOR! IT'S NOT MY FAULT YOU DIDN'T LISTEN!
HEY!
TELL HIM OFF FOR ME, THEO!
HOLPE!!
TO THE NORTH WEST!!
わくわく
Sparkle Sparkle
そわそわ
Scribble Scribble
OH NO, HE'S TOO EXCITED...
YOU SURE ABOUT THIS, THEO? THE MAGICIAN MIGHT NOT BE AROUND ANYMORE.
IT'S ENOUGH FOR ME! IF WE FIND HIM, GREAT! IF NOT, THERE SHOULD BE A REASON!
MR. TORAJI, DO YOU THINK YOU COULD DRAW ME A SIMPLE MAP TO HOLPE?
EH?!

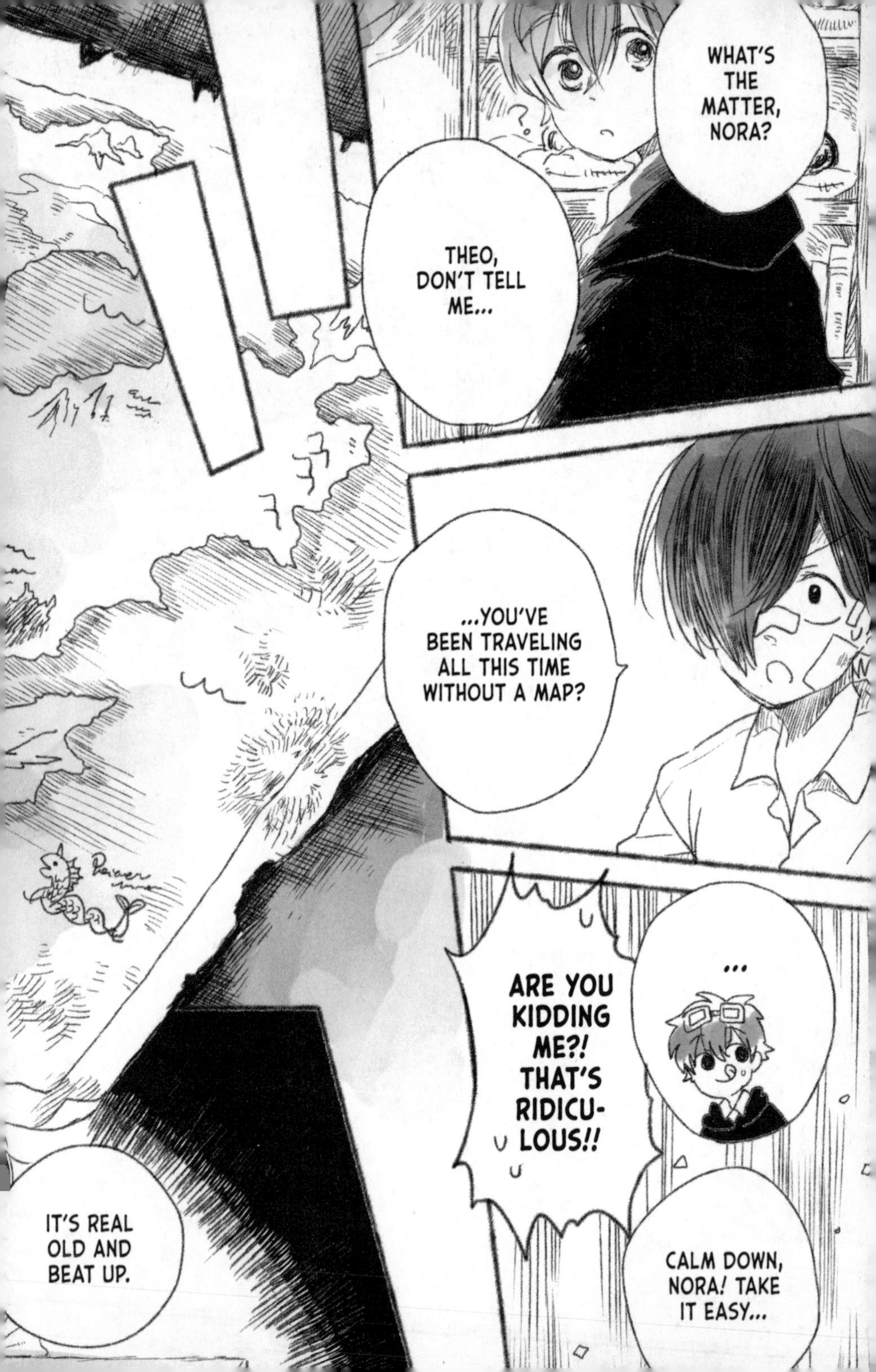
WHAT'S THE MATTER, NORA?
THEO, DON'T TELL ME...
...YOU'VE BEEN TRAVELING ALL THIS TIME WITHOUT A MAP?
...
ARE YOU KIDDING ME?! THAT'S RIDICU-LOUS!!
CALM DOWN, NORA! TAKE IT EASY...
IT'S REAL OLD AND BEAT UP.

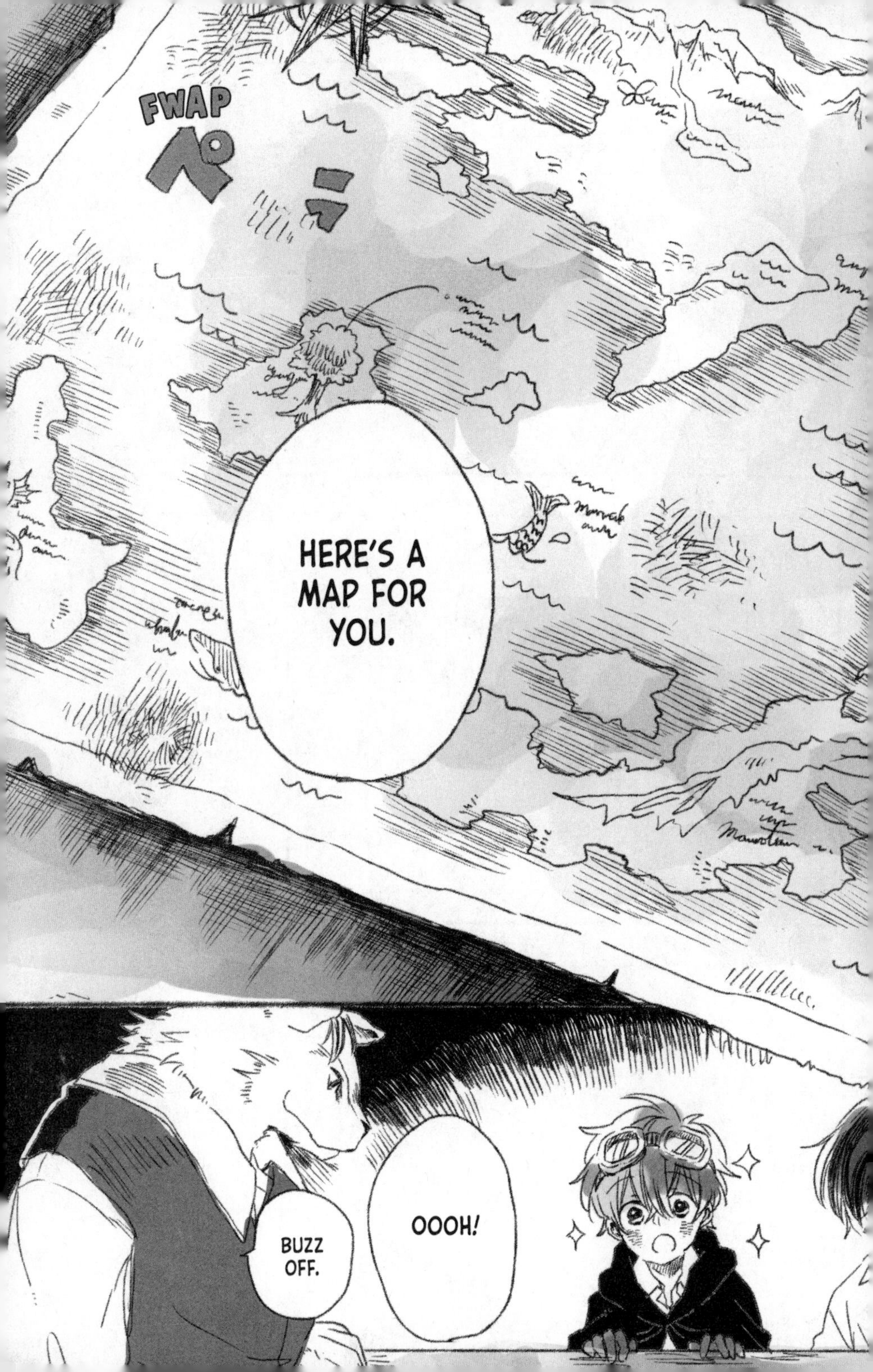
FWAP
HERE'S A MAP FOR YOU.
OOOH!
BUZZ OFF.

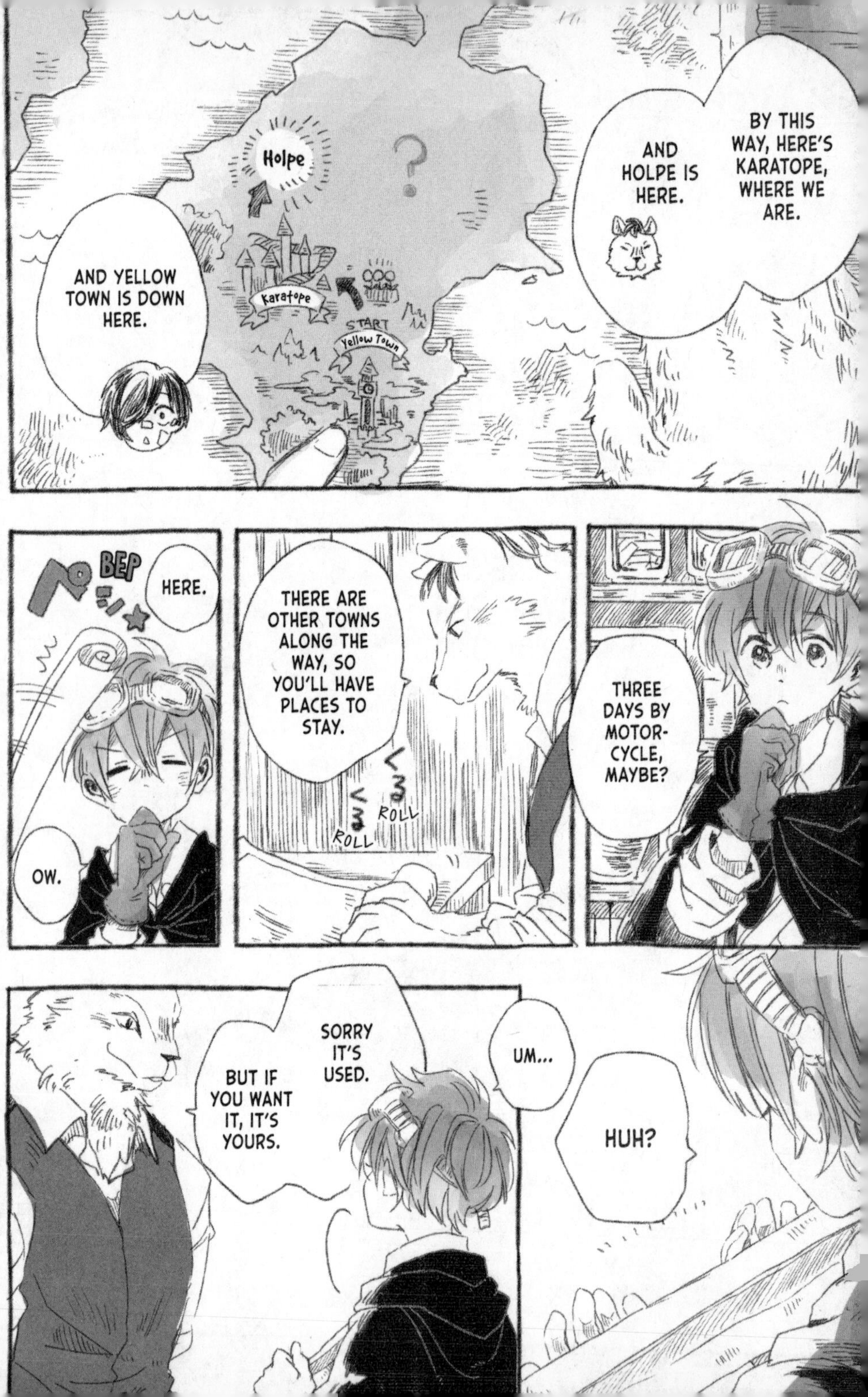
BY THIS WAY, HERE'S KARATOPE, WHERE WE ARE.
AND HOLPE IS HERE.
Holpe
Karatope
START
Yellow Town
AND YELLOW TOWN IS DOWN HERE.
THREE DAYS BY MOTOR-CYCLE, MAYBE?
THERE ARE OTHER TOWNS ALONG THE WAY, SO YOU'LL HAVE PLACES TO STAY.
ROLL
ROLL
BEP
HERE.
OW.
UM...
HUH?
SORRY IT'S USED.
BUT IF YOU WANT IT, IT'S YOURS.

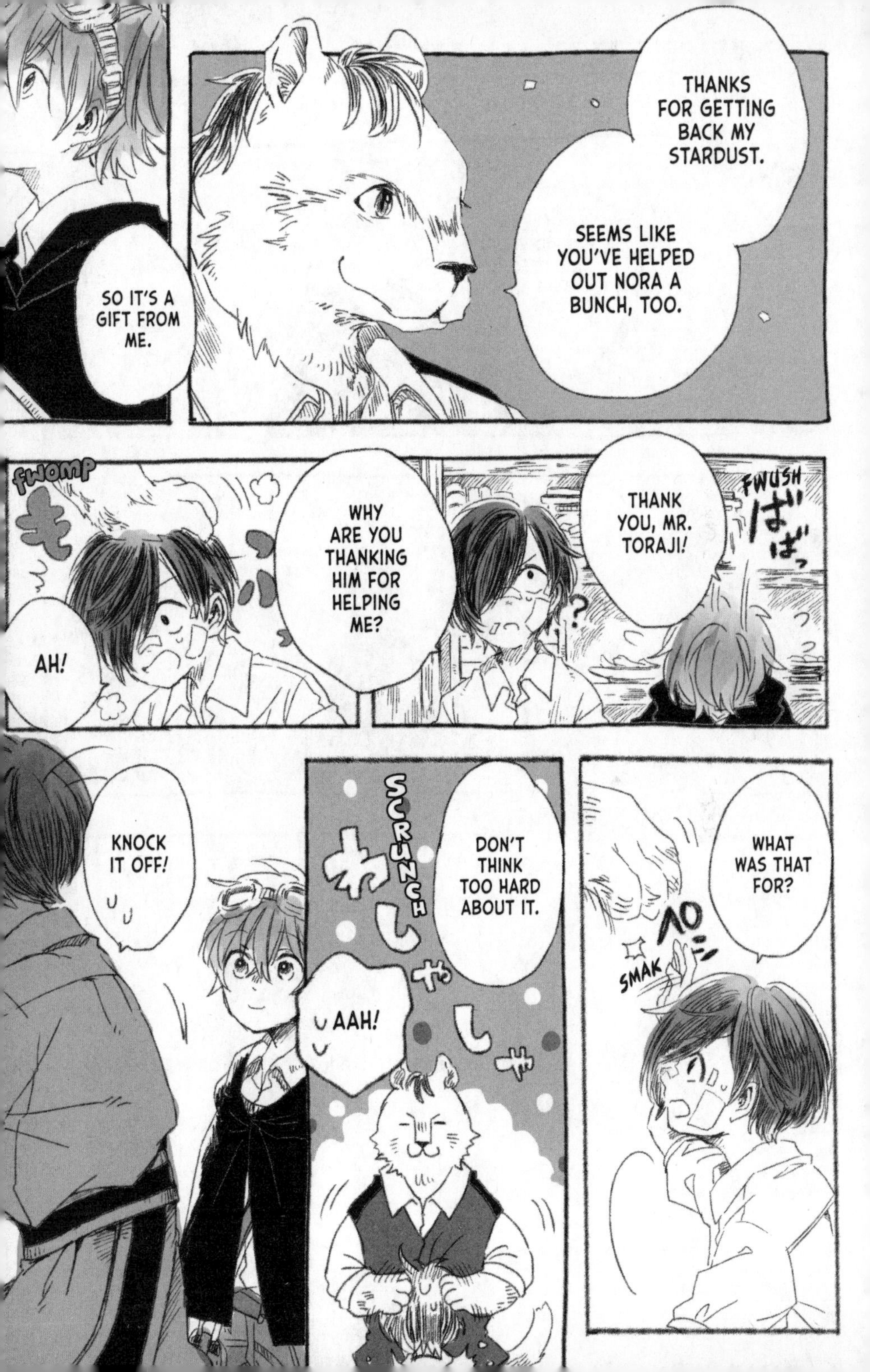
THANKS FOR GETTING BACK MY STARDUST.
SEEMS LIKE YOU'VE HELPED OUT NORA A BUNCH, TOO.
SO IT'S A GIFT FROM ME.
FWUSH
ばばっ
THANK YOU, MR. TORAJI!
WHY ARE YOU THANKING HIM FOR HELPING ME?
fwomp
も
AH!
WHAT WAS THAT FOR?
SMAK
SCRUNCH
わしゃしゃ
DON'T THINK TOO HARD ABOUT IT.
AAH!
KNOCK IT OFF!

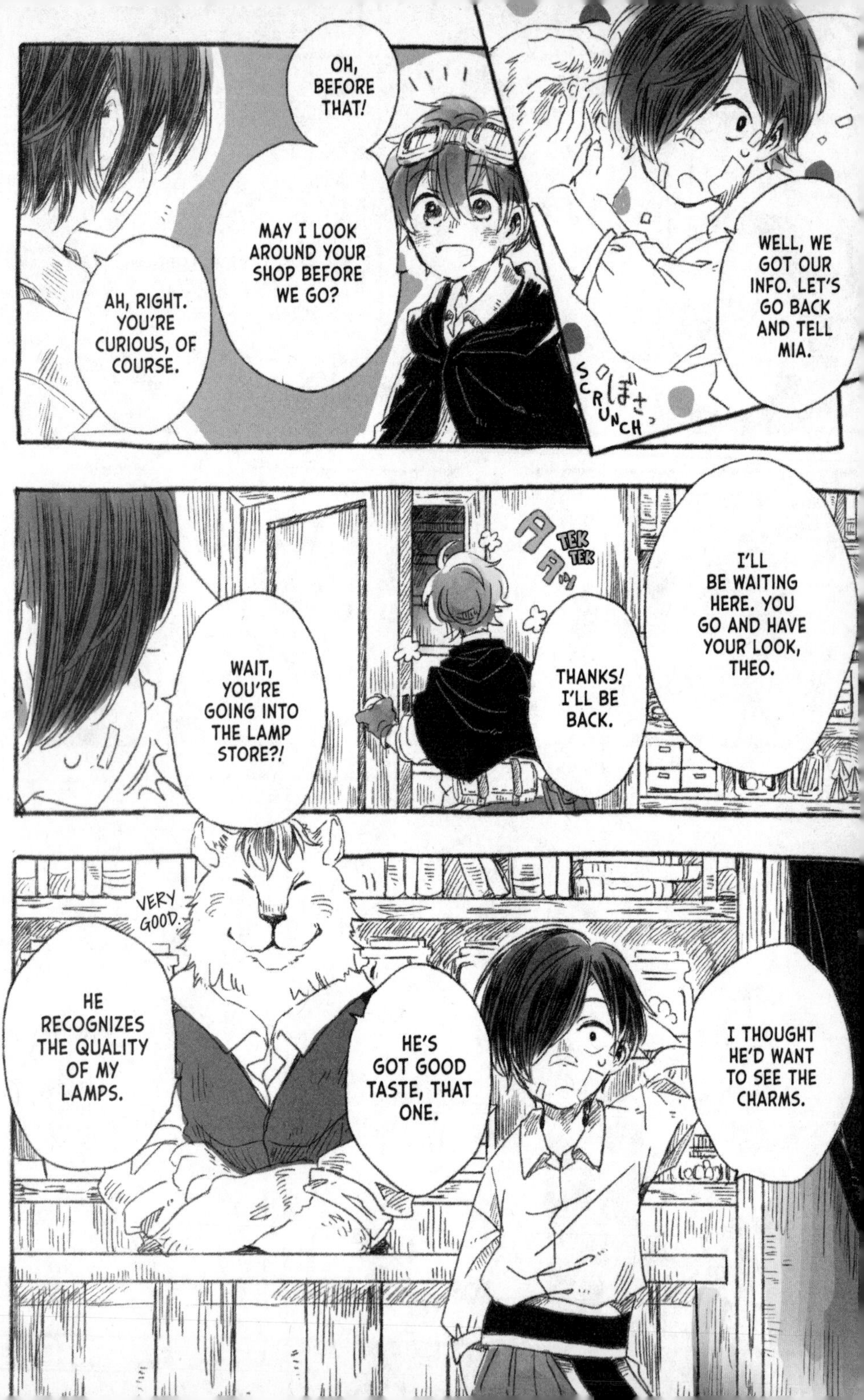
WELL, WE GOT OUR INFO. LET'S GO BACK AND TELL MIA.
SCRUNCH
OH, BEFORE THAT!
MAY I LOOK AROUND YOUR SHOP BEFORE WE GO?
AH, RIGHT. YOU'RE CURIOUS, OF COURSE.
I'LL BE WAITING HERE. YOU GO AND HAVE YOUR LOOK, THEO.
TEK TEK
THANKS! I'LL BE BACK.
WAIT, YOU'RE GOING INTO THE LAMP STORE?!
I THOUGHT HE'D WANT TO SEE THE CHARMS.
HE'S GOT GOOD TASTE, THAT ONE.
VERY GOOD.
HE RECOGNIZES THE QUALITY OF MY LAMPS.

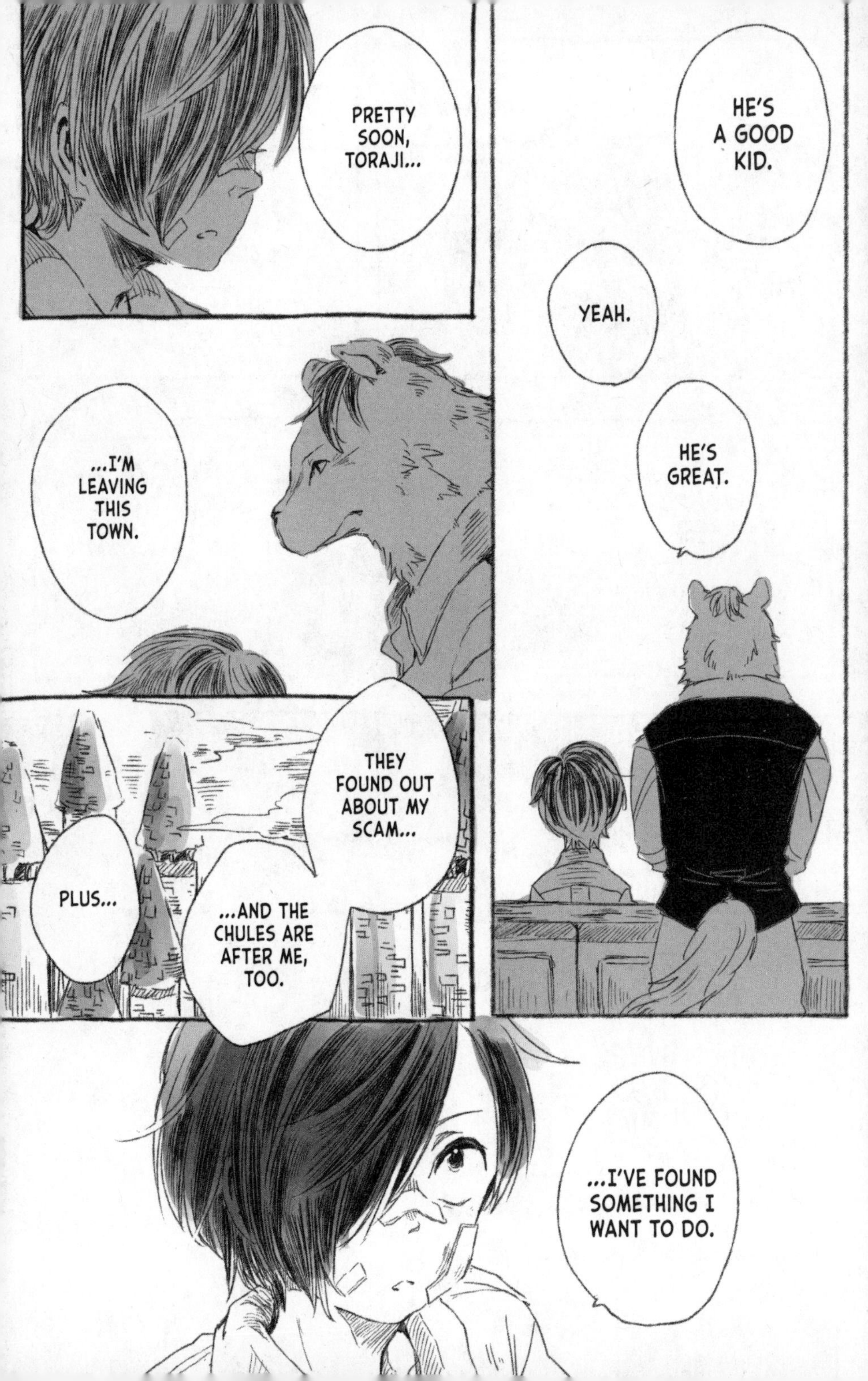

HE'S A GOOD KID.
YEAH.
HE'S GREAT.
PRETTY SOON, TORAJI...
...I'M LEAVING THIS TOWN.
THEY FOUND OUT ABOUT MY SCAM...
...AND THE CHULES ARE AFTER ME, TOO.
PLUS...
...I'VE FOUND SOMETHING I WANT TO DO.

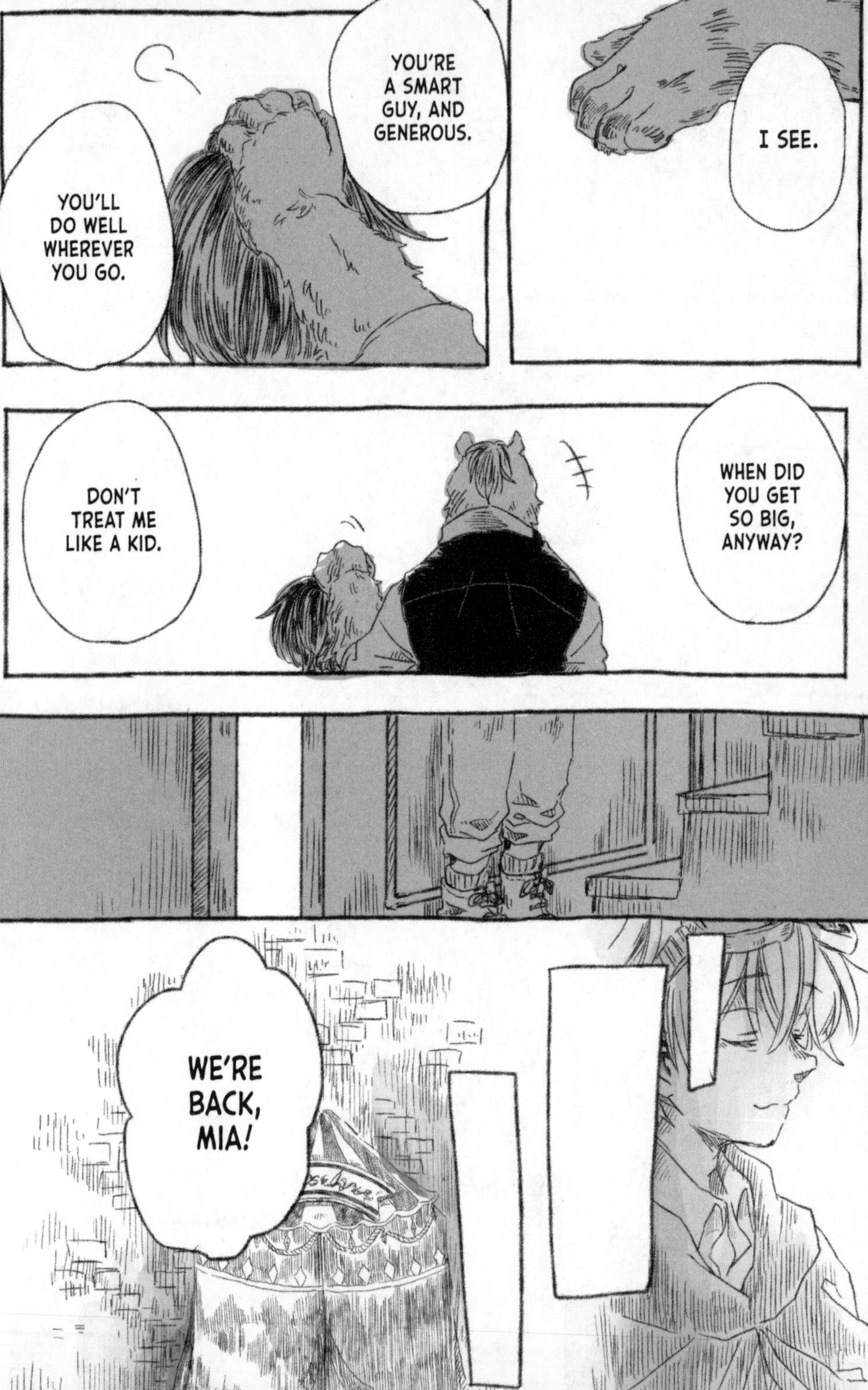
I SEE.
YOU'RE A SMART GUY, AND GENEROUS.
YOU'LL DO WELL WHEREVER YOU GO.
WHEN DID YOU GET SO BIG, ANYWAY?
DON'T TREAT ME LIKE A KID.
WE'RE BACK, MIA!

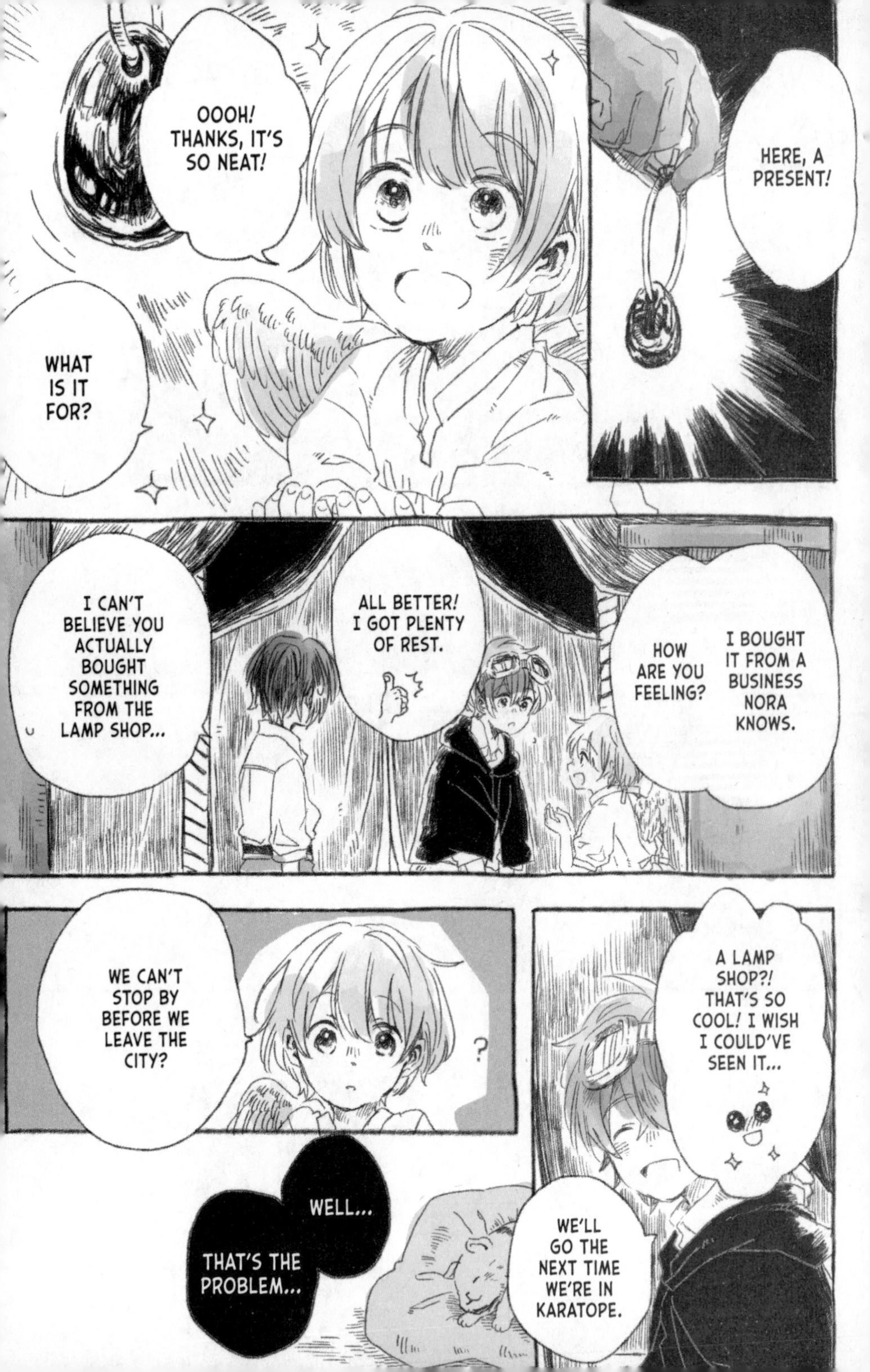
HERE, A PRESENT!
OOOH! THANKS, IT'S SO NEAT!
WHAT IS IT FOR?
I BOUGHT IT FROM A BUSINESS NORA KNOWS.
HOW ARE YOU FEELING?
ALL BETTER! I GOT PLENTY OF REST.
I CAN'T BELIEVE YOU ACTUALLY BOUGHT SOMETHING FROM THE LAMP SHOP...
A LAMP SHOP?! THAT'S SO COOL! I WISH I COULD'VE SEEN IT...
WE'LL GO THE NEXT TIME WE'RE IN KARATOPE.
WE CAN'T STOP BY BEFORE WE LEAVE THE CITY?
WELL...
THAT'S THE PROBLEM...

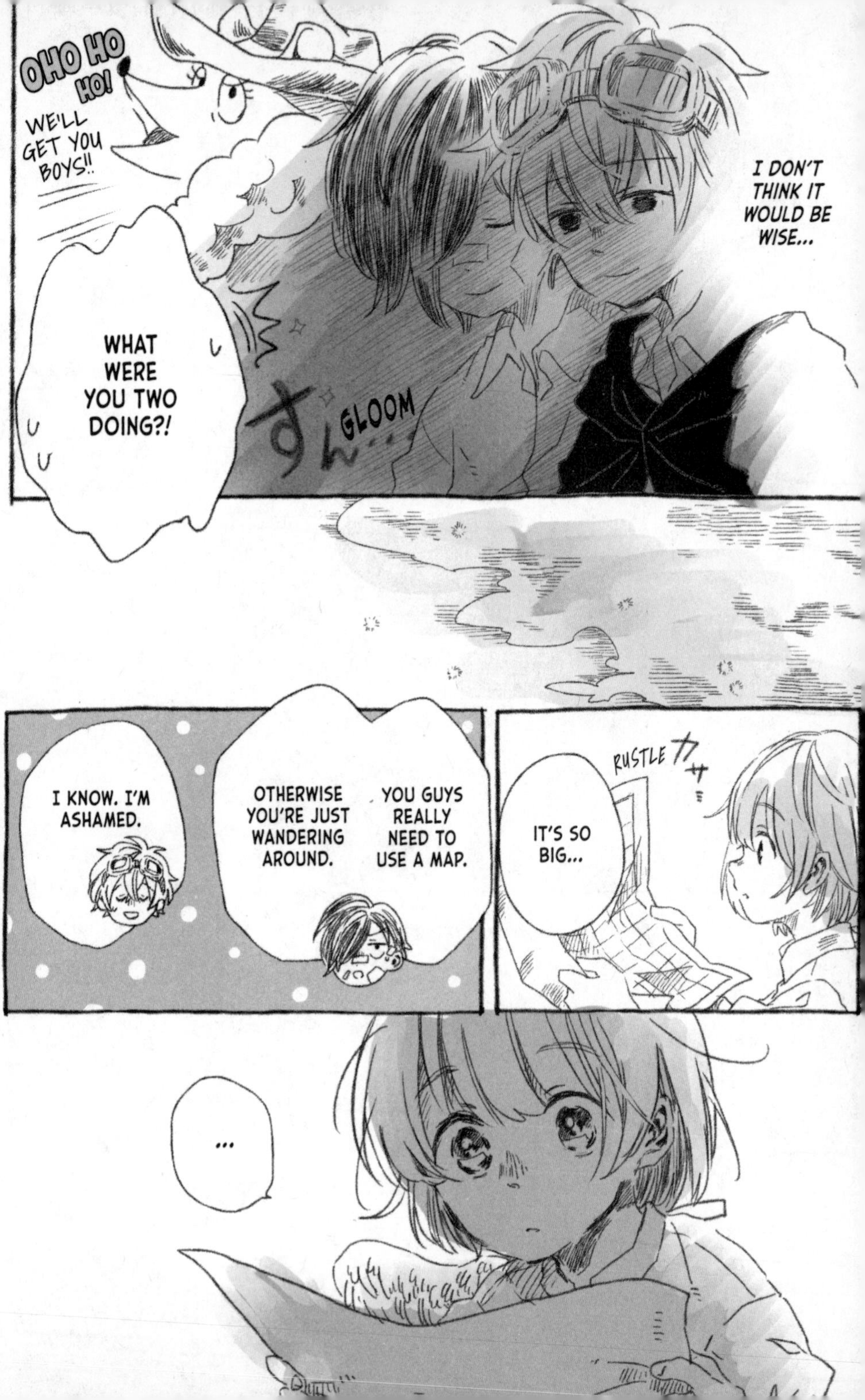
I DON'T THINK IT WOULD BE WISE...
OHO HO HO!
WE'LL GET YOU BOYS!!
WHAT WERE YOU TWO DOING?!
すん
GLOOM...
RUSTLE カサ
IT'S SO BIG...
YOU GUYS REALLY NEED TO USE A MAP.
OTHERWISE YOU'RE JUST WANDERING AROUND.
I KNOW. I'M ASHAMED.
...

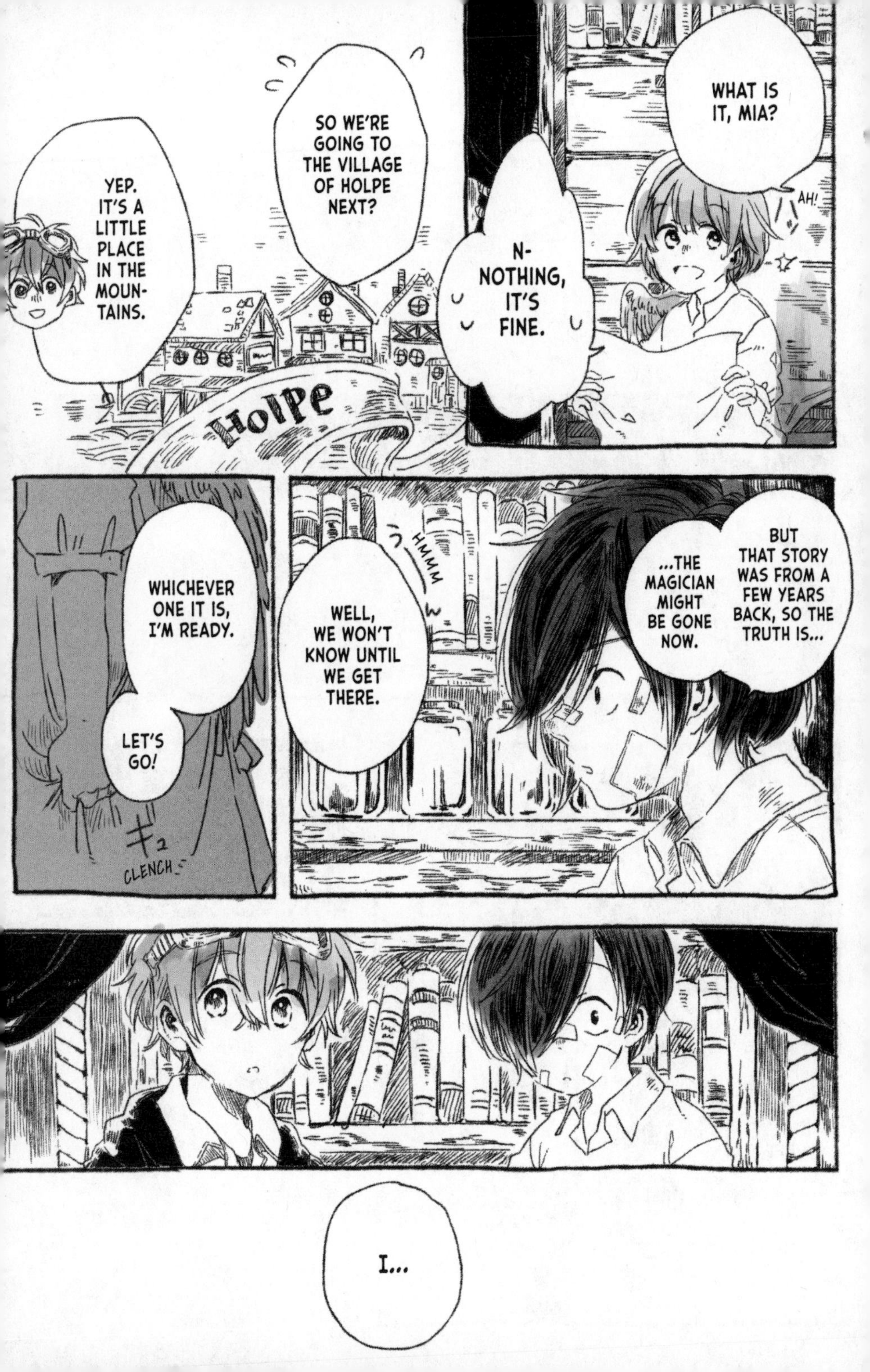
WHAT IS IT, MIA?
AH!
N- NOTHING, IT'S FINE.
SO WE'RE GOING TO THE VILLAGE OF HOLPE NEXT?
YEP. IT'S A LITTLE PLACE IN THE MOUNTAINS.
HOLPE
BUT THAT STORY WAS FROM A FEW YEARS BACK, SO THE TRUTH IS...
...THE MAGICIAN MIGHT BE GONE NOW.
HMMM
WELL, WE WON'T KNOW UNTIL WE GET THERE.
WHICHEVER ONE IT IS, I'M READY.
LET'S GO!
CLENCH
I...

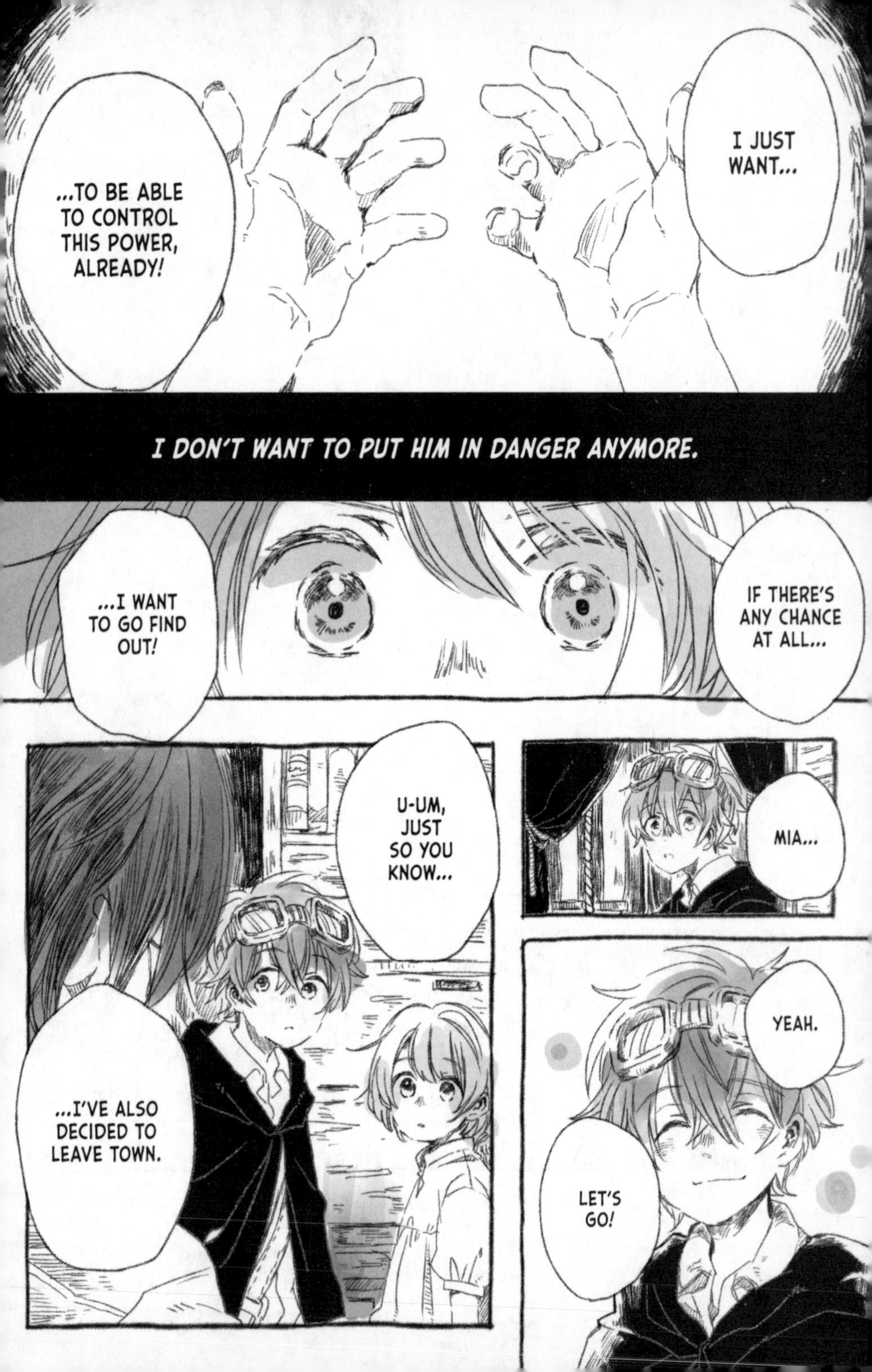
I JUST WANT...
...TO BE ABLE TO CONTROL THIS POWER, ALREADY!
I DON'T WANT TO PUT HIM IN DANGER ANYMORE.
IF THERE'S ANY CHANCE AT ALL...
...I WANT TO GO FIND OUT!
MIA...
YEAH.
LET'S GO!
U-UM, JUST SO YOU KNOW...
...I'VE ALSO DECIDED TO LEAVE TOWN.

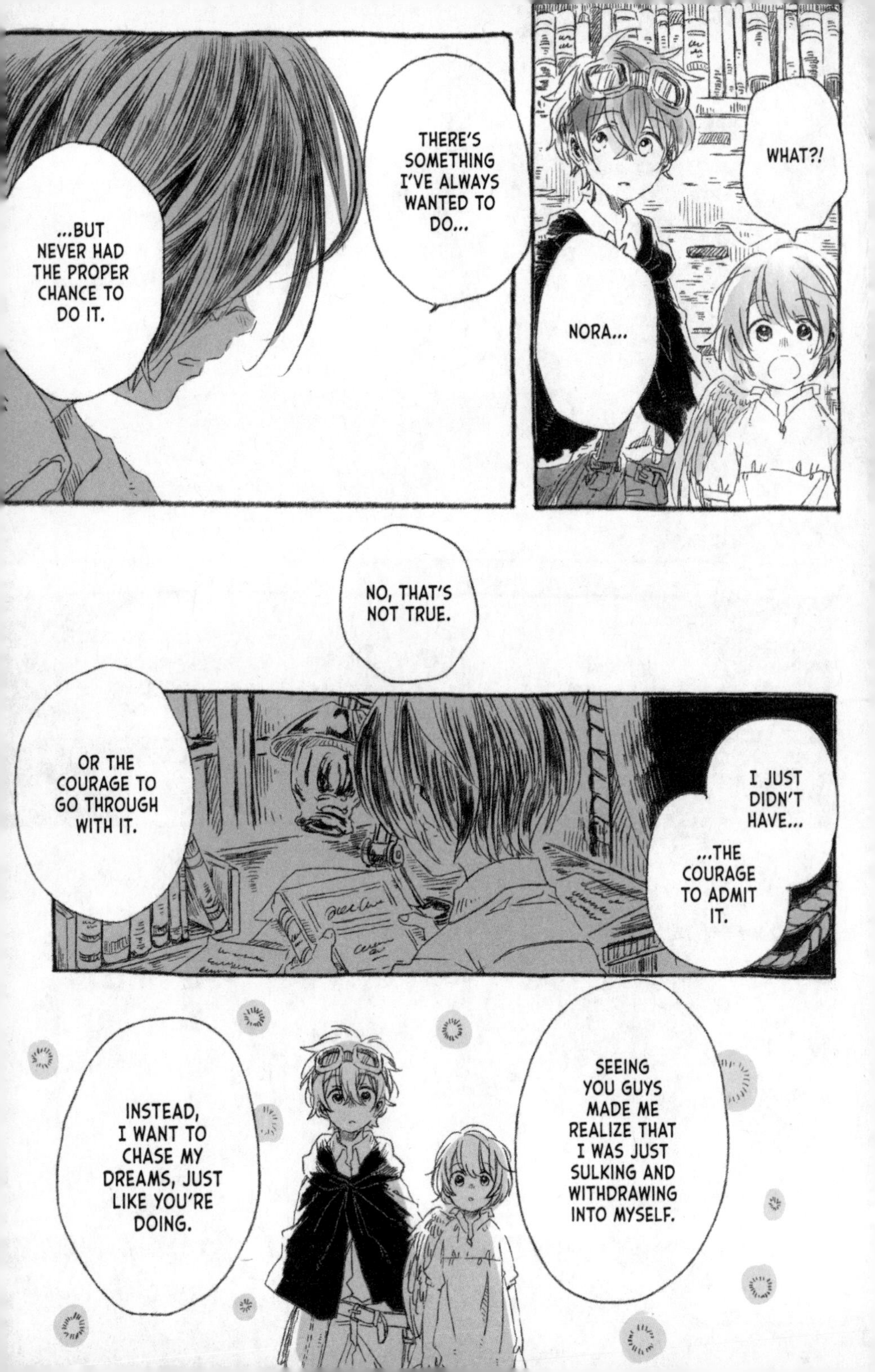
WHAT?!
NORA...
THERE'S SOMETHING I'VE ALWAYS WANTED TO DO...
...BUT NEVER HAD THE PROPER CHANCE TO DO IT.
NO, THAT'S NOT TRUE.
I JUST DIDN'T HAVE...
...THE COURAGE TO ADMIT IT.
OR THE COURAGE TO GO THROUGH WITH IT.
SEEING YOU GUYS MADE ME REALIZE THAT I WAS JUST SULKING AND WITHDRAWING INTO MYSELF.
INSTEAD, I WANT TO CHASE MY DREAMS, JUST LIKE YOU'RE DOING.

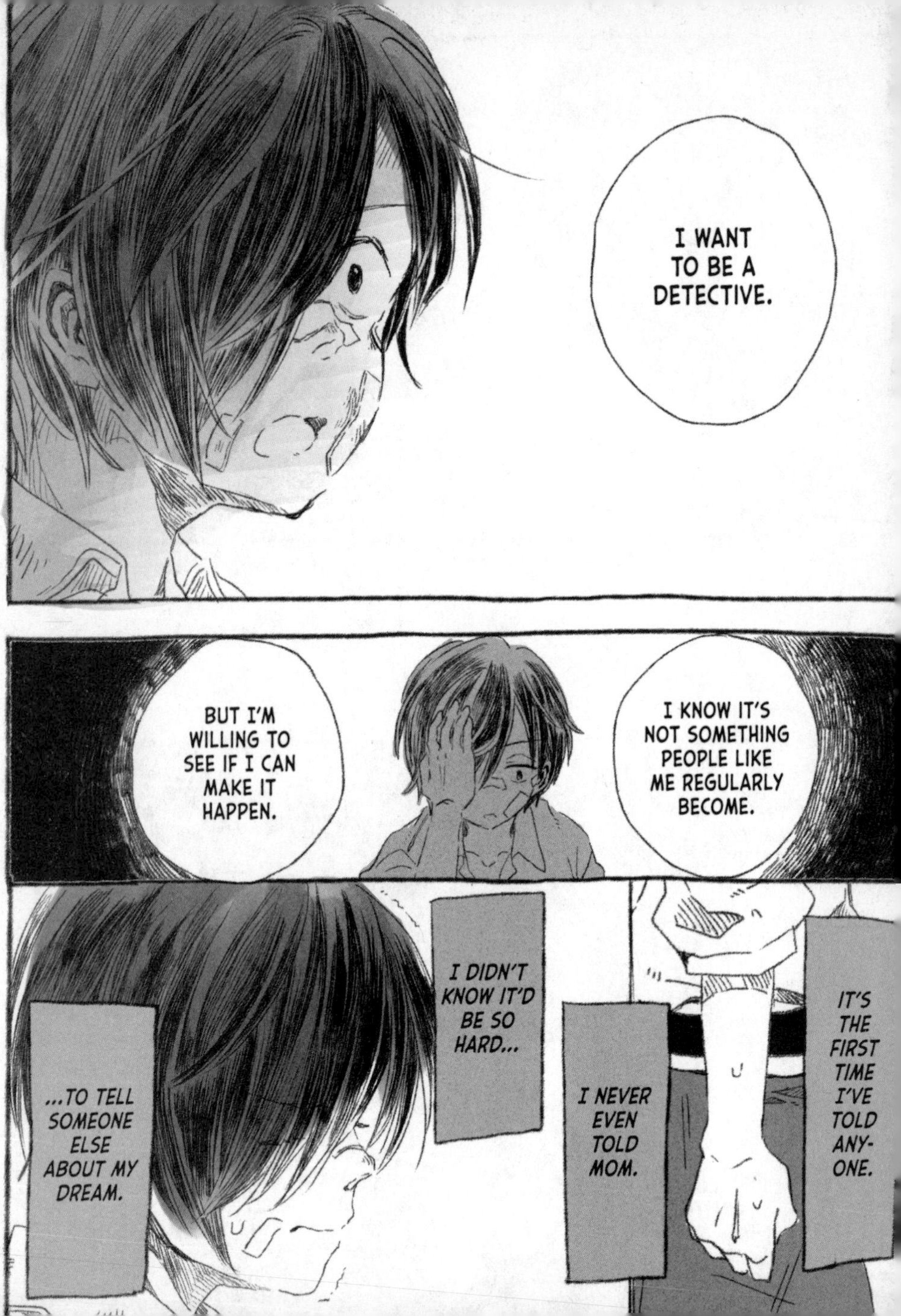
I WANT TO BE A DETECTIVE.
I KNOW IT'S NOT SOMETHING PEOPLE LIKE ME REGULARLY BECOME.
BUT I'M WILLING TO SEE IF I CAN MAKE IT HAPPEN.
IT'S THE FIRST TIME I'VE TOLD ANY-ONE.
I NEVER EVEN TOLD MOM.
I DIDN'T KNOW IT'D BE SO HARD...
...TO TELL SOMEONE ELSE ABOUT MY DREAM.

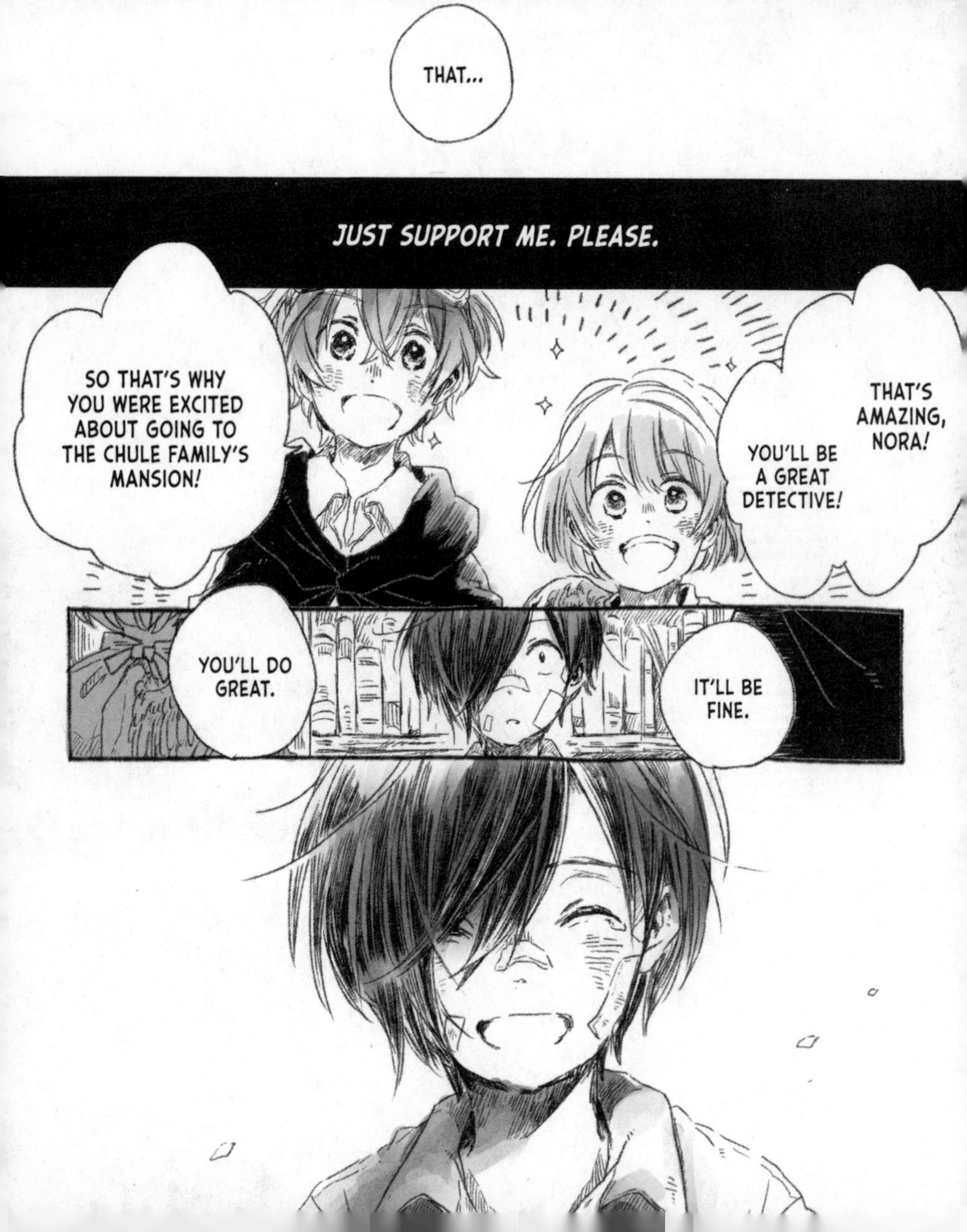
THAT...
JUST SUPPORT ME. PLEASE.
THAT'S AMAZING, NORA!
YOU'LL BE A GREAT DETECTIVE!
SO THAT'S WHY YOU WERE EXCITED ABOUT GOING TO THE CHULE FAMILY'S MANSION!
IT'LL BE FINE.
YOU'LL DO GREAT.

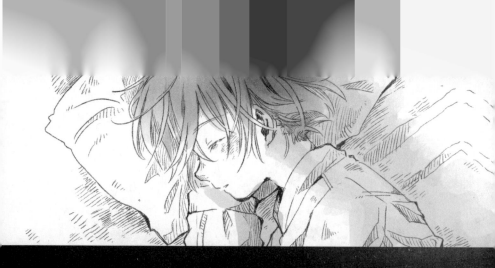

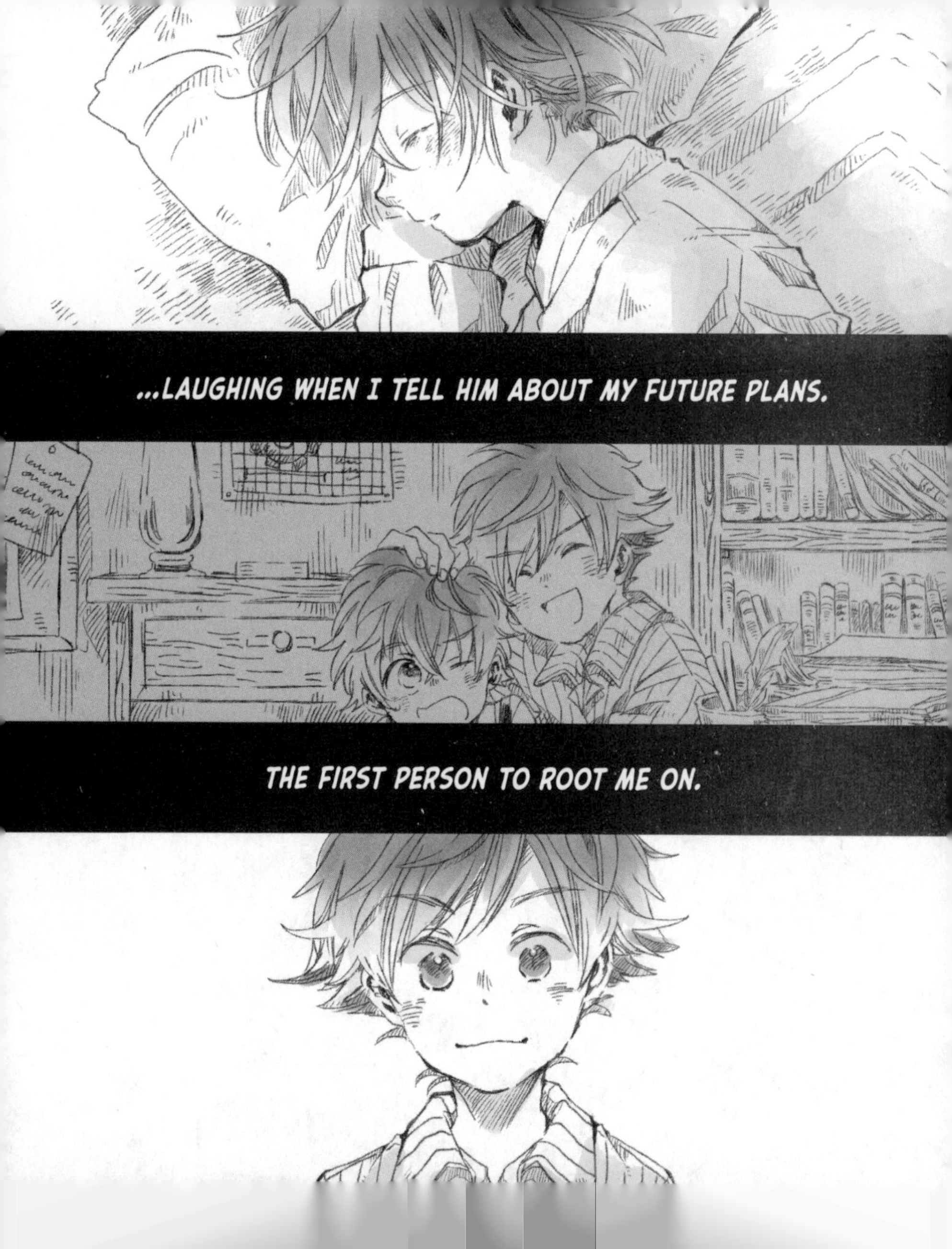
...LAUGHING WHEN I TELL HIM ABOUT MY FUTURE PLANS.
THE FIRST PERSON TO ROOT ME ON.

Chapter 20: A Mother's Warmth

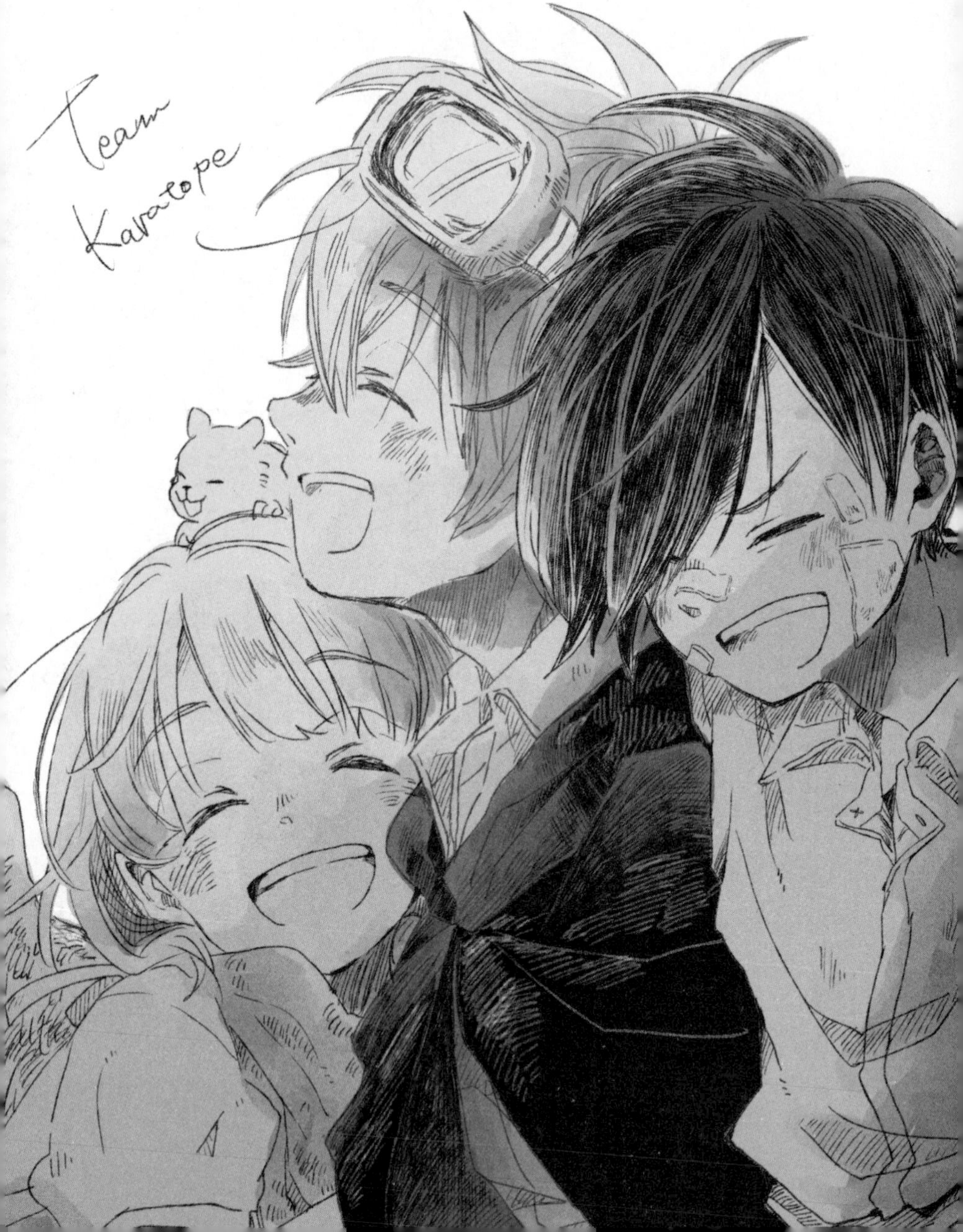
Team Karatope

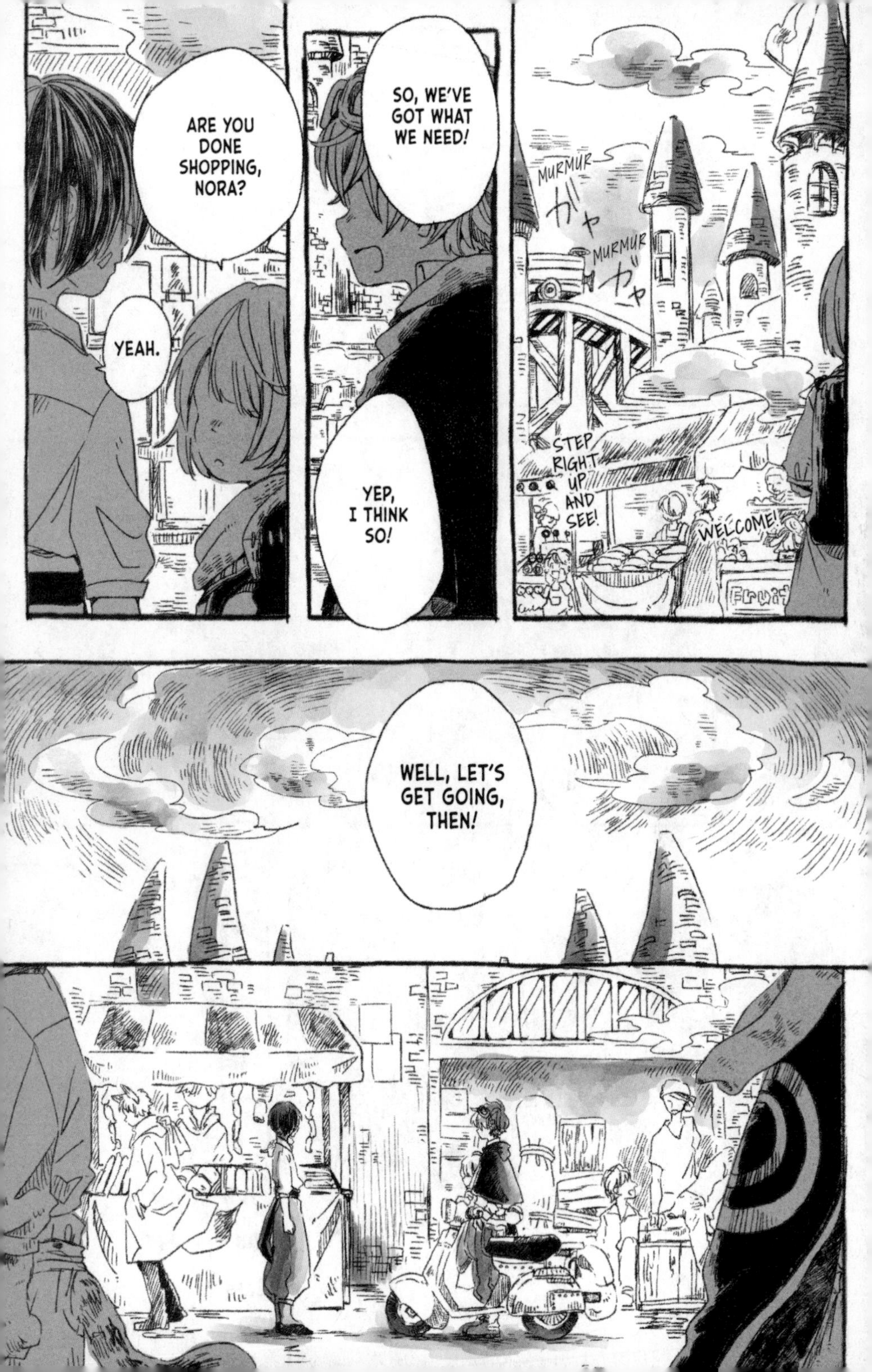
MURMUR
ガヤ
MURMUR
ガヤ
WELCOME!
STEP RIGHT UP AND SEE!
SO, WE'VE GOT WHAT WE NEED!
YEP, I THINK SO!
ARE YOU DONE SHOPPING, NORA?
YEAH.
WELL, LET'S GET GOING, THEN!

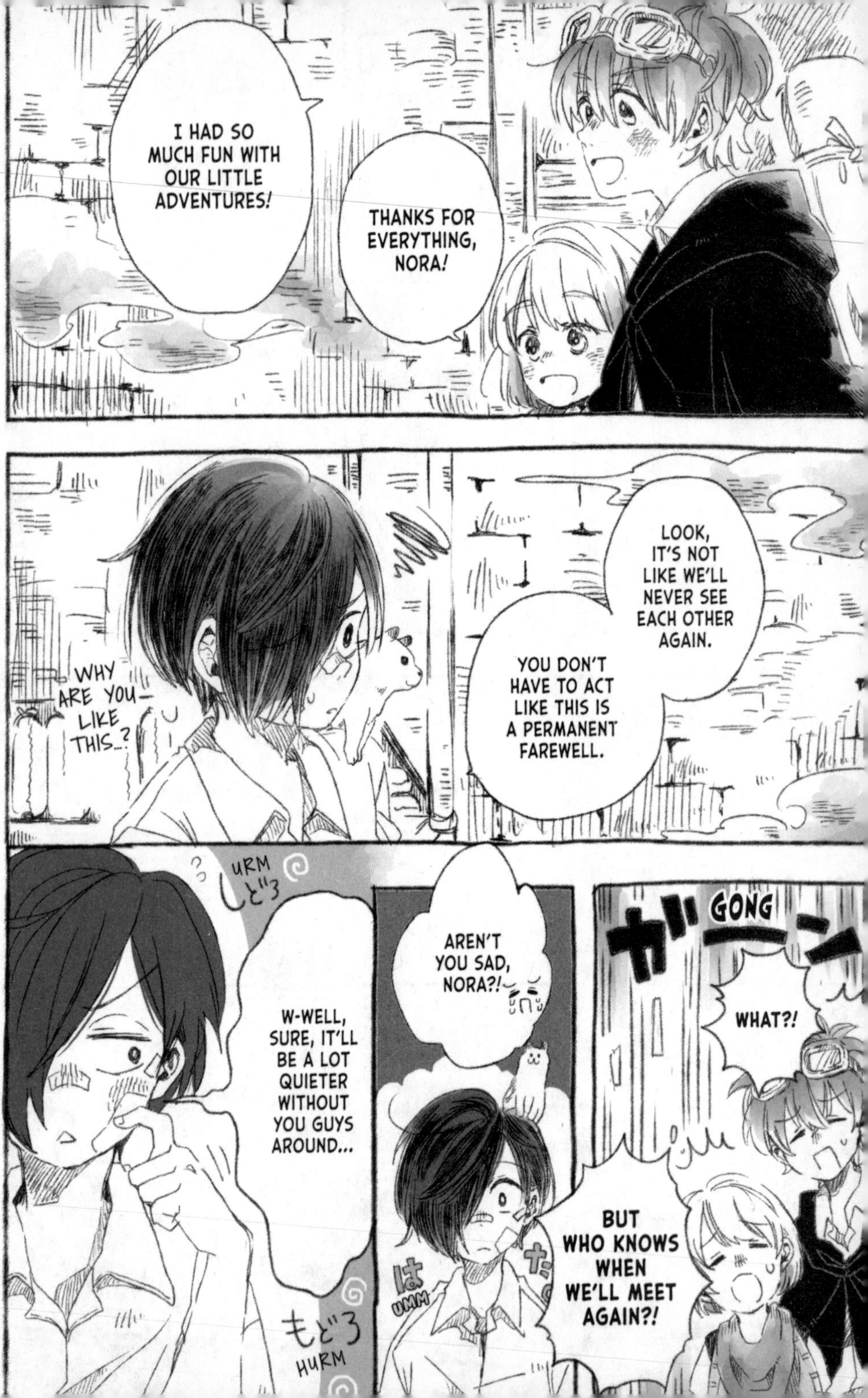
THANKS FOR EVERYTHING, NORA!
I HAD SO MUCH FUN WITH OUR LITTLE ADVENTURES!
LOOK, IT'S NOT LIKE WE'LL NEVER SEE EACH OTHER AGAIN.
YOU DON'T HAVE TO ACT LIKE THIS IS A PERMANENT FAREWELL.
WHY ARE YOU LIKE THIS...?
GONG
WHAT?!
AREN'T YOU SAD, NORA?!
BUT WHO KNOWS WHEN WE'LL MEET AGAIN?!
UMM
URM
W-WELL, SURE, IT'LL BE A LOT QUIETER WITHOUT YOU GUYS AROUND...
HURM

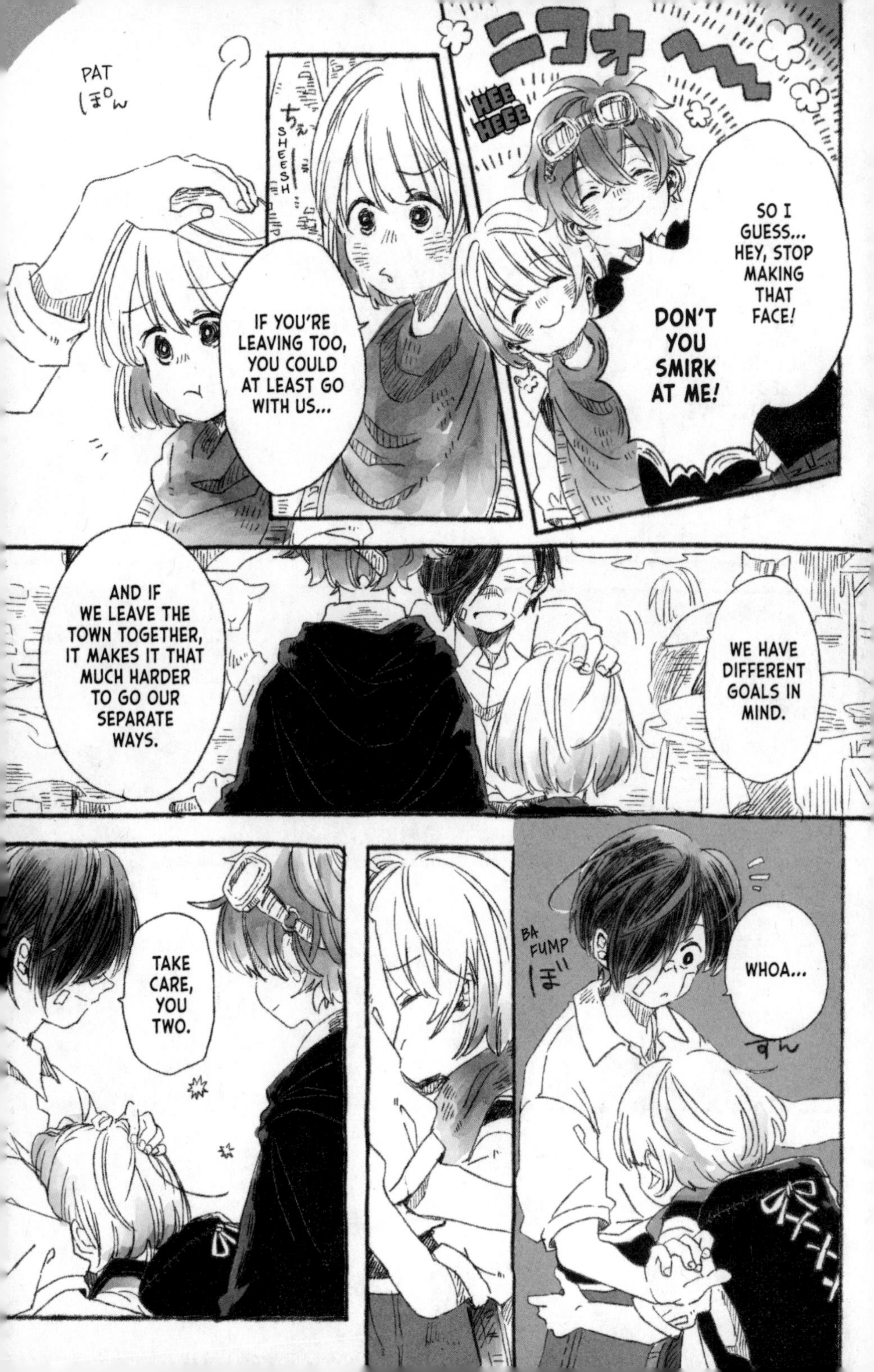
ニコォ へへへ
HEE HEEE
SO I GUESS... HEY, STOP MAKING THAT FACE!
DON'T YOU SMIRK AT ME!
ちぇ
SHEESH
IF YOU'RE LEAVING TOO, YOU COULD AT LEAST GO WITH US...
PAT
ぽん
WE HAVE DIFFERENT GOALS IN MIND.
AND IF WE LEAVE THE TOWN TOGETHER, IT MAKES IT THAT MUCH HARDER TO GO OUR SEPARATE WAYS.
WHOA...
BA FUMP
ぼ
すん
TAKE CARE, YOU TWO.

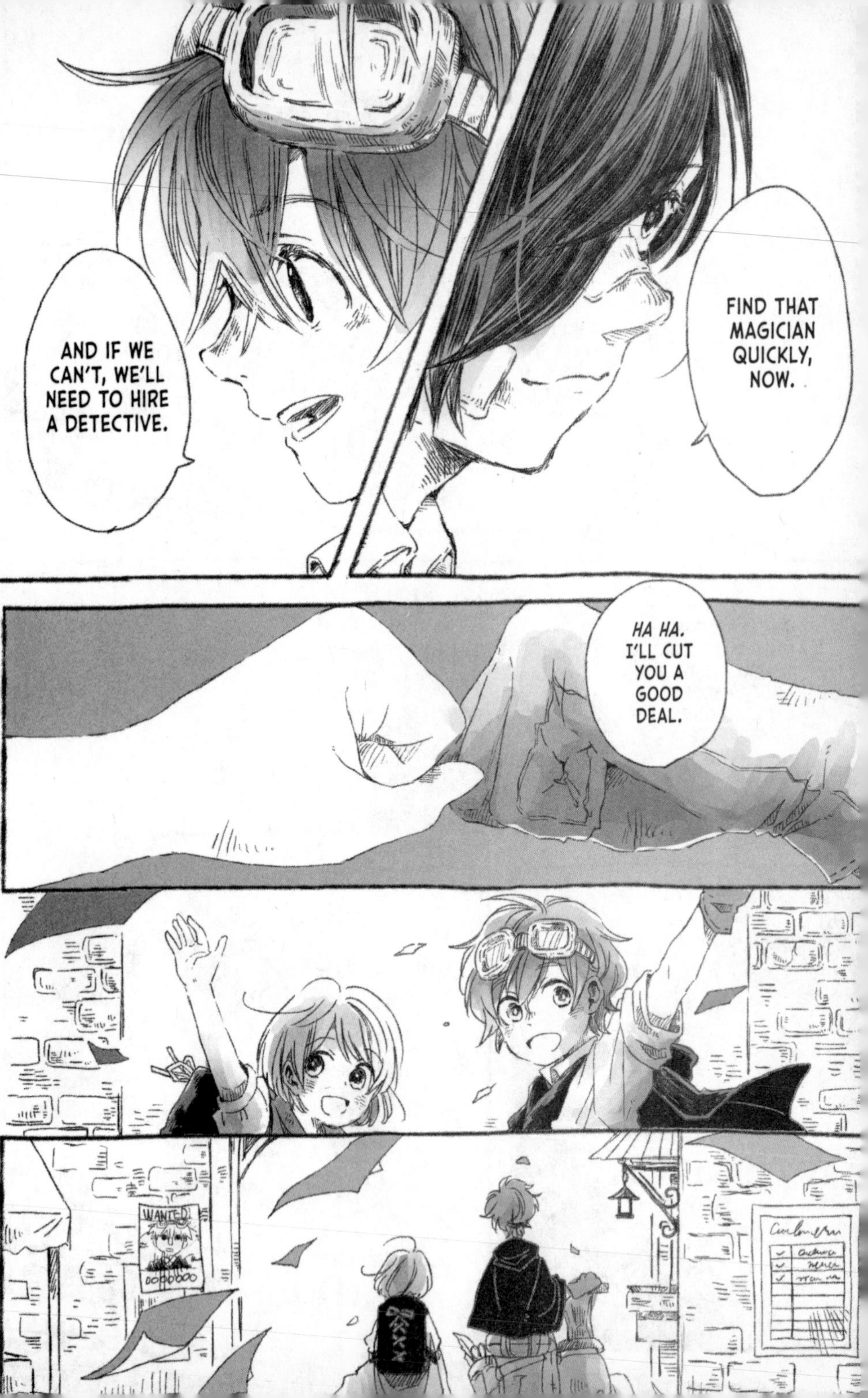
FIND THAT MAGICIAN QUICKLY, NOW.
AND IF WE CAN'T, WE'LL NEED TO HIRE A DETECTIVE.
HA HA. I'LL CUT YOU A GOOD DEAL.
WANTED

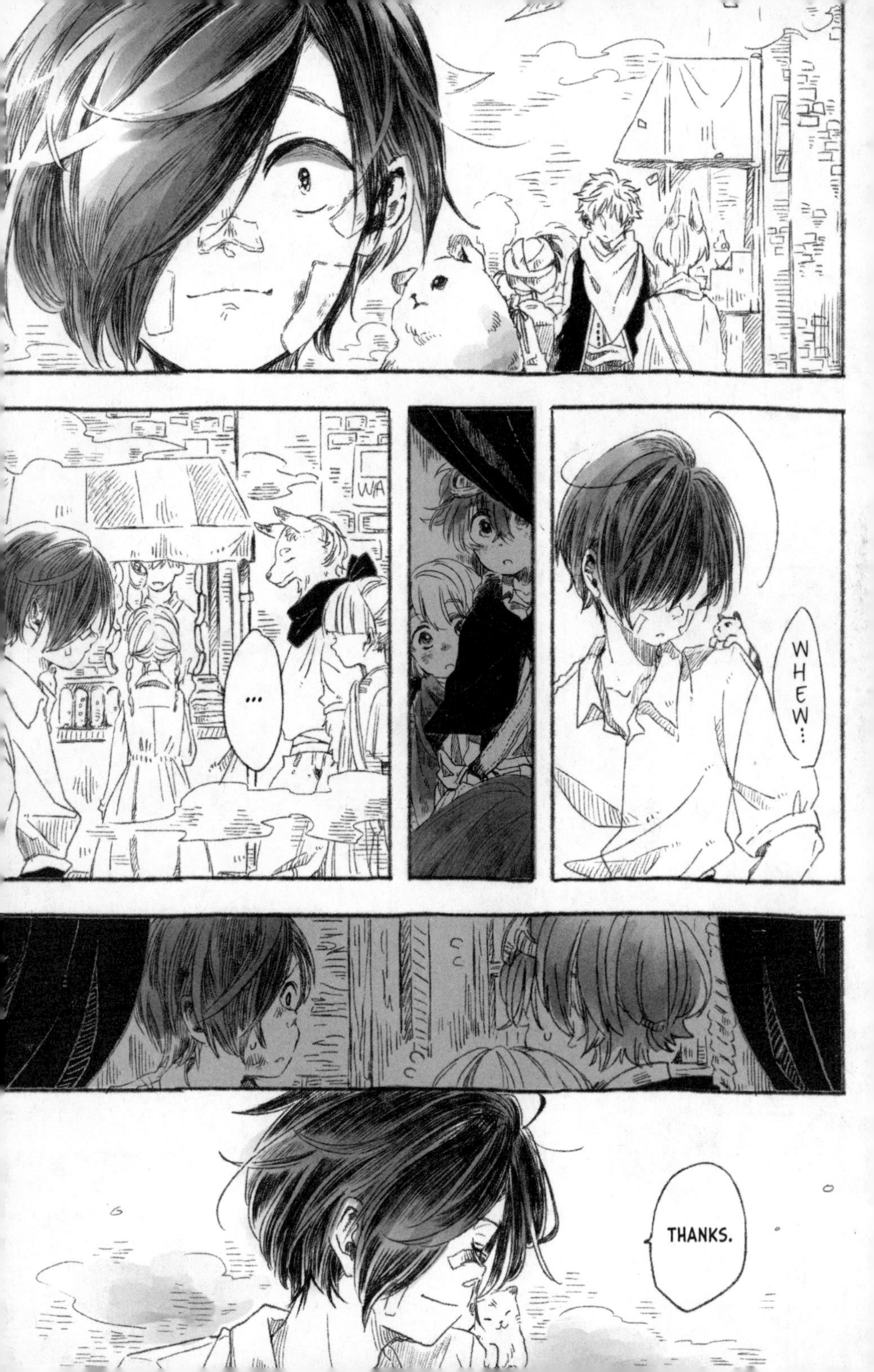
WHEW...
...
THANKS.

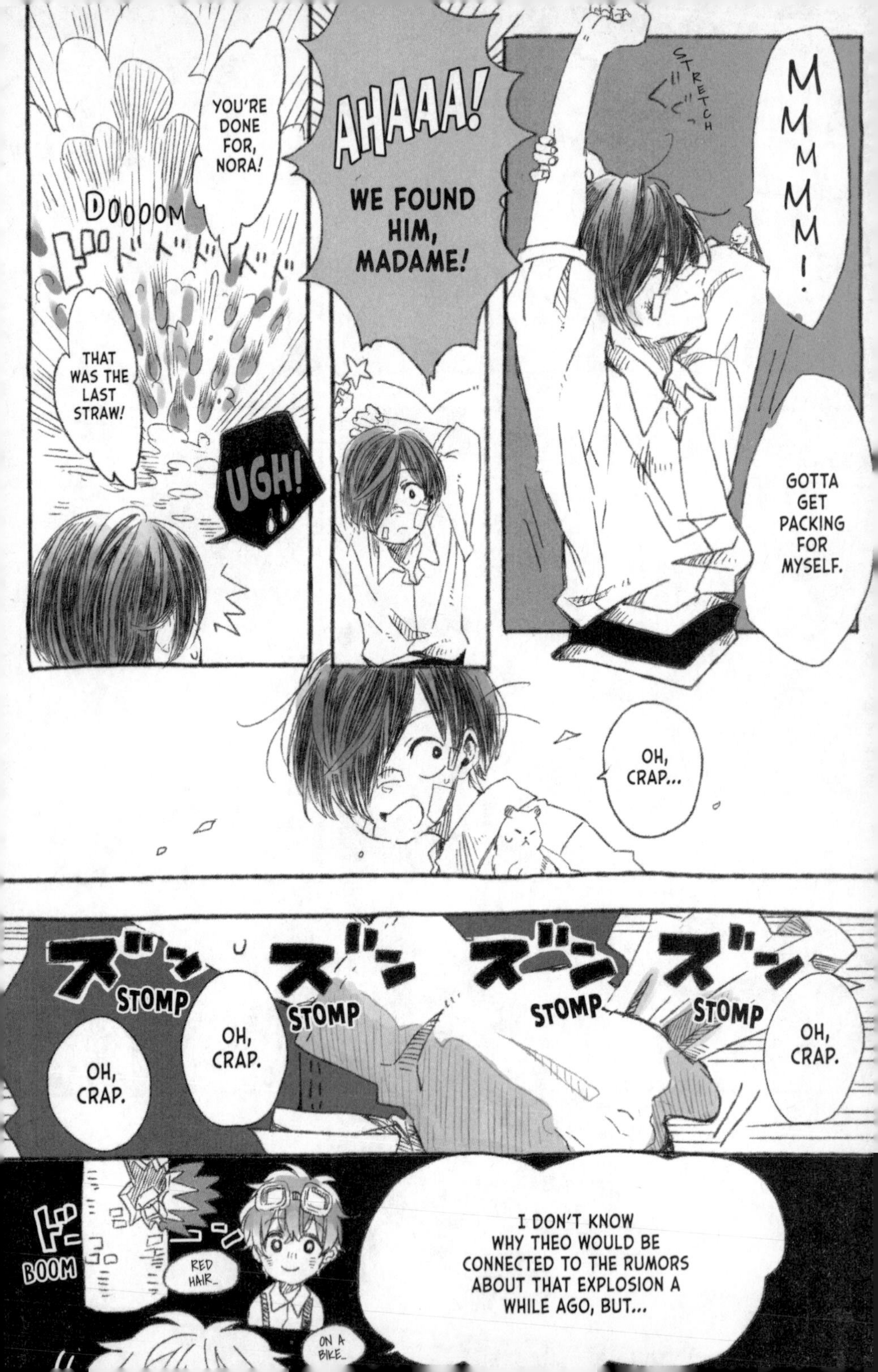
MMMMM!
STRETCH
GOTTA GET PACKING FOR MYSELF.
AHAAAA!
WE FOUND HIM, MADAME!
YOU'RE DONE FOR, NORA!
DOOOOM
THAT WAS THE LAST STRAW!
UGH!
OH, CRAP...
OH, CRAP.
STOMP
STOMP
STOMP
OH, CRAP.
STOMP
OH, CRAP.
I DON'T KNOW WHY THEO WOULD BE CONNECTED TO THE RUMORS ABOUT THAT EXPLOSION A WHILE AGO, BUT...
RED HAIR...
BOOM
ON A BIKE...

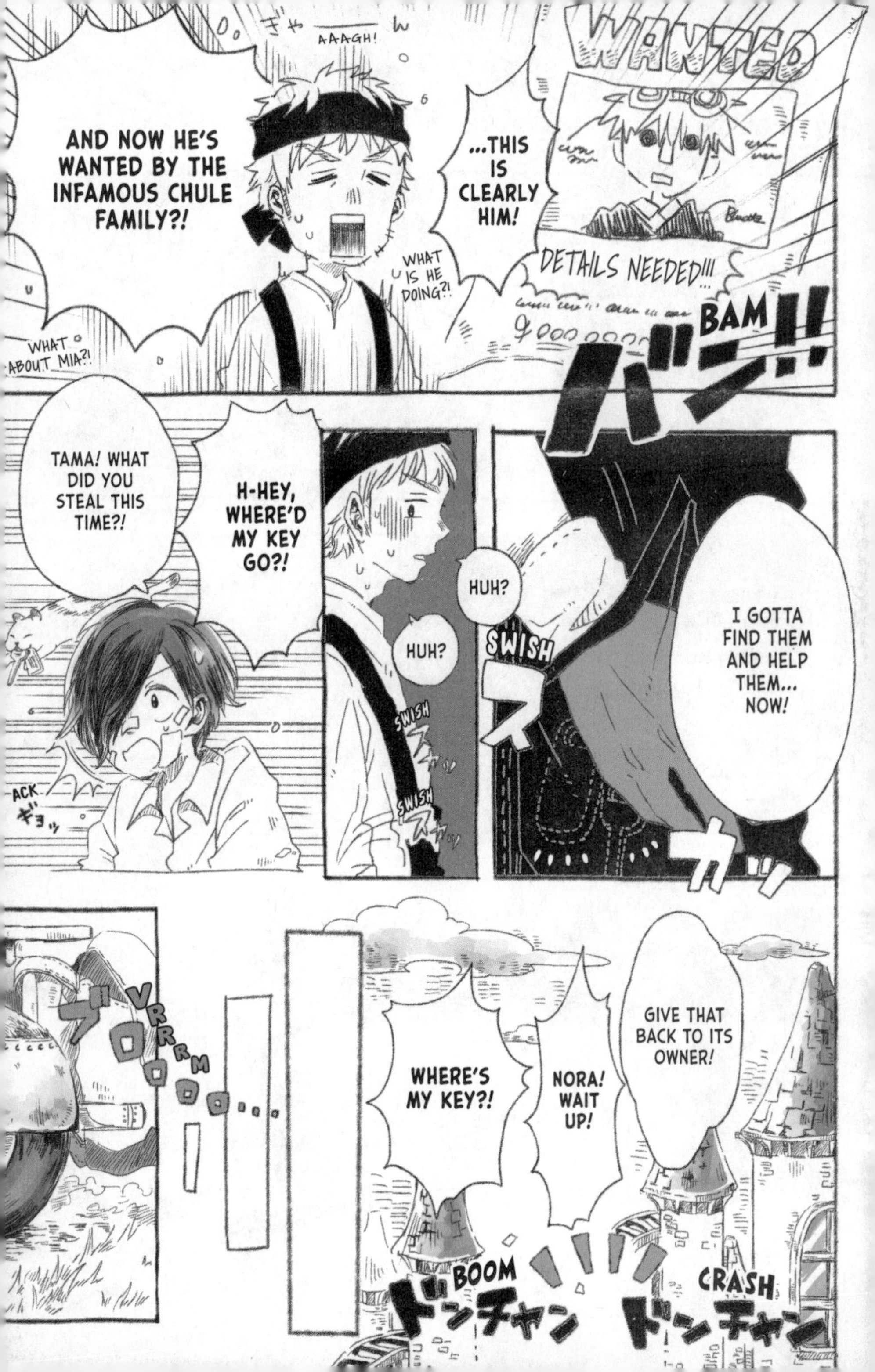
WANTED
...THIS IS CLEARLY HIM!
DETAILS NEEDED!!!
AAAGH!
AND NOW HE'S WANTED BY THE INFAMOUS CHULE FAMILY?!
WHAT IS HE DOING?!
WHAT ABOUT MIA?!
BAM
SWISH
I GOTTA FIND THEM AND HELP THEM... NOW!
HUH?
HUH?
SWISH
SWISH
H-HEY, WHERE'D MY KEY GO?!
TAMA! WHAT DID YOU STEAL THIS TIME?!
ACK
GIVE THAT BACK TO ITS OWNER!
NORA! WAIT UP!
WHERE'S MY KEY?!
CRASH
BOOM
VRRRM

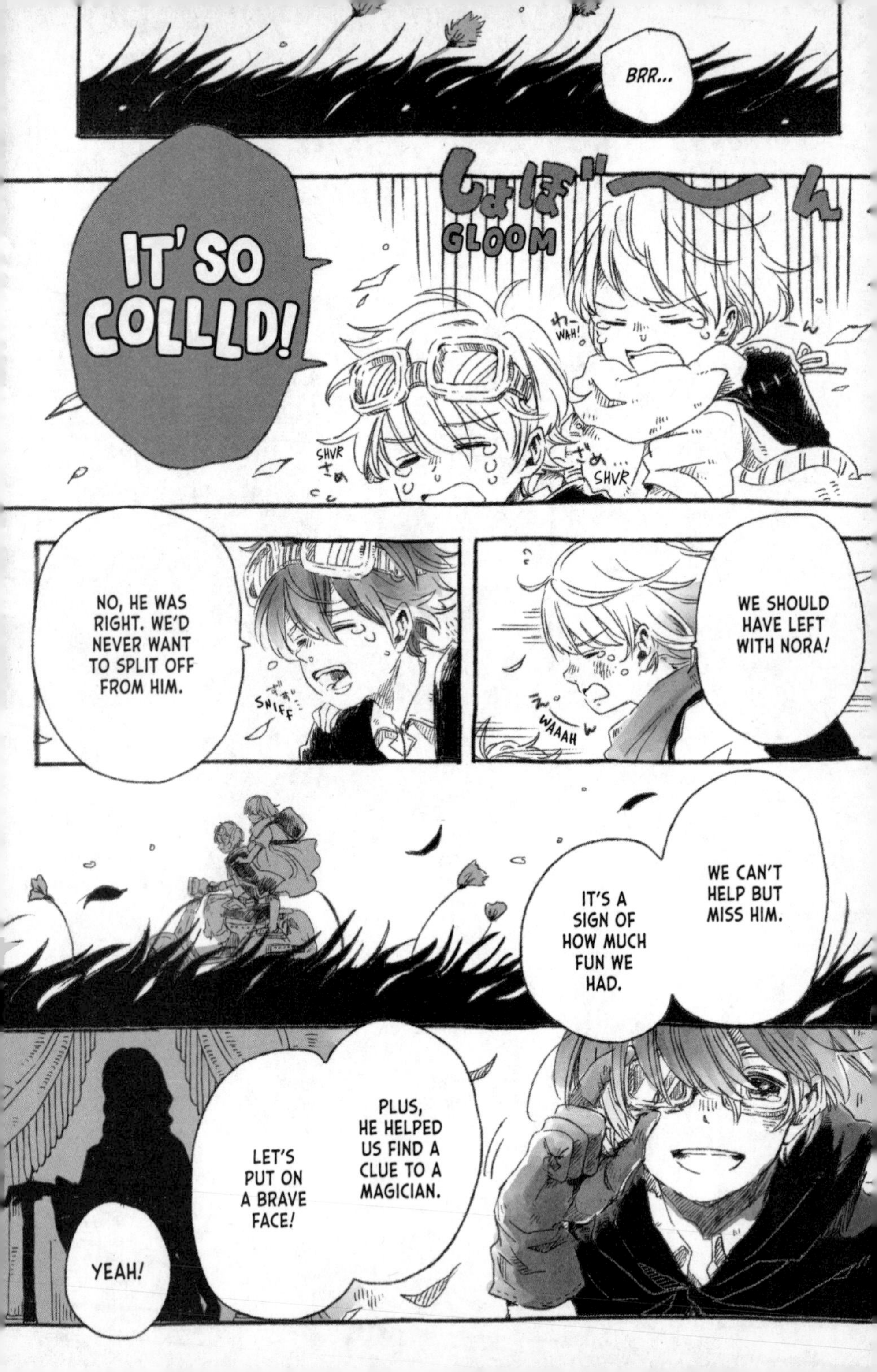
BRR...
しょぼーん
GLOOM
IT' SO COLLLD!
WAH!
SHVR
SHVR
WE SHOULD HAVE LEFT WITH NORA!
WAAAH
NO, HE WAS RIGHT. WE'D NEVER WANT TO SPLIT OFF FROM HIM.
SNIFF
WE CAN'T HELP BUT MISS HIM.
IT'S A SIGN OF HOW MUCH FUN WE HAD.
PLUS, HE HELPED US FIND A CLUE TO A MAGICIAN.
LET'S PUT ON A BRAVE FACE!
YEAH!

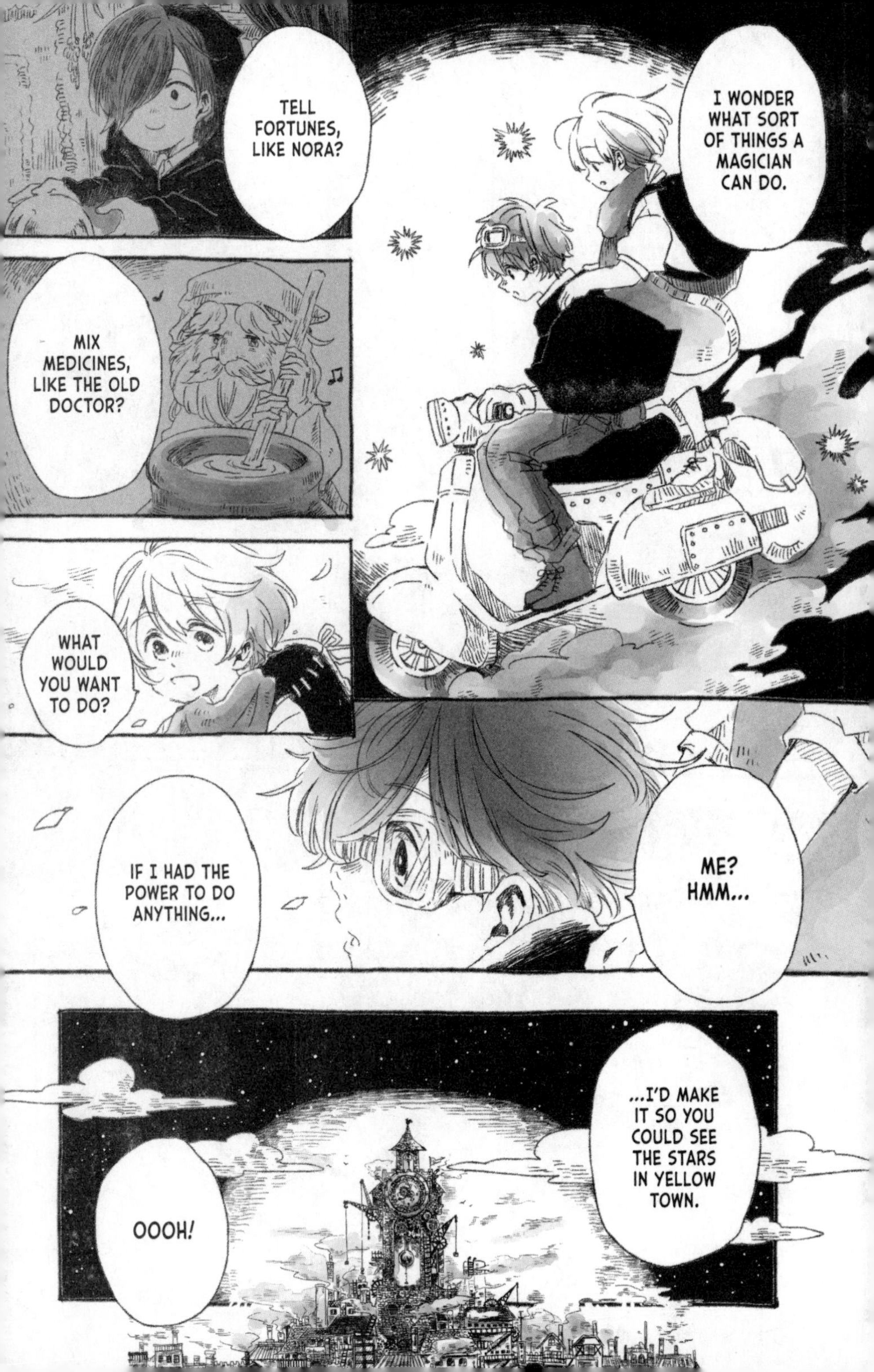
I WONDER WHAT SORT OF THINGS A MAGICIAN CAN DO.
TELL FORTUNES, LIKE NORA?
MIX MEDICINES, LIKE THE OLD DOCTOR?
WHAT WOULD YOU WANT TO DO?
ME? HMM...
IF I HAD THE POWER TO DO ANYTHING...
...I'D MAKE IT SO YOU COULD SEE THE STARS IN YELLOW TOWN.
OOOH!

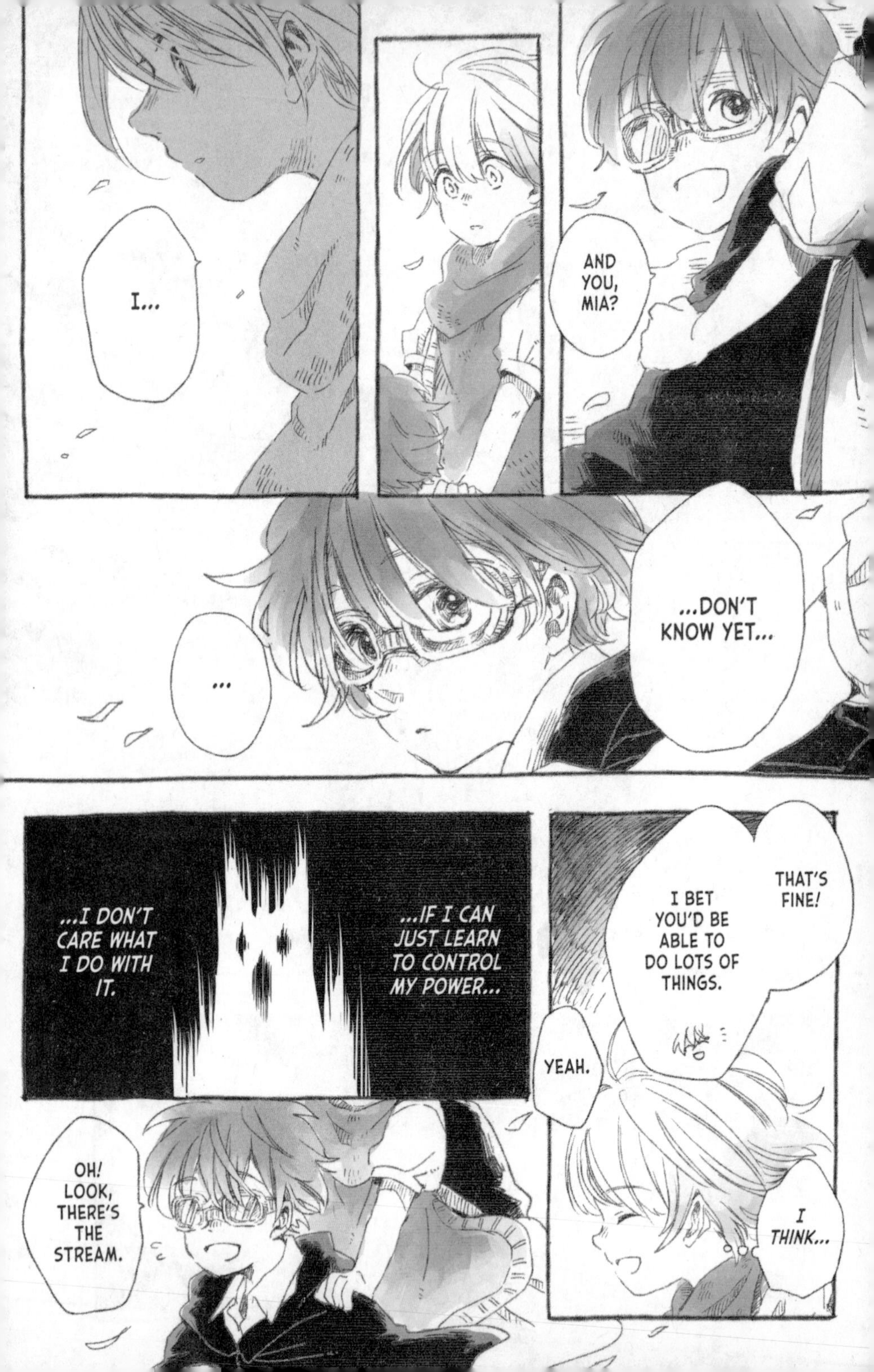
AND YOU, MIA?
I...
...DON'T KNOW YET...
...
THAT'S FINE!
I BET YOU'D BE ABLE TO DO LOTS OF THINGS.
YEAH.
I THINK...
...IF I CAN JUST LEARN TO CONTROL MY POWER...
...I DON'T CARE WHAT I DO WITH IT.
OH! LOOK, THERE'S THE STREAM.

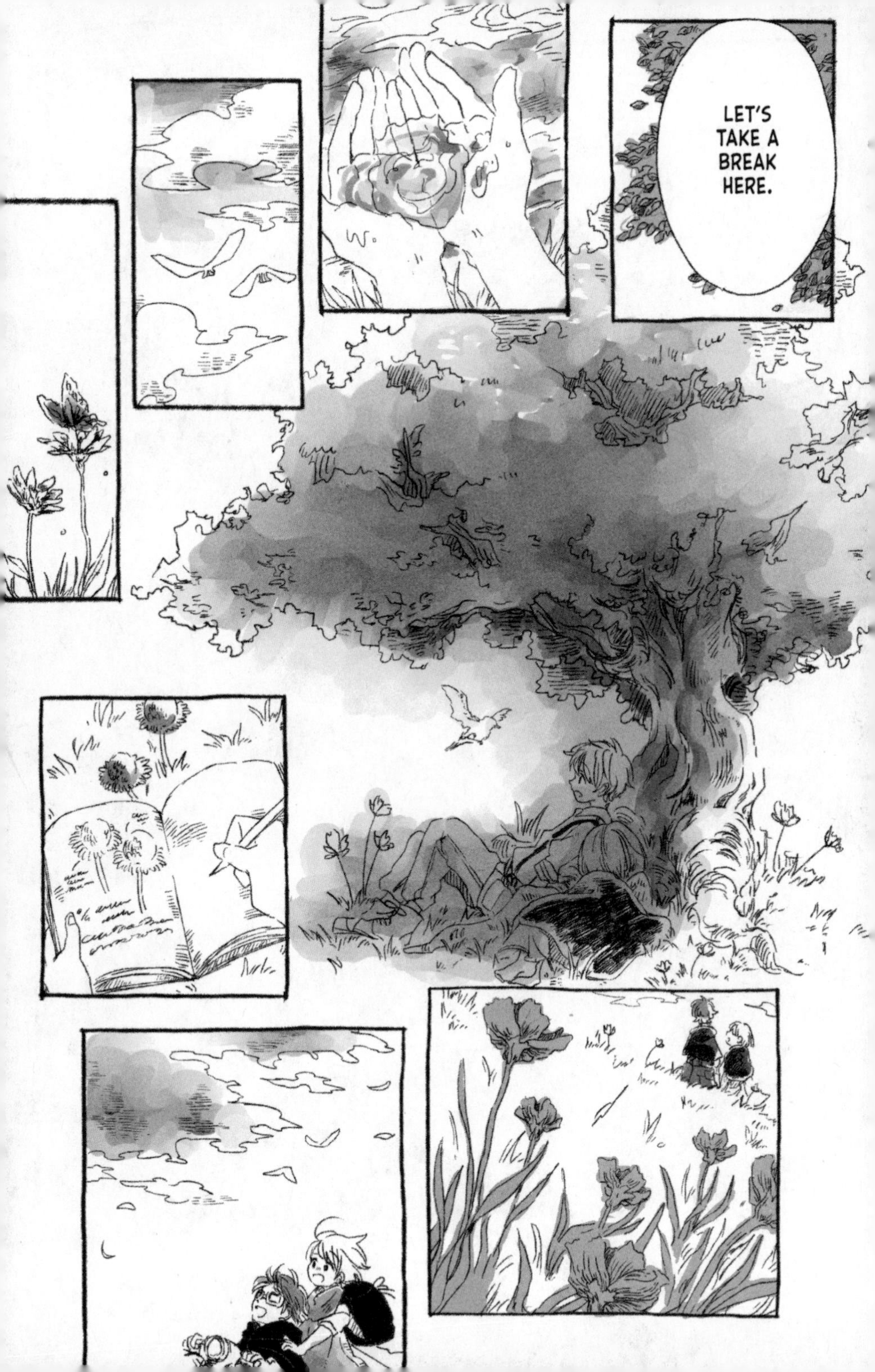
LET'S TAKE A BREAK HERE.

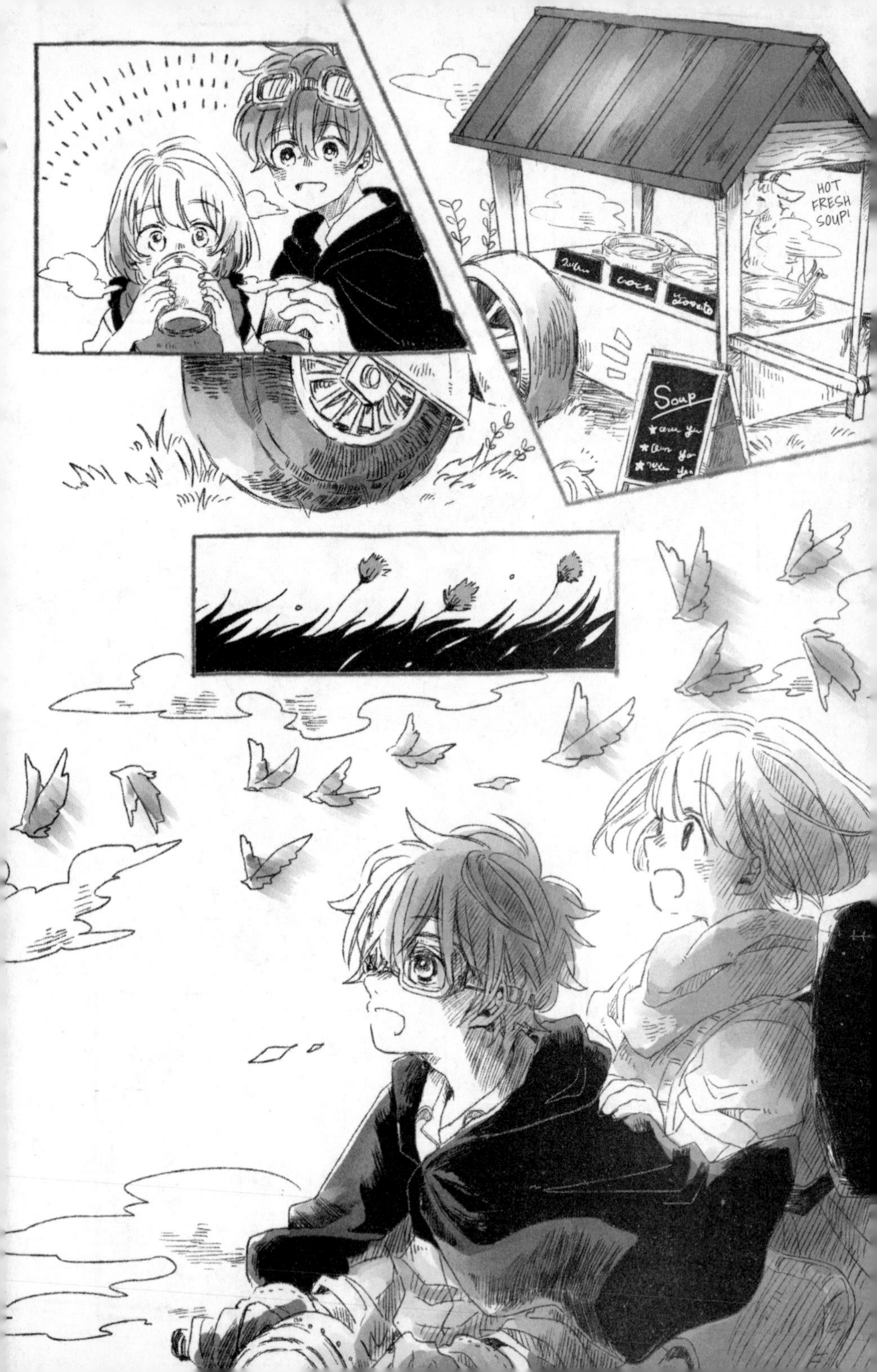
HOT FRESH SOUP!
Soup

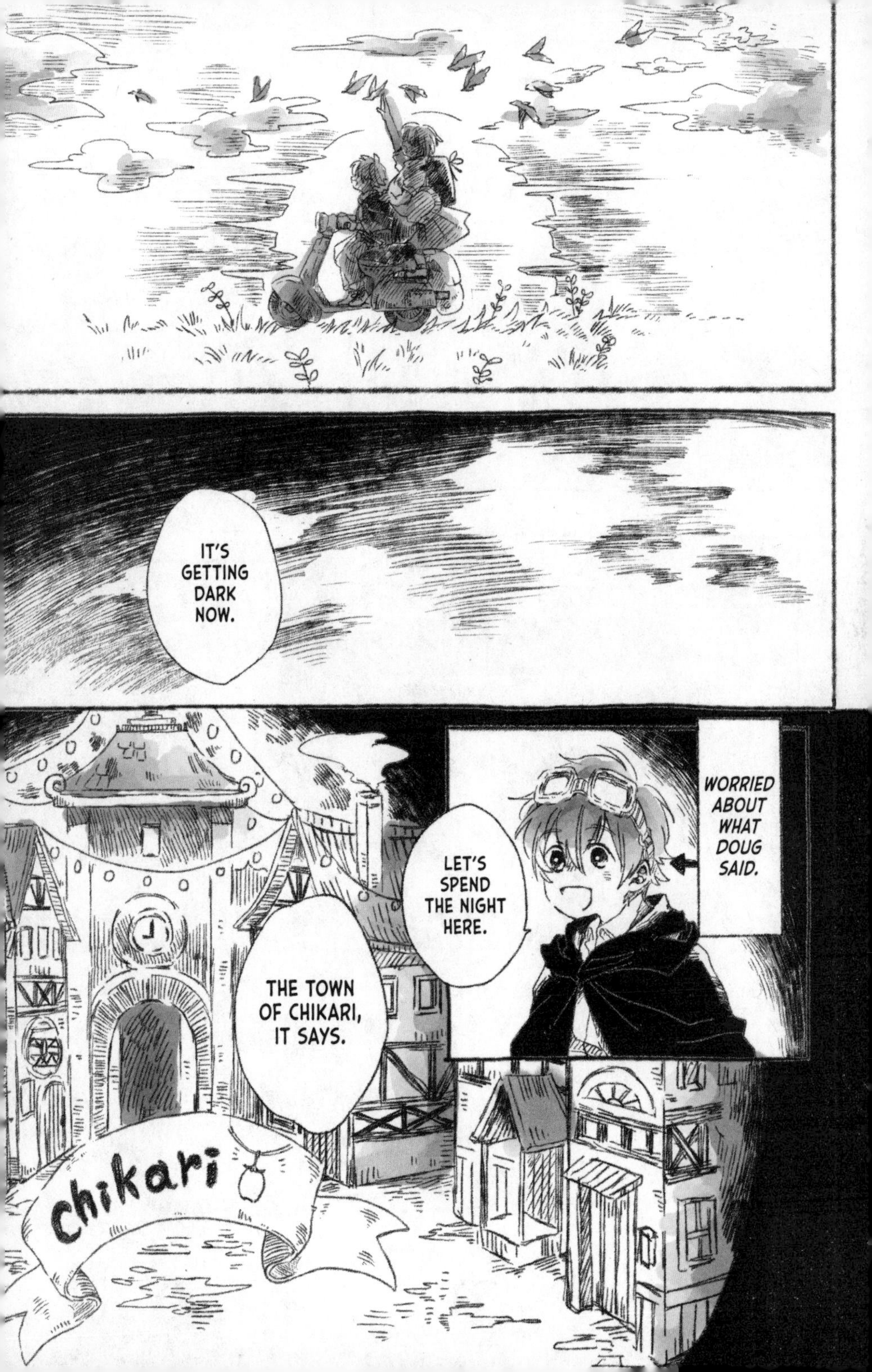
IT'S GETTING DARK NOW.
WORRIED ABOUT WHAT DOUG SAID.
LET'S SPEND THE NIGHT HERE.
THE TOWN OF CHIKARI, IT SAYS.
Chikari

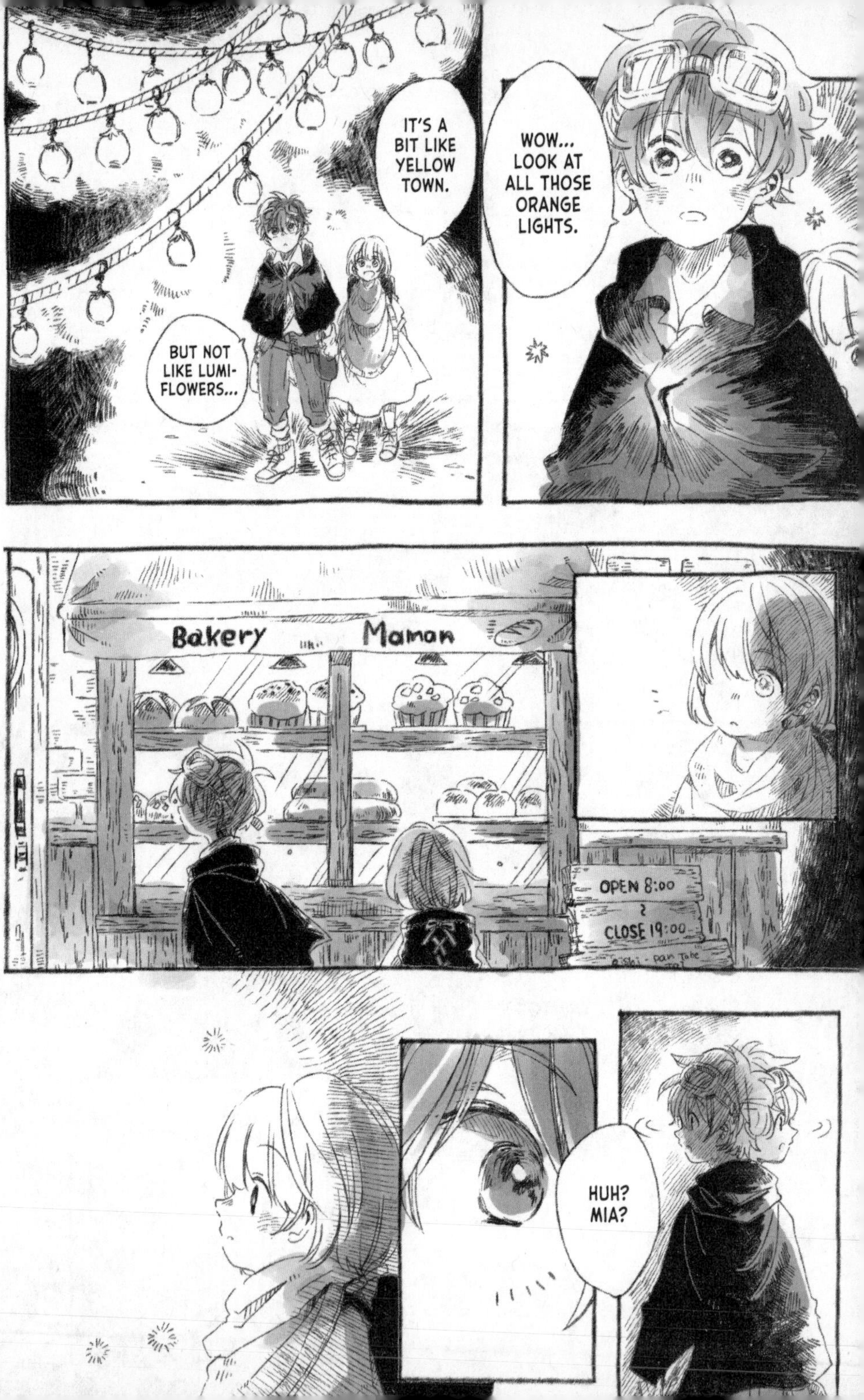
WOW... LOOK AT ALL THOSE ORANGE LIGHTS.
IT'S A BIT LIKE YELLOW TOWN.
BUT NOT LIKE LUMI-FLOWERS...
Bakery Maman
OPEN 8:00
CLOSE 19:00
HUH? MIA?

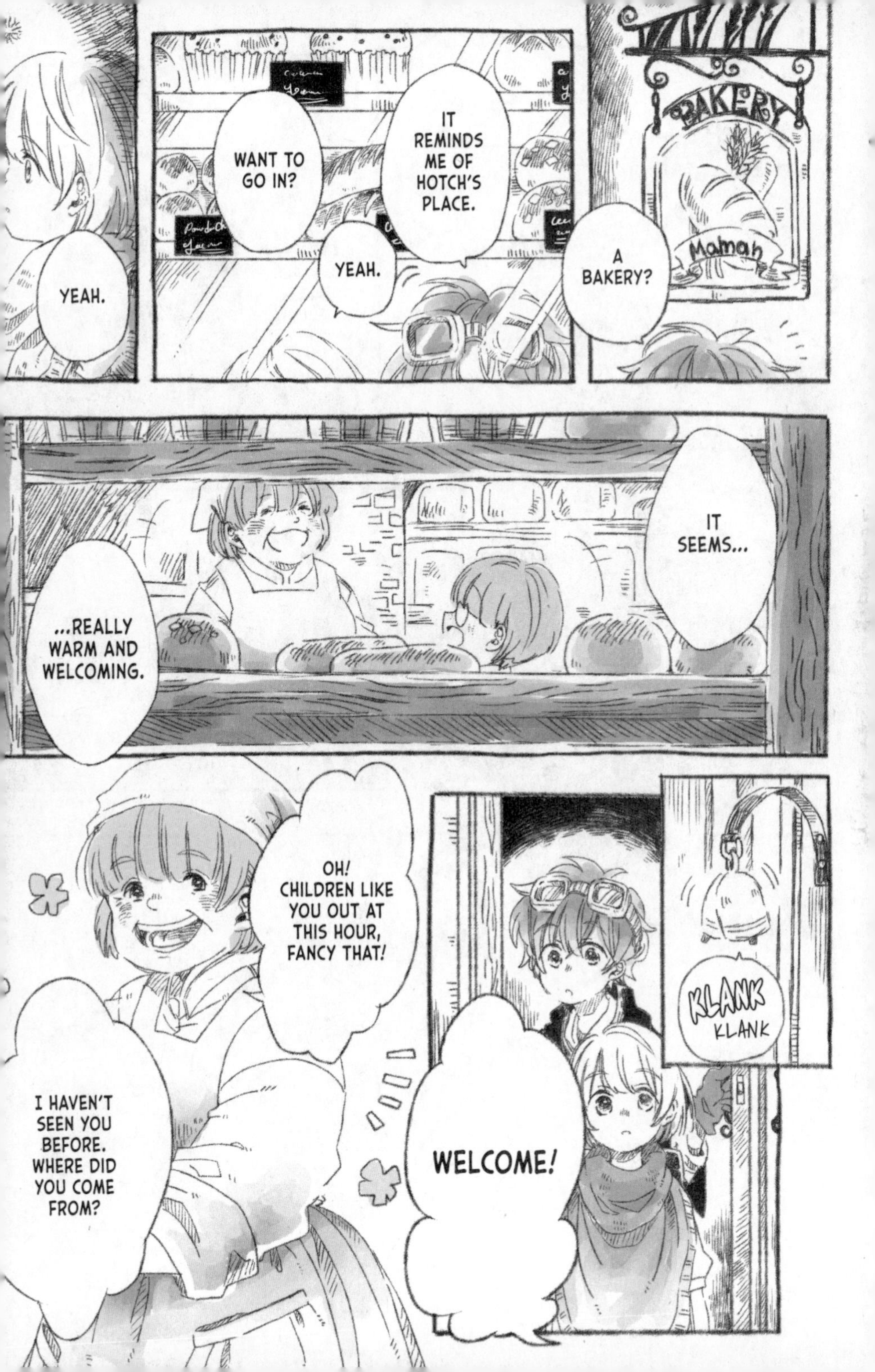
BAKERY
Maman
A BAKERY?
IT REMINDS ME OF HOTCH'S PLACE.
WANT TO GO IN?
YEAH.
YEAH.
IT SEEMS...
...REALLY WARM AND WELCOMING.
KLANK KLANK
WELCOME!
OH! CHILDREN LIKE YOU OUT AT THIS HOUR, FANCY THAT!
I HAVEN'T SEEN YOU BEFORE. WHERE DID YOU COME FROM?

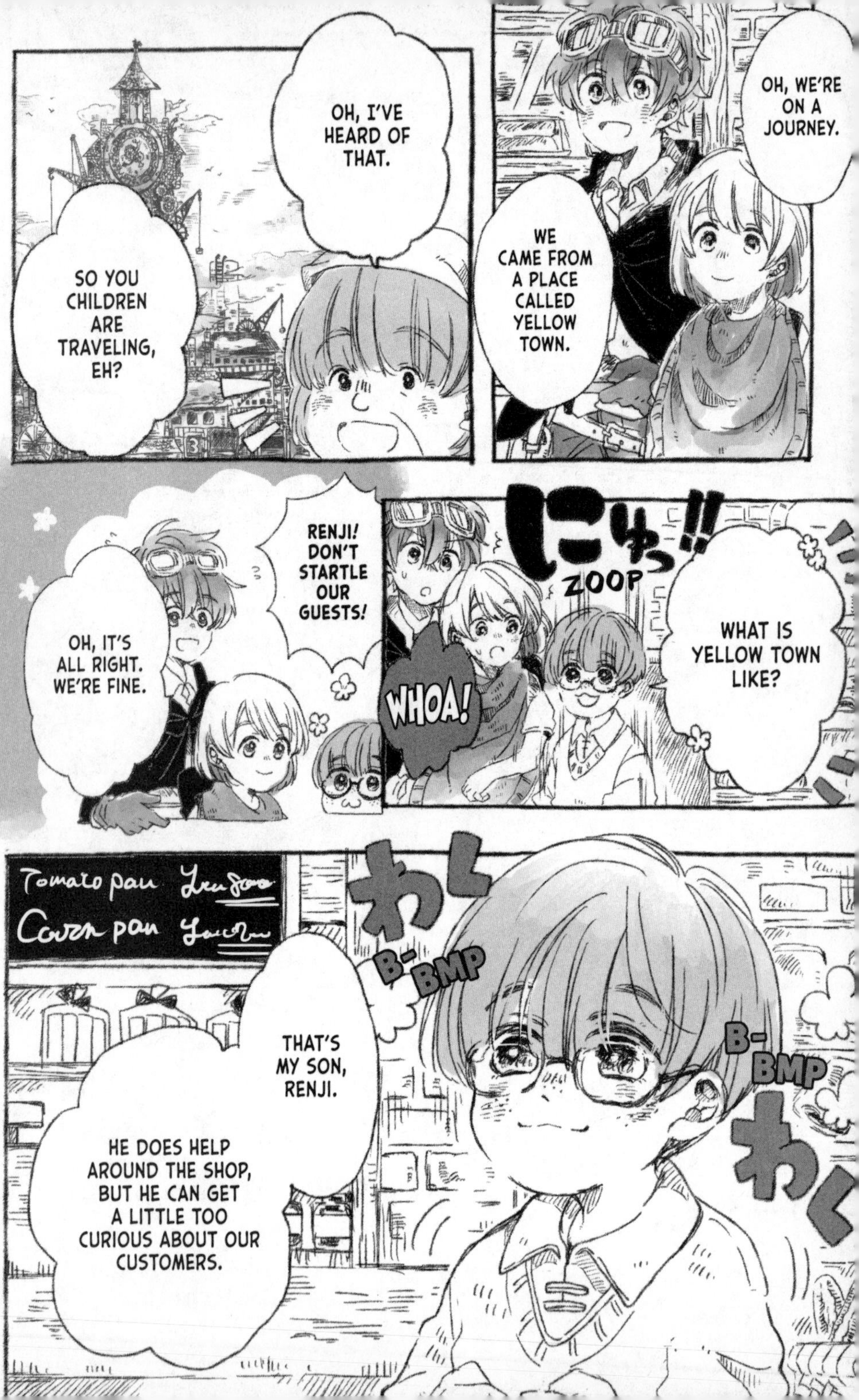
OH, WE'RE ON A JOURNEY.
WE CAME FROM A PLACE CALLED YELLOW TOWN.
OH, I'VE HEARD OF THAT.
SO YOU CHILDREN ARE TRAVELING, EH?
にゅっ!!
ZOOP
WHAT IS YELLOW TOWN LIKE?
WHOA!
RENJI! DON'T STARTLE OUR GUESTS!
OH, IT'S ALL RIGHT. WE'RE FINE.
わく
B-BMP
B-BMP
わく
Tomato pan
Corn pan
THAT'S MY SON, RENJI.
HE DOES HELP AROUND THE SHOP, BUT HE CAN GET A LITTLE TOO CURIOUS ABOUT OUR CUSTOMERS.

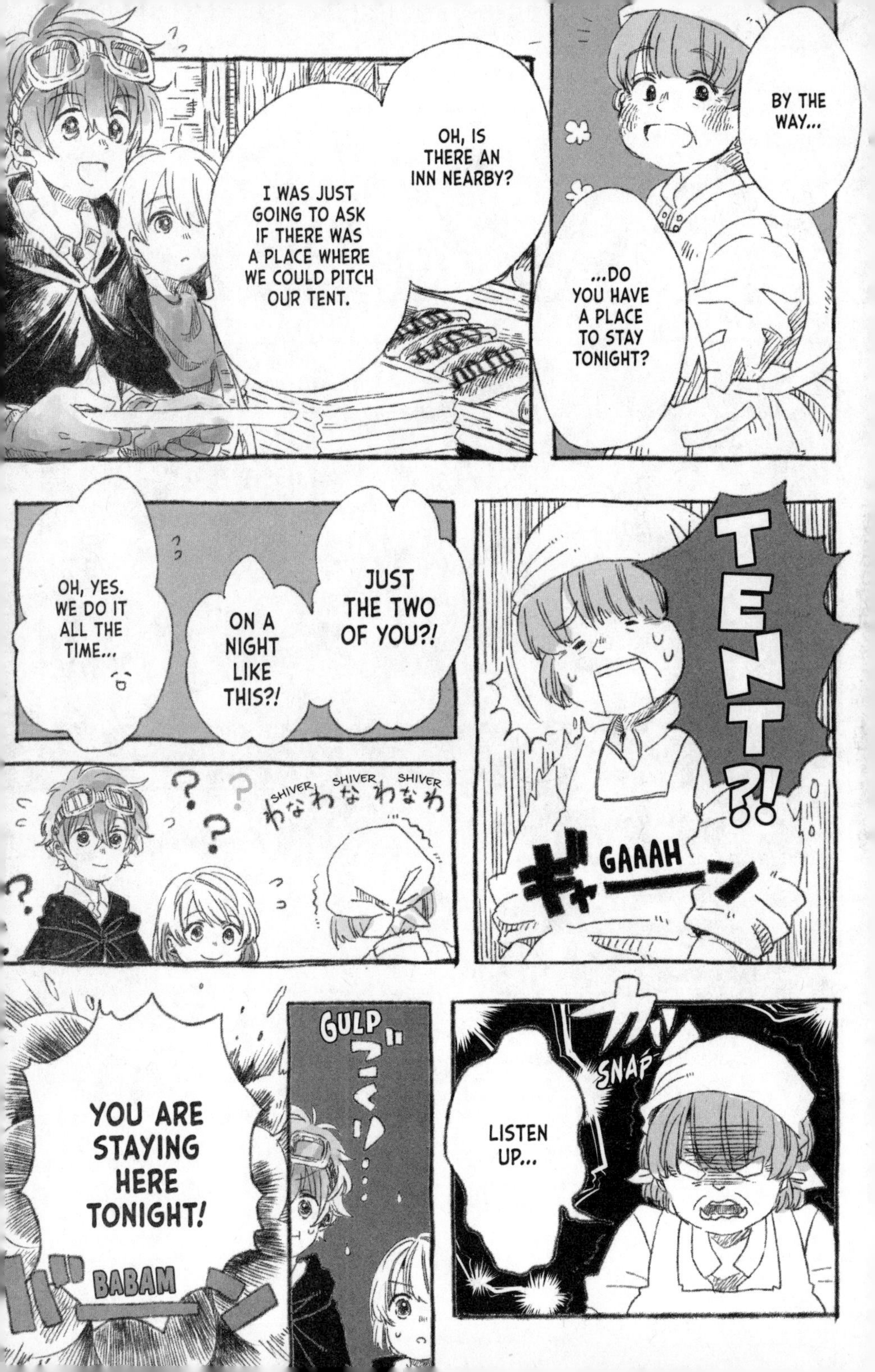
BY THE WAY...
...DO YOU HAVE A PLACE TO STAY TONIGHT?
OH, IS THERE AN INN NEARBY?
I WAS JUST GOING TO ASK IF THERE WAS A PLACE WHERE WE COULD PITCH OUR TENT.
TENT?!
GAAAH
JUST THE TWO OF YOU?!
ON A NIGHT LIKE THIS?!
OH, YES. WE DO IT ALL THE TIME...
SHIVER SHIVER SHIVER
SNAP
LISTEN UP...
GULP
YOU ARE STAYING HERE TONIGHT!
BABAM

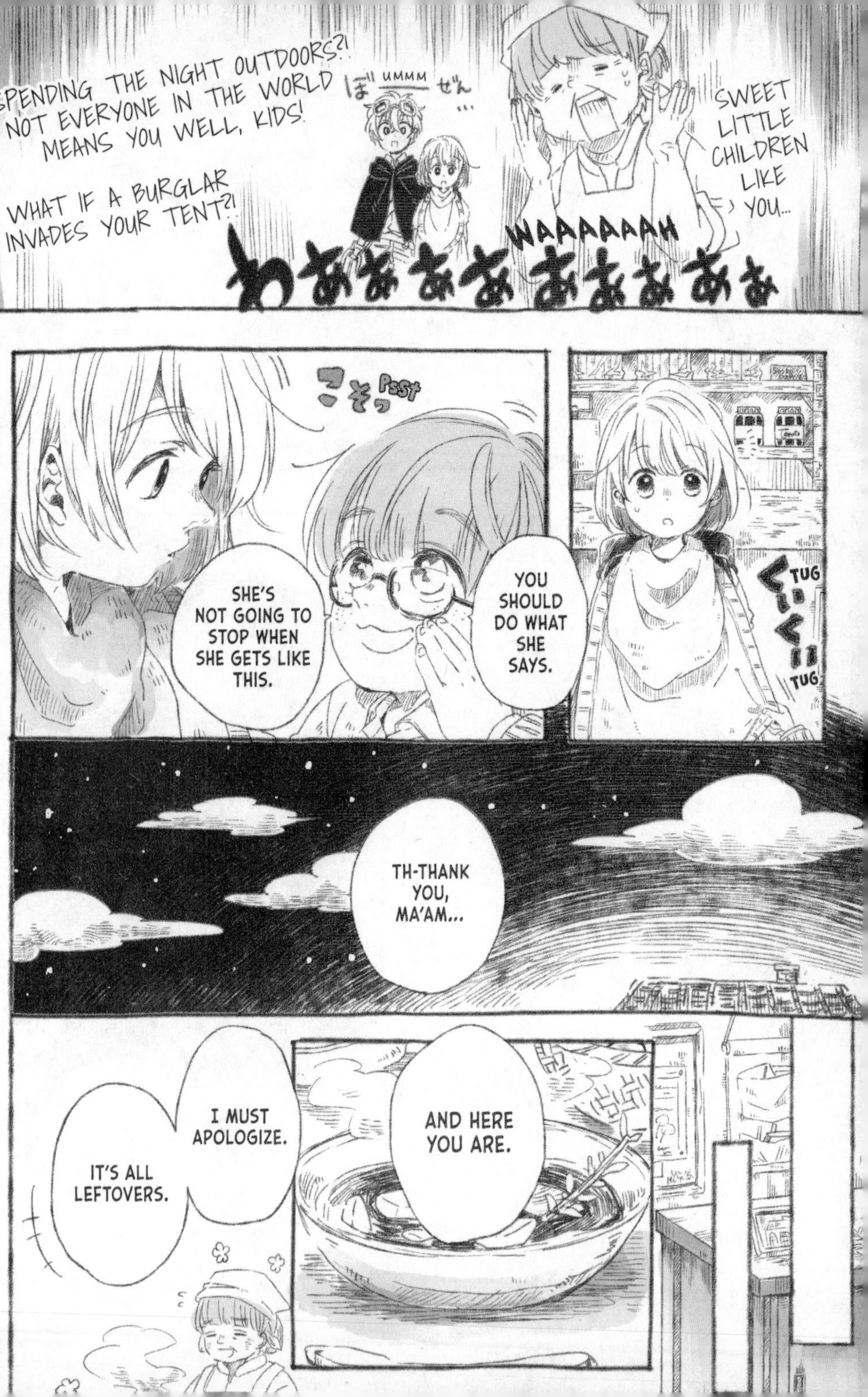
SWEET LITTLE CHILDREN LIKE YOU...
UMMM
...SPENDING THE NIGHT OUTDOORS?! NOT EVERYONE IN THE WORLD MEANS YOU WELL, KIDS!
WHAT IF A BURGLAR INVADES YOUR TENT?!
WAAAAAAH
TUG TUG
PSST
YOU SHOULD DO WHAT SHE SAYS.
SHE'S NOT GOING TO STOP WHEN SHE GETS LIKE THIS.
TH-THANK YOU, MA'AM...
AND HERE YOU ARE.
I MUST APOLOGIZE.
IT'S ALL LEFTOVERS.

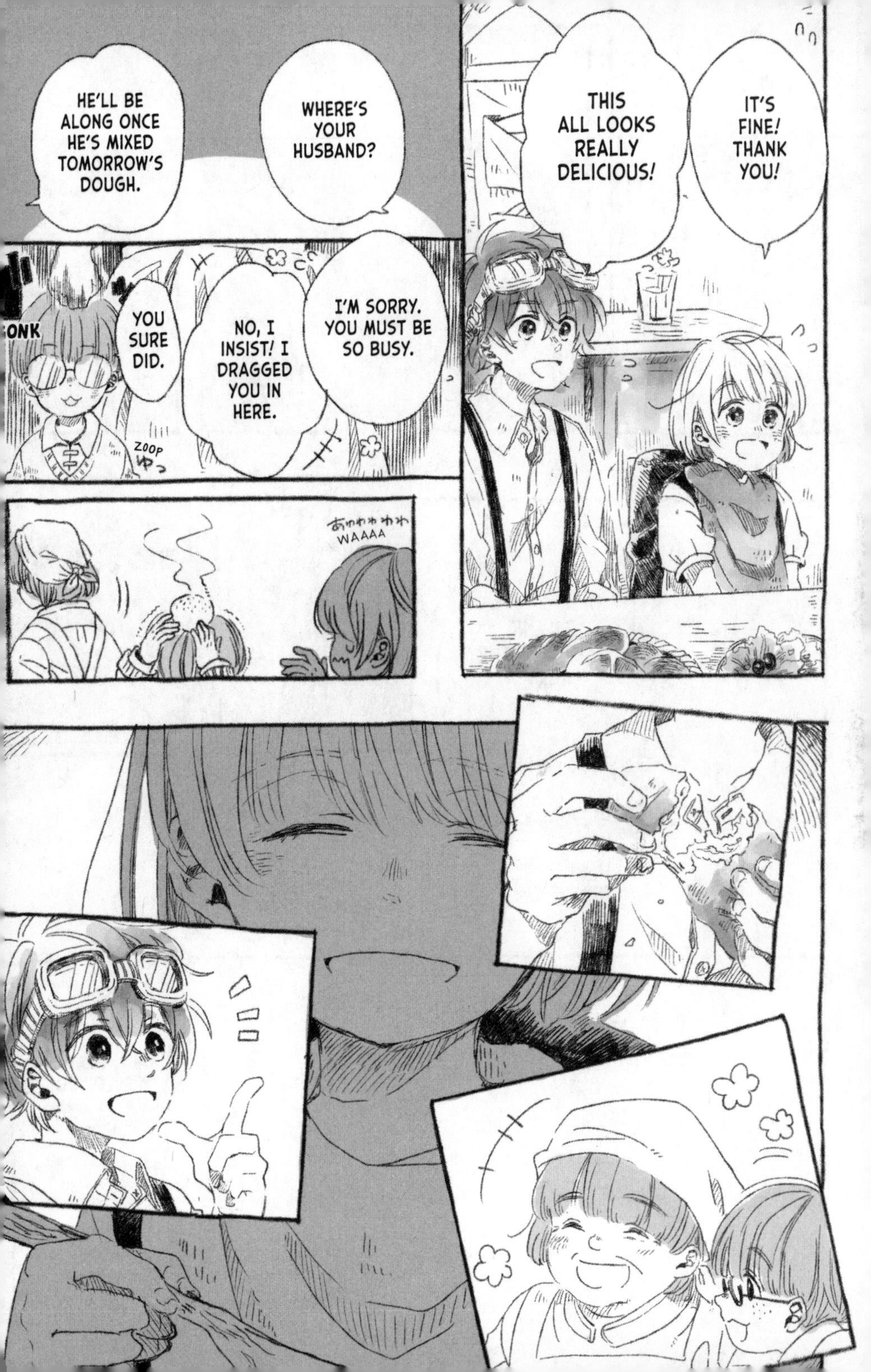
IT'S FINE! THANK YOU!
THIS ALL LOOKS REALLY DELICIOUS!
WHERE'S YOUR HUSBAND?
HE'LL BE ALONG ONCE HE'S MIXED TOMORROW'S DOUGH.
I'M SORRY. YOU MUST BE SO BUSY.
NO, I INSIST! I DRAGGED YOU IN HERE.
YOU SURE DID.
ZOOP
ゆっ
ONK
あわわわわわ
WAAAA

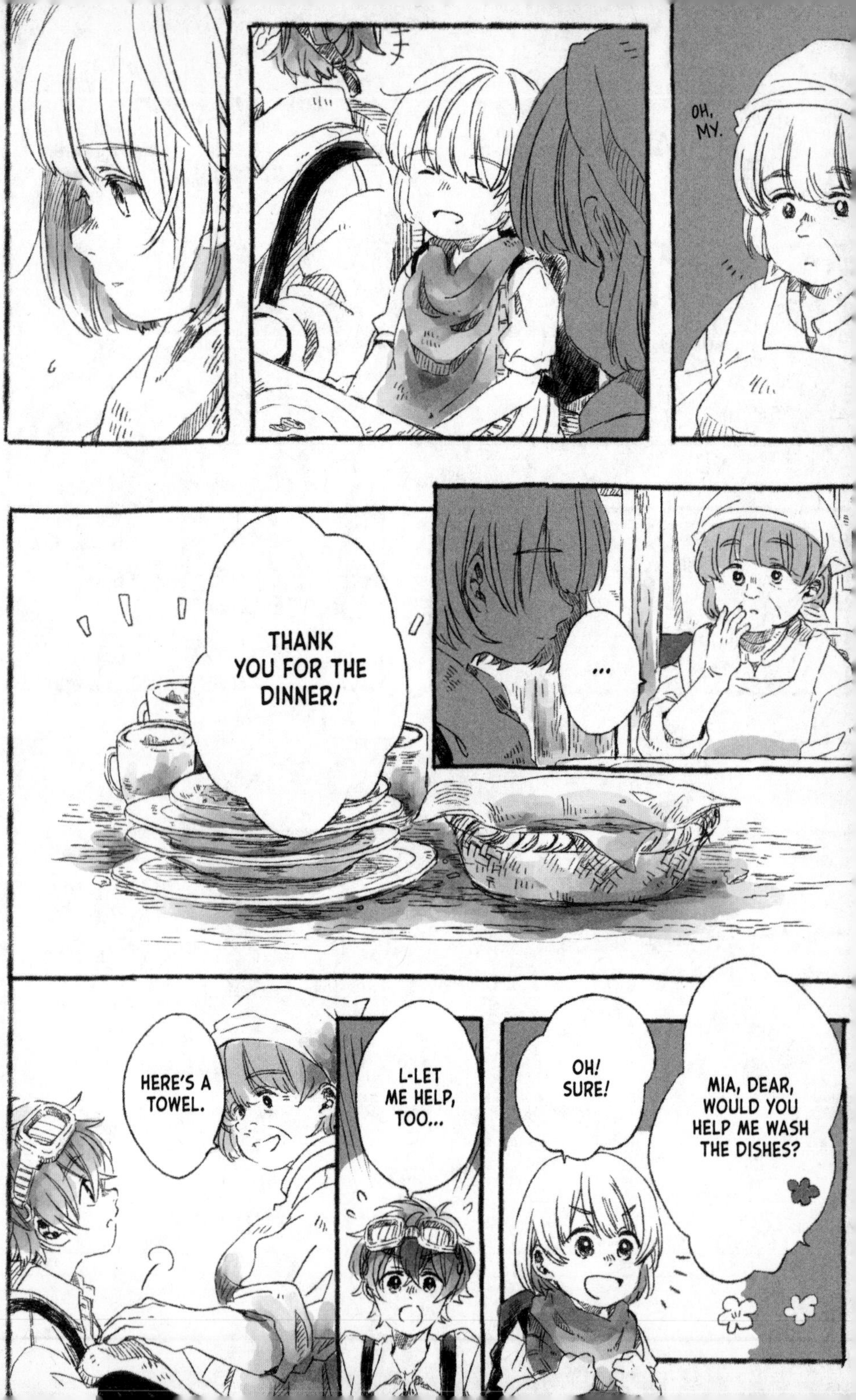
OH, MY.
...
THANK YOU FOR THE DINNER!
MIA, DEAR, WOULD YOU HELP ME WASH THE DISHES?
OH! SURE!
L-LET ME HELP, TOO...
HERE'S A TOWEL.

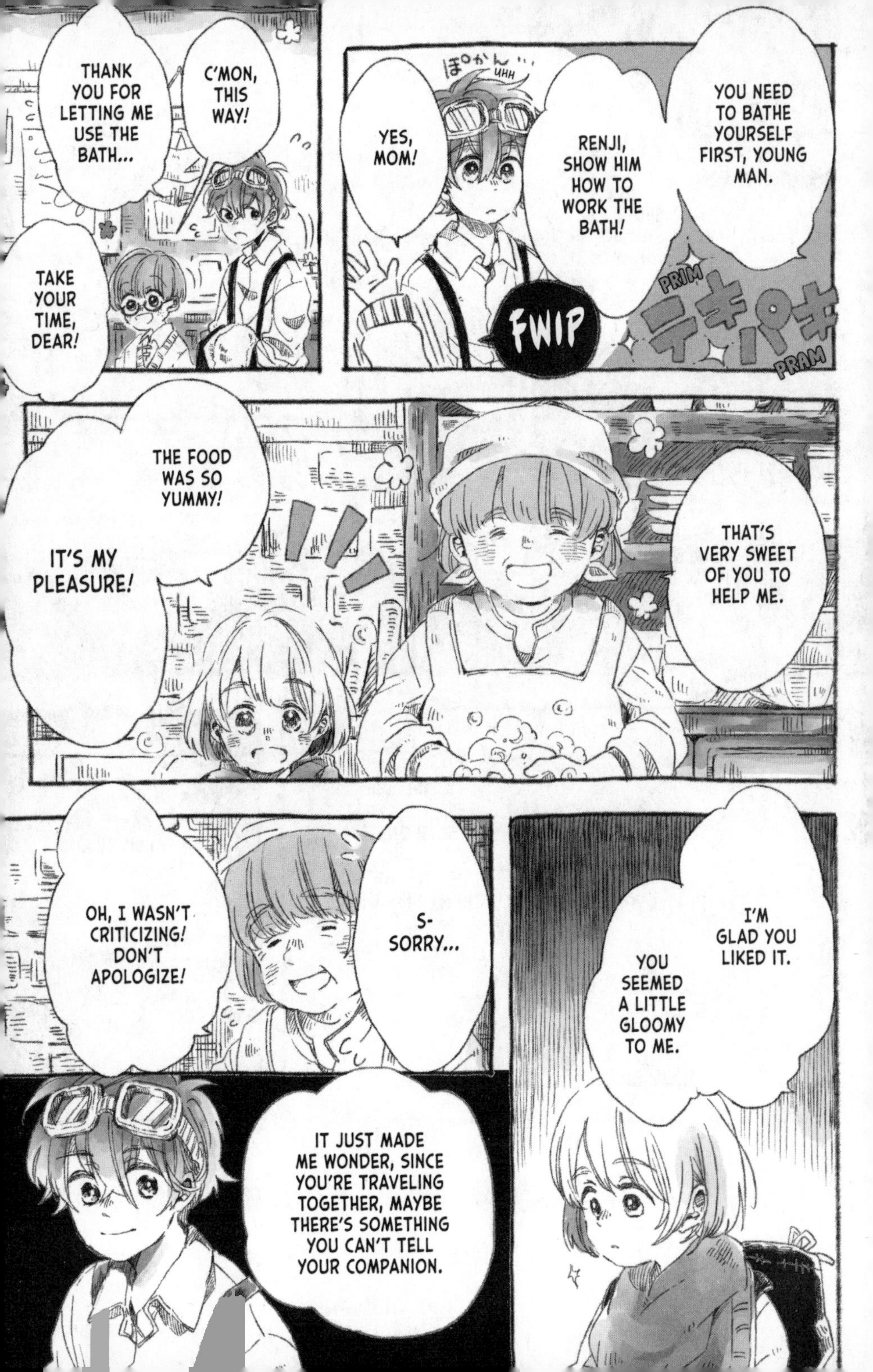
YOU NEED TO BATHE YOURSELF FIRST, YOUNG MAN.
RENJI, SHOW HIM HOW TO WORK THE BATH!
ぽかん UHH
YES, MOM!
FWIP
PRIM テキパキ PRAM
C'MON, THIS WAY!
THANK YOU FOR LETTING ME USE THE BATH...
TAKE YOUR TIME, DEAR!
THAT'S VERY SWEET OF YOU TO HELP ME.
THE FOOD WAS SO YUMMY!
IT'S MY PLEASURE!
I'M GLAD YOU LIKED IT.
YOU SEEMED A LITTLE GLOOMY TO ME.
S-SORRY...
OH, I WASN'T CRITICIZING! DON'T APOLOGIZE!
IT JUST MADE ME WONDER, SINCE YOU'RE TRAVELING TOGETHER, MAYBE THERE'S SOMETHING YOU CAN'T TELL YOUR COMPANION.

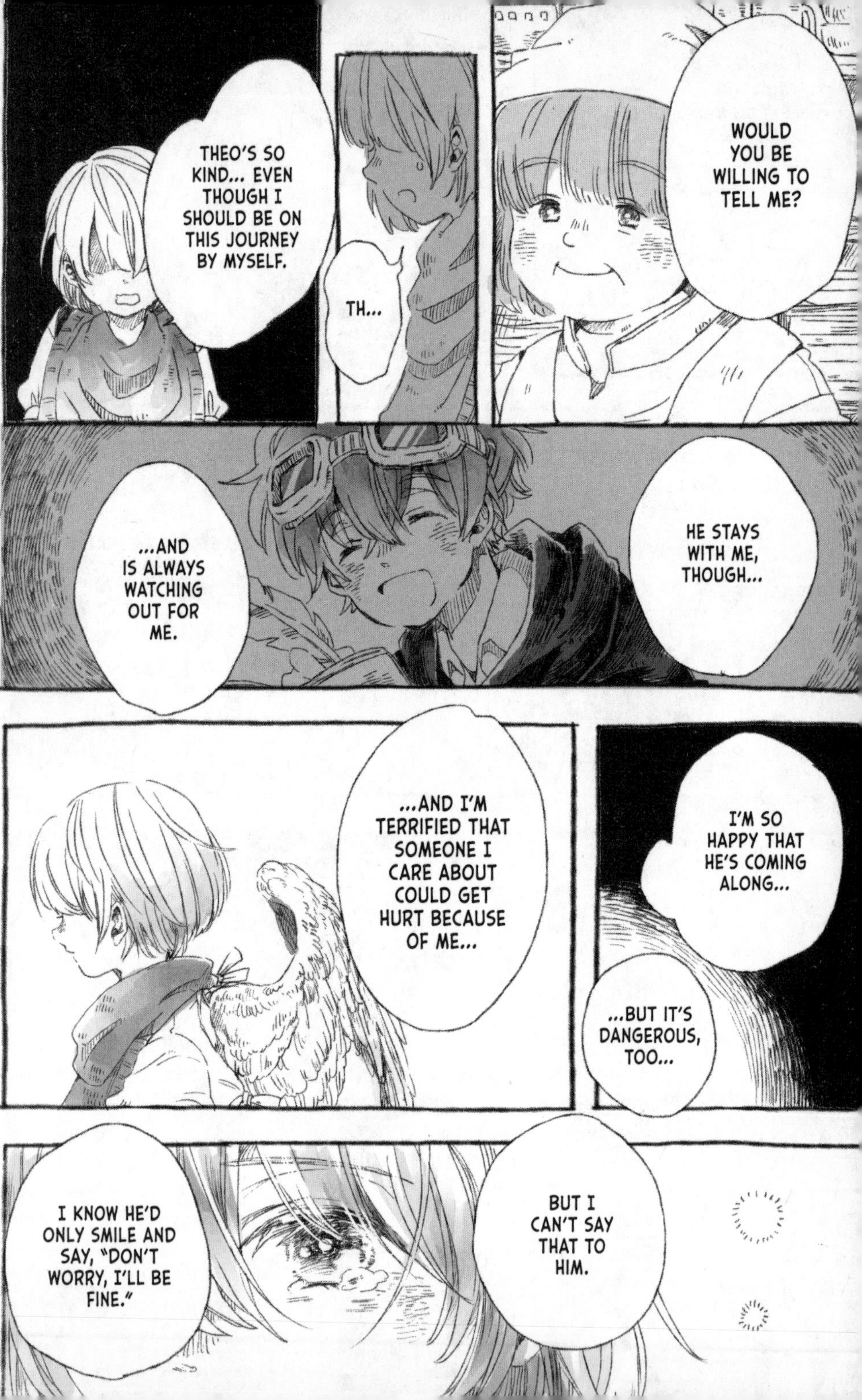
WOULD YOU BE WILLING TO TELL ME?
TH...
THEO'S SO KIND... EVEN THOUGH I SHOULD BE ON THIS JOURNEY BY MYSELF.
HE STAYS WITH ME, THOUGH...
...AND IS ALWAYS WATCHING OUT FOR ME.
I'M SO HAPPY THAT HE'S COMING ALONG...
...BUT IT'S DANGEROUS, TOO...
...AND I'M TERRIFIED THAT SOMEONE I CARE ABOUT COULD GET HURT BECAUSE OF ME...
BUT I CAN'T SAY THAT TO HIM.
I KNOW HE'D ONLY SMILE AND SAY, "DON'T WORRY, I'LL BE FINE."

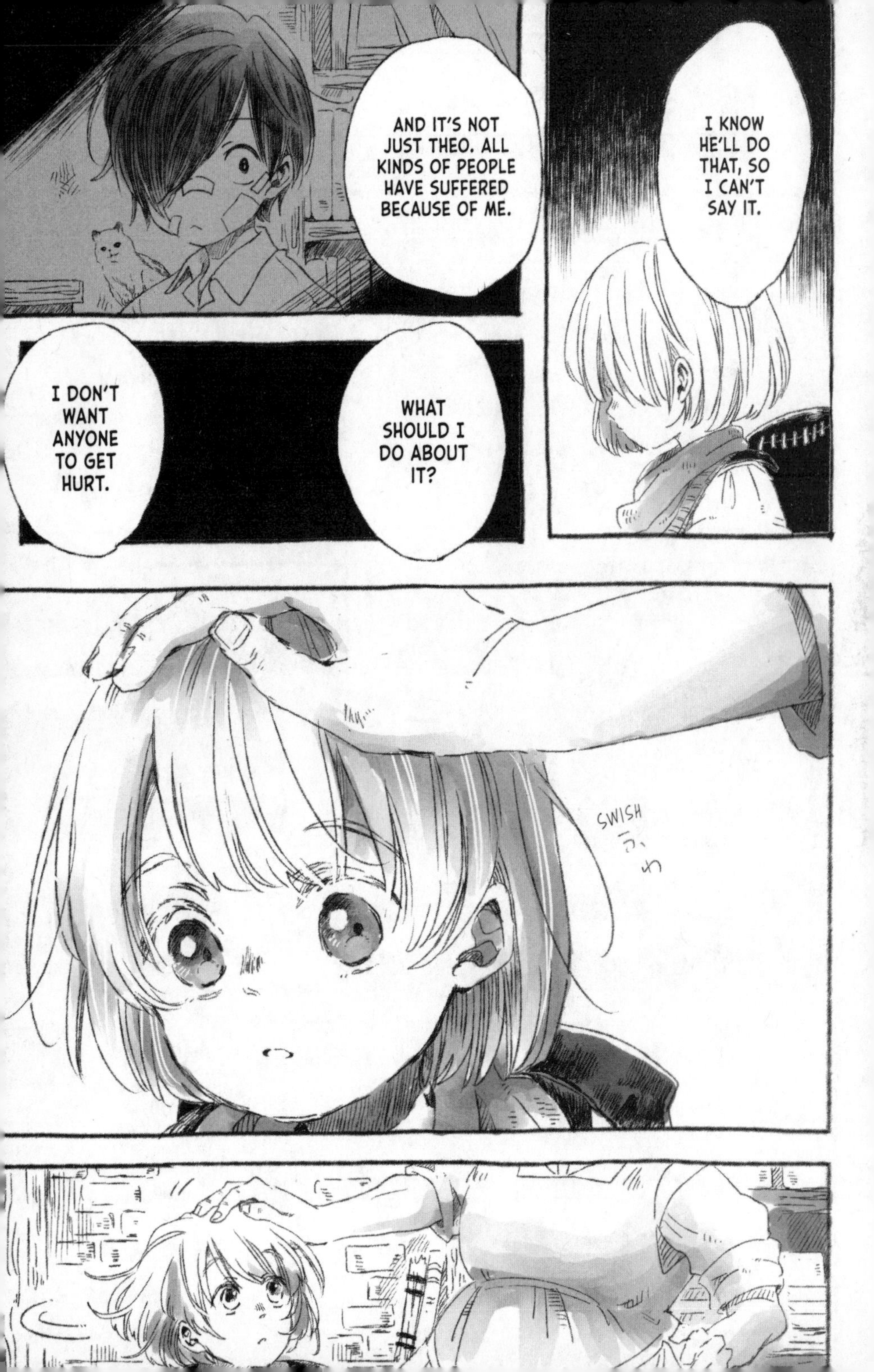
I KNOW HE'LL DO THAT, SO I CAN'T SAY IT.
AND IT'S NOT JUST THEO. ALL KINDS OF PEOPLE HAVE SUFFERED BECAUSE OF ME.
WHAT SHOULD I DO ABOUT IT?
I DON'T WANT ANYONE TO GET HURT.
SWISH
ふわ

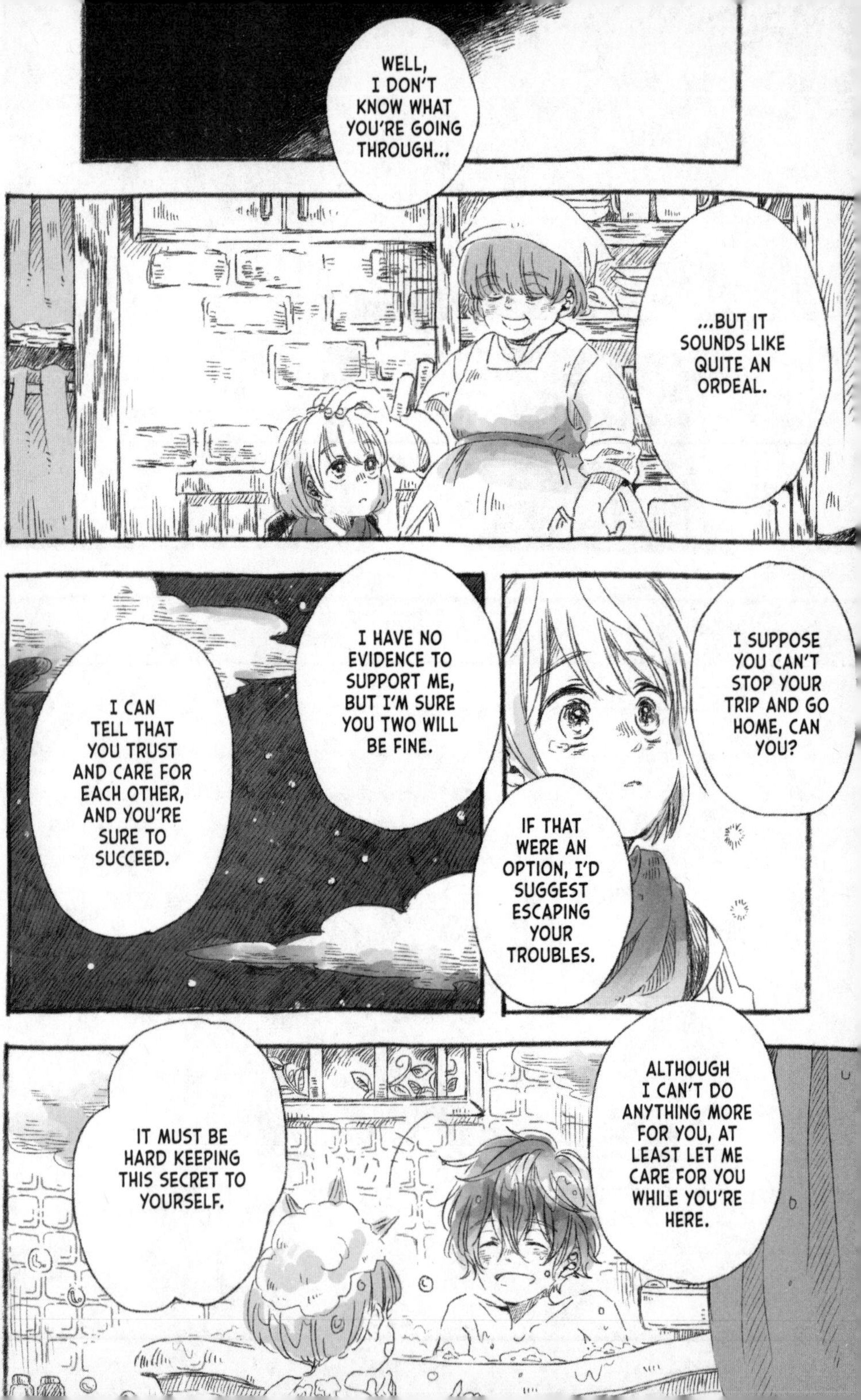
WELL, I DON'T KNOW WHAT YOU'RE GOING THROUGH...
...BUT IT SOUNDS LIKE QUITE AN ORDEAL.
I SUPPOSE YOU CAN'T STOP YOUR TRIP AND GO HOME, CAN YOU?
IF THAT WERE AN OPTION, I'D SUGGEST ESCAPING YOUR TROUBLES.
I HAVE NO EVIDENCE TO SUPPORT ME, BUT I'M SURE YOU TWO WILL BE FINE.
I CAN TELL THAT YOU TRUST AND CARE FOR EACH OTHER, AND YOU'RE SURE TO SUCCEED.
ALTHOUGH I CAN'T DO ANYTHING MORE FOR YOU, AT LEAST LET ME CARE FOR YOU WHILE YOU'RE HERE.
IT MUST BE HARD KEEPING THIS SECRET TO YOURSELF.

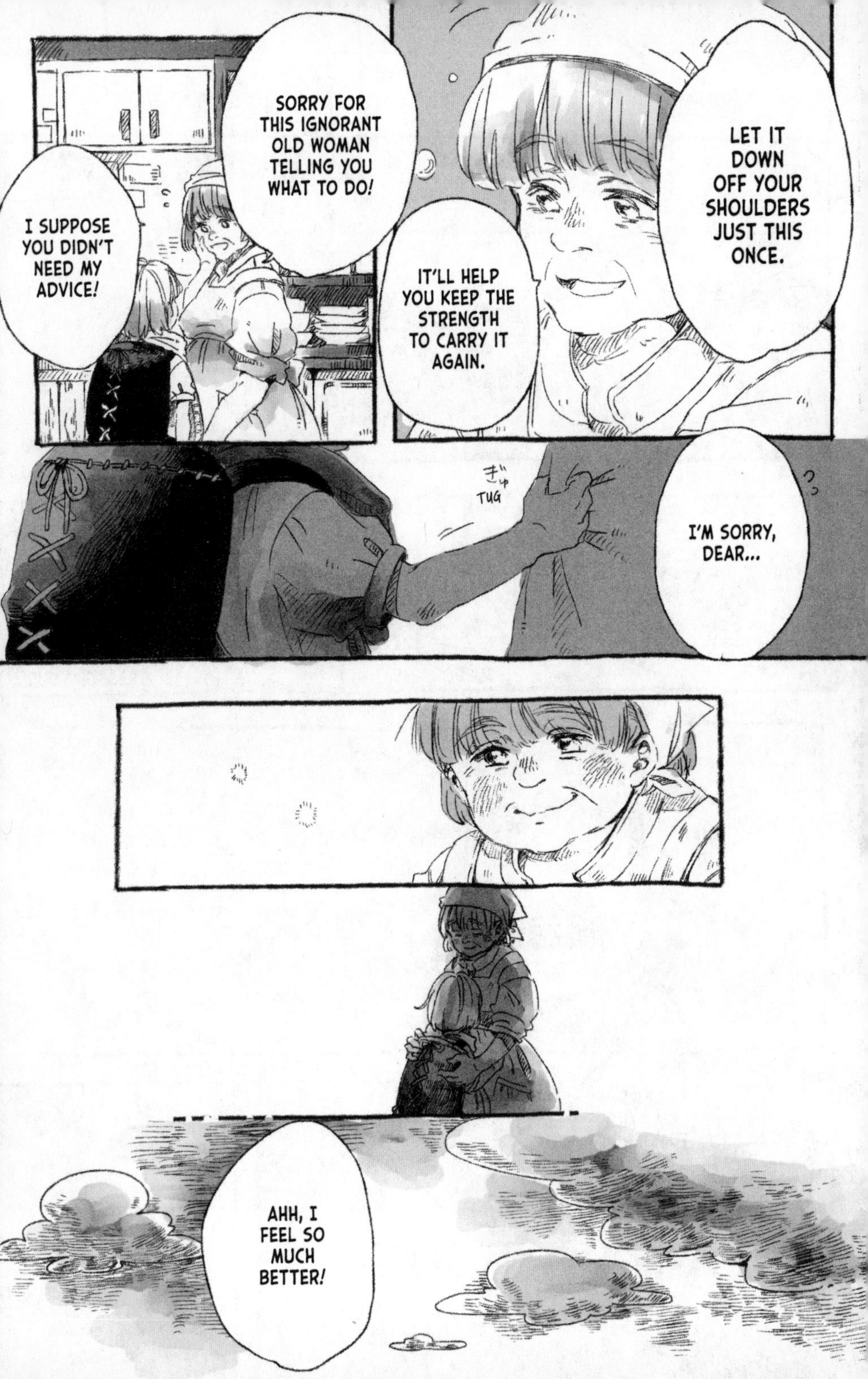
LET IT DOWN OFF YOUR SHOULDERS JUST THIS ONCE.
IT'LL HELP YOU KEEP THE STRENGTH TO CARRY IT AGAIN.
SORRY FOR THIS IGNORANT OLD WOMAN TELLING YOU WHAT TO DO!
I SUPPOSE YOU DIDN'T NEED MY ADVICE!
I'M SORRY, DEAR...
ぎゅ
TUG
AHH, I FEEL SO MUCH BETTER!

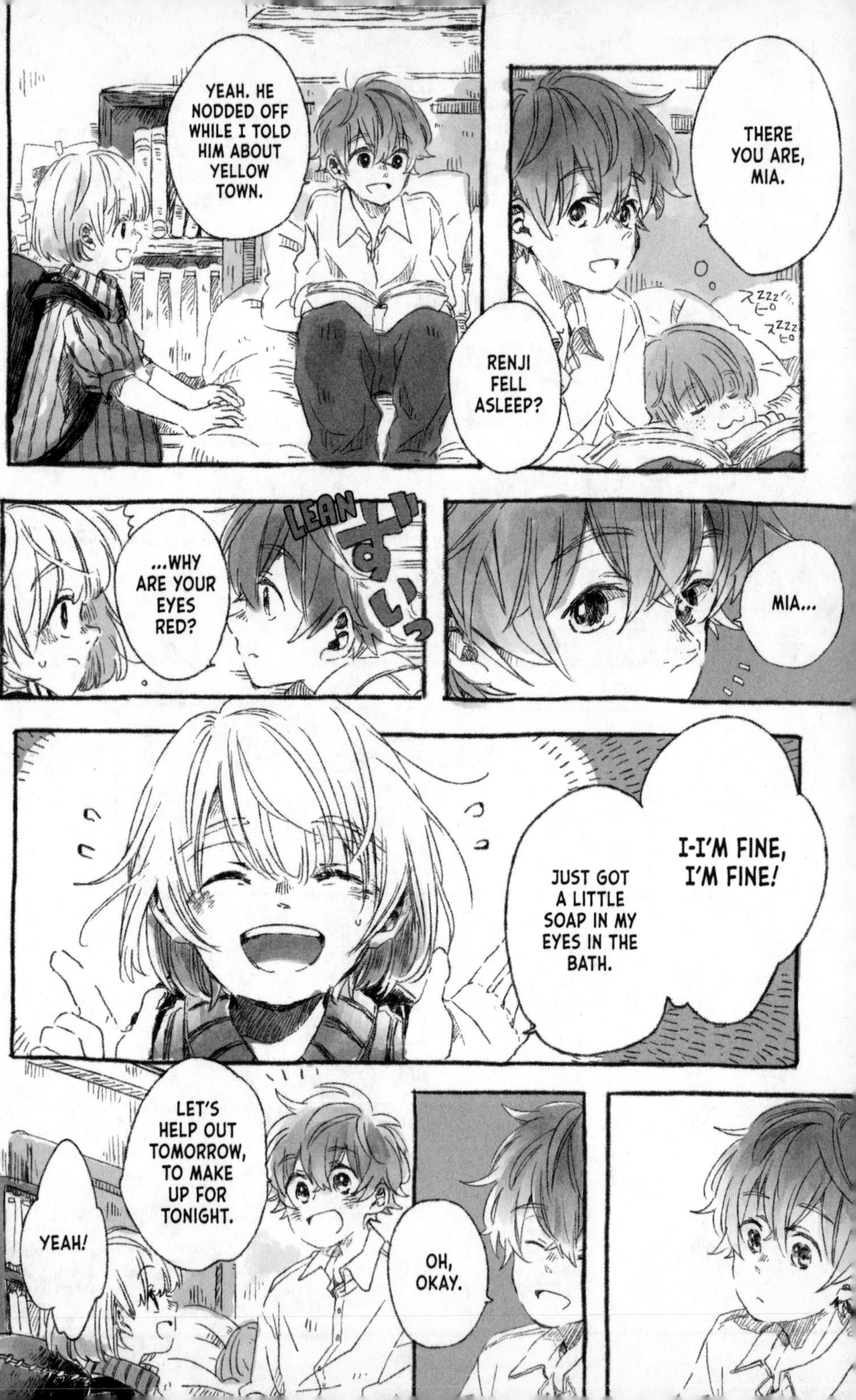
THERE YOU ARE, MIA.
RENJI FELL ASLEEP?
YEAH. HE NODDED OFF WHILE I TOLD HIM ABOUT YELLOW TOWN.
MIA...
LEAN
...WHY ARE YOUR EYES RED?
I-I'M FINE, I'M FINE!
JUST GOT A LITTLE SOAP IN MY EYES IN THE BATH.
OH, OKAY.
LET'S HELP OUT TOMORROW, TO MAKE UP FOR TONIGHT.
YEAH!

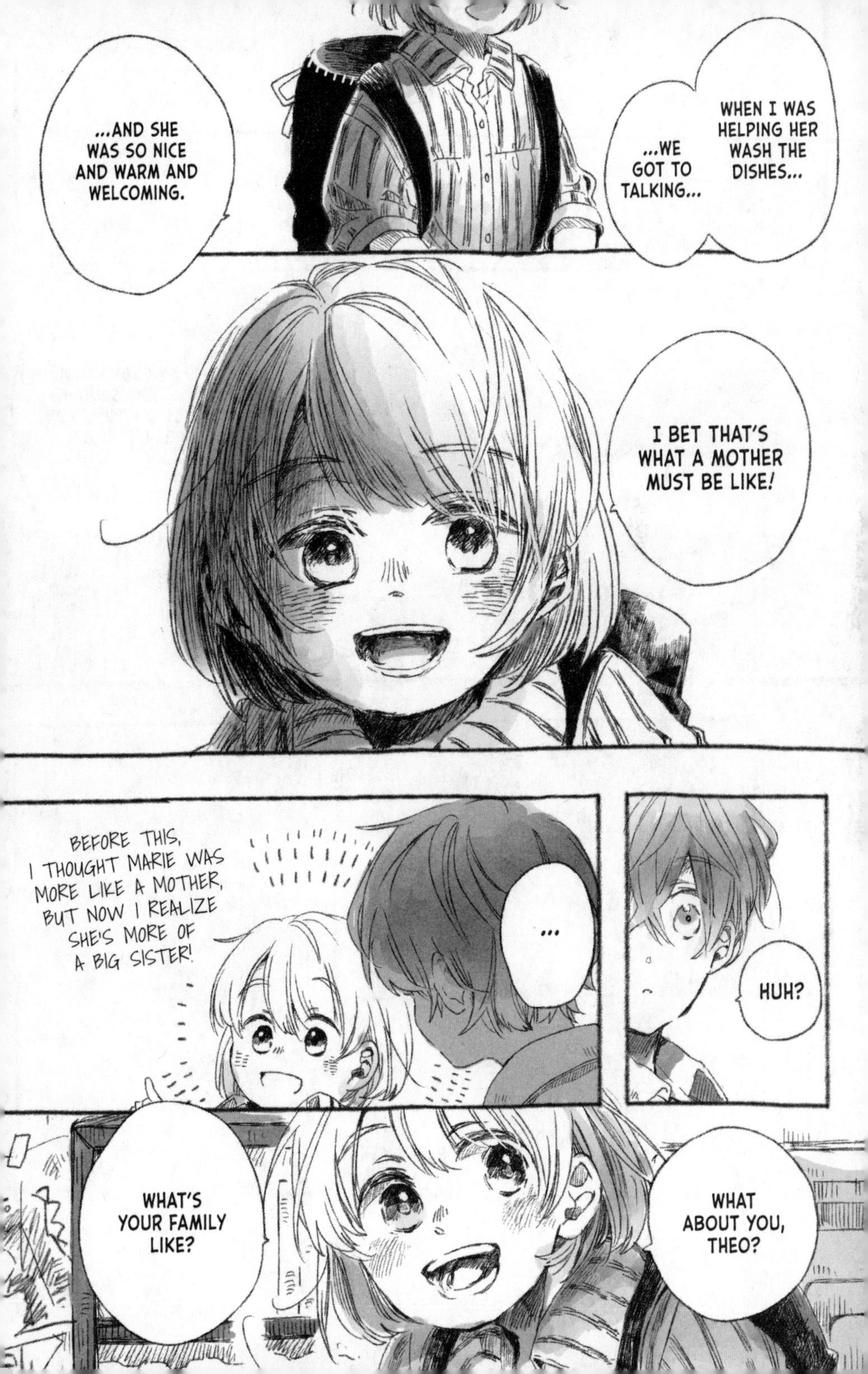
WHEN I WAS HELPING HER WASH THE DISHES...
...WE GOT TO TALKING...
...AND SHE WAS SO NICE AND WARM AND WELCOMING.
I BET THAT'S WHAT A MOTHER MUST BE LIKE!
HUH?
...
BEFORE THIS, I THOUGHT MARIE WAS MORE LIKE A MOTHER, BUT NOW I REALIZE SHE'S MORE OF A BIG SISTER!
WHAT ABOUT YOU, THEO?
WHAT'S YOUR FAMILY LIKE?

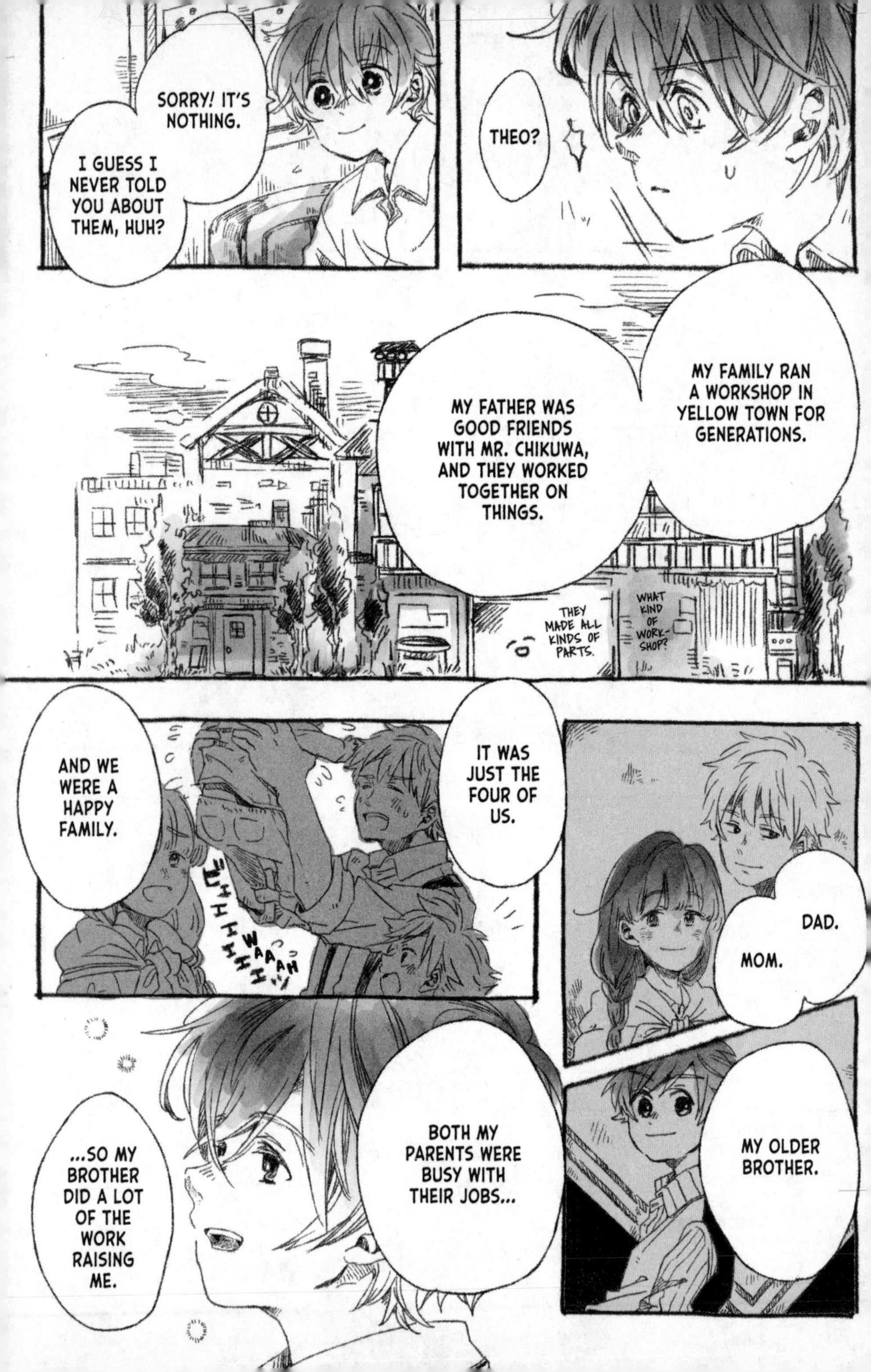
THEO?
SORRY! IT'S NOTHING.
I GUESS I NEVER TOLD YOU ABOUT THEM, HUH?
MY FAMILY RAN A WORKSHOP IN YELLOW TOWN FOR GENERATIONS.
MY FATHER WAS GOOD FRIENDS WITH MR. CHIKUWA, AND THEY WORKED TOGETHER ON THINGS.
WHAT KIND OF WORKSHOP?
THEY MADE ALL KINDS OF PARTS.
DAD.
MOM.
MY OLDER BROTHER.
IT WAS JUST THE FOUR OF US.
AND WE WERE A HAPPY FAMILY.
WAAAAH
BOTH MY PARENTS WERE BUSY WITH THEIR JOBS...
...SO MY BROTHER DID A LOT OF THE WORK RAISING ME.

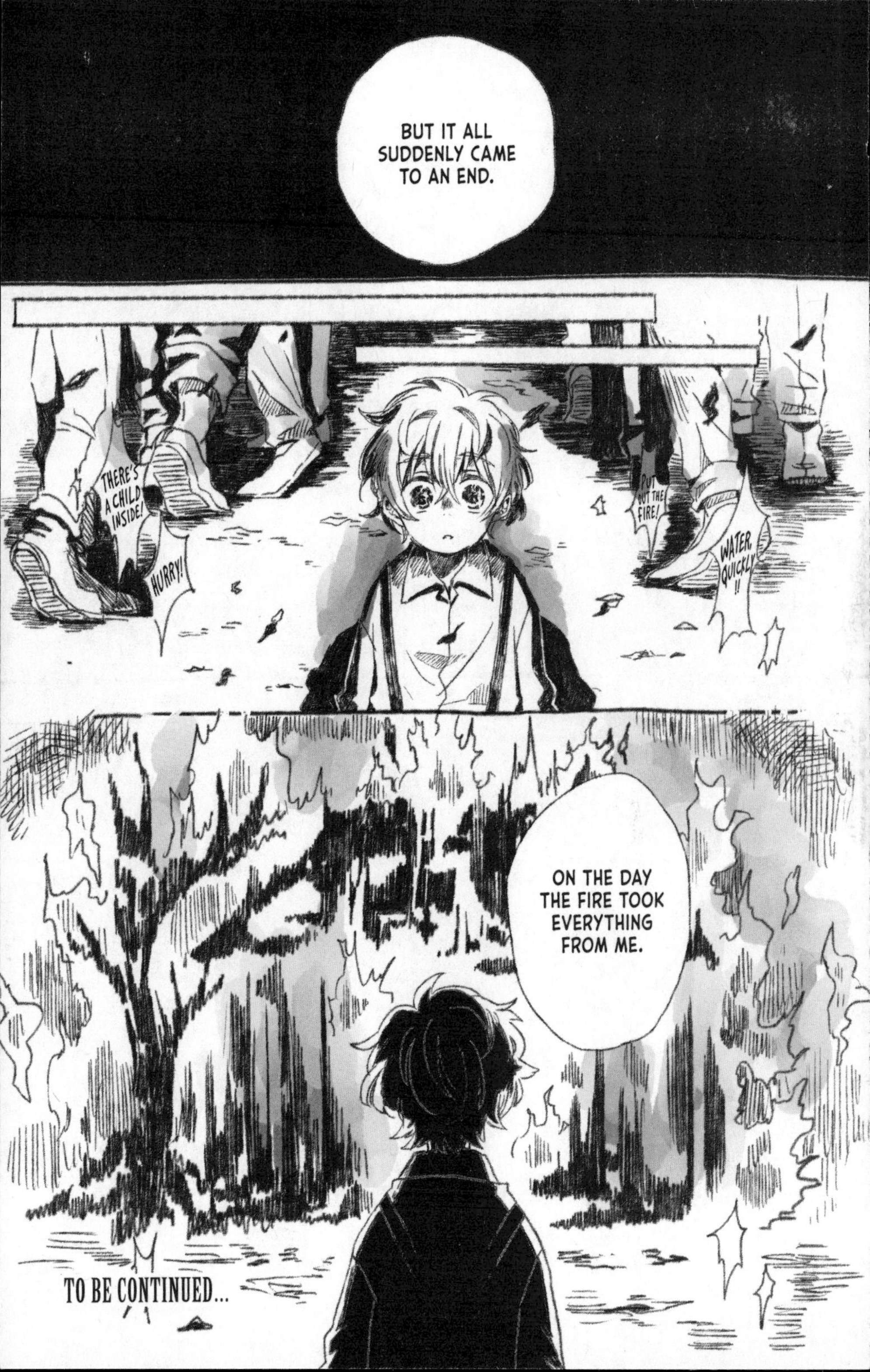
BUT IT ALL SUDDENLY CAME TO AN END.
PUT OUT THE FIRE!
WATER, QUICKLY!!
THERE'S A CHILD INSIDE!
HURRY!
ON THE DAY THE FIRE TOOK EVERYTHING FROM ME.
TO BE CONTINUED...

Beyond the Clouds

The Girl Who Fell From the Sky

The adorable new odd-couple cat comedy manga from the creator of the beloved *Chi's Sweet Home*, in full color!

Praise for Chi's Sweet Home

"Nearly impossible to turn away... a true all-ages title that anyone, young or old, cat lover or not, will enjoy. The stories will bring a smile to your face and warm your heart."

—School Library Journal

Sue & Tai-chan

Konami Kanata

Sue is an aging housecat who's looking forward to living out her life in peace... but her plans change when the mischievous black tomcat Tai-chan enters the picture! Hey! Sue never signed up to be a catsitter! *Sue & Tai-chan* is the latest from the reigning meow-narch of cute kitty comics, Konami Kanata.

A SMART, NEW ROMANTIC COMEDY FOR FANS OF *SHORTCAKE CAKE* AND *TERRACE HOUSE*!

Living-Room Matsunaga-san © Keiko Iwashita / Kodansha Ltd.

A romance manga starring high school girl Meeko, who learns to live on her own in a boarding house whose living room is home to the odd (but handsome) Matsunaga-san. She begins to adjust to her new life away from her parents, but Meeko soon learns that no matter how far away from home she is, she's still a young girl at heart — especially when she finds herself falling for Matsunaga-san.

PERFECT WORLD

Rie Aruga

A TOUCHING NEW SERIES ABOUT LOVE AND COPING WITH DISABILITY

An office party reunites Tsugumi with her high school crush Itsuki. He's realized his dream of becoming an architect, but along the way, he experienced a spinal injury that put him in a wheelchair. Now Tsugumi's rekindled feelings will butt up against prejudices she never considered — and Itsuki will have to decide if he's ready to let someone into his heart...

"Depicts with great delicacy and courage the difficulties some with disabilities experience getting involved in romantic relationships... Rie Aruga refuses to romanticize, pushing her heroine to face the reality of disability. She invites her readers to the same tasks of empathy, knowledge and recognition."
—Slate.fr

"An important entry [in manga romance]... The emotional core of both plot and characters indicates thoughtfulness... [Aruga's] research is readily apparent in the text and artwork, making this feel like a real story."
—Anime News Network

KC KODANSHA COMICS

A Kodansha Comics Trade Paperback Original
Beyond the Clouds 4 copyright © 2021 Nicke / Ki-oon
English translation copyright © 2022 Nicke / Ki-oon

Published in the United States by Kodansha Comics, an imprint of Kodansha USA Publishing, LLC, New York.

Publication rights for this English edition arranged with AC Media Ltd. through Tuttle-Mori Agency, Inc., Tokyo.

First published in France in 2021 by Ki-oon, an imprint of AC Media Ltd.

ISBN 978-1-64651-032-0

Printed in the United States of America.

www.kodansha.us

1st Printing
Translation: Stephen Paul
Lettering: Abigail Blackman
Editing: Aimee Zink
Kodansha Comics edition cover design by Phil Balsman

Publisher: Kiichiro Sugawara

Director of publishing services: Ben Applegate
Associate director of publishing operations: Stephen Pakula
Publishing services managing editors: Alanna Ruse, Madison Salters
Production managers: Emi Lotto, Angela Zurlo